CHAPLIN
Stage by Stage

by

"A.J" Marriot

Marriot Publishing

CHAPLIN – Stage by Stage

First published 2005
ISBN 978-0-9521308-1-9

This second print published October 2019
ISBN 978-1-78972-556-6-8

Marriot Publishing
Ciudad Quesada, Alicante, Spain
Text Copyright © by "A.J" Marriot 2005
Printed via "LULU"

Written, compiled, and designed by "A.J" Marriot. Layout by "A.J" Marriot
COVER DESIGN by "A.J" Marriot
Cover artwork by Paul Wood (TT Litho, Rochester, Kent. ME1 1NN. – www.ttlitho.co.uk)

PREFACE

In the autumn of 1978 I was into my fourth year as a professional comedian, when I was offered the position of Entertainment Director on a ship going on a world cruise. After four weeks of cruising up and down the straights of Alaska, the highlight of which was watching my clothes go round in a laundrette in Ketchikan, I returned home. Or, to be more accurate, I returned "home" homeless, and was put up temporarily by my manager. What started as "come round for dinner," turned into a nine-month stay. Long dinner. Some time during those months there was a season of Charlie Chaplin films, shown early evening each weekday on BBC2, I think. I had never seen Chaplin at the cinema, so a lot of these films were new to me. I would sit and watch them and laugh out loud, while my manager and his family would look at me in disbelief that I found any of it funny. But I knew this man Chaplin. I could instantly relate to the business he was performing, and I instinctively knew what he felt in his bones. Strange to say but, over the years, my capacity to laugh at his films has severely diminished, but my fascination for Chaplin "the man" has grown stronger – hence the dedication I have given to the research behind this book.

When I first voiced my intent to publish a book about Chaplin, the consensus of opinion seemed to be: "Surely, everything that *could* be written about Charlie Chaplin *has* been written." Well, I have to agree that there has been a voluminous amount written about Chaplin, but so much of what is to be found in magazine and newspaper articles, and more recently on dedicated web sites, is just junk. In these précis we often get the written equivalent of "Chinese whispers." One writer writes something about Chaplin, another picks it up but doesn't quite get it right, then the third writer re-writes it, a little more distorted, until the last writer has an article full of nonsense.

Within these pages you will find many quotes from contemporary sources. My feelings are: "If a quote is a quote – then quote it." And you can quote me on that. The theory behind this is that the nearer a biographer can get to the original source, the less chance there is that the words have become corrupted by the process mentioned. Obviously this method does not eradicate the quote which was written as a lie in the first place. There is also a certain arrogance in transposing first-person quotes into the third person. If Chaplin says "I was seventeen when I joined the Karno Company," and a biographer writes: "Chaplin was seventeen when he joined the Karno Company," then he is printing an inaccuracy whilst intimating that his source is correct. That is why, in nearly all cases, I have revealed my sources.

There have also been a lot of glaring inconsistencies written about Chaplin – most of them by Chaplin himself. When Chaplin sat down to write his biographies, it is doubtful that he had to hand the full list of dates he played whilst with the Karno Company; and so, as these numbered in the hundreds and occurred at the rate of up to three per night, he is rightly forgiven for any slight inaccuracies. One can also forgive Chaplin in instances where he has mistaken one London theatre for another. I, the author, was a club comedian for some fifteen years; in which time I too played thousands of dates at hundreds of venues. In my instance I had to find out the location of the venue in advance, plan my route, and then navigate my own way by car. Chaplin, however, had no such responsibility. All he had to do when playing in London, was to walk down to the Karno Fun Factory, in Camberwell, get aboard one of the special Karno buses, and be driven to the venue.

When you're not driving, you don't always pay attention to the route, and thus you can easily be unaware as to your location. Thus, when Chaplin says he was appearing at, say, Streatham, he might well have been appearing at Balham, and when he says "Woolwich", "Rotherithe" might well have been the venue. Failing that explanation, the passage of time between the actual appearances and the writing of his biographies must have clouded his memories. What further complicates accounts of Chaplin's movements is that many of these slip-ups have been carried on by latter-day biographers, who didn't have the recourse to check them out.

Past biographers have also underrated the time our eponymous subject spent in the Karno Company. In the biography *Remember Fred Karno?*, the author relates that Chaplin joined the Karno Company during a run of the sketch *The Football Match*, after which he went into *Jimmy the Fearless* – thus omitting at least half-a-dozen other sketches and jumping forward more than two years in the twinkling of an eye. Other authors make similar leaps.

Chaplin himself does not help. In his autobiography he omits to mention the first tour of three he made in *The Football Match*, thus giving the illusion that he was an immediate star in the Karno Company. Of the Karno sketch *Jimmy the Fearless*, Chaplin makes no mention whatsoever, despite his having played the lead role in it for some nineteen weeks.

This book has three aims:

The first is to destroy many of the myths and legends which surround Chaplin's stage career. Some can be dealt with here and now:

Firstly, there never was a sketch or a sketch company called: "*Fred Karno's Army*[1]." Neither was there a sketch or company called: "*Fred Karno's Circus.*" This is important to note as, in many previous accounts, Chaplin and Stan Laurel have been credited with being members of sketches and/or companies with these titles. Paradoxically, there were sketches called *Casey's Army* and *Casey's Circus* but, whereas the latter two Casey sketches have been forgotten with time, the mythical Karno ones are the first to trip off the tongue whenever the name "Karno" is mentioned.

There was no such sketch as "*Casey's Court Circus.*" There was a sketch called *Casey's Court*, which was set in a courtyard, and there was sketch called *Casey's Circus*, which was set in a mock-up of a circus ring.

Chaplin never appeared in *Casey's Court*.

Stan Laurel was never a member of *Casey's Court* or any other "Casey" Company.

Other myths, such as *The Eight Lancashire Lads* being in both *Giddy Ostend* and *Cinderella*, at the London Hippodrome; Charlie being a wolf in *Peter Pan*; when and where Charlie met Hetty Kelly; and when Chaplin was or wasn't caught on film for the first time, will be dealt with within the narrative.

The second aim is to put back many of the pieces of Chaplin's early stage work which he chose to leave out, and to remove from others the paint with which he retouched them when he wished to present a different image.

David Robinson, in *Chaplin – His Life and Art*, gives the opinion that: "Chaplin was an honest and truthful biographer." I can't agree. In my opinion, Chaplin has in many instances distorted

---

[1] The 1952 play "*Fred Karno's Army*" had nothing to do with the man, or his sketches.

the truth, changed the facts, fabricated evidence, and deliberately left out information which doesn't favour him. Also, the dates and years he gives are so inaccurate that, in at least fifty per cent of cases, it is best to ignore them. His most repeated inaccuracy is his age. When writing of his youth he constantly makes out is around twelve to eighteen months younger than he actually was. For instance, when he became 'Billy' in *Sherlock Holmes* he says he was twelve and a half, whereas he was fourteen; and when he became a principal comic in Karno's *The Football Match* he claims he was only seventeen whereas he was all-but nineteen. One can only surmise that he does this in an effort to be credited as the youngest to do this and the youngest to do that. I think Chaplin must have influenced the inept person who wrote the wording on the metal plaque beneath his statue in Leicester Square, London, for it makes out that he went into films when he was seventeen, whereas he was actually twenty-four.

A second oft-used ruse by Chaplin is to leave out anyone from his very early days who went on to become famous. For instance: if it weren't for the caption on two photographs – one in Chaplin's autobiography, and the other in *Chaplin – My Life in Pictures*, Stan Laurel would not have existed in Chaplin's records, despite their having spent four years together in the Karno Company. More "neglected" stars, *and* relatives, will be revealed throughout the book.

A third recurring inaccuracy is for Chaplin to make out that events which happened only once, happened repeatedly. In one instance he describes escorting Hetty Kelly to the tube station to attend an audition, then goes on to make out this happened four days running. In another he says his mother spent a week on tour with them, then doesn't "pull out" and tells us it was four weeks. His best one regards the time he was touring with the play *Sherlock Holmes*. Chaplin recounts his escapades in travelling with a pet rabbit, of which his guardian adds: "Once he let his rabbits run all over the landlady's sitting room, and of course they made a mess and annoyed the landlady." Chaplin's version of "once" is that this happened every week for a whole year.

The third, and main aim of the book, is to present a chronological account of all of Chaplin's stage appearances. This has been done in fragmented sections within the text, but then in full, date-sheet form in the tables at the back of the book. After more than six years of research I am still unable to present these as one hundred per cent complete. Obviously, some minor errors will be found in them, but I hope that the reader will realise the enormity of the task and seek to help to improve the listing, rather than take pleasure in highlighting mistakes or holes. After all, in the ninety-years-plus since Chaplin actually made these appearances, this is the nearest to a definitive record you can find.

In the article *A Comedian Sees the World*, written in September 1933, Chaplin himself revealed.

> *I am tired of love and people and like all egocentrics I turn to myself. I want to live in my youth again, to capture the moods and sensations of childhood, so remote from me now – so unreal – almost like a dream. I need to turn back time; to venture into the blurred past and bring it into focus.*

So, good readers, let us venture into the blurred past and bring it into focus.

Bouquets and brickbats to the author, 20 Oughton Close, Hitchin, Herts. SG5 2QY (no visitors) or e-mail: ajmarriot@aol.com.

Any suggestions, and amendments will be gratefully received, with a view to a proposed second edition.

ACKNOWLEDGEMENTS

I believe that, out of the hundreds of sessions I spent writing this book, there was never one during which I didn't think of the late-Olive Karno. When I met her, Olive was by then the widow of Fred Karno Jnr, whom she always referred to as "Freddie." I got to know her during the three-day *Stan Laurel Centenary Celebrations* I organised in Blackpool, in June 1990. We got on so well together that I kept in constant touch with her right up to the sad day she passed away. She was one of the strongest women I ever met, in that she never complained off any ailment, accident, or hurt she suffered, but just took everything that life threw at her as being the way life was. She had a wicked sense of humour, and a great twinkle in her eye, and I had lots of fun sharing our many conversations. If I'd published all the stories she told me of what Freddie had related to her about Chaplin, this book would have been a best-seller.

I never asked Olive for anything, but she would often make me surprise gifts of items that she knew were of interest to me. Among these were the scripts for the Karno sketches, some of which I am happy to share with readers of this book. Her son Michael was also generous enough to pass on further material to me, for which I am equally grateful. My gratitude also goes to Marian Daniels, a great-niece of Muriel Palmer's, who allowed me copies of the postcards, picturing the Karno Company, which Muriel sent home during the 1910-1912 U.S. Karno Company Tours.

Then there were the "professional" guardians of personal collections. To Kate Guyonvarch and Claire Byrski, from 'Associated Chaplin' in Paris, who provided me with pretty well everything in the Chaplin Archives up to and including 1913, I am greatly indebted for their extreme generosity. And to John Cahoon, Keeper of the 'Stan Laurel Collection' in the Los Angeles Natural History Museum, who allowed me images of the collection, I also acknowledge my appreciation. My thanks go to David Wyatt and Beth Werling for the tip-off regarding the existence of the latter.

And for the present-day photographs, my sincere thanks goes to my good friend Louis Mortier, who allowed me to drag him all over Lambeth, Kennington, Brixton, and Walworth to view and photograph the "Chaplin Locations." Thanks too to Tony Merrick, whose guide to the "Chaplin Walk" proved most useful.

For many of the reviews from Chaplin's UK tours I am especially beholding to Catherine Comerford, Managing Director of *The Stage* newspaper, and Trevor Davies Production Manager, who very kindly provided me with CD copies of relevant volumes.

Thanks also to the following "Sons of the Desert":- Bram Reijnhoudt, Editor of the Laurel & Hardy Dutch magazine *Blotto*; Rob Lewis – Editor of the UK *Laurel & Hardy Magazine*; and Wolfgang Guenther, Editor of the German *Two Tars* magazine; for their valued assistance.

Acknowledgments

And to the Libraries in England who were helpful in the extreme:

Stoke on Trent Archives – Janine Dawson; Portsmouth Central Library – Alan King; Wandsworth Local History – David Ainsworth; North Shields Local Studies – Eric Hollerton and Diane Leggett; Medway Archives – Jean Lear; Walsall Local History – Diana M. Wilkes.

And a Special Mention to the staff of the British Newspaper Library, Colindale, who, with unfailing grace, supplied me with literally thousands of newspapers.

In the United States:

When I realised that I wasn't going to be able to find all the dates on the U.S. Karno Tours, using solely British research sources, I had the choice of either flying to the States and visiting whatever libraries time and money allowed, or finding some person or people who could act in my place. I therefore printed an appeal in the *Laurel & Hardy Magazine* which, though published in the UK, is subscribed to by over two-hundred Americans. I was disappointed enough with the American contingent when only one of them responded to my appeal, until I learned that the one volunteer wasn't American at all, but a Scot, now resident in San Diego. (There's a message in there, somewhere.)

My initial frustration turned to pure joy however, when, over the next ten months, my newly-found Scottish friend, Bob Dickson, continually dispatched to me all the material that I could have hoped to have found had I gone to the States myself. And, whenever Bob himself couldn't get access to a required source he managed to persuade friends of his to do the work on his/my behalf. These people were: Spokane – Peter E. Nufer; Seattle – Samantha Everett; and Exeter – Carol Beers. Needless to say, without Bob and his friends' dedication in spending *weeks* in their various research centres, the account and date-sheets for the Karno US Tours would have been sadly depleted. So, to Bob, Peter, Samantha, and Carol, I cannot find words enough to show my gratitude. Bob's sole motivation was in assisting towards a more complete account of the early years of our beloved hero, Stan Laurel. He can now be justifiably proud of achieving that commendable aim.

The following U.S. Libraries were helpful in the extreme:

St. Paul Central Library – Mark Kile; Baltimore Enoch Pratt Free Library – Don Bonsteel; Baltimore County Public Library – Valentina Pickens; Milwaukee Public Library – Brian Williams-Van Klooster; Minneapolis Public Library – Nathalie Hart; Kansas City Public Library – Sara J. Nyman; Cincinnati County Library – Joan Luebering; Butte-Silver Bow Public Library – anon; Duluth Public Library – David Ouse; Beverley Hills, Academy of Motion Picture arts – Susan Oka.

And a big "Thank You" to the following two people who, for neither fee nor favour, volunteered to spend many hours searching for information that only I alone was to benefit from: New York – Hooman Mehran; and Cincinnati – Hank Sykes. You have my heartfelt appreciation.

To the *Ellis Island Foundation* I extend my utmost gratitude for access to the New York Immigration Records, which were invaluable in tracking the movements of the various Karno troupes across the great pond.

And lastly to:

Bob Dickson, Simon Louvish and Louis Mortier – by whose brilliant perceptions, and much appreciated suggestions, the text greatly benefitted.

CONTENTS

	PREFACE		i
	ACKNOWLEDGEMENTS		iv
	CONTENTS		vi
Chapter 1	**CHARLES THE SECOND**	(1889-1899)	1
Chapter 2	**CAPITAL GAINS**	(1899-1900)	14
Chapter 3	**JUNIOR DENIES SEE'N'YA** (Interlude 1)	(1898-1899)	26
Chapter 4	**TRAINING CATS AND DOGS**	(1900-1903)	32
Chapter 5	**HOLMES, SWEET HOLMES**	(1903-1904)	42
Chapter 6	**FROM RAGS TO RAGS**	(1904-1906)	55
Chapter 7	**CHARLIE FAILS TO APPEAR IN "COURT"**	(1906-1907)	64
Chapter 8	**CATCH A FALLING STAR**	(1907-1908)	77
Chapter 9	**HIS FIRST KICK IN THE PANTS**	(1908-1908)	85
Chapter 10	**WHEN HETTY MET CHARLIE**	(1908-1908)	95
Chapter 11	**THINGS BECOME SKETCHY**	(1908-1910)	108
Chapter 12	**TWO LOAVES AND SOMETHING FISHY**	(1910-1910)	120
Chapter 13	**VARIETY TO VAUDEVILLE**	(1910-1911 U.S.)	134
Chapter 14	**WAY OUT WEST**	(1911-1912 U.S.)	147
Chapter 15	**ONE GOOD TOUR DESERVES ANOTHER**	(1912-1912 U.S.)	161
Chapter 16	**AN ENGLISH SUMMER**	(1912-1912)	171
Chapter 17	**ANYBODY HERE SEEN KELLY?** (Interlude 2)	(1910-1912)	176
Chapter 18	**NEVER GO BACK**	(1912-1913 U.S.)	181
Chapter 19	**THE FINAL STAGE**	(1912-1913 U.S.)	195
Chapter 20	**FROM STAGE TO SCREEN** (The Epilogue)	(1913-1914 U.S.)	204
	BIBLIOGRAPHY		206

DATE-SHEETS

	INTRO and KEY	207
1898-1900	**"THE EIGHT LANCASHIRE LADS"** matched with **CHARLES CHAPLIN Snr.**	208
1900-1901	**"CINDERELLA"** matched with **"THE EIGHT LANCASHIRE LADS"**	213

"SHERLOCK HOLMES"

1903-1904	First Tour	214
1904-1905	Second Tour	216
1905-1906	Third Tour	217
1906	**"REPAIRS"** plus **"TEN LOONIES"**	219
1906-1907	**"CASEY'S COURT"** and **"CASEY'S CIRCUS"** matched with **SYD CHAPLIN**	220

FRED KARNO COMPANY TOUR DATES (U.K.)

1908	**"THE FOOTBALL MATCH"** – Chaplin's first Tour matched with **SYD CHAPLIN**	224
1908	**CHARLES** and **SYD CHAPLIN** – joint Tour plus **HETTY KELLY** in **"THE FATAL WEDDING"** and **"THE YANKEE DOODLE GIRLS"**	226
1908-1909	**"THE FOOTBALL MATCH"** – Chaplin's second Tour	227
1909	**KARNO SKETCHES** (Chaplin unconfirmed) plus **"THE FOOTBALL MATCH"** – Chaplin's third Tour	229
1910	**"SKATING"**	232
1910	**"JIMMY THE FEARLESS"** plus **"THE WOW-WOWS"**	233

FRED KARNO COMPANY TOUR DATES (U.S.)

	Introduction to U.S. Tours	235
	1910-1912 – first trip to U.S. (Tours 1-3)	236
	1912 – Summer in England	240
	1912-1914 – second trip to U.S. (Tours 4-5)	241

LAUREL & HARDY – The British Tours   244

Chapter 1

CHARLES THE SECOND

In the 1890s, the Hampshire town of Aldershot had a population of around thirty-thousand residents, complemented by twenty-thousand troops quartered on military camps. The town did have its own theatre, the Royal and Hippodrome, but the soldiers were encouraged to partake of on-site entertainment, and each division had a huge canteen at which music-hall artistes were engaged.

On one such night, a fading soubrette was having a bad time of it. Her voice had been deteriorating for a while but, that night, it went altogether. It is well-known, by show business professionals, that army audiences made up of members from the lower ranks are notoriously difficult to entertain. Other male-dominated audiences, such as members of the police force or the fire brigade, are wonderfully receptive and accept entertainers as they ought to – i.e. people who have come to take their minds off the job. The vast majority of squaddies however do not find release in light entertainment and view stage acts as the enemy, who are to be put down at all costs. Unsure of themselves, they maintain the pack principal and tend to frighten their quarry into submission. Thus it was that even this frail lady, in obvious distress, began to receive the baying of the pack.

This scene would be reminiscent of thousands before and thousands since excepting that, on this particular occasion, the mob was silenced by a six-year-old boy. Watching from the wings, he was unable to comprehend why his beloved mother was receiving such a hostile reception, and became even more upset when she was forced to leave the stage. Wanting to show the audience just what they were missing, he persuaded the officer-in-charge to let him continue with the act.

The first song, *'E Dunno Where 'E Are*, received loud applause, followed by a shower of coins – thrown as a show of approval, not derision. Fearing the money might not be there if he went off-stage and returned for it later, the boy called for a halt so that he might retrieve his "pennies from heaven." Whilst so doing he was coerced into performing a second song, for which he chose *Sergeant Riley*. This Irish marching song was from his mother's repertoire and, in delivering it, he included an impersonation of her, right down to the cracking voice. This added to the child's appeal, and led to his being encouraged to display his full repertoire of songs, dances, and impressions – previously performed only at family gatherings in the home. That night however, Charlie Chaplin had made his first-ever, public stage appearance.

Charles Spencer Chaplin, born on 16 April 1889 at his home in East Street, South London, was to have an horrendous upbringing. Although he was to write at length about the squalor, poverty and trauma he suffered in his childhood, he was to state in private that, had he revealed *all* of the depravation he had suffered, he would not have been believed. Sad to say, circumstances weren't going to allow further theatrical bookings to be secured by his mother. "That night was my first appearance on the stage and mother's last," he was to say in his autobiography.

If Charlie were indeed five years old, then his stage debut must have come between April 1894 and April 1895. However, in his book *My Life in Pictures* is a handbill for Hatcham Liberal Club, dated 8 February 1896, on which his mother, Hannah, is billed under one of her stage-names – Lily Chaplin. In his later writings, when speaking of *any* debut performance he made, Chaplin *always* knocked at least one year off his true age, in order to enhance his desired image as a child prodigy. One can safely assume therefore that Charlie was at least six when he debuted at Aldershot, which would bring the Hatcham Liberal Club booking into the time-line. Information from David Robinson's research revealed that Charlie had been enrolled at Addington Street School, in October 1895, whilst temporarily living at his grandfather's house at 164 York Road, both located off the Westminster Road. An entry in the records of Addington Street School gives us another time fix, as it reads: "Sydney Chaplin handed back to mother March 10, 1896. Charles, ditto."[1]

This last phrase would seem to indicate that Hannah had now found somewhere for her and her two sons to live together, as the children would hardly be handed over to their mother if she herself were in care. Likewise, the two boys would not be handed over to their mother if *they* were being boarded elsewhere. This narrows down the time-window considerably, and so a more acceptable time-frame for Charlie's first performance would be the following

1896

8 February	Lily Chaplin appears at Hatcham Liberal Club
10 March	Charlie is returned to his mother's care.
??	Lily's last performance – Charlie's first. Aldershot Canteen
16 April	Charlie's seventh Birthday.
30 May	Charlie and Sydney admitted to Newington Workhouse

There is at least one claim that Charlie appeared on stage when a babe-in-arms:

> The parents were often not on the same bill, nor even performing in the same town but, in between engagements, whenever she was free to, Mrs. Chaplin stood in the wings while her husband did his turn and, unseen by the audience, harmonized and echoed the refrain from off stage. She had an attractive voice, and one night the audience applauded so vociferously and insistently that Chaplin Snr. was forced to go to the wings and lead her on. Mrs. Chaplin was quite unprepared for this, either in make-up or in dress. In point of fact she had been nursing her child and had the few-days-old infant still in her arms. That was Charlie Chaplin's first appearance on any stage in the world.
>
> (*Picturegoer* – 4 October 1952)

Although this would count as his first on-stage appearance, if indeed it is factual, it could hardly count as his first performance. After the 1896 episode, there was to be a gap of three years before the child performer did secure paid stage work. A little of what happened in those interim years, and those which immediately followed, was revealed in a retrospective 1921 newspaper article:

---

[1] Charles Chaplin, A Comedian Sees the World, "Women's Home Companion," September, 1933

The nurse who assisted him on to the stage of life to make his bow to the world is Mrs. Harriet Tricks, who lives in a room at 141, Ethelred-street, Kennington. Mrs. Tricks, who was present at Charlie's birth, told the story of his early hardships.

"I saw him grow up, and he had a very hard life as a child," Mrs. Tricks said. "Many a slice of bread and butter and a cup of tea I have taken out to him when I was charring at Mr. Wentworth's (Mr. F. Wentworth, lamp manufacturer, Kennington-road). Mr Wentworth was then an elderly man, and is now dead, but he often found Charlie curled up asleep in his doorway."

"He was just a mischievous boy, but very funny, always up to monkey tricks, tripping himself up, climbing up fences, and falling down. I remember he used to climb the fence and steal apples from the orchard of a house in Kennington-lane, in which lived an old lady who was known as the 'Old Miser' because of her meanness. The house is now pulled down, but there was no doubt he could nip up her fence alright.

I used to call him 'Waggie'. He was always wonderfully fond of animals, and was a good pal to his dog."

(*The Star* – 2 September 1921)

The above article was written immediately prior to Chaplin's arrival in England, for a visit to promote his then latest film *The Kid*. Within three days of his stay Chaplin had amassed a reported seventy-three thousand letters and cards. Nearly seven hundred were from people claiming to be his relatives. Unbelievably, nine of the writers claimed to be his mother. Knowing this, one might feel justified in challenging if Mrs. Tricks is talking about the right boy, or just living up to her name, as Charlie being a dog-owner is not a partnership mentioned in his 1964 autobiography. However, in the 1933 article: *A Comedian Sees the World*, Chaplin reveals that he did indeed once own a dog. He acquired it in October 1903, after which he toured with it for over a year, so it looks as though Mrs. Tricks did observe Charlie during his early teens.

If we are further to believe that Mrs. Tricks was indeed present at Charlie's birth, then history will have to be rewritten as Ethelred-Street (formerly Regent Road) was adjacent to East Street, but this was not the East Street off the Walworth Road, but the East Street which ran between Kennington Road, and Lambeth Walk.

In 1952, another lady came forward to tell of her contact with the Chaplins. Mrs. J. Crane who, in 1898, had briefly been the family's landlady at 39 Methley Street, Kennington, recalled:

Mrs. Chaplin and her boys stayed at numerous addresses round and about the Horns Hotel, Kennington, Chester Street, Oakdon Street, Pownall Terrace, and Methley Street, many of them now gone in the blitz, were the kind of places they lived in for a few weeks when they had some money.

The family had a one-attic room with me. When she couldn't get singing engagements, poor Mrs. Chaplin worked all day at needlework, making blouses for a few pennies each. She had a hard job making ends meet.

The older boy worked for the Post Office[2], I think. Charles was rather a frail child with his mop of dark hair, his pale face and bright blue eyes. He was what I call a 'little limb' – out in the streets from morning to night.

I remember he was a regular one for finding a man with a barrel organ, and dancing to the music. He got a lot of extra money for the organ grinder and a few coppers for himself. I suppose that's how he started becoming an entertainer. Charlie was supposed to go to school in Kennington, but he was an awful truant.

(1952 article from *Charlie Chaplin*, by Peter Haining – original source unaccredited)

---

[2] The Post Office in question was in the Strand where, in the winter of 1898, Syd was working as a telegraph boy.

Note that Mrs. Crane appears to be testifying that Hannah Chaplin was still performing as a singer as late as 1898 but, considering the amount of time that Hannah spent in care in that year, because of her mental health, I believe this possibility can be dismissed. Mrs. Crane too, also presents us with a picture of Charlie as the lone, stray street child. But what of Sydney – Charlie's half-brother (Born: Sydney Hawkes – 16 March 1885) with whom Charlie spent a huge part of his earliest years, and yet he barely makes mention of their joint childhood escapades. The following is one missing from his own writings and, though it contains another account of his dancing in front of the organ grinder, there is one marked difference:

> The boys roamed the streets for diversion, Syd wearing a pair of shoes as "holey as Gruyere cheese," and a worn-out jacket, the sleeves of which had been replaced by sleeves from a green velvet jacket of his mother's. Charlie wore a pair of her red stage stockings and a shabby stocking-hat. How the other children laughed at them!
>
> When the familiar barrel organ began to play, Charlie, from the sheer joy of the music, danced to it. He was so small, and looked so pathetic, that a crowd soon began to collect, and Syd promptly passed his cap round the onlookers.
>
> The organ grinder's face beamed as he saw the pennies tumbling in, but, when he realized that the boys were collecting the money for themselves, he chased them away with foul oaths. Soon, all the organ grinders got wise, and Charlie had to do his dancing round the corner, out of sight.

(*Picturegoer* – 4 October 1952)

This second account of the same scene includes Sydney among the cast of players. As for the fourth family member, the father, Charlie definitely didn't spend much time with him as he had left the marital home when Charlie was in his second year. Charles Chaplin Snr.[3], too, worked the music halls, as a "comedian and descriptive vocalist." During the Christmas and New Year weeks of 1898-1899 Chaplin Snr. was appearing at the Tivoli Theatre, Manchester; while over at the neighbouring Theatre Royal, in the pantomime *Babes in the Woods*, were a troupe of clog dancers named *The Eight Lancashire Lads*. After popping across to the latter theatre and catching the boys' act, Chaplin went backstage to pay his compliments to the troupe's manager, William Jackson. Chaplin may well have known Jackson prior to this meeting as, in London, they were near neighbours – living at 289 and 167 Kennington Road, respectively.

During the conversation Chaplin was informed that one of the boys was about to leave, and a replacement was being sought. Taking advantage of the moment, he wasted no time in putting forward his son Charlie as a suitable new member. Chaplin's status as a performer was enough to convince Mr. Jackson that he need look no further and so, just one week later, Charlie was brought up from London *to prepare* to replace the outgoing member. Little Charlie was accompanied by his mother and, after an initial meeting between her and Mr. Jackson, it was agreed that Charlie was to receive free board and lodgings whilst touring, and that a half-a-crown a week would be sent home to her.

If Charlie believed he was leaving school to become a full-time performer, he very soon learned differently. "Interrupted" was one way to describe his education – "curtailed" was not.

> When touring the provinces we went to a school for the week in each town, which did little to further my education.

(Chaplin's 1964 autobiography)

Even during this sojourn in Manchester the rule applied and, on 9 January 1899, he was admitted to Armitage Street School, Ardwick, where he stayed until 22 February. For the full

---

[3] Charlie's father is named as Charles Chaplin "Snr." only to distinguish between the two in this account. He was never billed as "Snr." in real life.

seven weeks he and his mother were in Manchester they stayed in theatrical digs at 64 Morton Street, Longsight, a few minutes walk from Hyde Road.[4]

Babes in the Woods ran until Saturday 25 February 1899. The pantomime was a tremendous success and was proclaimed, contemporarily, as "the most successful of all time." It would appear from the above school dates that Charlie's rehearsal weeks with *The Eight Lancashire Lads* ended at the same time as the pantomime finished its run, whereas the original troupe stayed on for a return to the variety stage, with two weeks at the Manchester Grand. Maybe keeping Charlie and his mother in food and lodgings for the latter dates was considered an unnecessary cost.

Of Mr. and Mrs. Jackson's recent history, Charlie thought that both had been schoolteachers. From a previous marriage, Mr. Jackson had three sons between the ages of twelve and sixteen and a daughter aged nine. Mrs. Jackson, although getting on in years, had then presented Mr. Jackson with a fourth son, whom Charlie represented as still being nursed at the breast. Of the nine-year-old girl, Charlie said she had had her hair cut like a boy's in order to pass as one of the dance troupe. The haircut certainly did the trick as, in the photos of *The Eight Lancashire Lads* before, during, and after the time Charlie was a member, there is no-one who so much as resembles a girl. For another member, however, the requisite haircut was confirmed by Albert Jackson, one of the three Jackson brothers:

> He [Charlie] was living with an aunt and his brother Sydney above a barber's shop in Chester Street, off the Kennington-road. He was a very quiet boy at first, and, considering that he didn't come from Lancashire, he wasn't a bad dancer. My first job was to take him to have his hair, which was hanging in matted curls about his shoulders, cut to a reasonable length.
>
> (*The Star* – September 1921)

Now returned to London after the Christmas season in Manchester, the troupe should have had a well-earned three-week break before their next engagement, but it was such a major booking that Mr. Jackson wisely punctuated the rest period with a one-week booking, in Portsmouth. Here he could make absolutely certain that the new boy had mastered the routines. Totally synchronised steps had to be achieved, otherwise all eight dancers would look bad and, at the venue where William Jackson had booked them next, nothing less than perfection was going to be good enough.

The Oxford Music Hall, in London's Oxford Street, was arguably the number-one of the capital's numerous music halls. It booked not only the largest number of acts but also the biggest stars. Here *The Eight Lancashire Lads* would be performing not just where some of the greatest acts from the music-hall stage *had played*, but would actually be performing with them. Getting it wrong would seriously jeopardise future bookings – getting it right would give the troupe the prestige needed to secure work at any theatre in Britain. But first things first. Charlie's trial week at the Portsmouth Empire was on 20 March 1899, of which the *Portsmouth Evening News* said:

> The Eight Lancashire Lads won hearty approval with their smart clog dancing.

Charlie remembered:

> After practising six weeks [in Manchester] I was eligible to dance with the troupe. But now that I was past eight years old[5] I had lost my assurance and confronting the audience for the first time gave me stage fright. I could hardly move my legs. It was weeks before I could solo dance as the rest of them did.

Everything was now in place. Charlie had rehearsed with the troupe whilst in Manchester; had overcome his homesickness by a return to London and a visit to his mother, both before and after

---

[4] Manchester Evening News article – 12 September 1921
[5] This is a strange choice of phrase: "But now that I was past eight years old." Charlie was just four weeks short of his tenth birthday.

(Marriot Collection)

Typical bill during The Eight Lancashire Lads' seven-week
season at the Oxford Music Hall, London.
(3 April to 20 May 1899)

THE REFEREE

9 APRIL 1899

(w/c 10 April 1899)
THE OXFORD

"THE PROGRAMME OF LONDON"

7:25	OVERTURE
7:30	HARRY CHASE
7:35	DAISY JAMES
7:40	AUSTIN RUDD
7:45	MARIE WILTON
7:50	TOM WHITE'S ARABS
8:00	LEONARD BARRY
8:05	KATIE COHEN
8:10	GEORGE LASHWOOD
8:15	LENA VERDI
8:20	EDWARD HOWLAND
8:25	THE LEONARDS
8:30	VERA VERE
8:40	WALTER BELLONINI
8:50	HARRIET VERNON
8:55	GEORGE MOZART
9:00	MUSICAL AVOLOS
9:10	EUGENE STRATTON
9:20	THE McNAUGHTONS
9:30	ELDORADO GIRLS
9:35	BRANSBY WILLIAMS
9:45	BERT GILBERT
9:55	BILLIE BARLOW
10:00	HARRY RANDALL
10:10	EIGHT LANCASHIRE LADS
10:20	GEORGE ROBEY
10:30	MILLIE HYLTON
10:40	JAMES and MARIE FINNEY
10.55	COSMAN COUPLE

HAMLET
by
BRANSBY WILLIAMS
Impersonating well-known Actors and Variety
Celebrities as it is done and might be done.

Doors Open 7:00   Commence 7:15
Manager Mr. HARRY LUNDY

the week in Portsmouth; and had a full week of professional performances under his belt. *The Eight Lancashire Lads* were now ready to take their first steps onto one of music-hall's biggest stages.

Music Hall was at its peak in 1899, with twenty artistes and more appearing nightly at the top venues, and performances running continuously from 6:00 p.m. till going on midnight. It might have helped the eight young boys if they had been allocated an earlier performance time, thus reducing the amount of time spent quivering with stage nerves; but "get in – get it done – and get out" was not going to be allowed. The troupe's six-minute slot was at 10:40 p.m. – a time when the audience could be feeling low, because of having tolerated a load of bad acts, or were high, in expectation of the acts getting better as the show went on. Extra pressure was added by the opening night landing on the Easter Bank Holiday Monday, a night when people who hadn't been able to get away for the weekend were relying on these acts to finish off their holiday with something special.

All obviously went well, as the one-week booking was extended – not to two weeks, not three weeks but, incredibly, SEVEN weeks. For the boys to be retained for this length of time, at this legendary music hall, was a testimony that *The Eight Lancashire Lads* were now an act deemed worthy of a place on the biggest stages, with the biggest acts around. But how had *The Eight Lancashire Lads* managed to get the booking at the Oxford in the first place? Is it a coincidence that, just four weeks earlier, Charles Chaplin Senior had played the same venue?

Having completed the seven weeks at the Oxford, the troupe moved on to do a tour of the provinces. First stop was two-hundred and forty miles away, in the North-East town of Middlesbrough; followed by a two-hundred and ninety mile diagonal cross-country route to Wales, for a week in Cardiff and Swansea respectively. This is hardy travelling in geographical sequence, and the conditions endured, and the hours spent, on what should have been a day-off, must have been gruelling for all involved. As there was not yet any automotive form of road transport, the only way to get to and from railway stations was by horse-drawn cart, and loading and unloading such a large party of people, plus all their luggage, would have been an arduous exercise.

Sharing the bill in both of the Welsh cities was Wal Pink and Company, a team of athletic comedians who specialised in knockabout sketches. There were many like comedy troupes around at the time – such as The Bogannys, with their sketch *The Lunatic Bakers*; The Five Foys in *The Excursion Depot*; The Leopolds in *Frivolity*; and The Boissets in *The Bricklayers* – but Wal Pink's Company was one of the best, and young Charlie must have been not only impressed by them, but desirous of being one of them – a desire he was to realise some seven years later.

After Swansea came a rest week, then a trip to the North-West coast to the seaside town of Blackpool – the undisputed number-one resort in Britain for summertime entertainment. Here, for their "First Appearance in Blackpool" *The Eight Lancashire Lads* performed for two weeks at the Pavilion Theatre, in the Winter Gardens complex. The boys must have felt they had landed in paradise, for all around them was entertainment of every diversity. Firstly, there were shows in the other theatres within the complex; plus other theatres on or near to the seafront, such as the Grand, the Alhambra, and the Empire, all of which they could visit. Add to this the world-famous Blackpool Tower, completed only five years previous, with its surrounding vast indoor entertainment buildings, including a ballroom, a circus, and zoological gardens. And not forgetting the three piers – the North, the Central, and the Victoria – each with its own attractions, such as bands, singers, variety artists, orchestras, and dancing. And, as an added bonus, the thrill of riding on the "Gigantic Jolly Wheel" – a Ferris-type wheel with passenger cabins the size of railway carriages, located adjacent to the Winter Gardens.

The domed entrance to the Winter Gardens complex, in Church Street, Blackpool.

BLACKPOOL

GAZETTE & NEWS

20 JUNE 1899

WINTER GARDENS
BLACKPOOL
MAMMOTH PROGRAMME
The Greatest and Grandest in Blackpool
OPEN ALL DAY.
6d   ADMISSION   6d
Reserved Seats (Pavilion Stalls 1s 6d. 2000 Free Seats.
Remember, SIXPENCE now admits to the whole
of the Winter Gardens, including the Empress
Ballroom, Indian Lounge, Enchanting Ferneries,
Palm Houses, Floral Halls, Ornamental Gardens
etc. from morning till night.
The most Extensive and Magnificent Palace of
Amusement in the World, and only SIXPENCE.

WINTER GARDENS
BLACKPOOL

General Manager - JNO. R. HUDDLESTONE.
MONDAY, JUNE 19th, 1899,
And until Further Notice.
MAGNIFICENT
ENTERTAINMENTS
IN THE GRAND PAVILION AT 2-0 AND 7-0
First appearance in Blackpool of Miss
FANNY WENTWORTH
Character Vocalist and Refined Entertainer.
THE LADY GROSSMITH
Return visit of
ALEXANDRA AND BERTIE
In their Novel Refined Aerial Act, the Horizontal
Balancing Ladder on the Single Trapeze.
First Appearance in Blackpool of
THE PERMANE TRIO
Comedians, Vocalists, and Dancers.
CLOWN ZERTHO
And His Marvelous Performing Dogs, from the
Palace Theatre, London.
Return Visit of
VASCO, The Mad Musician,
In his Great Novelty Specialty Act, from the
Alhambra, London
First appearance in Blackpool of
HELENE AND EMILON,
In their Great Novelty Trapeze and Wire Act,
from the Alhambra, London.
First appearance in Blackpool of the
EIGHT LANCASHIRE LADS,
Speciality Dancers and Vocalists.
First appearance in Blackpool of the
DEZMONTE AND MORA TRIO
In their Comical and Original Triple Bar Pantomime.

GRAND OCHESTRA
Conductor .... Mr. Arthur Grimmett

Before anyone questions the boys' ability to pay the entrance fee for all these attractions, let me acquaint you with the following: There has always been an unwritten law in show business circles that an artiste appearing at venue A, be allowed into venue B, or C, or D, to watch the show for free. Theatre managers realise that their venue alone is not the single attraction which draws holidaymakers to the resort, but the combined wealth of talent at all venues, and so free entry is their way of acknowledging the artistes as being part of the draw.

Following the two week stay in Blackpool the troupe had no booking. As the engagement after that was in the North-West port of Liverpool, only a short ride down the coast, the company might well have stayed on in Blackpool to enjoy their free time. There is also good reason to believe they went to a performance of the Tower Circus, which commenced its summer show that week. Cyril Critchlow – Blackpool resident, and the man who knows more about Blackpool than anyone else I know – tells that, to earn a little money to maintain their keep, *The Eight Lancashire Lads* busked on the beach at the neighbouring resort of Lytham St. Annes.[6]

After Blackpool, they played two weeks at the Parthenon Theatre, in Liverpool, and during the second week doubled at the Pavilion Theatre in the seaside resort of Southport, some nineteen miles North of Liverpool:

(w/c 10 July 1899)

SOUTHPORT, Winter Gardens, Pavilion

The Eight Lancashire Lads give an excellent exhibition of clog-dancing – pretty and effective – and prove that they have musical voices in a well-rendered glee.

(*Southport Visiter* – 10 July 1899)

The Pavilion Theatre, Seafront, Southport, Lancashire.

Most in-land theatres close during the month of July, as this is the hardest month to get clientele into theatres. Many local residents are away on holiday and, of those who stay home, few wish to spend hot summer evenings cooped up inside a stuffy theatre. The theatres in the Midlands, however, must have worked on a locality-based holiday rotary system, as it was in three of the major Midland cities that the troupe next played. First off was the Empire, Nottingham. Normally, different reviews for the same show are similar but, here, the second of two reviewers thought the Lancashire Lads would be better advised to drop their singing, which is in sharp contrast to the review from the previous week, in Southport:

---

[6] Later troupes named "The Eight Lancashire Lads" played Blackpool, so it is not possible to say if it was Charlie's troupe in this instance.

(w/c 17 July 1899)

NOTTINGHAM, Empire

The Eight Lancashire Lads give a clever exhibition of step-dancing, and quickly establish themselves as favourites.

(*The Era* – 22 July 1899)

The Eight Lancashire Lads form an attractive little outlet of dancers and vocalist, who would do well to stick to dancing alone. They danced charmingly in response to the loud demands of their admirers.

(*Nottingham Daily Express* – 17 July 1899)

For some reason, known only to himself, Chaplin didn't mention in his 1933 or 1964 writings that singing was a part of *The Eight Lancashire Lads'* repertoire, and yet it was nearly always featured in their bill matter. It was only in a 1921 article that he chose to mention this integral part of the act.

I found the Lancashire dialect hard at first but, thanks to my powers of mimicry, it came easier in the end and soon I was able to sing and dance to the satisfaction of my employer. The life was not as attractive as it might be, but I felt that I was getting on by degrees and kept to it in the hope that it might prove the next step to something better.

(*Weekly Record* – 10 September 1921)

Chaplin may have thought the singing side of the act was hardly worth a mention, whereas a third review for Nottingham gave the vocal aspect first billing.

An attractive turn is provided by vocalist and dancers *The Eight Lancashire Lads*; and a performance by the Fred Karno Company is a rich treat and highly appreciated.

(*The Magnet* – 17 July 1899)

The above review also contains another important milestone in Chaplin's life: that of seeing Fred Karno's Comedians appearing 'live' on stage, the sketch being *Jail Birds*. In his biography he mentions only once having seen them in his youth, when he fell in with some woodchoppers who worked in a mews at the back of Kennington Road.[7]

One night the boss decided to treat us to a twopenny gallery seat at the South London Music Hall. I was thrilled because Fred Karno's comedy Early Birds (the company I joined years later) was playing there that week.

(Chaplin's 1964 autobiography)

An alleged third significant event in Charlie's life was to take place that week, a competitive twenty-mile walk, with a first-prize of twenty-five pounds. In his autobiography Charlie boasts of his prowess in not only competing in the walk, not only of completing the walk, but of being the actual winner. The *Nottingham Daily Express* has comprehensive accounts of scores of sporting events for that week, from the most trivial to the most major, but nowhere to be found is mention of a twenty-mile walk. Even if the event didn't make the papers, there are still limitations that make Chaplin's involvement seem questionable. Just how did a tiny, ill-nourished ten year-old boy beat older, larger, and fitter competitors over an estimated five-and-a-half hour walking race? Then you have to ask: "If you were William Jackson, would you have allowed Charlie to go on the walk knowing that, in the evening, you would be relying on his performing a synchronised dance routine?"

---

[7] This is estimated to be in the Spring of 1903, although the sketch he names could not be traced to that particular venue, at that time.

And if Charlie did win this staggering amount, what did he spend it on? He was currently receiving twopence a week pocket money from Mr. Jackson, and a further two shillings and sixpence was being sent to his mother. Twenty-five pounds, therefore, is equivalent to FOUR years' earnings and yet, during the next four years he, his mother, and Syd often went without food for the want of sixpence.

Some seven years later Chaplin was still including his sporting feat, and sporting feet, in his CV. The following is an entry in *Who's Who on the Stage – 1906* (aka: *The Green Room Book*) which is an annual biographical record of the dramatic, musical, and variety world:

> CHAPLIN, Charles. impersonator, mimic and sand-dancer; b. London, April 16th. 1889. s. of Charles Chaplin; brother of Sidney Chaplin; cradled in the profession, made first appearance at the Oxford, as a specialty turn, when ten years of age, has fulfilled engagements with several of Charles Frohman's companies (playing Billy in "Sherlock Holmes"), and at many of the leading variety theatres in London provinces; won 20-miles walking championship (and £25 cash prize) at Nottingham.
>
> Address: c/o Ballard MacDonald, 1, Clifford's Inn, E.C.

There are those who might find it remarkable that Chaplin was included in this book, amongst the elite and the great. I don't. In compiling any work under the umbrella title *"Who's Who,"* no-one would sit down and write a list of the top names in the given profession, then pursue sources which might contain their CV. All that happens is that the compiler approaches the top agencies and asks who they've got on their books. The agencies then hand over all their artistes' publicity material and CVs, and the compiler copies them out. Thus it's quite common to find the greatest actors, singers, musicians, or variety artistes of the day listed alongside someone who has done little more than once having walked across a stage.

All in all, the entry for Chaplin in *The Green Room Book* is pretty accurate, so it's a pity that his engagement as a "step-dancer" was corrupted to "sand-dancer." Or was it a corruption? There may yet be a good reason for this entry, which will be revealed in good time. The entry for his first appearance at the Oxford, however, is spot on. He had done a try-out week at Portsmouth, before making his big London debut on 3 April 1899, just two weeks before his eleventh birthday.

On with the show: From Nottingham it was only a short walk – well for one member at least – to Birmingham, where the eight young boys topped the bill at the Gaiety Theatre. One week later and another short stroll brought them to Wolverhampton, for an appearance at the Empire.

It seems that William Jackson was now finding work harder to come by. After the long run at the London Oxford, one would have thought the troupe would have been in ever-increasing demand. Maybe, as they were now a top-of-the-bill act, Jackson had increased their fee and priced them out of some theatres. One couldn't blame Jackson for wanting more money. After all, he had to maintain a travelling company of ten fast-growing children, plus two adults, and a baby. Of just how hard a feat this was, Charlie tells the story:

> I remember playing on the same bill with two young acrobats, boy apprentices about my own age, who told us confidentially that their mother received seven and sixpence a week and they got a shilling pocket money put under their bacon and egg plate every Monday morning
>
> "And," complained one of our boys, "we only get twopence and a bread and jam breakfast."
>
> When Mr. Jackson's son, John, heard that we were complaining, he broke down and wept, telling us that at times, playing odd weeks in the suburbs of London, his father only got seven pounds a week for the whole troupe and that they were having a hard time making both ends meet.
>
> (Chaplin's 1964 autobiography)

The Eight Lancashire Lads
(Photo taken *circa* May 1899)
Although Chaplin has never been officially identified in this photograph, I would venture
to say he is standing fourth from left. (Compare the inset taken less than two years later
which IS confirmed as being Chaplin.)
Charlie described his costume as follows:
"A white linen blouse, a lace collar, plush knickerbocker pants, and red dancing shoes."

BEFORE:
The Eight Lancashire Lads
(*circa* July 1898)
So which one did Charlie replace?
And which one is a girl?

AFTER:
The Eight Lancashire Lads
(July 1908)
So which ones are the originals?
Which are the Jackson Boys?

Next county of call was Yorkshire, which had scores of theatres where one would have thought they could have secured engagements; such as those in Barnsley, Halifax, Huddersfield, Leeds, and Sheffield. But, after a stay of just one week only, in Bradford, the company headed way up North; in fact over the Scottish border. Here too, in Scotland, the rich vein of theatres was not exploited and so, after just one week in Dundee, and one in Aberdeen, the troupe headed back into Yorkshire for a week's appearance at the Alhambra, in Hull.

Although willing to take work regardless of distance, the company found itself with no engagement for two weeks, and so wearily wended its way back to London for some rest and rethinking. It's hard to understand the reason for the company's poor number of bookings in the provinces. On their most recent travels to and from Scotland they had not stopped off to play *any* Lancashire towns, and had played only two in Yorkshire; and yet here in London they were engaged by the biggest theatres, and were kept over for multiple weeks. As the troupe were scheduled to spend all but three weeks of the next five months in London, let us hope it was about to remain kind to them. If it didn't, they would be finished.

Chapter 2

CAPITAL GAINS

'*The Eight Lancashire Lads*' first booking after their break was at Barnard's Palace in Chatham, Kent. This was one of the lesser theatres on the circuit, but would do to refresh the act before returning to the capital. The review from Chatham ran:

(w/c 24 September 1899)

CHATHAM – Barnard's Palace of Varieties

The Eight Lancashire Lads – Characteristic Championship Clog Dancers, Vocalists etc.

The Music Hall Stage possesses a group of accomplished dancers in the really first-rate combination of dancers *The Eight Lancashire Lads*, who form a great attraction. Their movements when they are dancing together, are executed with precision, while their individual performances are equally clever and meritorious. Crowded audiences have cheered the lads enthusiastically, and demanded repetitions

(*Chatham News* – 25 September 1899)

Upon examining all past reviews and bills, one observes that *The Eight Lancashire Lads'* actual performance time varies from three minutes to around ten. This would have been governed by their performing one dance – or two; and one song – or no songs. Now, here at Chatham where the boys were the top-of-the bill, and the number of acts on the bill was very low, they would have had to do longer. One of their party-pieces was to stand on their heads and tap-dance on a board above them. It was also during weeks like this that the boys did solo routines. To reiterate what Charlie had said about his debut: "It was weeks before I could solo dance as the rest of them did."

The Chatham engagement was an almost identical set of circumstances to the time Charlie had made his debut at the Oxford: a two week gap; a try-out week outside of London, followed by a season in London. It's a good bet, therefore, that Chatham would have been where Charlie performed his first-ever solo dance.

I was not particularly enamoured with being just a clog dancer in a troupe of eight lads. Like the rest of them I was ambitious to do a single act, not only because it meant more money but because I instinctively felt it to be more gratifying than just dancing.

(Chaplin's 1964 autobiography)

Although they had already conquered the London Oxford, *The Lancashire Lads* would now have to turn in an equally impressive performance at a theatre of almost equal prominence – namely the Canterbury Music Hall. In addition to the prestige of working the latter theatre, finances would be considerably helped by their being allowed to do a second show each evening at another venue – the Paragon Theatre, in the Mile End Road, East London. At the Canterbury the eight apprentice music-hall stars were again able to observe the grand masters – stars such

THE REFEREE

8 OCTOBER 1899

(9 October 1899)
THE CANTERBURY
WESTMINSTER BRIDGE ROAD

OLD-ESTABLISHED
GRAND COMPANY
GREATEST SHOW ON STAGE

PAUL MARTINETTI and CO.
in
ROBERT MACAIRE

LEONI CLARKE'S CLEVER	HARRY ANDERSON
BOXING KANGAROO	GEORGE ROBEY
THE LEOPOLDS	EDWIN BARWICK
SISTERS LEVEY	DUNBAR TRIO
MARIE KENDALL	ARTHUR LLOYD TRIO
SISTERS CASELLI	QUEENIE LAWRENCE

REZENE and ROBINI

VESTA TILLEY

EIGHT LANCASHIRE LADS	THE SALAMBOS
ATHAS and COLINS	OLIVETTE

KITTY CORBETT

Doors open 7.30. Saturday 7.
Manager, Mr. FRED HOLDEN

THE MAGNET

14 OCTOBER 1899

THE PARAGON
Mile 'End-road
Manager Mr. Fred Miller

ATHAS and COLLINS

HARRY ANDERSON

EDWIN BARWICK

WILLIE BENN

PAUL COURTNEY and Co.

TOTS DAVIS

GODWYNNE PEARL

EDGAR GRANVILLE

HANVAAR

MARIE KENDALL

EIGHT LANCASHIRE LADS

OLIVETTE

GEORGE ROBEY

REZENE and ROBINI

THE SALMBOS

TILLER'S "Harvest Home"

THE REFEREE

5 NOVEMBER 1899

MONDAY - November 6, 1899
THE OXFORD

"THE PROGRAMME OF LONDON"

Important engagement of
BRANSBY WILLIAMS
In a Dramatic Sketch, entitled
A NOBLE DEED,
Adapted from Charles Dickens's Novel
"A Tale of Two Cities"
Sydney Carton .... Bransby Williams

EUGENE STRATTON
In his Latest Success
MY LITTLE OCTOROON

7:20	OVERTURE
7:25	JENNY LYNN
7:30	JOE ARCHER
7:35	LILY LENA
7:40	THE NINE ROSEBUDS
7:45	PAT RAFFERTY
7:50	KATIE COHEN
7:55	HERBERT LA MARTINE
8:00	VERA VERE
8:05	ELAINE RAVENSBERG
8:10	ALBER CHRISTIAN
8:15	DONALDSON BROS. and ARDELL
8:25	EIGHT LANCASHIRE LADS
8:30	THE TWO BOSTONS
8:40	MARIE KENDALL
8:45	THE POLUSKIS
9:00	FRANTZ FAMILY
9:10	GEORGE LASHWOOD
9:15	J. A. WILSON
9:25	BRANSBY WILLIAMS
9:50	THE TWO McNAUGHTONS
10:00	EUGENE STRATTON
10:10	GEORGE MOZART
10:20	CHIRGWIN
10:30	BALE TROUPE
10:40	CONSTANCE MOXTON
10:50	JAMES and MARIE FINNEY

CHIRGWIN
The White-Eyed Kaffir

GEORGE MOZART, THE POLUSKIS
GEORGE LASHWOOD

Doors Open 7:10   Commence 7:30
Matinees every Saturday at 2:15
Manager Mr. ALBERT GILMER

Bills for three different music halls being played by *The Eight Lancashire Lads*, during October and November 1899.

as: George Robey, Paul Martinetti, Arthur Lloyd, The Leopolds, and Vesta Tilley.

All these weeks playing in London must have been very comforting to Charlie, as he was able to see his mother at the weekends. There was no compulsion however for him to stay at his mother's home, as the rules of his contract were that he was to receive board and lodgings, whilst touring. Alfred Jackson confirmed the situation:

> He [Charlie] came to stay with us at 167 Kensington Road, and slept with me in the attic under the tiles. While we were in London we all went to the Sancroft-street Schools (opposite Kennington Cross), and he began to brighten up as he got to know us better.

(*The Star* – September 1921)

167 Kennington Road (with the black front door, next-door-but-one to
The Ship public house) were Charlie slept in the attic under the tiles.
(Photo 2005 by *Mortier*)

After four weeks at the Canterbury and the Paragon, the troupe shot up to the Lancashire town of Bolton, only to shoot back down to the capital after just one week. This marked a return to the Oxford, where they played for an impressive six weeks, after which they were offered yet more work in London, but this time in a different medium. Mr. Jackson had secured parts for the boys in a pantomime, to run over the Festive Season at the New Alexandra Theatre in Stoke Newington, North London. Some crossed-wires have led to these seven weeks containing a mystery – wires which can happily be uncrossed right here. Some biographers have worked on the theory that Chaplin also appeared at the London Hippodrome, concurrent with the Stoke Newington pantomime, in a play called *Giddy Ostend*. This is wrong on two counts: 1) It wasn't a play and 2) Chaplin wasn't in it. To expound:

The name "Hippodrome" is part misnomer. This London venue, which opened on 15 January 1900, might better have been named the 'Aqua-Hippodrome,' as the horse-ring had a special feature housed below it. The ring would be lowered into a massive circular tank, which was part-filled with water. Within a few short minutes the one-hundred-thousand gallon capacity, eight foot deep tank was then topped-up with warm water, pumped in at a rapid rate, which allowed for aquatic shows and displays to be performed. With the audience being seated three-quarters-in-the-round, conventional shows could not be staged; so many of the variety acts were handpicked to work in or around the pool. Thus 'Woodward's Sea-Lions,' 'Lockhart's Plunging Elephants,' and the swimming act 'The Finneys,' were literally in their element.

As microphones had not yet been invented, it would have been impractical, if not metaphorically suicidal, for any patter comedian to perform there. The resident principal comic was Marceline, who overcame the need to be heard by working as a 'dumb' act. One of the comedy sketches on the Hippodrome bill was *Giddy Ostend*, the star of which was 'Little Tich.' There *were* some children who acted as extras in 'the beach' scene in *Giddy Ostend* but, as the sketch ran for only a few minutes, transporting *The Eight Lancashire Lads* from Stoke Newington to fill these roles would not have been cost worthy. Timing, to play parts in both shows, would also have been too great a risk to contemplate. Far better to use children who belonged to the artistes, or the staff at the Hippodrome.

The theory of *The Eight Lancashire Lads* being in this panto probably originated because of the appearance on the Hippodrome bill of an act called 'The Jacksons'[1] – a group of musicians, with the bill matter: "The Jackson Family – in their Refined Drawing-Room Musical Entertainment." Because the backbone of *The Eight Lancashire Lads* was also 'the Jackson Family,' I believe that somewhere along the line a biographer saw 'The Jacksons' on the bill and assumed it referred to 'Jackson's Eight Lancashire Lads.' To demonstrate the exact process take a look, below, at an extract from an article written to coincide with Chaplin's 1921 visit to England.

> Charlie Chaplin has made several appearances in Blackpool. The first time he appeared at the Palace Variety Theatre[2] was about twenty years ago, when he came with the Jackson Family, a group of Lancashire dancers of Bolton origin.
>
> (*Blackpool Gazette and Herald* – 10 September 1921)

I know Chaplin says in his autobiography that he appeared with Marceline at the Hippodrome but, as Marceline played the Hippodrome for four consecutive years, there is nothing to place Chaplin here during this particular panto season, as we shall yet see.

So now we know where the lads *weren't*, let's look at where they *were*. Stoke Newington is a borough of London, four miles North of the Thames. There, the Alexandra Theatre closed for rehearsals w/c 18 December 1899, and opened the following Tuesday, Boxing Day, with the pantomime *Sinbad the Sailor*. It gained some great reviews for its staging and production values:

> .... Bright, tuneful, and magnificently staged.
>
> (*Sun* – December 1899)

> ..... One of the funniest and most picturesque pantos seen in North London for years.
>
> (*Morning Post* – December 1899)

Charlie and the rest of *The Eight Lancashire Lads* played members of Captain Bowlines' crew:

---

[1] 'The Jackson Family (aka: 'The Jacksons') had previously shared the bill with The Eight Lancashire Lads at the Theatre Royal, in Manchester, in the pantomime Babes in the Wood, during the Christmas season of 1898/99.
[2] The Lancashire Lads did appear at the Palace Theatre, but that was w/c 19 December 1904, long after Charlie had left.

Where *The Eight Lancashire Lads* were ....

.... and where they weren't.

NEW ALEXANDRA THEATRE
STOKE NEWINGTON, N.

SINBAD THE SAILOR

Sinbad the Sailor has many gorgeous scenes, tableaux, processions and ballets, exquisite costumes, and some remarkable electric lighted scenery. It teems throughout with fun and jollity.

Audiences have seldom seen so blithe and jolly a 'Sinbad' as Miss Lola Hawthorne. Then, too, dainty Miss Lydia Flopp as 'Lady So-and-So' and 'Mary the Housemaid' has quite won the ear and admiration of all North London, while 'Mrs. Sinbad' and 'Binbad' (Messrs. Fred Eastman and F. W. Colman) have many new practical jokes and burlesque scenes to cause laughter, both at the time and after. The prison scene with eccentric cookery lingers funnily in the memory.

Mr. Charles Bignell has now quite shaken down into his part as 'Capt. Bowline,' and has introduced many fresh wheezes which 'go' immensely. So, too, is the clog dancing and hornpipe dancing—and foot playing—for it comes to that, since they give tune and variations easily with their feet of the 'Eight Lancashire Lads;' while the Harlequinade, including an excellent clown and pantaloon and a very funny and very corpulent policeman gains an interest from being conducted on skates by the splendid 'Ashley Team,' but loses nothing of its fun and comicality.

MATINEES MONDAY, WEDNESDAY, THURSDAY, and SATURDAY, January 8th, 10th, 11th, 13th, 15th, 17th, 18th, 20th; and every Monday, Thursday, and Saturday. Prices of Admission 6d. to £2 2s.

(w/c TUESDAY January 15, 1900)
THE LONDON HIPPODROME
GIDDY OSTEND - or
The Absent-Minded Millionaire

Petrolio Vanderstor	Little Tich
Mrs. P. P. Vanderstor	Miss Elsie Carew
Columbia Vanderstor	Miss Marie Finney
De Wolfhopp Von Sineth	Mr. Fritz Rimina
Nikola Nonoofa	Mr. Kenneth Altamont
Simpkin Spudkins	Mr. M. R. Morand
Yaurelia Saveranna	Miss Blanche Wolseley
Neddy	Mr. S. Asher

Giddy Ostend, termed an "amphibious burletta," introduces once more to London audiences Little Tich - in fact it is round the diminutive but clever comedian, and the swimming performance of Mr. James and Miss Marie Finney, that the piece is constructed. The scene is Ostend and the millionaire desires to lose his wife, and disguise himself, whilst his daughter, not caring to marry a certain Count who pesters her, throws himself in to the sea to drown herself, but, being rescued, takes advantage of the the opportunity thus offered and gives a swimming entertainment. In these circumstance one can understand how Mr. Chance Newton, the librettist, must have been hampered in his work. With no straw he could turn out very few bricks. There are one or two good songs, notably a parody on "The Absent-Minded Beggar" and a Volunteer song which starts off its chorus with the words "Off to Pretoria." Two pretty little ballets, one danced by the bathers, are supplied with tuneful music, in which one can trace Mr. Georges Jacobi's graceful style without the authentication of the programme. Mr. Jacobi's ballet music has always such a captivating turn that to dance badly to it would be an impossibility. The backcloth to the scene gives a very good and truthful view of the the Kursaal. Little Tich, with his nimble dancing, eccentric tricks, and mannerisms causes endless amusement. He really sustains the piece. Supporting him are Miss Elsie Carew and Blanche Wolseley; Messrs. Fritz Rimina, Kenneth Altamont, M. R. Morand, and S. Asher; while M. Finney and Family's clever performance constitutes the "amphibious" portion of the burletta.

Scene three: the deck of 'the Saucy Puss Puss' before the catastrophe. A capital dance by *The Eight Lancashire Lads* with clogs is admirably done, and highly appreciated.

(*The Stage* – 4 January 1900)

> In the ship scene is introduced a troupe of boys hailing from the North of England who, first as sailors with a hornpipe, and next as clog-dancers, brought the house down with some wonderful dancing.

(*London Daily Chronicle* – 27 December 1899)

The seven-week run in Stoke Newington ended on the 10 February 1900, from whence *The Lancashire Lads* travelled to the North-East, for a week in the Teesside town of Middlesbrough. The last journey they had made from London to Middlesbrough, was followed by an even longer trek to Wales, but this time they had the blessing of playing theatres in close proximity, namely the Tyneside cities of Newcastle and South Shields. Then came one week each in the Scottish cities of Glasgow and Edinburgh.

Whilst at the Glasgow Empire, Charlie nightly observed the stage performance of Bransby Williams, in his portrayal of 'celebrated characters from Charles Dickens.' The character which Charlie particularly took to was Bransby's interpretation of "Little Nellie's" grandfather in *The Old Curiosity Shop*, in 'the death scene with Nellie.' Off-stage, Charlie began to do what he thought was a mean impersonation of Bransby's 'old man', and took every opportunity to try it out with members of the troupe. "Every opportunity" might not be an exaggeration as this is what Alfred, youngest of the Jackson boys, had to say:

> He [Charlie] was a great mimic, but his heart was set on tragedy. For weeks he would imitate Bransby Williams in The Old Curiosity Shop wearing an old grey wig and tottering with a stick, until we others were sick of him.

(*The Star* – September 1921)

Finally, the impression was seen by Jackson senior who was impressed enough to let Charlie perform it on stage. On the allotted evening, as soon as 'the Lads' had finished their clog-dancing routine, Jackson walked out on stage to introduce this 'extra turn' from "one of his talented company." With that, Charlie returned wearing the said grey wig, which was the only addition to the costume he had just danced in. Chaplin's account continues:

> Although I had a large head, the wig was larger; it was a bald-headed wig, fringed with long, grey stringy hair, so that when I appeared on stage bent as an old man, the effect was like a crawling beetle, and the audience endorsed the act with titters. It was difficult to get them quiet after that. I spoke in subdued whispers: "Hush, hush, you mustn't make a noise or you'll wake my Nelly."

> But I went on feebly whispering, all very intimate; so intimate that the audience began to stamp. It was the end of my career as a delineator of Charles Dickens' characters.[3]

Again, Charlie's account is at odds with the available information (see photograph on Page). As a postscript: on 7 February 1955 Chaplin was Guest Speaker at the Dicken's Fellowship, at the Café Royale, London, and in his speech said:

> I am very happy to have the honour of proposing the toast to the immortal memory of the great master of letters Charles Dickens. There is somebody whom I wish were here tonight, because he was a man who was responsible for inspiring, and I should say, enlivening, a young boy's interest in literature.

---

[3] Chaplin says he saw Bransby Williams in Glasgow, then impersonated him in Middlesbrough. But the Middlesbrough engagement was four weeks before the one in Glasgow. The most likely venue for Charlie's impersonation was the Edinburgh Empire, or even the Birmingham Empire, some three weeks later, as Alfred did say Charlie was driving them mad for weeks with the impersonation.

I remember at the age of eight[4], when I was with The Eight Lancashire Lads, a troupe of clog dancers, standing in the wings of the Empire Music Hall, Glasgow, and I stood there enthralled, as I watched a world for the first time, a new world of romance, mystery and wonderment, enacted by a very handsome gentleman imitating characters from Charles Dickens.

The gentleman responsible for those moments was Mr. Bransby Williams. I am truly sorry that he is not here tonight, for he is one of the few persons I can say I remember when I was a little boy.

(Peter Haining – unaccredited 1955 article)

The above is rare praise indeed. In his writings Chaplin makes few mentions of the music-hall stars he saw on stage and, when he does, it is not usually to give credit. In his 1964 autobiography the longest list of acts he gives revelations about is a number of comedians who shot themselves; thus dismissing everything they achieved in their career in preference to informing us just how they ended it.

The week in Edinburgh was followed by a two-week run in Birmingham, after which it was back to London. The recent runs to Yorkshire and Scotland must have been hardly financially worthwhile, and were certainly exhausting; but now – between 16 April and 15 September 1900 – *The Eight Lancashire Lads* were to enjoy an almost five month unbroken run of London venues. Charlie must have been hoping that word of his Bransby Williams impersonation hadn't followed him to London, as he was to share the bill with the man himself for the next five weeks. At least the other *Lancashire Lads* had the comfort of the seeing the act being performed properly.

Another legendary act they worked was Marie Lloyd. Maybe as she did not fall into the category of "male comedians I must remember not to mention," Chaplin allowed us a little insight into her, although even this wasn't actually praising:

> The famous Marie Lloyd was reputed to be frivolous, yet when we played with her at the Tivoli, in the Strand, never was there a more serious and conscientious artist. I would watch her wide-eyed, this anxious, plump little lady pacing nervously up and down behind the scenes, irritable and apprehensive until the moment came for her to go on. Then she was gay and relaxed.

Although *The Eight Lancashire Lads* did play the Tivoli, w/c 21 May 1900, they doubled at another theatre each evening, and it was at the second, the Metropolitan in the Edgware Road, where they shared the stage with Marie Lloyd. What baffles me is not that Chaplin got the venue wrong, but that his archives don't, I believe, carry a copy of the review for the Metropolitan. Within the pages of this book you will become acquainted with instances where Chaplin has re-written newspaper reviews, in order to give himself undue praise. However, in this instance, he couldn't have written a better one himself:

A VISIT TO THE MET'

> Proudly the Metropolitan continues to hold its own with its West-End rivals. This week a fine array of talent is to be found. Marie Lloyd comes along with plenty of songs. Eugene Stratton proves what a wonderful 'darkie' he is. One of the best turns, however, is provided by The Eight Lancashire Lads, a troupe of really finely trained dancers; the boys really understand their work, and we have seen nothing more delightfully novel and attractive for a long time. George Robey does his best to live up to his reputation.

(*The Magnet* – 26 May 1900)

---

[4] Here we go again! Charlie wasn't eight. He was actually just four weeks short of his ELEVENTH birthday.

This is a stunning piece of testimony to the talents of *The Eight Lancashire Lads*. They have been singled out for praise above three of the biggest names in music-hall history, and yet Charlie fails to bring it to our attention. But what of the greatest-of-all music-hall acts, legendary comedian Dan Leno? Did Chaplin ever work with him, or see him work? Well he states in his autobiography:

> Dan Leno, I suppose, was the greatest English comedian since the legendary Grimaldi. Although I never saw Leno in his prime, to me he was more of a character actor than a comedian. His whimsical character delineations of London's lower classes were human and endearing, so Mother told me.

Considering Charlie's movements between 16 April and 15 September, one would have to question not only his recollection, but his honesty, for he shared the bill with Leno on no less than FIFTEEN of those twenty-two weeks. One might try to make a case that, in instances where *The Lancashire Lads* were working other theatres on the same night, they might not have been in the common theatre at the same time. However, for six of the fifteen weeks the troupe shared the bill with Leno, they were working only the one theatre and, because of their position on the bill, could not have already left the theatre when Leno arrived.

If one then defends Chaplin by saying that he doesn't claim he never saw Leno, only that he never saw him "in his prime," then that too would be a flawed defence. In 1900, Leno was in no way passed his prime. In fact, he was probably at his peak. Witness the following contemporary reviews:

> This week at the London Tivoli Dan Leno has the warmest of welcomes, and never has been in better form. His two latest songs, "I'll Fit You," and "Man is Not Complete," wildly extravagant as is their humour, are decidedly entertaining. The last-mentioned song is particularly good, and Mr. Leno's blackboard illustrations of man, simply bring down the house.
>
> (*The Stage* – 26 April 1900)

And again from the Tivoli, just four weeks later.

> Dan Leno, with his "Incomplete Man," now given with fresh and excruciatingly funny "diagrams," as he puts it, and his "Bootshop" song, goes "immense."
>
> (*The Stage* – 24 May 1900)

Another four weeks later on, and Leno is back at the Tivoli:

> After leading his audience in highly amusing fashion through the intricacies of "Incomplete Man," and causing them to laugh as heartily as possible, Dan Leno proceeded to earn further distinction as a comedian with his "Bootmaker" song.
>
> (*The Stage* – 21 June 1900)

And from the Oxford theatre, itself.

> Dan Leno's new song here is entitled "The Huntsman," and is full of quaintness and "funnisms" that make the audience roar with laughter. Leno's description of a visit to the house of "a friend I owe money to" for the purpose of hunting, and without having the faintest idea of what he's got to hunt, is excruciatingly funny. His second song, "The Bootmaker," goes even better than before.
>
> (*The Stage* – 16 August 1900)

These are hardly the reviews of a comedian past his best. So just why did Charlie omit these encounters from his records? By using "I suppose" in the above résumé of Leno, Chaplin is again reserving praise; and the phrase "so my Mother told me" seems to have been appended as a defence, in case an interviewer might ask: "How would you know, if you never saw him?"

Music Hall's two greatest-ever comedians – DAN LENO and GEORGE ROBEY – whom Chaplin never worked with. Unless, that is, you count the fifteen weeks he shared the stage with Leno, and the ten weeks with Robey.

The reason Chaplin forgot about working with them was because they had nothing memorable about them. Leno's character of a working-class man trying to look like an upper-class gent, in his rounded hat, tight jacket, baggy trousers, and carrying a gamp, had little interest to Chaplin.

As a postscript: when Chaplin was visiting London in 1921, Fleet Street journalist Hannen Swaffer went walkabout with him. One stop was at Sharp's photographers' shop, on Westminster Bridge-road, where Charlie was drawn inside by a photo of Dan Leno on display in the window. Swaffer recorded that Chaplin there and then confessed that, to him, Leno was a God. To hold Leno in such status, Chaplin must have had first-hand knowledge of Leno's work, and studied him at close quarters. So why deny it? One theory I have is that, if Chaplin said he hadn't seen Leno, he couldn't be accused of any form of plagiarism. But if any such accusation were totally unfounded, why bother to cover it up?

June was a great month for *The Eight Lancashire Lads*, with all four weeks being spent at the legendary Canterbury Music Hall. There they caught the attention of a journalist from *The Magnet* who, from an interview with William Jackson, later did a huge write-up on them. The first half of his article is so inaccurate that, were it to be reproduce it here, it would then take a full page to correct it. The remainder, however, gives a good insight into the troupe and its manager:

THE LANCASHIRE LADS

The head of the troupe is William Jackson, and with this gentleman I had an interview recently.

"How long do you stay in town?"

"Until September, when we go to the provinces, where we appear until pantomime period; afterwards we come back to Town, opening on March 18th, 1901, at the [Holborn] Royal."

"Of course you are well booked?"

"Until 1902; and we still receive offers."

"Did the troupe appear in pantomime last Christmas?"

"Yes; at the Alexander Theatre; and the troupe were to appear also at Drury Lane, being engaged by Mr. Arthur Collins; but unfortunately the arrangement fell through: so the lads only worked Stoke Newington." [So no *Giddy Ostend* at the Hippodrome, then?]

"Are any of your sons among the lads?"

"Yes, two of them are included in it; and the other six are my pupils.[5] They have all been trained under my personal supervision, and in this direction my wife gives me much assistance."

Of the boys' performance, the article continued:

A bright and breezy turn, with a dash of true "salt" in it, is contributed to the Variety stage by that excellent troupe, *The Eight Lancashire Lads*, whose speciality act we cannot speak too highly of. Mr. William Jackson presents to the public eight perfectly drilled lads, who treat the audience to some of the finest clog dancing it is possible to imagine. The turn is a good one, because it gets away from the usual, and plunges boldly into the sea of novelty. The Lancashire Lads are fine specimens of boys, and most picturesque do they look in their charming costumes; indeed, they are useful as well as ornamental, and treat us to a most enjoyable ten minutes' entertainment.

(*The Magnet* – 14 July 1900)

One would have thought that, following a four-week stay at the Canterbury and the publicity given by the write-up in *The Magnet*, William Jackson would have been able to fill their date sheet with bookings, but this was far from the case. July turned out to be an absolute stinker of a

---

[5] No mention here of William Jackson's daughter being in the troupe. Some sources say he had TWO daughters amongst the eight, but these accounts can be instantly dismissed. The Jacksons had only the one daughter, and she was too young for the troupe.

THE MAGNET

2 JUNE 1900

THE TIVOLI
The Strand
Manager: VERNON DOWSETT

Joe Archer
Albert Christian
Eight Lancashire Lads
Will Evans
Annette Fengler
Gotham Quartette
Glinseretti Troupe
Lil Hawthorne
Dan Leno
Sisters Levey
The Leo Tells
George Mozart
Constance Moxon
Minnie Palmer
George Robey
Austin Rudd
Harry Randall
Ernest Shand
Vesta Tilley
Baroness Valmar
Ada Willoughby
Bransby Williams

METROPOLITAN
Edgware-road
Manager: J.W. EDGAR
Managing Director: HENRI GROSS

Asher Sisters
Anglo-American Bio-
  Tableaux
Bale Troupe
Sisters Caselli
Eight Lancashire Lads
Ethairien Brothers
Rose Elliott
May Evans
The Hulines
Lillian Lowe
Marie Lloyd
George Mozart
Newham and Latimer
George Robey
Bert Shepherd
Ernest Shand
Fred Walton & Edith Bruce

ROYAL STANDARD
Pimlico
Manager: FRED LAW

Albert & Edmunds Troupe
Herbert Campbell
The Sisters Chester
Kitty Corbett
Lois Du Cane
Darnley Brothers
Eight Lancashire Lads
Chas. E. Edwards
Minnie Mario
Fred Neiman
The Phantos
Ricardo Troupe
Tom Woottwell

Bills for three different music halls being played each evening by *The Eight Lancashire Lads*, during week commencing 28 May 1900.
Among the stars they shared the stage with can be found Dan Leno, George Robey, Harry Randall, Vesta Tilley, Bransby Williams, and Marie Lloyd.

month. To continue in work, the troupe had to travel almost literally from the toe to the top of England. Firstly, they made their way down to the South-West coast, for just a one-week engagement in Plymouth, only to return to London for the following two weeks, in Woolwich. There, the Theatre Royal, a small-time drama theatre, decided to change its policy for just those two weeks and stage Variety. A one-week holiday was then had by the company; one day of which would have been lost in having to take the trip of some two-hundred and eighty-five miles to the Lancashire town of Barrow-in-Furness, for the next booking. Seven days later, the exact same trip was made in reverse for the start of another long run in London. Just *why* Jackson bothered to take single-week bookings, which necessitated journeys of five hundred miles plus, when taking a week out would seem the more prudent, seems incomprehensible.

Back in London, meant being back in the "big-time." They were returning to the Oxford, the venue at which they could do no wrong, and again gained better reviews than three of the greatest comedians in music-hall history:

(w/c 10 September 1900)

LONDON – Oxford Music Hall

We appreciate the show given by the Lancashire Lads, a splendid troupe of boys who are quite the smartest clog dancers we have seen. We all know the turns of Leno, Knowles, and Robey but, like the town-crier, we ask for a little bit more novelty, and a little less "reputation."

(*The Magnet* – 15 September 1900)

During the six-week run at the Oxford, *The Lancashire Lads* were able to make up for the loss of earnings in July by doubling, in successive weeks, at theatres in the boroughs of Camberwell, Walham Green, Clapham Junction, and Shoreditch; plus a short out-of-town run to Croydon. In fact, during the first week they worked three theatres per night. For a normal, healthy eleven-year-old boy this was a strength sapping schedule. For Charlie it must have been absolutely exhausting but, to his credit, he speaks only of it affecting his facial demeanour.

Audiences liked the Eight Lancashire Lads because, as Mr Jackson said, we were so unlike theatrical children. It was his boast that we never wore grease-paint and our rosy cheeks were natural. If some of us looked a little pale before going on, he would tell us to pinch our cheeks. But in London, after working two or three music halls a night, we would occasionally forget, and look a little weary and bored as we stood on the stage, until we caught sight of Mr Jackson in the wings, grinning emphatically and pointing to his face, which had an electrifying effect of making us suddenly break into sparkling grins.

(Chaplin's 1964 autobiography)

Then came yet another of those several hundred-mile journeys just to play one week, this time in Hull, followed by a return to London to play Clapham. On the bill at the Grand Theatre, Clapham Junction, was an act that one would have thought Chaplin ought to have gone out of his way to mention in his autobiography. Not only did he fail to do so, but he further tried to cover up their shared week by stating that he only ever saw this person once on the stage, some years earlier at the Canterbury Music Hall. The circumstance regarding Chaplin omitting to mention sharing the bill with Dan Leno has already been covered, but this person was a much more important part of Charlie's life – for the act was none other than his father.

Chapter 3 (Interlude one)

JUNIOR DENIES SEE'N'YA

Charles Chaplin Senior was a "descriptive vocalist," a type of act commonly referred to as a "lion comique." To "sell" the song to the audience Chaplin would get into the part of the characters the songs were written around, typical of which were a coster, a Jew, and a dude. Ted Hughes, a comedian who saw Chaplin Senior work, said of him:

> In those days salaries were very small, and Charles Chaplin senior did not earn much more, but he was a good singer, and a very capable actor, too.
>
> (*Blackpool Gazette and Herald* – 10 September 1921)

Charles junior stated that his father, at the peak of his career, was earning the princely sum of forty-pound per week. However, in the years 1898-1901 Chaplin senior was averaging a booking around only one week in four. Apply this average and forty-pound per week becomes, in reality, forty-pound per month. From this he had to pay household bills plus, when working in the provinces, transport and accommodation costs. Then take out the money spent keeping his current lady friend in the lifestyle she expected, and forty-pound starts to look hardly enough. And we haven't yet deducted his biggest outlay – his drinks' bill. The management of the theatres thought forty-pound per week no great outlay, as a large percentage of the money would end up being paid back over the bar by the star himself.[1] Is it little wonder that Hannah Chaplin and her two sons hardly ever, if ever at all, received the fifteen shillings maintenance the courts had decreed the father should pay them?

Charlie later defended his father's drinking habits, when he reflected:

> It was difficult for vaudevillians not to drink in those days, for alcohol was sold in all theatres, and after a performer's act he was expected to go to the theatre bar and drink with the customers. Thus many an artist was ruined by drink – my father was one of them.

But it wasn't just vaudevillians who drank in those days – everyone drank. They drank for one simple reason: it was safer to drink beer than it was to drink the water. Workers in mills and factories were known to drink in excess of ten pints of beer during one shift which, so long as they didn't show any outward signs of drunkenness, was quite acceptable. However, it was the

---

[1] A common arrangement was for theatre managers to actually pay artistes "part money – part drinks."

untoward effects brought about by drinking that was the cause of Charles Snr. not being allowed into the family home. It was also, ultimately, to be the cause of his sad end.

In September 1898, the Board of Guardians were seeking to make Charles Chaplin guardian of his son Charlie and step-son Sydney, but he was away in Hull. Whilst there he received a review which might well indicate that the pressure in his private life was beginning to affect his stage work.

HULL, New Alhambra

Audiences for a long time past have been so surfeited with "eccentric" vocalists with extravagant make-up and songs to match, that they seem, just at present, to be incapable of appreciating the work of a singer who appears in evening dress and condescends to give them sensible humour. Perhaps this explains to some extent why Mr. Charles Chaplin, who tops the Alhambra bill, does not seem to meet with the warm reception he might expect. His songs are real good stuff, especially The Ostler's Story; English, French, and German; and Winning and Losing; and descriptive work which needs histrionic capability. He sings four songs in all.

(Hull Entr'Acte – 26 September 1898)

It's almost unknown for a trade paper to print a negative review of a professional act, especially a headliner. So the above review of Chaplin's performance can be interpreted as a review of a man who was not connecting with his audience; which can in turn be interpreted as he "died." For anyone unfamiliar with the term "dying on stage," it means simply that the audience do not appreciate the act. Their reaction can be either that of derision, or stony silence – which depends upon whether or not they retain any sympathy for the artiste.

In October, Chaplin was back working in London but, in contempt of the court order against him, failed to enrol Charlie and Syd in school. Hannah was desperate to rectify the situation but wasn't in any position to do so as, in September 1898, she had been committed to Cane Hill Asylum. However, after being released in mid-November, she was determined to run her husband to ground. Her chance came a few weeks later, when Chaplin had a two-week engagement at the Canterbury Music Hall. The boy Charlie remembered going with her, and sitting in a red plush seat while watching his father perform. The reason Hannah had come, however, was not to see how plush the seats were, front of stage, but to see how flush her husband was, backstage. Once there, she obviously made it quite clear to Charles that she and Charlie were in dire straits, and that it was up to him to address the matter.

At Chaplin's very next engagement, at the Manchester Tivoli, a way out of his commitment to wife and son must have been fresh in Chaplin's mind, as it was there and then that he obtained the position for Charlie in *The Eight Lancashire Lads*. This was not the result that Hannah had played for. She had wanted the money to come from her husband's earnings, but having a son who could bring in some money, even though it was a fraction, had to be considered as the second-most favourable outcome. Her husband, however, most likely considered it the best.

At a time when things just weren't going right for him, Chaplin accepted the challenge of returning to the Hull Alhambra where, only four months earlier, he had "died." Going back to a venue where you have previously been rejected is not normally advisable, but Mr. Chaplin must have been of strong character, for this is how he was received on his return:

(w/c 30 January 1899)

HULL, New Alhambra – CHARLES CHAPLIN. The Popular Star Vocal Comedian

That old favourite and sound comedian Mr. Charles Chaplin is premier among "stars" and makes his usual success with a strong vocal repertory, including "Dear Old Pals", and "Duty Calls", which necessitated him singing four songs to satisfy the audiences requirements.

(Hull Entr'acte – 4 February 1899)

DEAR OLD PALS

Dear old pals, that nothing can alter,

Staunch old pals, pals that are always true

Let the weather be rough, you know,

Give me the pal who will always go,

Through hail, rain, fire, and snow

For a dear old pal.

WHAT'S THE ROW?

What's the row, old chappie, what's the row?'

You've given him a hiding anyhow,

You've made both his eyes look shady,

And I say, 'Boy, who's the lady?'

What's the row, old chappie, what's the row?

"OUI TRAY BONG!"

or "MY PAL JONES"

Jones and I, with two good boys, Tom and Harry,

Have returned from a visit to 'Gay Par-ee'

We thought we would see the sight of it,

But we made some fair old night of it;

Still I can assure you, we've enjoyed ourselves immense I say boys!

CHORUS

Through the streets we marched along,

Shouting ev'ry comic song;

Hip, hooray! Let's be gay!

Boom diddy ay! Ta-ra-ra!

To each little Frenchy dove

Standing drinks and making love,

We fairly mashed the ladies with our Oui! Tray bong!

Just three of the songs for which Charles Chaplin Senior was famous.

Ted Hughes, a comedian who worked with Chaplin Senior may times, rightly pointed out:

They don't sound very much. They're out of date now, of course. But they went well when the late Charles Chaplin sang them, and he always carried a good chorus with him.'

(*Blackpool Gazette and Herald* – 10 September 1921)

Top marks to Chaplin here, who had totally revamped his act with a change of songs. Sad to say, the willingness to change and the will to work proved not to be enough to gain Chaplin regular engagements. In February he was booked to appear for a full four weeks at the newly-opened Bedford Theatre, in Camden. However, although billed, his name does not appear in any of the available reviews. The second week in March then signalled the start of a rapid decline in the frequency of senior's engagements. Any chance of an upsurge was dealt a resounding blow when Chaplin senior's brother, Spencer Chaplin, died and Charles had to take over the position of licensee at the *Queen's Head* public house in Broad Street, Lambeth. In July 1899 Chaplin managed to obtain three weeks work, but after that came an even bigger decline in his fortunes, as it would appear that during the remaining five months of 1899 his only engagement was the Christmas/New Year week – a week when "every act and his brother" can find work. Sharing the bill with him, and I believe this is no coincidence, was Leo Dryden, father of Chaplin's step-son Wheeler Dryden, and a similar kind of music-hall singer.

The New Year brought no prosperity. Chaplin had just one week's work in February, and then absolutely nothing until 6 August 1900, the week he shared with his son. Some listings seem to indicate that Chaplin Snr. did a second week with *The Eight Lancashire Lads* at the Grand Theatre, Clapham, although this couldn't be confirmed. Young Charlie may well have been embarrassed by witnessing his father's stage performances at Clapham, or had just found his condition all too sad to bear. No doubt the young Chaplin had been telling the other members of *The Eight Lancashire Lads* what a big star his father was but, now that they too had seen his sad state, the experience had become too embarrassing for all parties – which is one probable reason for his omitting the whole episode from his later memoirs.

Song-sheet for Leo Dryden's most famous number:
"The Miner's Dream of Home"

Senior next spent the last week of August and the first week of September at the Camberwell Palace, after which Leo Dryden again stepped in to assist him to find further work. He had seen the state of Charles's health when the two of them had shared the bill at the Granville Theatre, Clapham, over the New Year week 1899-1900. It was back at this very theatre some nine months later that Dryden persuaded the management to re-engage Chaplin. The proviso was that if Chaplin were unable to complete his act on any evening, for whatever reason, Dryden would fill the vacant time on the bill, in addition to doing his own act.

After the Clapham engagement, Chaplin senior began calling in favours from theatre managers he had done well for in the past; like those at the Manchester Tivoli, Leicester Empire, and the Portsmouth Empire, to name but three. All of them cried shy, except for the manager of the latter who engaged him for week commencing 31 December 1900 – Yes! that time of year when, because of demand, every act in the country can get work. This was the only paid booking that Chaplin is known to have had in the last three months of that year. It also turned out to be his final one. What little hope Hannah and Charlie had of ever getting Chaplin Senior to bale them out was now well and truly scuppered. Mother and son may have been dreaming of a white Christmas, but it could hardly have been blacker, and the start of the New Year was not about to bring prosperity. Not only had Chaplin's bookings ebbed away but, within four months, so too would the life of the man himself.

Sometime during his last months a Benefit Night was held for Chaplin Senior; an event mentioned by Charles Junior in the memoirs of his 1931 visit to England.

> On my way back [to the Ritz Hotel] I stopped at *The Horns* [2] for a drink. It had been rather elegant in its day, with its polished mahogany bar, fine mirrors and billiard room. The large assembly room was where my father had had his last benefit.

In his autobiography, Chaplin furnishes further information about the event:

> Three months before I left the troupe we appeared at a Benefit for my father, who had been very ill; many vaudeville artists donated their services, including Mr Jackson's Eight Lancashire Lads. The night of the benefit my father appeared on the stage breathing with difficulty, and with painful effort made a speech. I stood at the side of the stage watching him, not realising that he was a dying man.

The only other mention he makes of seeing his father is at nearby venue.

> *The Three Stags* in the Kennington Road was not a place my father frequented, yet as I passed it one evening an urge prompted me to peek inside to see if he was there. I opened the saloon door just a few inches, and there he was, sitting in the corner! I was about to leave, but his face lit up and he beckoned me to him. I was surprised at such a welcome, for he was never demonstrative. He looked very ill; his eyes were sunken, and his body had swollen to an enormous size. He rested one hand, Napoleon-like, in his waistcoat as if to ease his breathing. That evening he was most solicitous, enquiring after Mother and Sydney, and before I left took me in his arms and for the first time kissed me. That was the last time I saw him alive.

(ibid)

It's not for me to try to re-write Chaplin's history using sheer speculation or invention, but it is my aim to try to put misplaced pieces back where they belong. In the above two instances I believe Chaplin has confused two known events. The image he has of standing in the wings watching his father making a speech on stage, is far more likely to be what he remembers of the time he shared the bill at the Grand Theatre, Clapham. Note that Chaplin says that *The Eight Lancashire Lads* were on the bill, and it was held three months before he left the troupe. As they were in Clapham in September 1900, and Charlie was to leave the first week in December, this would fit the chronology.

And the last meeting of father and son is far more likely to have occurred in *The Horns* tavern, on the night of the benefit at *The Horns Assembly Rooms*. May be Chaplin later wrongly recalled the pub as being *The Three Stags*. After all, they were both corner-pubs on the Kennington Road.

In Charlie's accounts of Chaplin Snr.'s last days he has left out any mention of Syd, as if he wants us to believe that all the hardships were born by him, and him alone. And yet, for nearly a whole year of the two years leading up to Chaplin Senior's death, Charlie was away on tour, whilst Syd was at home caring for their mother. It took a piece in a 1952 magazine article which, though it is out by some seven years on Syd's age, does at least provide a picture of his presence in the home:

---

[2] *The Horns Tavern* was on the corner of Kennington Park Road and Kennington Road. The "Benefit" Chaplin goes on to mention was at the adjacent *Horns Assembly Rooms,* the entrance to which was in Kennington Road. The latter was licensed for singing and dancing.

Charlie's father was seriously ill and had been away in hospital for months; after a long spell of suffering, he died. His mother, also very ill, had been carrying on bravely, taking in sewing and mending for her neighbours so that there should be some money coming in. Often, however, there was nothing.

Then Sydney, about nine at the time, would go and fetch some free soup from a church in the Waterloo Bridge Road, a few doors from the Old Vic [theatre]. It was pea soup with shredded meat in it. Seated on the mattress, Mrs. Chaplin and her two children would drink the soup. Nothing the boys have had since in the de-luxe restaurants of the world has ever tasted so good.

(Picturegoer – 4 October 1952)

Chaplin senior died on 9 May 1901. The only personal effects he left his widow were the clothes he had been taken to the hospital in, and a half-sovereign. Whatever monies had been raised at the Benefit Night at The Horns had probably gone where most of Chaplin's money had gone – over the bar. It was left to the deceased's youngest brother to pay the funeral expenses.

The Stage newspaper said only of his passing:

We learn with regret that Mr. Charles Chaplin died in St. Thomas's Hospital of dropsy on Thursday last. He had been some fifteen years on the variety stage. The height of his success was attained about six years back. Of late he had had but poor luck, and misfortune had done much to break up his health.

(16 May 1901)

Charles Chaplin Senior had died in life as he had died on stage: no plaudits, no friends around him, and no money. Next!

Chapter 4

TRAINING CATS AND DOGS

Back in August 1900, over at the Oxford Music Hall, *The Eight Lancashire Lads* were sharing the bill with some of the biggest music-hall stars that ever trod the boards – acts like: Gus Elen; R.G. Knowles; Harry Champion; G.H. Chirgwin; Dan Leno, again; and George Robey – second only to the great man himself. Charlie would have been able to learn something from all of these artistes, but especially the latter three.

G.H. Chirgwin – 'The White-Eyed

G.H. Chirgwin was billed as 'The White-Eyed Kafir' – a reference to his striking blacked-up face, on which he painted a white patch over one eye. His act consisted of comedy but, when the laughter was at its peak, he would bring it right down with a song that turned the laughter to tears. His most notable success in this category was *The Blind Boy,* which he sang in a falsetto voice, and which audiences constantly requested him to perform throughout his long career. This was the second lesson in changing laughter to tears that Charlie had had from a master, the first being from Leno, and was a mechanism he would later repeatedly use in films.

From Robey he would have learned the power of stage presence, and how to command an audience. Robey was quiet spoken and inoffensive, with no form of attack should his act go wrong. However, it seldom did, owing to his ability to command order, respect and, most of all, laughter. In the 1933 article *A Comedian Sees the World,* Chaplin said of his affection for Robey:

> Robey was my idol as a boy. I remember how I used to wait outside the stage door at the
> Tivoli and follow him along to Trafalgar Square, where he caught his bus.

In his account of following Robey around, haplin makes no reference to actually working with his idol, which he did many times; including at the said Tivoli. Strange that Chaplin should give such praise to Robey, and yet deny Leno any acknowledgement whatsoever, although in Chaplin's 1964 autobiography the Robey quote is omitted.

With summer well and truly over it was back to the provinces, for *The Lancashire Lads,* with weeks in Hull, Sheffield, Leeds, and Bradford. Yorkshire had finally adopted them. Next, they travelled over the Pennines for one week in Liverpool, and then over the Irish Sea to Ireland, for three weeks, split between Dublin and Belfast. This must have been a very exciting trip for the young boys. They had only recently made their first trip to the seaside, but now they were actually travelling overseas to another country. From Ireland, it was back to London for one week at the New Cross Empire, which brought them right up to panto time. And here Chaplin was to create another situation for biographers to puzzle over.

Of this 1900-1901 Christmas season, Chaplin was to write that *The Eight Lancashire Lads* had parts in the pantomime *Cinderella,* at the London Hippodrome. I am willing to accept that Charlie may have been in this panto, but for *The Eight Lancashire Lads* to have been in it raises far too many unanswered questions:

Because of the irregular layout at the Hippodrome, it was not possible to stage regular theatre productions, such as the ones at the Drury Lane theatre. At the Hippodrome, the pantomime was more of a pageant and words were *almost* non-existent, making it just about the only theatre that produced a pantomime which fitted its literal meaning – "all mime." The pageant lasted only around thirty minutes, and was presented as the Grand Finalé to the usual weekly bill of variety artistes. If indeed *The Eight Lancashire Lads* had been a part of the pantomime then, without question, they would have had to perform their clog-dancing act prior to partaking in the finalé. But they aren't listed on any of the weekly bills of variety artistes; whereas acts such as the Aquamarinoff Troupe of Russian Dancers one week, and Rosow's Midget Dancers on another, are. Why would the management of the Hippodrome book a troupe of dancers for the variety bill, if they already had eight highly skilled and well-known dancers on their payroll?

Add to this the next stumbling block: *Cinderella* ran until 13 April 1901, whereas *The Eight Lancashire Lads* were back touring from 11 February onwards. This meant that if they ever had been in the panto, it could have been only for the first seven weeks of its sixteen in total. Which begs the question: "Why would the management engage them, knowing they would have to be replaced less than half-way through?" The most obvious answer seems to be that *The Eight Lancashire Lads* weren't there at all – only Charlie was. If we apply this theory, we get a more feasible record of events: Charlie leaves the troupe at the conclusion of the week in New Cross, and goes into rehearsals at the Hippodrome, in time for the opening on Boxing Day. Meanwhile, during the nine weeks between Charlie's departure and their next booking, "The Seven Lancashire Lads" spend time finding and training his replacement.

Although not giving any clue as to when exactly he did leave *The Eight Lancashire Lads,* Charlie did at least give the reason:

> Mother thought I looked pale and thin and that dancing was affecting my lungs. It worried her so much that she wrote about it to Mr. Jackson, who was so indignant that he finally sent me home, saying that I was not worth the bother of such a worrying mother.

So, if Charlie did indeed spend the Christmas season at the London Hippodrome, what drew him there? To answer that we first need to look at the urges that were tugging at him. He was at a very impressionable age and would have wanted to emulate some of the acts who had particularly impressed him. He even informs us of one idea for an act he wanted to devise:

> My ideal was a double act, two boys dressed as comedy tramps. I told it to one of the other boys [Tommy Bristol] and we decided to become partners. It became our cherished dream. We would call ourselves 'Bristol and Chaplin, the Millionaire Tramps', and would wear tramp's whiskers and big diamond rings.

The tramp character was *en vogue* around that time. It would seem that anyone who wanted to be a stage character would adopt the guise of a tramp. There was W.E. Ritchie – the tramp cyclist (of whom we shall hear more of, under his more familiar name of Billy Ritchie). Then there was Camplin – tramp cyclist; Bert Woodward – tramp and trick cyclist; and Charlie Edwards – 'The Happy Tramp;' to name but a few. Charlie had other desires, too:

> I wanted to be a comedy juggler, so I had saved enough money to buy four rubber balls and four tin plates, and for hours I would stand over the bedside practising.

Here he was inspired by Zarmo – 'Tramp Juggler.' Yes! Another 'tramp.' So Charlie saw in Zarmo two identities he coveted. But it was to be some fifty years later before Chaplin was to show off his proficiency; when he juggled cup and saucer, in his film *Monsieur Verdoux*. As for the tramp character maybe, in later life, Charlie could get a little more mileage out of that too.

While in this "I want to be like him" mode, Charlie became fascinated with Marceline, the resident clown at the London Hippodrome. Ready to do anything to get near him, Charlie, if one

Marceline on-stage   ..... and off-

The London "Aqua" Hippodrome Extant theatre on the
corner of Leicester Square and Cranbourn Street

is to believe his earlier account, secured for himself the most minor of roles in the current pantomime in which Marceline was starring. Although the minor role would receive only a minor wage to suit, Charlie was aware that his real payment would come in being able to observe the great clown at close quarters.

Marceline, born in Spain in 1873, had worked in continental circuses since the age of ten, before first coming to England in 1892 with Lockhart's Circus. Here he joined other circuses, including an eighteen-month engagement with Hengler's.

> When I first came to England in 1892 I could not speak a word of your language; that's – whispered the great clown – why I became a 'dummy.'

> (*The Magnet* – 10 November 1900)

Off-stage, though, Marceline was certainly no dummy. Although still trying to master the English language he could, in addition to his native Spanish, converse in Portuguese, Italian, French, German, and Dutch. The same article revealed more:

> Marceline is a wonderful little fellow – such humour; such somersaulting abilities, over tables, over chairs, over the very backs of the arena attendants – over goes Marceline.

> "Of your somersaulting, which do you consider your most difficult feats?"

> "The tumble backward and then forward. This took me six years to practise, and even now the strain upon the feet is so great that the tendons of the ankles may break any evening. I take care not to overstrain my strength, and of course it is the great art of a clown to know how to fall without injury."

> If you have not seen Marceline somersault you have missed one of the best sights in London.

Most of the spectacle within this panto can be visualised from the information contained in the reviews below:

"CINDERELLA" AT THE HIPPODROME

SCENE 1 – A FOREST GLADE.

> To better our enjoyment of the spectacle, all the wide arena is carpeted in green so that the 'Prince' and his followers, and the foresters and Cinderella may come out to dance and sing and talk before our eyes. In this scene we are introduced to the 'Baron' and his 'ugly daughters' and 'page'. We must not forget to mention the Hippodrome favourite, Marceline who, as the Baron's page-boy 'Buttons', made great sport.

> (*The Topical Times* – 29 December 1900)

And for the same scene, *The Stage* noted:

> With the beginning of the pantomime the arena, which becomes a forest glade for the nonce [*sic*], is filled with the Prince's followers in hunting costume, and singing a hunting chorus of very tuneful quality by George Jacobi. Then follow the traditional incidents of the forest scene, the principal characters entering from the rear of the stage. Cinderella acts the Good Samaritan to the old woman picking sticks, encounters the Prince, and so on.

> (*The Stage* – 27 December 1900)

* * * *

SCENE 2 – THE BARON'S KITCHEN

> The next scene – 'the Baron's Kitchen' – is chiefly remarkable for a charming looking-glass song by Miss Farrell [Cinderella]; some excellent fooling from the comedians; and Cinderella's dream – portrayed by the bio-tableaux.

> (*The Topical Times*)

The 'Baron's Kitchen' scene and the above phrase: "some excellent fooling from the comedians," pin-points where Chaplin's alleged big moment came.

With scene two, the Baron's kitchen, comes a novelty in the shape of a cinematographic representation of the Fairy Godmother's magic transformation of pumpkin, mice, etc., but otherwise the story is enacted on familiar lines.

(The Stage)

*   *   *   *

SCENE 3 – THE GATES OF THE PALACE

Then we are transported to 'the Gates of the Palace,' wither there arrive presently many princes and ambassadors from foreign lands – each travelling in accordance with the custom of his country, and accompanied by several retainers; considerably attired. The Indian group – with its great elephant; the Japs with their ricksha; the Chinese, with their palanquin; and the Abyssinian visitors were perhaps the most admirable constituents of this truly novel and delightful procession.

(The Topical Times)

Outside the Palace we are treated to a very picturesque procession of "The Colonials" in the guise of guests at the Prince's Ball, with their characteristic conveyances, such as the jinricksha of India and the sledge of Canada. In costume and other details this procession appears to have been prepared with great care and accuracy, but it is impossible to understand why Japan should be included, and the appearance of a contingent of Boers occasions much mingled cheering and hissing.

(The Stage)

*   *   *   *

SCENE 4 – THE PRINCE'S BALLROOM

Then comes the scene-of-scenes; a wonderful conceit and a great success: quicker, almost, than thought, great gilded poles are brought into the arena. Festoons of flowers are hung between these and therefrom to the very roof of the house. Silk settees are set round between these and the barricade. A beautiful back-scene is dropped. Then – pff! – thousands of electric lamps are set going, and you see a light which is worth taking a journey upon the South-Eastern Railway to gaze upon.

(The Topical Times)

With the ball scene the pantomime culminates in a feast of light and colour which, of its kind, has probably never been surpassed, if equalled, on the stage. From the high roof of the *Hippodrome* pendants of roses, surmounted by a gorgeous coronet, are suspended and connected with festoons of the same flowers encircling the great arena. This is the Prince's ball-room; and when filled with the richly-dressed crowd of dancers and illuminated by myriads of artistically arranged electric lustres, it aroused the audience to a somewhat rare pitch of enthusiasm.

(The Stage)

SCENE 5 – THE AQUA SHOW

Fairy fountains, a comic water panto, and all sorts of good things follow.

(The Topical Times)

..... there will be a funny water-spectacle, called "The Village Wedding."

(The Topical Times Pantomime Supplement – 15 December 1900)

There is also, of course, an excellent variety programme. But it is "Cinderella" which counts – with its luxuriant dresses; charming music (by Mr. George Jacobi), and magnificent setting.

* * * *

Sadly, in panto, the action in the classic comedy scenes is seldom written down, not even in the actual script, and phrases like "business with cake," are the only clues. The business is left off the script not only to dispose with pages and pages of complicated directions, but also to protect the personal input which the principal comic provides, and allow him to keep it as his own for future pantos. However, some thirty years later a small part of the business Charlie allegedly performed with Marceline was finally put down on paper, after Chaplin's chance reunion with two of the Jacksons in Paris in 1931.

I had heard that Alfred Jackson, an old associate of mine, was working at the Folies Bergère with his troupe of dancers. Jackson and I were kids together in his father's troupe called *The Eight Lancashire Lads*. Upon arriving at the Folies Bergere, I met his father also, and after a warm greeting we started to reminisce.

William Jackson in later life. (*circa* 1925)

"My lad," said Jackson's father, "I remember the very first laugh you got from an audience."

And then he recalled an incident that occurred at the London Hippodrome. I was about eight at the time. The troupe was engaged to play cats and dogs, in the pantomime Puss in Boots. I was dressed as a dog. It was the first performance and on we came.

Wanting to give a little touch of nature to my portrayal of the canine species, I ran lambent over to the corner of the scenery and proceeded to go through the motions of absolute realism that my childish impressionable mind had seen other little dogs do.

The house came down in an uproar. With the laughter and appreciation of the audience, I was inspired to go further and so I started to take a sniffing interest in the other little dogs on the stage. This also was most realistic and brought forth another burst of laughter. I would sniff, then look suddenly at the audience. This action was most successful.

It appears that my dog's mask wore a startled expression. At each sniff the audience would laugh and I would look at them. There was a sort of tempo to it, the laughter, the look and the sniff. This seemed to work the audience into a state of hysteria. I was feeling very happy and encouraged until my attention was drawn to the side of the wings. There were Mr. Jackson and several gentlemen in white shirt fronts, all protesting violently, shaking their heads and making motions for me to exit. This left me bewildered and somewhat discouraged, so I put my tail between my legs and slunk off the stage to the tune of laughter and applause.

"What on earth are you doing?". they all said. "You'll have the police close up the theatre if you carry on like that."

I thought everybody ungrateful after giving such a splendid characterization.

(*A Comedian Sees the World – 1933*)

It's hard to take the above account seriously for several reason: Charlie says he was about eight, whereas the date of the pantomime would have made him going-on twelve. He then names the panto as *Puss in Boots,* whereas the supposed one was *Cinderella.* His 1964 autobiography does nothing to clarify the situation:

> In the [Baron's] kitchen scene I was given a little comedy bit to do with Marceline. I was
> a cat, and Marceline would back away from a dog and fall over my back while I drank milk.
> He always complained that I did not arch my back enough to break his fall. I wore a cat-
> mask which had a look of surprise, and during the first matinée for children I went up to
> the rear end of a dog and began to sniff. When the audience laughed, I looked surprised at
> them, pulling a string which winked a staring eye. After several sniffs and winks the house-
> manager came bounding back stage, waving frantically in the wings. But I carried on. After
> smelling the dog, I smelt the proscenium, then I lifted my leg. The audience roared –
> possibly because the gesture was uncatlike. Eventually the manager caught my eye and I
> capered off to great applause. "Never do that again!" he said, breathlessly. You'll have the
> Lord Chamberlain close down the theatre.

No major differences there, except that *The Eight Lancashire Lads* don't get a mention, William Jackson has been replaced by the house-manager, Charlie has metamorphosed from a dog into a cat, and the Lord Chamberlain has become a police officer. I fully appreciate that Chaplin could not possibly accurately recollect all his childhood memories, but I do get the feeling that on many occasions the account suffers not from memory loss, but from an intent to embellish or deceive, and that is why I so often challenge his accounts throughout this tome.

The Census of 31 March 1901 shows that Charlie was no longer staying with the Jackson family at 167 Kennington Road but was then at 92 Ferndale Road, off the Brixton Road, Lambeth. However, the Jackson connection was still there, as the householder's name was registered as "John Jackson, age 17" – this being one of William Jackson's boys. It might well be the Jackson connection that led Charlie to later fool himself into believing he was still with *The Lancashire Lads* at that time.

If Charlie were indeed in this panto, his portrayal as the cat/dog creature during his short apprenticeship as a clown, would have ended in mid-April 1901. So what did Charlie do next? Well, one of the first things to happen was that he was laid low by recurring attacks of asthma. Charlie disclosed that, at times, these were so severe he was almost tempted to jump out of the window to relieve the agony. His one piece of comfort came when he was informed by the family doctor that he would one day grow out of it.

However, of events between the Spring of 1901 and the Spring of 1903 Charlie's recollections were a blur, of which he could offer only:

> My memory of this period goes in and out of focus. The outstanding impression was a
> quagmire of miserable circumstances. I cannot remember where Sydney was; being four
> years older, he only occasionally entered my consciousness. He was possibly living with
> Grandfather to relive mother's penury. We seemed to vacillate from one abode to another,
> eventually ending up in a small garret at 3 Pownall Terrace.

One known abode during the said period was "2, Paradise Street," which was, and still is, just off the southern approach road to Lambeth Bridge. This is confirmed on the school records which show that Charlie was enrolled at his new school on 16 September 1901, which might well indicate that his bout of illness was between his finishing at the Hippodrome in April, and enrolling at school for the winter term.

Another dwelling appears to have been in Munton Road, off Rodney Road, the existence of which was brought to light some years later by his schoolboy friend Bert Herbert:

> He was an ingenious kid. I remember often going to his house in Munton-road and playing
> with a farthing-in-the-slot, which he had made. It was an excellent miniature model of the
> 'penny-in-the- slot' machines seen at fairs, etc., and worked admirably.

(The Star – 3 September 1921)

School register showing Charles Chaplin's enrolment on 9 September 1901.
His address is given as "2, Paradise Street" and his last school as "Kennington Lane Bd."

(By kind permission of Associated Chaplin)

In his autobiography Chaplin acquaints us with a long list of temporary jobs he undertook in this period. They weren't *meant* to be temporary, it's just that he turned out not to be suitable for any of them. However, Charlie did have skilled hands and so, between times, he busied himself making and selling model ships, and the like. Charlie's solo money-making schemes suited him much better than all his other work, and had striking points of similarity: 1) He was his own boss. 2) There was no one to criticise him. 3) He didn't have to work with members of a team he hadn't chosen. 4) He didn't have to socialise with anyone. Yes indeed, at just twelve years old Charlie Chaplin had laid out the way he was going to cut the cloth in his adult life.

But it was back to the skill in his feet that Charlie reverted to next. The following is a great story, but one which is missing from Chaplin's autobiography. Is it because he doesn't come out as the winner, or perhaps that he can't see the funny side of it?

> A year or so later, after Charlie had left the [*Eight Lancashire Lads*] troupe, the family faced again the crisis of having to pay the rent for their one room and of buying food. They hadn't a penny in the world. Charlie saw a way out when the old Canterbury Music Hall staged a clog-dancing contest for amateurs only. The prize offered was a five-pound note.
>
> Charlie put on an old ragged cap, tied a handkerchief round his neck and entered for the contest. Nearly all the others had done their turn when Charlie went on. Some of them danced extremely well for amateurs, so Charlie was taking no chances. He worked in some of the most intricate steps; he could easily have won with those steps alone.
>
> But the thought of the rent made him work up to a tremendous crescendo of nerve-dancing, one of the most difficult things for even a highly skilled professional. The applause was tumultuous-but that finale was Charlie's undoing.
>
> The judge was Vesta Victoria's father. He had been a champion clog-dancer himself in his time. He took Charlie quietly to one side and asked: "What's your line of business?"
>
> "Paper boy," replied Charlie. "I sell news-papers at the foot of Westminster Bridge."
>
> "Don't lie to me," said Vesta's father. "I remember you now. You were one of *The Eight Lancashire Lads*. Get out of here!" – and, suiting the action to the words, he eased Charlie through the stage door with the toe of his boot. The Chaplins went to bed hungry that night.
>
> (*Picturegoer* – 4 October 1952)

However, Charlie's talents had been seen and noted, with the result that he was asked to join another clog-dancing troupe. This time, though, the numbers would be slightly reduced – to three. How this came about can be found in the following account, told to *The Star* newspaper by comedian Bert Herbert:

> My introduction to Charlie Chaplin was through my uncle. After Charlie had left *The Lancashire Lads* he brought him to our house (Thrush Street, Walworth), and asked my parents if they would agree to my brother and I joining another boy to tour as a dancing trio.
>
> My people agreed, and Charlie took over his duties straight away. Charlie was an excellent dancer and teacher, but I am afraid we did more larking about than dancing – we were between 10 and 14 years.
>
> Eventually we mastered six steps (the old six Lancashire steps), and got a trial show at the *Montpelier,* in Walworth, at that time, I believe, a Mr. Ben Weston was the proprietor.
>
> I remember that we had no stage dresses, and went on in our street clothes. Charlie and my brother wore knickerbockers and, as I had long trousers, I had to tie them up underneath at the knee to make them look like knickers.
>
> How Charlie laughed when I went wrong, because one leg of my trousers started to come down as soon as I commenced to dance.

My uncle then went to America, and as we had no money to carry on, we had to let the Trio fall through. It was to have been called *Ted Prince's Nippers*.

(*The Star* – 3 September 1921)

Charlie, himself, passed off the whole scenario in just one short line.

... and my own contribution of five shillings weekly, which I earned giving dancing lessons, had suddenly ended.

(Chaplin's 1964 autobiography)

But Bert Herbert and his brother weren't the only boys with whom Chaplin practised clog dancing:

Some of the lads Charlie used to knock about with were Fred Ernest, Gus Elton, Fred Leslie, Harry Wharton and Nigger Heaton. They had a bit of roller shutter and practised tap-dancing on it by the old King's Hall, and at the back of the South London Palace.

(1952 article written from an interview with a Mr. W.C. Sherrington. Reproduced in *Charlie Chaplin,* by Peter Haining – original source unaccredited)

And yet another story of Charlie showing off his tap dancing skills was brought to light by one of his former boyhood pals:

I remember he used to act and dance in a shed at the back of Clayton's buildings to an audience of boys and girls, and charge a farthing admission. He was very good at mimicking the late-Barnie Goodwin's Piccanninies. [1]

(Harry Charmain interviewed for *The Star* – 2 September 1921)

Maybe during Charlie's absence from show business he came to realise that, unacceptable as many of the terms of employment were, the rewards were easier to achieve, more regular, more substantial, and less of a gamble. He therefore put his principles on hold and made periodical calls at Blackmore's Theatrical Agency, in the Strand, to stand in line with other would-be thespians in the hope of being offered an acting role. Having registered at Blackmore's, but not really believing anything would come of it, Charlie was one day surprised by the arrival of a postcard requesting that he call at the agency's office. There, Mr. Blackmore himself gave Charlie a letter of introduction and instructed him to go and see a Mr. Hamilton at the offices of Charles Frohman. Once there, Charlie was told he had been chosen for the role of a cheeky cockney boy in a play that was about to tour in the late-summer of 1903.

Fate had finally set the little street urchin on the right road. From this small beginning Charlie was to remain in almost continuous stage-work for the next ten years, after which would come worldwide fame, and fortune.

---

[1] Harry is referring to 'Bonnie' Goodwin's Piccaninnies, a tap-dancing quartette; usually billed as 'Bonnie Goodwin's Famous four Real Apollo Piccaninnies.'

Chapter 5

HOLMES, SWEET HOLMES

Charles Frohman was a legendary impresario. Whereas many theatrical promoters would struggle to fill dates for just one touring production, he could generate full date-sheets for several productions, plus have two or three different companies touring concurrently with the *same* play. In the summer of 1903, Frohman recruited the first of two companies to play in *Sherlock Holmes*. One was to tour the northern circuit of theatres, and the second the southern circuit.

Charlie's part was that of 'Billy,' Sherlock Holmes' page-boy, for which he was to receive two-pound ten-shillings (£2.50p) per week during the play's run. Mr. Hamilton told Charlie he might have second part for him, in a play called *Jim* – subtitled: A *Romance of Cockayne* – which was to be staged immediately prior to the opening of *Sherlock Holmes*. The part of 'Holmes' was to be played by H.A. Saintsbury, who was also the star and writer of *Jim*. Hamilton sent Charlie to the Green Room Club, in Leicester Square, so that Saintsbury might have a look at him. The latter was suitably impressed and, there and then, confirmed his acceptance of Charlie in both roles. Of the meeting with Hamilton in the Frohman office Charlie commented:

> Mr. Hamilton was amused and surprised to see how small I was. Of course I lied about my age, telling him I was fourteen – I was twelve and a half.

> (Chaplin's 1964 autobiography)

No Charlie! You were fourteen. You were born in April 1889, and you got the job in June 1903. That's fourteen years and two months. Just how Charlie worked out he was twelve-and-a-half is mind numbing. If you're going to lie about your age, keep the month the same but change the year. Picking a month which is six to eight months away from the real one causes mathematical complications, and you're bound to trip up, as Chaplin so often did.

Nowhere in Chaplin's lengthy account of his obtaining these roles does he mention giving any kind of audition or performance. He does say he was relieved that Saintsbury didn't ask him to read for the part, which would have been embarrassing as he was almost unable to read. However, that he got the part on looks alone, is hard to accept.

After the confirmation of his engagement on the Sherlock Holmes' tour, Charlie went home on the bus in a daze of happiness. In the absence of his mother, who back in April had been committed to Cane Hill Asylum, Charlie broke the news to Sydney who, in turn, became teary-eyed at the thought that this was a turning point in their lives.

Saintsbury had given Charlie a copy of the script for *Jim* to learn at home, which he set about doing with the help of Sydney:

> Sydney read the part to me and helped me to memorise the lines. It was a big part, about thirty-five sides, but I knew it all by heart in three days.

Jim – A Romance of Cockayne ran for just two weeks, commencing 6 July 1903, at the Royal County Theatre, Kingston-upon-Thames, with the second week at the Grand Theatre, Fulham. The full review of the debut of the play, as printed in the broadsheet the Topical Times would run to around four pages if reprinted here so, for the purposes of this book, it was considered that a few extracts would suffice. Of the play in general it said:

JIM - A ROMANCE OF COCKAYNE

Cast:

Roydon Carstairs	H. A. Saintsbury
James Seton Gatlock	James C. Aubrey
Walter Jenifer	Mr. Blake Adams
Inspector Grint	Mr. Caleb Porter
Inspector Bradstreet	Mr. Harry Payne
Bill Caffle	Mr. Charles Rock.
Sharpe	Mr. Graham Herington
Sam	Master Charles Chaplin
Alma Treherne	Miss Beatrix de Burgh
'Jim'	Miss Dorothea Desmond

ACT 2: The Garret of Mrs. Putherby's Lodging-house in Drury Lane

DETECTIVE GRINT IS LOOKING IN A CUPBOARD.
ENTER SAM, THE NEWSBOY.

SAM	Oi, you! Do you know that's a lady's bedroom?
GRINT	What! That cupboard? Come here!
SAM	The cool cheek of him.
GRINT	You stow that. Come in and shut the door.
SAM	[WALKING TOWARDS HIM] Polite, ain't you, inviting blokes into their own drawing-room?
GRINT	I'm a detective.
SAM	What! A cop? I'm off.
GRINT	I'm not going to hurt you. All I want is a little information that will help to do someone a good turn.
SAM	A good turn indeed! If a bit of luck comes to anyone here, it won't be through the cops!
GRINT	Don't be a fool. Would I have started by telling you I was in the Force?
SAM	Thanks for nothing. I can see your boots.
GRINT	Who lives here?
SAM	The Duke.
GRINT	Yes, bit what's his real name?
SAM	I don't know. The Duke is a "non de guerre" as he calls it, though blow me if I know what that means.
GRINT	And what does he look like?
SAM	As thin as a lath. Grey hair, clean shaven, wears a top hat and an eye-glass. And blimey, the way he looks at you through it.
GRINT	And Jim - who's he?
SAM	He? You mean SHE!
GRINT	Ah! then she's the lady who....
SAM	.... sleeps in the cupboard. This here room's ours, mine and the Duke's ....

(continued)

(w/c 13 July 1903)

"Jim" at the Fulham Grand

Mr. H.A. Saintsbury's play, *Jim,* is described on the programme as "A Romance of Cockayne," not "cocaine," as some of the earlier preliminary announcements had it, so there was disappointment in store for those who had been looking forward to a study of the drug habit. [1] *Jim* really belongs to what I call a 'domestic melodrama,' and is a very fair specimen of its class.

(Topical Times – 18 July 1903)

The Stage offered some of the action from Act 2:

KINGSTON, Royal County

The next scene is the Garret of Mrs. Putherby's Lodging-house in Drury Lane. Detective Grint is tracing Carstairs, with a view of informing him that he is Gatlock's heir, but Sam, the newspaper boy, thinking, by past experience, that his visit is not a friendly one, fences with him most cleverly, and succeeds in entirely mystifying him.

(The Stage – 9 July 1903)

Just how Charlie, as 'Sam', mystified Detective Grint can be found in the script, reproduced on the previous page. *The Topical Times* lavished much more praise on Charlie's contribution:

In the second act we see Carstairs living in a Drury Lane garret, where his co-lodgers call him 'the Dook.'

One is 'Sam', a newspaper boy, a smart London street Arab, responsible for much of the comic part of the play, which comic part, if not in anyway new, is yet decidedly good. 'Sam' was made vastly amusing by Master Charles Chaplin, a bright and vivacious child actor, absolutely free from that air of being an automaton, mechanically devised to carry out stage manager's instructions which makes the ordinary child actor such an unmitigated nuisance.

The other is 'Jim' (Miss Dorothea Desmond), a flower girl, Alma's long-lost daughter. She is in love with 'the Dook', although but for the accident of Alma's marrying some one else, he might have been her father, and, as far as appearance goes, would not have been doubted if he had said he was her grandfather.

(Topical Times – 18 July 1903)

In his autobiography Chaplin quotes from memory the paragraph, in bold, in the review above as follows:

But there is one redeeming feature, the part of **'Sammy', a newspaper boy, a smart London street Arab, much responsible for the comic part. Although hackneyed and old-fashioned, Sammy was made vastly amusing by Master Charles Chaplin, a bright and vigorous child actor.**

I have never heard of the boy before, but I hope to hear great things of him in the near future.

(Chaplin's 1964 autobiography)

One has to admit that the above is pretty good recollecting on Charlie's part. However, the line Chaplin has tagged on is somewhat lacking in accuracy and representation, for this is how the original article actually reads:

It only remains to add that Miss Dorothea Desmond, as 'Jim' was delightful. I don't remember having seen this promising actress before; but I hope soon to see her again.

(Topical Times – 3 July 1903)

What a striking example of how Chaplin would always deflect praise towards himself, while denying others their due.

---

[1] Author's note:- Jim – *a Romance of Cockayne* resurfaced in 1908 but, to stop any misunderstandings, was re-titled simply *"Lucky Jim"* – which may in turn have caused further confusion with the Kingsley Amis novel of the same name.

After *Jim* came one week of rehearsals for *Sherlock Holmes*. According to a 1921 newspaper article, Syd wasn't called upon to assist Charlie to learn his lines for this part, as Charlie had roped in a neighbour, Harry Charmain, who said:

> We were pals as boys, and I held the book of words while he rehearsed the part of 'Billy – the Page' in *Sherlock Holmes*. Charlie was living at 3, Pownall-terrace, and we lived at No. 6. Charlie was badly off at that time, and he was always in and out of our house, and my mother gave him food and often shelter in cold and wet weather.

> Outside No. 3 Pownall-terrace are six steps, and it was on these he first practised his antics on the stairs, going up one and falling back two. He was always funny, and he used to make all the boys and girls laugh. He used to perform plays in our house.

> When he was working up his part as 'Billy – The Page,' and I was holding the book of words, to give dramatic effect he took up an old revolver, and held it to my head for a lark.

> I was scared, and I seized him by the neck, and we had a struggle which resulted in both of us tumbling down the stairs and into another tenant's room.

(The Star – 2 September 1921)

Sherlock Holmes then made its debut at the Pavilion Theatre, in the Whitechapel Road, Mile End, East London.

(w/c 27 July 1903)

MILE END, Pavilion E.

William Gillette and Sir Arthur Conan Doyle's famous, Sherlock Holmes, is being played this week. That Mr. Isaac Cohen's enterprise is appreciated is abundantly proved by the large houses which are being attracted. The play presented by Mr. Charles Frohman's excellent company is admirably staged in every respect. A better Sherlock than Mr. H. A. Saintsbury it would be difficult to imagine. He thoroughly enters into the spirit of the character, and presents a neat, meritorious calm, cool, and collected study of Dr. Doyle's famous detective. He is seen to particular advantage in the 'Gas Chamber' scene, and also in the scene with 'Alice Faulkener'. In the latter character Miss Grete Hahn is charming and sincere, and convincing. 'Professor Moriarty' finds a powerful exponent in Mr. Robert Forsyth, who does justice to the character. Some particularly good work is done by Mr. Kenneth Rivington, who gives a typical impersonation of 'Holmes's chronicler' and friend. His performance in the 'Consulting Room' scene is worthy of especial mention. A faithful portrait of 'Billy' is given by Master Charles Chaplin, who shows considerable ability, and bids fair to develop into a capable and clever actor.

(The Stage – 30 July 1903)

This is fantastic review for the debut of a show, but what is even more remarkable is the amount of praise given to Chaplin for what was only a minor role. Consider, too, that it was Chaplin's debut as an actor. If only Charlie had quoted this review, instead of falsifying the one for *Jim,* he would have achieved his objective in proving how clever he was as a little boy, instead of how deceptive he was an older man.

With the second company preparing to hit the southern theatres in September, Saintsbury's company headed north, stopping off en route to play the Midlands' town of Burton-on-Trent, before reaching Newcastle in the North East. They then turned around and headed southwards to play Sheffield, Manchester, Reading [unconfirmed], Northampton, and Wolverhampton. At the latter, Charlie's harsh Cockney accent was highlighted.

Pownall Terrace, viewed from across Kennington Road.
No.3 is the third doorway from the right.

Photo from "CHARLIE CHAPLIN –
My Autobiography"

"Outside No.3 Pownall-terrace are six steps, and it was on these Charlie first practised his antics on the stairs, going up one and falling back two." (Harry Charmain)

(w/c 14 September 1903)

WOLVERHAMPTON – Grand

"Sherlock Holmes"

The rapidity of speech and actions of Master Charles Chaplin, as 'Billy', interested the audience greatly.

(14 September 1903)

Although Charlie had toured extensively before, one must remember that he was still a very young boy so, to comply with the laws of "Employment of Child Actors," a guardian had to be allocated to look after him at all times. The person chosen was the wardrobe mistress, Edith. In 1931 Edith, who by then had become Mrs. Scales, wrote at length about her memories of the young Charlie – memories I am happy to include in this account:

> I first met Charlie when, as a boy of fourteen he played the part of 'Billy – the page,' in Charles Frohman's Company. We opened the tour at the Pavilion Theatre, Mile End-road, in July 1903. I became his guardian a week later when we went to Newcastle to play at the Theatre Royal.
>
> Charlie was all right while we were in London, because he was at home, but when we started touring he had no one to look after him. There was a matinée on the Saturday, but Charlie, who had failed to leave his [lodgings'] address, knew nothing about the matinée and, when he did not turn up for the opening, we had to get his understudy into his clothes. The show had started when up came Charlie, proudly carrying under his arm a 5s. [2] camera he had just bought.
>
> Poor boy, he started to cry when he heard he was late for a matinée, but I told him to dry his eyes, and dashed off to get his understudy out of the clothes again. Charlie was not due on until the second act, and so I rushed him into the ladies dressing-room, and we got him ready in time.
>
> No one offered to look after him, however, and so I said I would take charge of him if he would promise to behave himself, and I did actually take charge of him for about six months. Then his brother, Syd, joined the company and relieved me of him.

(*Empire News* – 8 March 1931)

Not for the first time, and certainly not for the last, Charlie's account varies from those who were witness to his movements.

> On my first tour, the management decided that I should live with Mr. and Mrs. Green, the carpenter of the company and his wife, the wardrobe lady. This was not very glamorous. Besides, Mr. and Mrs. Green drank occasionally. Moreover, I did not always want to eat when they did, or eat what they ate. I am sure my living with the Greens was more irksome to them than to me. So after three weeks we mutually agreed to part, and, being too young to live with other members of the cast, I lived alone. I was alone in strange towns, alone in back rooms, rarely meeting anyone until the evening performance, only hearing my own voice when I talked to myself.

After Wolverhampton, the company played weeks in Coventry, Birkenhead, Blackburn, Huddersfield, Bolton and Wigan, from three of which Edith Scales retained stories of Charlie:

> But whatever he might do, Charlie was a real business man and an economist at heart. With the camera he bought at Newcastle he took lots of photographs, especially among working-class people, and used to sell them for 3d. and 6d. each.
>
> The 3d. ones were just plain snaps, but he framed them in penny cardboard frames if you were willing to pay sixpence. Whenever we went to new rooms Charlie would ask the landlady "Have you got a dark room, Ma?"

---

[2] 5s. is five shillings pre-decimal money = 25p. decimal coinage; 1d = 1 penny = 1/2p.; 3d. = threepence = 1 1/2p.; 6d. = sixpence = 2 1/2p

1   2   3

The above photos are obvious representations of Master Charles Chaplin as:

   (1)   'Sam' – the Newsboy', in *Jim*

   (2)   as 'Billy – the Page boy', in *Sherlock Holmes*

   (3)   again as 'Billy – the Page boy,' but from a later tour.

But when one scrutinises the photos in detail, there are several perplexing discrepancies:

In photo 1 Sam is a street urchin, but is wearing highly polished shoes, whereas in photo 3 he is wearing scruffy, dull shoes, in direct contrast to photo 2. Plus, the shoes in 3 are on the wrong feet.

From Chaplin's facial characteristics one can see that photos 2 and 3 were taken some time apart, possibly a couple of years – and yet the body and leg positions are *exactly* the same, the shadows and finger positions on both hands are *exactly* the same, as are the buttons on the tunic. Mystifying!

Photo 3 does however appear to be free from any form of manipulation, and is even signed by the boy himself.

Once at Coventry I remember returning to the lodgings for dinner, and when it was served asked the landlady where Charlie was. She said he had gone upstairs.

I went to find him, but as he did not appear to be in the upstairs rooms I called out. Then I heard a knocking at the wardrobe door.

"Don't open the door," called Charlie. "You'll spoil my plates if you do." I was very much annoyed and he came out, then I discovered he had burnt the bottom of the landlady's wardrobe with his candle. "It will be jolly fine if she charges you for the damage before we go," I told him.

"Don't worry, she won't notice it," said Charlie. "I'll put a piece of clean paper in the bottom and cover it over." He did, and we heard no more about it.

He knew how to make money, too. One day while we were at the [Hay]Market Hotel, Blackburn, he went into the sitting room and delighted all the farmers by singing to them. It was market day and the place was full. He finished up by showing them the Clog Dance, and he could do that dance, too. But the farmers had to pay for the entertainment!

Yes! Charlie went round with the hat when he had finished. I got hauled over the coals for allowing him to do that, but I wasn't there to stop him.

When at Wigan, Charlie bought two tame rabbits. He went to the property man and asked him where he could leave them until he got a box made. The stage carpenter, a very kind-hearted man, made him a box, covered over with some old canvas. Charlie had a great affection for his two pets, and kept them for several months. When one got worried [attacked] he vowed vengeance and searched all over for the cat or dog that had done it, walking through all the streets in the district, but of course he did not find it.

He took the rabbits wherever he went, and when we were travelling used to put them on the luggage rack and take the cover off the box to give them plenty of air. Once he let his rabbits run all over the landlady's sitting room, and of course they made a mess and annoyed the landlady. That was the only time I had really to chastise him. He could make those pets do all sorts of tricks.

(Empire News – 8 March 1931)

Charlie's account almost matches Edith's:

> For company, I bought a rabbit and wherever I stayed I would smuggle it into my room unknown to the landlady. It was an endearing little thing, though not house-broken. Its fur looked so white and clean that it belied its pungent odour. I kept it in a cage hidden under the bed. The landlady would cheerfully enter the room with my breakfast, until she contacted the odour, then she would leave, looking worried and confused. The moment she was gone I would release the rabbit and it would lope about the room.

(Chaplin's 1964 autobiography)

And that, one would think, is a pretty comprehensive account by Chaplin of the time he kept a pet rabbit. However, Edith Scales says he had two rabbits. But then from the 1933 account of Chaplin's 1931 visit to England we get a *third* account of just what pets he owned. The first discovery comes in the line:

> I made my way to Blackburn, the town where as a boy I had bought the pup and the rabbit.
> I had a general idea of the large market square, the Haymarket and the [White] Bull Hotel.

The visit set Chaplin reminiscing, during which he comes up with a *fourth* account of his animal acquisitions:

> When a boy of fourteen I was a member of Sherlock Holmes Touring Company. I lived alone, being too young to mix or room with the older members of the cast. So to alleviate my loneliness I decided to purchase some companionship – a rabbit and a dog.

I used to carry my grips to and from the station. And now I added my new friends to my paraphernalia. As the dog grew up I trained her to follow me until we were nearing the depot. Then she would crawl into a grip and I would steal her past the station master. Later the dog had five pups and so I became a walking menagerie.

What a problem it was to get them by the landlady. I developed a technique for this. I would engage a combined sitting-room and bedroom and would say nothing about the family which I kept hidden. Later when the landlady discovered her room had been turned into a zoo, I would smile disarmingly, picking up one of the puppies and exclaiming enthusiastically, "Isn't he sweet? When they're a little older I'll give you one."

This good will and generosity would usually dispel any objections she might have. But towards the end of the week the odour of the animals would lessen the landlady's tolerance. But I managed to tour with them for over a year.

(A Comedian Sees the World – 1933)

Apart from the above cutting, and the brief mention by Ethel Tricks of Charlie owning a dog [see Chapter 1], there seems to be no other reference to Charlie having a dog, how long he had the dog, or what happened to it – if indeed it ever existed. The truth lies somewhere between: Charlie had one rabbit; Charlie had two rabbits; Charlie had one rabbit and one dog; Charlie had one rabbit, one dog, and a litter of puppies; Charlie had a vivid imagination. Take your choice.

Note that I've deliberately avoided calling Edith 'Mrs. Green' throughout this section. That's because I have a sneaky feeling she wasn't married to Mr. Green. First flag was waved when I saw she had become 'Mrs. Scales.' Second flag was when she said: "The stage carpenter, a very kind-hearted man, made him a box," whereas you would expect to have said: "My husband, the stage carpenter, made him a box." But that's by-the-by. Let's hear what other incidents Edith tells of the 1903 tour, which continued through Ashton-under-Lyne, Stockport, Burnley, Rochdale, Broughton, and Bury:

I remember well the occasion we were at Ashton-under-Lyne. I was resting in the lodgings one afternoon when in rushed Charlie and awakened me. He said a man was hitting him, then he dashed off again. Of course, thinking a lot about the boy, I was up like a shot and followed him into the kitchen.

There was Charlie with a heavy poker in his hand, and the landlady was just putting a man out of the house. Apparently the man had come into the house and accused the landlady of having her chimney on fire. He had got some jugs of water and emptied them on the fire before she could stop him.

When I got there the landlady had got the man out of the house, but he had kicked her on the leg and injured her badly. The police were brought, the man was arrested, and Charlie and I were told we would have to give evidence.

Charlie in the Box

We were at Stockport the following Monday when they sent for us to appear in court, and we had to return to give evidence. Charlie first went into the witness box, but no one could understand his cockney accent.

The sergeant kept touching him on the shoulder and saying: "Will you please speak a little more clearly, please?" But Charlie was very excited and indignant about the man kicking the landlady. After a lot of fun he got his story out, however, and the man was sent to prison. I believe for about three months.

Then Charlie asked the sergeant, "What about our expenses?" The sergeant replied: "There's no fine, and so there's no pay." Charlie was very vexed but, despite his indignation at such treatment, the court allowed us no expenses. Charlie chattered and grumbled about this all the way to the station, and it took him a long time to forget it.

"To think we have had to come all this way and pay our own fares!" he complained.

(Empire News – 8 March 1931)

It's interesting to note the above quote from Edith Scales that: "Charlie first went into the witness box, but no one could understand his cockney accent." Here was a boy who was playing theatres in all parts of the country and yet, in this instance, couldn't be understood. So just when and how did Chaplin lose the strong South London accent, and cultivate the non-descript voice we recognise him for, from his later films? Another question would be: "*Why* did he cultivate his speech?" for he barely used his speaking voice in any of his stage work, and it was to be 1940 before he was heard to speak on screen. Chaplin himself refers to being taught the rudiments of speaking properly by his mother, when he was just a small child:

> Living as we did in the lower strata, it was very easy to fall into the habit of not caring about our diction, But Mother always stood outside her environment and kept an alert ear on the way we talked, correcting our grammar and making us feel that we were distinguished.

> (Chaplin's 1964 autobiography)

But here, at fourteen-and-a-half, Charlie appears not to have tempered his speech one iota. It is also interesting to note that Charlie stated he had left the guardianship of "Mrs. Green" after just three weeks, but the Accrington incident was four months into the tour and he is still clearly under her care. That he shied away from members of the cast is undeniable. He himself admitted:

> I got accustomed to living alone. But I got so much out of the habit of talking that when I suddenly met a member of the company I suffered intense embarrassment. I could not collect myself quickly enough to answer questions intelligently and they would leave me, I am sure, with alarm and concern for my reason. Miss Greta Hahn, for instance, our leading lady was beautiful, charming, and most kindly; yet when I saw her crossing the road towards me, I would quickly turn and look into a shop window or go down another street in order to avoid her.

> (Chaplin's 1964 autobiography)

Edith's account continued:

> Charlie was an expert at getting round landladies, though. When it was baking day they could never resist his appeals for hot cakes; but for all that he was still the economist. When the time came to settle with the landlady he would inspect the bill, and knock out any item he had not had. He allowed no overcharging. If he had been out to tea, for instance, he would deduct the amount chargeable for one tea from the bill. But everybody liked Charlie. He was a wonderfully clever boy, and had perfectly beautiful teeth and hair.

> (*Empire News* – 8 March 1931)

Monday 21 December 1903, when the company played Dewsbury, marked the five-hundredth performance of the play *Sherlock Holmes,* for which each paying entrant at the Monday night houses was presented with a souvenir programme. Don't ask how the number of five-hundred was calculated. It couldn't have been based on the number of performances on this tour alone, as that would have meant they were averaging twenty-two shows a week.

It was also around this date that Charlie's brother, Syd, joined the company. Working and travelling together provided marked benefits for the two brothers. As well as the obvious financial rewards for them, and their mother, it meant that Charlie was able to leave the charge of Edith, and share time with someone whom he knew, loved, and valued the company of. The more immediate benefit was that, though away from home, the two brothers would not have to spend Christmas alone.

Come the New Year the tour continued from Barrow, through Wakefield, Leeds, Halifax, Gateshead, York, Harrogate, Jarrow, Middlesbrough, Sunderland, and Birmingham. Whilst in Birmingham, w/c 29 February (it was a leap year), the leading man, H.A. Saintsbury, was taken ill and the understudy had to stand in. The illness must have been pretty bad as Saintsbury was out for seven weeks, during which time Daziel Heron played 'Holmes' in Scarborough, Aberdeen, Dundee, Paisley, Carlisle, and Hanley. Finally, when the company opened in Hull, w/c 18 April 1904, Charlie got his old friend back. Chaplin said of Saintsbury:

> Mr. H.A. Saintsbury, who played Holmes on tour, was a living replica of the illustrations in the *Strand* magazine. He had a sensitive face and an inspired forehead. Of all those who played Holmes he was considered the best, even better than William Gillette, the original Holmes and author of the play.

> (Chaplin's 1964 autobiography)

Next came Hartlepool West, then Nottingham – where Charlie got yet another excellent review:

(w/c 2 May 1904)

NOTTINGHAM, Grand – "SHERLOCK HOLMES"

... a special word should be devoted to Master Charles Chaplin who makes a perfect study of the part of 'Billy,' Holmes' page-boy.

(Nottingham Daily Express – 5 May 1904)

David Robinson quotes records which show that Hannah Chaplin had been released from Cane Hill Asylum on 2 January, but Charlie places the event much later, and even claims some involvement in the arrangements.

> Sydney wrote to Mother every week and towards the end of our second tour we received a letter from Cane Hill Asylum stating that she had fully recovered her health. This was indeed good news. Quickly we made arrangements for her discharge, and made preparations for her to join us in Reading.

> (Chaplin's 1964 autobiography)

This is another piece that has been cut to the wrong shape. Charlie's choice of Reading can't be right as they didn't play there on this tour. Charlie was to play Reading on the next tour, but Syd *wasn't,* so all three Chaplins being in the same place at the same time must have occurred in a town they visited on this tour. The one which best fits both time and area is Aldershot which, like Reading, is within a forty-five mile radius west of London. All other places on the tour were much further distanced. Charlie said of his mother's visit which, if my choice of Aldershot is correct, would have been following the week in Nottingham, w/c 9 May 1904:

> Sydney and I waited for her at the railroad station, tense and happy, yet I could not help feeling anxious as to how she would fit into our lives again, knowing that the close ties of other days could never be recaptured.

The boys had reserved a special de-luxe apartment: a sitting-room complete with a piano, and two bedrooms – hers bedecked with flowers. However, within a short time of them being re-united, an uneasy silence fell:

> It was uncomfortable and in spite of my wanting to be happy I found myself fighting back a depression. Poor Mother, who wanted so little out of life to make her gay and cheerful, reminded me of my unhappy past – the last person in the world who should have affected me this way.

Of her behaviour later in the week, when they had adjusted to each other, Charlie tells:

> On tour she did the shopping and catering, bringing home fruits and delicacies and always a few flowers. For no matter how poor we had been in the past, when shopping on Saturday nights she had always been able to buy a pennyworth of wallflowers. Occasionally she was quiet and reserved, and her detachment saddened me. She acted more like a guest than our mother.

MR. H. A. SAINTSBURY,

"Mr. H.A. Saintsbury, was considered the best, even better than William Gillette, the original Holmes and author of the play." (Chaplin 1964)

(w/c 27 July 1903) **MILE END, Pavilion E.**	
SHERLOCK HOLMES	
Charles Frohman Company	
Sherlock Holmes	Mr. H. A. Saintsbury
Professor Moriarty	Robert Forsyth
Dr. Watson	Kenneth Rivington
James Larrabee	Ernest Ruston
Madge Larrabee	Theodora Diehl
Sidney Prince	Harry Stafford
John Forman	Ernest Wallace
Billy	Master Charles Chaplin
Sir Edward Leighton	Harold Broughton
Count von Stahlberg	F. Clive Ross
Alice Faulkner	Grete Hahn
Mrs. Faulkner	Mariette Hyde
Thérèse	Lilla Nordon
Mrs. Smeedley	Alice Farquar
Parsons	H. S. Davis
"Lightfoot" McTague	M. M. Loomis
Thomas Leary	James F. Anson
Jim Craigin	W. F. Stirling
Alfred Bassick	George Henry
John	E. H. Fairburn

(w/c 11 April 1904) **HANLEY – Royal**	
SHERLOCK HOLMES	
Charles Frohman Company	
Sherlock Holmes	Dalziel Heron
Professor Moriarty	Robert Forsyth
Dr. Watson	Fred Inwood
James Larrabee	Ernest Ruston
Madge Larrabee	Theodora Diehl
Sydney Prince	Pelham Rayner
John Forman	F. Clive Ross
Billy	Master Charles Chaplin
Sir Edward Leighton	Harold Boughton
Count von Stahlberg	Sydney Chaplin
Alice Faulkner	Marjorie Murray
Mrs. Faulkner	Mariette Hyde
Thérèse (French Maid)	Katherine Del Rey
Mrs. Smeedley	Dorrie Roberts
Parsons	George Henry
"Lightfoot" McTague	M. M. Loomes
Thomas Leary	James F. Anson
Jim Craigin	W. F. Stirling
Alfred Bassick	H. S. Davies
John	E. H. Fairburn

Two cast lists, one from the opening week of the tour, and the other ten months later, showing the considerable changes in the cast members – one of which allowed Syd Chaplin to join the company.

Chaplin says she stayed with them on the tour for a month which, if Aldershot was indeed the starting point, means she also had a week each in Bradford, Blackpool, and Eastbourne. I hope she did, but I must say "I doubt it." Here is woman who was now so used to solitary confinement that sharing the hectic and peripatetic life of her sons would have been particularly bewildering, if not frightening. She did express her anxiety, and her wanting to return to London, citing to Charlie that she was becoming a financial burden on the boys, and would be better employed getting their lodgings ready for when the tour finished. It is probably nearer to the truth, though, that she wanted to get home as she felt totally alien to her environment.

Regardless of how many Chaplins stayed on the tour, the last three weeks must have been a pleasure. A week at the North West seaside resort of Blackpool, was followed by a week in the South Coast resort of Eastbourne. The company then completed the loop by returning to London, where the tour ended at the West London Theatre, in the Edgware Road, on 11 June 1904. Charlie summed it up as follows:

After forty weeks in the provinces, we returned to play eight weeks around the suburbs of London. Sherlock Holmes, being a phenomenal success, was to start a second tour, three weeks after the first one.

Anyone using Charlie's records, above, to try and track down the tour venues would be guaranteed to hit a few dead ends. Firstly, the tour lasted forty-eight working weeks – not forty. Secondly they played just one week in the London suburbs – not eight; and finally, the second tour was to start twelve weeks after the first one – not three. Who'd be a chronologist?!?

Chapter 6

FROM RAGS TO RAGS

It was the summer of 1904 and, though he was out of work, Charlie had sufficient savings to enjoy his freedom and the activities that warm weather affords to a fifteen-year-old youth. Hannah Chaplin was living in Chester Street, in the flat over the barber's shop, where the family had lived five years earlier. Whilst touring with the Sherlock Holmes' company, Syd and Charlie had been sending her one twenty five shillings a week, to help towards purchasing furniture. It's as well they did for they ended up spending the summer with her.

Although Charlie himself may not actively have been seeking work, wheels were being set in motion for his next engagement. Ernest Stern, after having seen him in *Sherlock Holmes,* had offered Charlie the star role in a play he was intending to put into production; for which, in mid-August, the advanced publicity advert ran:

Spring Tour – Starts Boxing Day
MR. ERNEST STERN'S CO.
"FROM

RAGS

TO

RICHES"

By Chas. Taylor.

Specially Selected Company including
Master CHARLIE CHAPLIN
as 'NED NIMBLE'

NOW RUNNING IN AMERICA TO
ENORMOUS BUSINESS.
Vacant Dates, apply,
John A. Atkin,
Bramcote Lodge, Sunbury-on-Thames.

THE STAGE

11 AUGUST 1904

These adverts ran for thirteen weeks, but the play Charlie next went into was not *Rags to Riches* but a second run of *Sherlock Holmes.* As for *Rags to Riches,* it never got past being 'rags.' The tour was to commence 31 October 1904, with every actor but Charlie being new to the cast. Charlie admitted rather guiltily that, although he was happy to have spent some time with his mother, he was pleased to be getting out of the flat, and into the more comfortable accommodation of theatrical digs. The living arrangements in the flat may well have become even more uncomfortable during Charlie's last ten days there, as Hannah's father Charles Hill had probably moved back in after a seven week spell in Renfrew Road Workhouse.

The opening performance of the new tour of *Sherlock Holmes,* was in the Berkshire town of Reading, forty miles due west of London. Syd however was not on this tour, as he was about to go to sea just ten days later. If Chaplin's recollection of Reading is correct, then Syd and his mother must have joined Charlie here, to spend a bit of quality time together, before they went their separate ways. You choose! Charlie and the company then headed northwards to hit Shropshire then Lancashire, before turning southwards for towns in Cheshire, and Derbyshire.

(w/c 21 November 1904)

ILKESTON – Royal

Mr Charles Frohman's company occupy the boards with *Sherlock Holmes*. Mr. Kenneth Rivington appears in the title-rôle, his impressive style being much appreciated by the audience. Miss Florence Radcliffe as 'Alice Faulkner' plays with much feeling and finish. Mr. Fred Inwood as 'Dr. Watson' is a capable exponent, and Mr. Charles. E. Scutt is worthy of mention as 'John Forman'. Mr. Charles Chaplin is notably smart as 'Billy'. The other artists are highly suitable to the work allotted to them, and the general and scenic effects leave nothing to be desired.

(*The Stage* – 24 November 1904)

Three weeks in Yorkshire towns brought them up to the Christmas and New Year weeks, which the company appear to have had off; after which the tour restarted in Darlington. Next it was over the border into Scotland for a total of five weeks, some of which were split – Monday to Wednesday in one town, and Thursday to Saturday in another.

(Mon to Wed 16-18 January 1905)

KIRKCALDY – King's

Mr Charles Frohman presents *Sherlock Holmes* for three nights. In the part of 'Holmes' Mr. Kenneth Rivington proves himself to be a strong and a capable actor. Mr. Arthur B. Murray plays 'Moriarty', and is appreciated. 'James Larrabee', played by Mr. Ernest Gray, is portrayed to the life. Mr. Harry G. Wright as 'Sydney Prince' supplies the humorous element in a creditable manner. Mr. Fred Inwood as 'Dr. Watson' has a good stage appearance: he is a very natural actor. Praise is due to Master Charles Chaplin, who plays 'Billy' cleverly. The scenery and effects are all that could be desired.

(*The Stage* – 19 January 1905)

The trail then turned around and headed south into the North-West of England, where they remained for three weeks; then on into Staffordshire for one week, and through into Wales. Here, during the last two weeks in March and the first two weeks in April, 1905, the company played small mining towns in the Welsh valleys, with some weeks again being split. The first week was spent in Merthyr Tydfil, but no engagement was traced for week two. The first-half of the third week began in Tonypandy:

(Mon to Wed 3-5 April 1905)

TONYPANDY – Royal

A return visit is paid for the first three nights of this week by *Sherlock Holmes*. Mr. Kenneth Rivington again appears in the title-*rôle* with unqualified success. Mr. Ernest Gray as 'James Larrabee' adopts a tone of frank brutality which quite suits the part. Miss Carrie Lacey as 'Madge Larrabee' is very good. Miss Florence Radcliffe as 'Alice Faulkner' acts in a natural manner. Mr. Fred Inwood makes an effective 'Dr. Watson'. Mr. Charles Chaplin as 'Billy' is distinctly good. 'Professor Moriarty' is well portrayed by Mr. Arthur B. Murray. Crowded houses are the rule. For Thursday, Friday and Saturday an excellent company of variety artists have been engaged.

(*The Stage* – 19 January 1905)

If Chaplin's recollection is correct, it was whilst staying in Tonypandy that his one-year run of playing "the cute little boy, with the cute little bunny" finally ran into an unsympathetic audience. Charlie himself tells of the tragic ending:

Before long I had it trained to run to its box every time there was a knock at the door. If the landlady discovered my secret I would have the rabbit perform this trick, which usually won her heart, and she would put up with us for the week. But in Tonypandy, Wales, after I showed my trick, the landlady smiled cryptically and made no comment; but when I returned from the theatre that night my pet had gone. When I enquired about it, the landlady merely shook her head. 'It must have run away or someone must have stolen it.' She had in her own way handled the problem efficaciously.

Hope she hadn't boiled it in a saucepan. No engagement was traced for the second-half of week three, but Charlie does say that, after playing Tonypandy on the first three nights of the week, the play switched for the next three days to Ebbw Vale. And it is from there that Chaplin tells of an animal story of a very different nature.

Most of the company stayed at a small hotel, but Charlie stayed in a miner's house. The man of the house went to see the play on the second night, and afterwards engaged Charlie in conversation back home. Thinking that Charlie might be just the right kind of lad to introduce his son into show business, he took him into his confidence with the leading line: 'Ever seen a human frog?' With that, he led Charlie into the kitchen to where a curtain covered the bottom part of a dresser, and called out: 'Hey Gilbert, come on out of there.'

A half man with no legs, an oversized, blond, flat-shaped head, a sickening white face, a sunken nose, a large mouth and powerful muscular shoulders and arms, crawled from underneath the dresser. He wore flannel underwear with the legs of the garment cut off to the thighs, from which ten thick, stubby toes stuck out.

(Chaplin's 1964 autobiography)

The miner then ran poor Gilbert through a series of acrobatic tricks, which included hopping; jumping high in the air; then climbing onto a rocking chair and doing a handstand on its arms. Charlie stood and watched, unable to speak. When the repertoire was finished he gave what the father and son thought to be enthusiastic applause and compliments. Secretly though, he was horrified, a feeling which was hardly diminished when the father asked: "How do you think he'd fit in with a circus – 'The Human Frog'?" Charlie's revulsion was added to when he later realised that he was sleeping in what would usually be Gilbert's bed.

On his first tour with the *Sherlock Holmes* company Chaplin claimed that he had been released from the guardianship of the wardrobe lady after just three weeks and, outside of the theatre, had isolated himself from the rest of the cast members. This was proved not to be true, as Edith Scales had continued as his guardian until Syd took over the role, six months in to the tour. If one now applies his reminiscences of isolation from the company here, they sit all that much better.

On this second tour things must have seemed very strange for Charlie. The whole cast had been changed, including his casual friends Robert Forsyth and H.A. Saintsbury, and gone were his guardians – Edith, and Syd. The latter was now an assistant steward aboard the *SS Dover Castle*. Charlie himself had also undergone huge mental and physical changes in metamorphosing from a fourteen-year-old boy, to a sixteen-year-old youth, so it is quite understandable why he felt it difficult to connect with the others.

From Wales was an unwanted and, seemingly, unwarranted trip to Scotland for one week in Perth, followed by a free week. The last week of this twenty-seven week tour came at the beginning of May 1905, and ended, as did the last tour, in London. The first thing Charlie did when he got back was to go and visit his mum in Cane Hill Asylum, where she had been readmitted on 18 March. She was to remain there for the next seven-and-a-half years.

(w/c 1 May 1905)

EALING – The New

Mr Charles Frohman's company in *Sherlock Holmes* are playing a farewell visit this week, and, as before, are doing good business. Mr. Kenneth Rivington gives an excellent impersonation of Holmes, which is greatly appreciated. As 'Dr. Watson', Mr. Fred Inwood is good. Mr. Arthur B. Murray portrays 'Professor Moriarty' in an able manner. Mr. Ernest Gray and and Miss Carrie Lacey as 'James' and 'Madge Larrabee' add much to the interest by their capable handling of the parts. Harry G. Wright as 'Sydney Prince' also does very well. Mr. Chas. Chaplin as 'Billy' is good, but overdoes the part a little.

(*The Stage* – 4 May 1905)

During June and July, Charlie must have worried that further stage work may not come his way as Frohman had dropped *Sherlock Holmes,* but not offered Charlie a part in any of his other productions. But then theatrical impresario Harry Yorke bought the performing rights of *Sherlock Holmes,* set up a tour to start almost immediately, and, to Charlie's surprise, invited him to join the company. Rehearsals were held at the Theatre Royal & Opera House, Blackburn, where Harry Yorke happened to be the proprietor, and where the play then opened on 14 August 1905.

(w/c 14 August 1905)

BLACKBURN – Royal

(Proprietor, Mr. Harry Yorke; Manager, Mr. Reginald C. Yorke) – Mr. Yorke, the proprietor of this house, having secured the provincial rights of Conan Doyle and Wm. Gillette's play *Sherlock Holmes,* opened his theatre on Saturday after the usual summer vacation, with that attraction. The company are one of the best seen in Blackburn in this play, and in every respect the production is all that could be desired. The title-*rôle* is filled by Mr. H. Lawrence Leyton, who gives a really fine portrayal of the nonchalant detective, and compares very favourably indeed with any of his predecessors in the part. Mr. W. F. Stirling has been seen before as 'Professor Moriarty', and he is convincing as ever in the part. Mr. Ernest Gray as 'James Larrabee' is also good, while as 'Sydney Prince' Mr. Philip Renouf raises many a laugh by his eccentricities. Miss Beatrice Marsden acts charmingly as 'Alice Faulkner' and, along with Mr. Leyton, has been the recipient of well-deserved applause from large holiday audiences. Miss Gertrude Harrison is clever as 'Madge Larrabee', while Mr. J. P. Kirkwood as 'John Forman', Mr. Edward Heanley as 'Dr. Watson', and Mr. Charles Chaplin as 'Billy' also act well. The scenery and electrical effects are all new.

(*The Stage* – 17 August 1905)

The venues were on the No.2 theatre circuit and so, because future box-office receipts were unlikely to match those of the Froham productions, Charlie had to accept a drop in salary from £2.10s [= £2.50p] to just thirty-five shillings [= £1.75p] per week. There was little about the tour to make up for the loss of earnings. Charlie described it as follows:

> It was a depressing come down, playing the small towns of the North with an inferior company.

When one looks at the first four places the company played, one would have to question Charlie's use of 'small towns', for they were Blackburn, Hull, Dewsbury, and Huddersfield. Charlie had played all four of them before whilst with the Froham Company, so it was a bit unfair of him to select them for criticism this time around. However, his feelings that the present company were inferior to the Frohman's may have been well-founded. Unfortunately, Charlie made his feelings all too obvious, as he himself confessed:

> This comparison I tried to conceal but, at rehearsals, in my zeal to help the new director, who would ask me about stage directions, cues and business etc., I would eagerly tell him how it was done in the Frohman Company. This, of course, did not make me particularly popular with the cast, and I was looked upon as a precocious brat.

If any of Charlie's fellow actors were contemplating saying to him; "If you think you're so much better than us, how come you're in the same company?" they were soon made to choke on their words, when Charlie received an invite to join "the elite." No less a person than William Gillette, the great Sherlock Holmes portrayer and co-writer of the play, sent a telegram asking if Charlie could come and join him in London. No snoop has ever been cocked so well.

Gillette had opened at the Duke of York's, in St. Martin's Lane, London, on 13 September in a self-penned comedy entitled "*Clarice,*" after a production try-out week at the Shakespeare Theatre, Liverpool. Then, for the fourth week onwards of the London run, he decided to add a curtain-raiser. This was to be another play he himself had written, entitled *The Painful Predicament of Sherlock Holmes,* and was described as "A fantasy in one-tenth of an act" – the latter being a tilt at the shortness of the play itself.

Duke of York's Theatre
ST MARTIN'S LANE W C

CHARLES FROHMAN

PRESENTS

William Gillette

IN HIS NEW COMEDY

"CLARICE"

WITH A CAST AS FOLLOWS

JUDITH CLANCY	LUCILLE LA VERNE
CLARICE MARLAND	MARIE DORO
DR CARRINGTON	WILLIAM GILLETTE
MR TRENT	THOMAS H BURNS
MRS TRENT	ADELAIDE PRINCE
H FORSYTHE DENBEIGH M D	FRANCIS CARLYLE
BELL BOYS AT THE BENBOW ARMS	GORO KODAMA HARRY HILLMAN

A VILLAGE IN SOUTHERN VIRGINIA
ABOUT A NIGHT'S RAILWAY RUN
FROM WASHINGTON
THE SECOND AND THIRD
OF JUNE 1904

FIRST ACT — MORNING   THE LIVING ROOM AT DR CARRINGTON'S

SECOND ACT
    SCENE I — AFTERNOON   MR AND MRS TRENT'S PARLOUR AT THE BENBOW ARMS
    SCENE II — EVENING   LIVING ROOM AT DR CARRINGTON'S

THIRD ACT — NEXT MORNING   THE SAME ROOM

FOURTH ACT — THE FOLLOWING EVENING   THE SAME

PRECEDED AT 8.30 BY

"THE PAINFUL PREDICAMENT OF SHERLOCK HOLMES"
A FANTASY — IN ABOUT ONE-TENTH OF AN ACT

GWENDOLYN COBB	MISS IRENE VANBRUGH
SHERLOCK HOLMES	MR WILLIAM GILLETTE
BILLY	MASTER CHARLES CHAPLIN

Advert for
"CLARICE"
and
"The Painful Predicament of Sherlock Holmes"
at the Duke of Yorke's Theatre, London.

Charlie had had a few anxious days while a replacement was being sought so that he could be released from the Northern tour. But then, at the end of September 1905, he was able to make his merry way from Warrington back to the capital in time for rehearsals. Just two days and one night later the curtain rose on *The Painful Predicament of Sherlock Holmes*. Along with Gillette as 'Holmes', and Charlie reprising his role as 'Billy,' was Irene Vanbrugh playing the part of Gwendolyn Cobb.

THE STAGE — 5 OCTOBER 1905

THE DUKE OF YORK'S

On Tuesday evening 3 October 1905, *Clarice* was preceded by a fantasy — in about one-tenth of an act — entitled: —

The Painful Predicament of Sherlock Holmes.
Gwendolyn Cobb ...... Miss Irene Vanbrugh
Sherlock Holmes .... William Gillette
Billy .... Master Charles Chaplin

It all transpires in Sherlock Holmes' Baker Street apartments about the date of day before yesterday. The time of day is not stated.

Apparently to strengthen the bill at the Duke of York's *Clarice* was on Tuesday preceded for the first time by a whimsical skit on *Sherlock Holmes*, rightly described as a fantasy, though more than a tenth of an act, as taking some ten or fifteen minutes to play. In this Mr. William Gillette, who very possibly may be the author of an ingenious *jeu d'esprit*, for once appears in a thinking part, leaving all the talking to be done by Miss Irene Vanbrugh (warmly welcomed on making her reappearance), who has to represent a poor, crazy woman, excitable, impulsive, and tremendously voluble, who, in spite of the zealous efforts of "Billy", the page, bursts like a whirlwind into the sanctum of the great detective. Unusual, rather than painful, should be styled the predicament of Sherlock Holmes, who, whilst smoking and brooding placidly in his familiar Baker Street apartments, has to put up with the vagaries of such a strange invader. Gwendolyn Cobb, as the name is given on the programme, hurries in, eagerly shaking hands with the man whose exploits have apparently turned her brain, nearly pokes out his fire, upsets his lamp, tears down his prints, and generally causes havoc, whilst she is breathlessly gabbling out some incoherent nonsense about an extraordinary case on which she wants to consult him. She succeeds in making clear only that her lover has been lodged in gaol at her own father's instigation, and Holmes listens attentively and smokes peacefully whilst this queer visitor rambles on. Once, when she fancies she hears unearthly noises, he scribbles on a bit of paper "There are plumbers in the house," and later on, when she has worked herself up into a fury because someone had called her incarcerated sweetheart "a right-angled triangle," he calmly makes another memorandum, which he sends out by Billy. Two stern-faced men in uniform appear, evidently attendants from a lunatic asylum, and the poor creature is marched off, back to captivity again. The woman's madness is not made absolutely plain until near the end of this amusing but rather *outré* joke, which may be too clever by half for some playgoers. Mr. Gillette was as imperturbable as ever as the Doyle-detective, and Master Charles Chaplin was duly boisterous as the harmless, necessary page. Miss Vanbrugh gave a capital *tour de force* as the maniac, whose jumbled-up harangues and quick, erratic movements she cleverly made consistent with eccentric insanity as long as possible. As a curious piece of stagework *The Painful Predicament of Sherlock Holmes* may be worth seeing.

The Painful Predicament of Sherlock Holmes ran for just two weeks and then made way for Gillette's original version of *Sherlock Holmes*. It has been suggested that Gillette wrote and introduced *The Painful Predicament* just to have a go at the theatre critics, but this seems not to stand up as Gillette had successfully played *The Painful Predicament* in New York, some six months earlier – with the leading lady being no other than Ethel Barrymore. It has also been suggested that The Painful Predicament was taken off because the joke misfired but, as can been seen from the above review, it certainly wasn't panned.

So now it's on with the show: with the original and ever-popular version of *Sherlock Holmes* as the main play, and *Clarice* switching to being the curtain raiser. Charlie was absolutely thrilled to be back on the London stage, especially at such a prestigious venue. A different type of thrill, however, was afforded him at the first morning's rehearsal when he set eyes upon the leading lady, Marie Doro. Of her looks Charlie commented:

THE PAINFUL PREDICAMENT OF SHERLOCK HOLMES
A Fantasy in One Act - by WILLIAM GILLETTE

(Enter Billy at door up R, very excited. He pulls the door shut after him, and holds it while he turns to speak to Holmes)

      BILLY I beg pardon, sir ---
(The door is pulled from outside and Billy turns to hold it, but turns again quickly to Holmes)
      (Same business)
      I beg pardon, sir - If you please, sir! - It's a young lady 'as just came in, an' says she must see you - she's 'ere now, sir, a-tryin' to pull the door open - but I don't like 'er eye, sir! . . . I don't like it at all, sir!
      (Holmes rises and moves up LC. Turns up lamp. Lights on.)
      'Er eye is certainly bad, sir! An' she - she don't seem to be able to leave off talkin' long enough fer me to tell 'er as 'ow she can't see you, sir!
(Holmes moves toward C carrying pipe in left hand and watches Billy and the door with interest)
      I tried to tell 'er as you give orders not to see no one. I shouted it out tremendous - but she was talkin' so loud it never got to 'er - so I run up to warn you - an' she come runnin' after me - an' - an'
(Door suddenly pulled upon from outside while Billy is talking to Holmes)
      An' . . . an' 'ere she is, sir!
      GWENDOLYN
      (Entering joyously)
      Oh! There you are! This is Mr. Holmes, I know! Oh - I've heard so much about you! You really can't imagine! (going toward Holmes). And I've simply longed to see you myself and see if . . . oh, do shake hands with me. (they shake hands. Isn't it wonderful to realize I'm shaking hands with Sherlock Holmes! It's simply ripping! To think that I've lived to see you this day! (looks at him) Of course, I suppose you're the real one - detectives have so many disguises and things that it might be you were only pretending - but still, why should you?
(He motions her to seat, she does not pause for an any business)
      Oh, thank you. Yes - I will sit down.
(She moves down C to R C to chair at R of table and sits on arm of it)
      (Holmes motions Billy to go)
      (Exit Billy)

William Gillette
In characteristic pose as 'Sherlock Holmes'

She was so devastatingly beautiful that I resented her. I resented her delicate, pouting lips, her regular white teeth, her adorable chin, her raven hair and dark brown eyes. I had just turned sixteen, and the propinquity of this sudden radiance evoked my determination not to be obsessed by it. But 'Oh! God' she was beautiful! It was love at first sight.

It is interesting to note that less than eighteen months earlier, when Charlie first got the part of Billy, he had wanted everyone to believe he was just twelve-and-half but, now that there was a lady whom he wished to impress, he admitted to his full age. I could have forgiven Charlie if, at times, he had lied about his age by adding years, but this was an untruth he never went in for. Quoting an older age on occasion may have achieved some reward but, by only ever making himself out to be younger, it makes it appear as though it were only ever sympathy he craved.

The highlight of the play's run came on 20 November 1905, when a Royal Gala Performance of *Sherlock Holmes* was attended by Queen Alexandra, accompanied by the King of Greece, and Prince Christian. *Sherlock Holmes* then finished its run on Saturday 2 December 1905, a little earlier than had been scheduled. This was due, some say, to Gillette pulling out after being upset by some of the critics' reviews. The newspapers revealed only scant information:

> What is the real reason of Mr. William Gillette's sudden departure from the Duke of York's Theatre, London? Business was good, says a contemporary, so that lack of that can't have been the cause of his departure. When invited by an interviewer to explain the 'how, why, and wherefore' of the abrupt ending of his season, and his resolve never to play in England again, Mr. Gillette said: 'I have nothing to say.' And, unlike the average man who starts this way, he said it! His card advertisement in Saturday's Era appeared thus:

> William Gillette – No Address

> (Liverpool Weekly – 15 December 1905)

Whatever the cause of Gillette's departure, the certainty was that he would not be persuaded to return for, just four days after quitting, he boarded the *SS Majestic* and sailed for New York. Nor was there any chance of his being substituted, as with him went fellow cast members Adelaide Prince, Francis Carlyle, George Sumner, and Marie Doro – among others.

With the departing cast members went thirty-one year-old William Postance, Gillette's stage manager. During Charlie's short stay at the Duke of York's theatre he had developed a real fondness for Postance; a fondness that stayed with him throughout his life and which he acknowledge by naming one of the characters in the 1952 film *Limelight* 'Mr. Postant'. The name may have been wrongly spelled – but the gesture was well meant.

Charlie may well have hoped that Gillette would take him to America, to make him a star, but his time would come. Meanwhile, back at the Duke of York's, the mystery of Gillette's non-appearance in *Sherlock Holmes* then spawned the mystery of Charlie's alleged appearance in the pantomime which followed. *Peter Pan* opened on 19 December 1905, for which some early chroniclers have claimed that Charlie took on the role of a wolf. If one is to accept this claim as feasible, then the question "Why would he take up such a minor role?" needs to be answered.

Having speculated on this, one would then need to overcome the fact that, at the beginning of the third week of the run of *Peter Pan,* Charlie was in Doncaster where he had been recalled to play 'Billy' in Harry Yorke's company. Not since its original conception in Aesop's fable has the use of the phrase "never cry wolf, when there is no wolf to be seen" been so applicable.

Changing companies from the "Duke of York's" to plain "Harry Yorke's" might have been a comedown for Charlie, but at least he was back in work. Again he had to endure dank, dark Northern towns like Doncaster, Sheffield, Crewe, and Rochdale but, as these were equally spaced either side of a four-week run in London Boroughs, the weeks away from home would not have been so hard to bear.

Charlie records that Sydney was also engaged on this tour. However, the first entry found for Syd was in a programme from the New Theatre, Cambridge, w/c 15 January 1906, although it is quite possible he had joined a little earlier, probably at the start of the New Year along with Charlie. In total, the tour ran for a further nine weeks only, then it was all over. But, for Charlie, there could be no regrets. He had been recalled for a second tour by both the Frohman and the Yorke companies; had played opposite four different actors in the eponymous role; and had ridden through the harsh trials of trying to get on with all the crew, cast and management of four different companies. Of future value to him would be the stagecraft, timing, delivery, projection, acting, and upstaging he had learned. And, on a physical level, he had joined as a vulnerable boy but was leaving as a mature youth. Yes indeed, as the old adage goes:

"There's no play like Holmes."

Chapter 7

CHARLIE FAILS TO APPEAR IN "COURT"

Around the turn of the nineteenth century Dan Lipton was to be found touring the variety halls as 'a witty and amusing comedian.' He then opted for the less-demanding role of songwriter, for which he took up residence in London, sharing a flat with C.W. Murphy. Murphy had a good track record, being the composer of such popular music-hall songs as *Kelly, Oh! Oh! Antonio,* and *Put Me Amongst the Girls,* but Lipton had yet to score a hit. In 1921 Mr. Ted Hughes, a retired comedian living in Blackpool, gave some background to Lipton's new career:

> Mr. Dan Lipton and Mr. Murphy used to write songs in Walcot Gardens, a block of flats in Kennington Road, London S.E., where they were often disturbed by a small crowd of youngsters in the courtyard at the back of the flats. The chief imp was the young Charlie Chaplin, who attracted their attention by his natural gift for mimicry. The boys' performances prompted Mr. Dan Lipton to write the sketch *Casey's Circus,* and eventually Charlie Chaplin himself was secured for a part, that of the principal comedian.
>
> (*Blackpool Gazette and Herald* – 10 September 1921)

Another article, printed at the time of Chaplin's 1921 visit to England, seemed to back up the claim with first-hand recollections:

> Charlie Chaplin was a small, thin boy, with dark eyes when he was 'discovered' by a simple, kind-hearted man, named Dan Lipton. The talented youngster used to give al fresco performances to his admiring comrades in Walcot public gardens.
>
> "Even if he had never leapt into fame, I couldn't forget that mischievous boy," said Dan, "for the noise that came from his outdoor show used to disturb me and my pal who were writing comic songs."
>
> "We lived in a flat that overlooked the gardens, and these boys made such a row that I often had to go out to quiet them."
>
> (*Daily Graphic* – 1 September 1921)

Had Dan Lipton really witnessed the young Charlie or had he, in looking back eighteen years, just convinced himself the young boy he had observed then was Chaplin? Well, in the Spring of 1903, the Chaplin's moved into 3 Pownall Terrace, which was just two blocks away from Walcot Gardens. So now we have the time and the place. Let's hear from Charlie, to see if the story stands up. He begins one account by informing us of the McCarthy family, who came to live in Walcot Mansions.

> Their son, Wally McCarthy, and I were the same age. As little children, we used to play at grown-ups, pretending we were vaudevillians, smoking our imaginary cigars and driving in our imaginary pony and trap, much to the amusement of our parents.
>
> Wally and I formed an inseparable friendship. As soon as I was through with school I

would race home to mother to find out if she needed any errands done, then race up to the McCarthy's. We would play theatre at the back of Walcott Mansions.

Dan Lipton's story continues, now all the more believable to readers of this tome:

Charlie was about thirteen then, and his acting and mimicry were so extraordinary that my friend and I decided to write a show for him.

(Photo 2005 by *Mortier*)

WALCOT GARDENS
(Corner of 135-136 Kennington Road and Fitzalan Street).
"The McCarthys came to live in Walcot Mansions. Their son Wally and I were the same age. We formed an inseparable friendship. As soon a school was over I would race up to the McCarthys. We would play theatre at the back of Walcot Mansions."
(Chaplin's 1964 autobiography)

(Photo 2005 by *Mortier*)

Exterior view of the rear of WALCOT GARDENS
"Mr. Dan Lipton and Mr. Murphy used to write songs in Walcot Gardens, a block of flats in Kennington Road, London S.E., where they were often disturbed by a small crowd of youngsters in the courtyard at the back of the flats."
(*Blackpool Gazette and Herald*)

A rare photograph of the setting of Casey's Court, with 'Mrs Casey' seen left. There appear to be about twenty-six children in this scene, but look closely and you will see that some of them are actually cut-outs. The two children in minstrel costume and make-up might well be doing an impersonation of 'The Two Daniels,' whose act was described as follows:

"As versatile Negroes, furnish attractive turns, first on stilts. They afterwards provide a big boot dance and song, while one of them, in a step dance to the twanging of the old banjo, shows remarkable vigour in the activity and length of his dancing."

The most fascinating aspect of the picture above is the scenery. We have already read that Dan Lipton wrote the sketch after watching children playing in Walcot Court. If there are any doubters of this, then doubt no more. Just compare the scenery, above, with the photograph of Walcot Court, below. Got it?

Photo from 1921 London newspaper.

(Photo 2005 by *Mortier*)

Gone is the terrace across the road, but the Court itself is virtually unchanged.

The 'show' entitled 'Casey's Court' was produced by [Harry] Cadle, but, much to Dan's chagrin, Cadle would not have the young Charlie, because he knew nothing about him.

His Seven Parts in 'Casey's Circus'

Before Charlie appeared in Dan's burlesque, 'Casey's Circus,' he toured with the 'Eight Lancashire Lads,' and several other shows.

By this time, Cadle was convinced of the boy's ability, and 'Casey's Circus,' in which Charlie, then about seventeen years of age, played no fewer than seven different parts, proved a huge success. It was produced at Woolwich, Charlie's salary being £4 a week.

(Daily Graphic – 1 September 1921)

So Lipton's account is pretty accurate: he puts Charlie at being thirteen when he first saw him, which ties in with Charlie coming to live in Pownall Terrace in the Spring of 1903; and seventeen when he finally landed a part in *Casey's Circus* – which is also correct.

In his autobiography, Chaplin dismisses his time in *Casey's Circus* in just one paragraph. Considering that this constituted some sixty-one weeks of continuous work, one might conclude that Chaplin was again denying credit to those who had developed his character and repertoire. Thankfully, in 1921, more chroniclers came forward to fill in the blanks in the 'Casey' tours, all of which make very interesting reading, and will be featured throughout this chapter. Firstly, though, let's nail down exactly which sketch Charlie was in, as confusion has abounded in previous accounts:

On 11 January 1906 Harry Cadle placed the following advert in *The Stage* trade paper.

Wanted, Boys over 14 (small for age).
Boy Actors, Boy Comedians,
Boy Vocalists, Boy Acrobats, Boy Musicians,
Exceptional opportunities clever Boys.
Cadle's Agency – 105, Strand

At the auditions which followed, the cast members were picked for a sketch titled *Casey's Court*, which made its debut at the Richmond Theatre, Richmond, on 6 March 1906. The 'Court' referred to in this instance was, as we have just read, a courtyard at the back of a block of flats. The theme of the sketch was based on the ever-popular premise that children behaving as adults are most amusing. The type of entertainment being referred to is to be found in the later *Just William* books, in which William Brown and his gang regularly put on plays for the enjoyment of friends, family and locals. We can also witness the same premise on film: in the Hal Roach comedies of the 1930s featuring children known as *The Little Rascals* (aka: *Our Gang*). The following reviews will give some idea as to the entertainment featured.

OLDHAM, Gaiety – "Casey's Court"

'Mrs. Casey' [played by Bob King] is a theatrical wardrobe dealer and the queen of her court, which is not too clean. The company, comprising 30 youngsters, organise an amateur variety show for the benefit of the inhabitants, and refuse to allow admittance to any one from a neighbouring court. The make-up of the numerous artistes is laughable in the extreme. All the youngsters enter heartily into the fun of the thing, each filling his humorous part to perfection.

(The Stage – 19 April 1906)

WALTHAMSTOW, Palace

A great success is made by a new eccentric sketch, *Casey's Court,* in which a few "grown up" actors, surrounded by a perfect phalanx of boisterous juveniles, keep the ball rolling with unabated vigour from start to finish. The entire production is brimful of grotesque merriment, and is received with every mark of favour. The singing and dancing of some of the young people are both excellent, and no expense has been spared to place the sketch on the stage.

(*The Stage* – 26 April 1906)

NOTTINGHAM, Empire

Ventriloquism, conjuring, coon songs, and choruses were introduced in this street urchins' idea of a variety entertainment.

(*Nottingham Evening Post* – 3 September 1906)

BRADFORD, Empire

Casey's Court, by 30 clever boys and girls. The funniest skit on a Variety Show yet seen. Simply side-splitting.

(*Bradford Daily Telegraph* – 15 May 1906)

The last reviewer seems to be claiming that *Casey's Court* actually featured girls. The recruitment adverts asked for boys only, but the figure on the extreme right of the photograph of *Casey's Court* does look like a girl – as opposed to a boy in girls clothing. The following review then adds confirmation to the presence of at least one girl in the cast:

NEW CROSS, Empire

Special mention must be made of *Casey's Court* in which a number of children hold high revel in the court or alley from which the Show takes its title. A little girl who sang a "Sweep Song" showed distinct aptitude both as a vocalist and dancer, and the show is full of quaint business and clever touches.

(*The Referee* – 2 September 1906)

And, finally, a review which reveals a little more of the premise and plot:

SUNDERLAND, Palace – 'CASEY'S COURT'

By the Midget Mimes – 30 in Number

For the first time in Sunderland Harry Cadle's production of *Casey's Court* was submitted. It is a ragged burlesque, founded on an idea worked upon in a comic illustrated paper. The performers are about 30 children and an adult, and the youngsters pose as slum children holding a mimic music-hall entertainment. Curious devices are brought into use, a bath tin, for instance, representing a private box to accommodate a young Eton toff, and a wringing machine the pay office. The children are ragged and dirty, their grotesque business is entertaining, and some fun is obtained out of a persistent slovenly-dressed little Scot, who doesn't belong to the court, and is constantly being chased away as an intruder.

(*Sunderland Echo* – 9 October 1906)

Casey's Court was an instant hit, and generated such a demand for bookings that Harry Cadle, placed a second advert in *The Stage,* the background to which was provided by Will Murray:

I first met Charlie when I was running the sketch "Casey's Court (Circus)". These sketches, which were pure burlesque, met with a great measure of success throughout the country.

To carry out a second edition of the sketch I found it necessary to advertise for a number of boys between fourteen and nineteen years of age. Amongst the applicants was one little lad who took my fancy at once. I asked him his name and what theatrical experience he had. "Charlie Chaplin, sir," was the reply. "I've been one of 'The Eight Lancashire Lads,' and just now I've got a part in the sketch [sic] 'Sherlock Holmes.'[1]

I put him through his paces. He sang, danced, and did a little of practically everything in the entertaining line. He had the makings of a "star" in him, and I promptly took him on salary, 30s per week.[2]

(*Weekly Record* – 10 September 1921)

---

[1] Charlie obviously applied for the part before *Sherlock Holmes* ended its run on 3 March, which means he must have acted upon the first advert, which was for *Casey's Court.* The latter commenced on 6 March.

[2] 30 shillings (£1.50p), sounds a more convincing figure than the £4 wage Dan Lipton purported Chaplin to be on.

Murray is slightly mistaken in the above statement where he speaks of "To carry out a second edition of the sketch I found it necessary to advertise," as he did actually set up a second company playing *Casey's Court,* which commenced touring on 2 April. *Casey's Circus* was therefore the *third edition,* and made its full debut at the Olympia theatre, Liverpool, on 21 May 1906, with Will Murray himself taking the lead role of 'Mrs. Casey.' There are some biographers who wish to claim that Chaplin actually appeared in *Casey's Court,* when it played Bradford the previous week. However, in the weeks leading up to his joining *Casey's Circus,* Charlie had been otherwise engaged. His brother Syd had obtained employment for both of them in Wal Pink's Company of Comedians.

In his 1964 autobiography, Chaplin wrote not a single word about his participation in Wal Pink's Company – nor even of his brother Syd's. He does mention that Syd joined Charlie Mannon's troupe of knockabout comedians, and adds that Fred Karno saw Syd with them and signed him up, but the latter part is incorrect. And why Charlie should then go on to mention three other similar-type troupes and leave out Wal Pink's is yet another of those mystifying omissions in Chaplin's accounts.

There is a saying that "A good liar must have a good memory." Likewise, someone who is trying to hide a secret must have a good memory, otherwise he is likely to forget what he is hiding, or who he is hiding it from. So, in 1921 when Chaplin was on a visit to London, he made what must have been for him a major gaff when talking to former actor Hannen Swaffer. Swaffer showed Charlie a photograph of an action freeze from the sketch *Repairs* and asked him if he was the little guy at the front-centre, chopping wood. "Yes! That's me," said Chaplin, "and that's Syd on the ladder." So the truth was out – and big time. Hannen Swaffer, since leaving the stage had became a newspaper theatre critic. The next day the photo was featured in a major London broadsheet, with Chaplin's confirmation as the caption. Chaplin may have omitted his involvement with this sketch from his autobiography, but this was one source he couldn't erase.

The sketch *Repairs* featured 'Wal Pink's Workmen' wallpapering and decorating a room in 'Muddleton Villa.' One reviewer described it as "a capital knockabout, pantomimical sketch after the manner, in scenic effects, of *The Jerry Builder;* whilst *The Magnet* recycled the programme notes and came up with: "Top-of-the-bill Wal Pink's Workmen in *Repairs* is a skit on the house decorator, and shows how it should not be done."

The sketch opened in Southampton:

(19 March 1906)

SOUTHAMPTON, Hippodrome

Wal Pink's Workmen in Repairs give a satirical burlesque on very broad lines of the hopeless inefficiency and nerve-racking attributes of the modern house painter and decorator. The sketch is a clever example of the low comedy school of humour. The cast number close on a dozen, and one and all worked thoroughly hard last night.

(*Southern Daily Echo* – 20 March 1906)

From Southampton the company was scheduled to make a short trip along the South Coast to play a week in Portsmouth, and then Boscombe, but no record was found of them performing in either town. In the third week the sketch came to London, then went all the way up to Glasgow. One week later and a very short boat trip from Stranraer then took the company to Belfast, Northern Ireland, where they opened on Easter Monday at the Palace Theatre. Here an on-stage incident happened which is said to have offended Irish nationalists. Part of Chaplin's stage costume was a green tam o'shanter hat. At some point in the business he was performing he used to take off the hat and stamp on it. This allegedly enraged a section of the audience, who felt his actions were disrespecting the Irish tartan. However, this innocent action hardly developed into an international incident. In fact it appears not to have registered at all with the reviewer from the *Belfast Morning News:*

Charlie Chaplin (using the hammer) as he appeared in a sketch called "Repairs," acted by Wal Pink's Workmen. His brother, Sydney, is standing on the ladder.

A previously unpublished photo of a freeze from the sketch Repairs – played by "Wal Pink's Workmen." On his 1921 visit to England Chaplin was shown this photo by former actor-turned-journalist Hannen Swaffer, to whom he confirmed that he was indeed the character stage centre, chopping wood, and added: "And that's Sydney on the ladder".

Chaplin is clearly not wearing the Tam O'Shanter, the trampling of which had agitated the audience in Belfast, but what appears to be a soft, felt hat. My guesstimate for when this photograph was taken would be w/c 30 April 1906, at the Hammersmith Palace.

WAL PINK – prolific sketch writer and producer, and the man who had both Chaplin Brothers in his company, and let them go. How many sleepless nights did he spend wondering what could have happened if he'd kept them on his books?

(w/c 16 April 1906)

BELFAST, Palace

Easter Monday – Matinee at 2-30 p.m. Evening 7 and 9 p.m.

A funny turn was that supplied by "Wal Pink's Workmen," who appear in an amusing rough and tumble acrobatic sketch entitled *Repairs,* written by Wal Pink with music by Tom Kent. The production is well set, and evoked hearty laughter from crowded audiences at both performances.

For the return to England, the company took a ferry to Liverpool, followed by a short train ride to Manchester, for a week at the Palace Theatre. It was then back to London:

(w/c 30 April 1906)

HAMMERSMITH, Palace

In a wildly new whirling sketch, written by Mr. Wal Pink, and entitled *Repairs.* In this piece you see the Plumber, the Paperhanger, the Whitewasher, the Carpenter, and their various assistants all engaged in their respective fell tasks, breaking windows faster than they mend them, whitewashing the tenants rather than their house, painting themselves rather than the wainscots, or sleeping at their work, but very wide awake at meal-times, and especially Beer Times. But why attempt to describe? All Refereaders know (alas! too well) how a certain class of "British Workmen"-so-called because he won't work-comports himself under such circumstances.

In Mr. Pink's sketch there are superadded strange orations from a boozy painter, terrible pugilistic displays by a huge plumber, a combined worship of Bacchus chorus around a beer barrel, and an extraordinary sand dance for Omnes, who in this connection uses sawdust for sand purposes. The little interlude is one long roar, and the acrobatic actors (who also speak) are as smart a crowd as can be found around Variety Land. I would suggest, however, that in order to avoid an anti-climax, which causes the piece to end a little mere tamely than it deserves to do, the aforesaid screamingly funny and quite indescribable dance should be used as the finale.

(*Referee* – 5 May 1906)

In leaving us the above account of the business in *Repairs,* the reviewer has unknowingly supplied information about the Chaplin brothers' roles. One would surmise that Syd was the 'huge plumber' and that Charlie, who was as far away from the walls as it was possible to be – thus eliminating him as paperhanger or whitewasher – was the carpenter. His chopping wood also points to this. We then come to the 'sand' dance. Seeing as how sawdust was used en lieu of sand, one might conclude that the source emanated from some wood being sawn by the carpenter. It might also explain why, in his entry in *The Green Room Book* – which was published just a few months after he had first joined *Repairs* – Charles Chaplin was described as a "sand-dancer." It might!

The following week the company remained in London to play the Clapham Grand, at the completion of which Charlie quit. Seeing as how Charlie left Wal Pink's company on Saturday 12 May, and *Casey's Court* played Bradford w/c 14 May, it would seem to be more than a little 'unlikely' that Chaplin appeared there. Neither Chaplin nor Will Murray made the claim about Bradford, so why should others? Remember! – "Don't cry 'wolf'." Oh yes! There's one more obstacle preventing Charlie from having played Bradford. Remember Dan Lipton saying:

'Casey's Circus,' in which Charlie, then about seventeen years of age, played no fewer than seven different parts, proved a huge success. It was produced at Woolwich.

(*Daily Graphic* – 1 September 1921)

Well, a quick check revealed that *Casey's Circus* played a production try-out week at the Royal Theatre, Woolwich, w/c 14 May 1906 – which is the very week that *Casey's Court* was in Bradford. I told you not to cry "Wolf!" Charlie must have been rehearsing *Casey's Circus* during the day at Woolwich, in readiness for the change-over to the new sketch, before shooting off to Clapham to make the evening's performance of *Repairs*.

The staging of *Casey's Circus* varied slightly from *Casey's Court* in that it was set within a mock-up of a circus ring. And, whereas *Casey's Court* was an 'all singing – all dancing' kind of show, *Casey's Circus* featured sketches and parodies of well-known music-hall acts. A later review will ably confirm:

TURNS AT THE BLACKBURN, PALACE

There is bright and breezy entertainment at the Blackburn Palace Theatre this week, some excellent comedy being supplied by various artists, including W. J. Churchill. Then there is another of the 'Casey Court' series of burlesques. This week the juvenile artists give a street urchins' idea of a circus entertainment, and their antics are decidedly funny, while their imitations of well-known music hall turns are extremely apt.

(*Northern Daily Telegraph* – 4 December 1906)

Will Murray revealed the name of one of the well-known music-hall turns being parodied:

Included among the subjects we burlesqued were several famous music-hall stars. I particularly wanted a good thing made of Dr. Bodie. Chaplin seemed the likeliest of the lot for the part, and he got it. Rehearsals were numerous, and Charlie always showed a keen desire to learn. He had never seen Bodie's turn, but I endeavoured to give him an idea of the Doctor's little mannerisms. For hours he would practice these in front of a mirror. He would walk for long spells backwards and forwards cultivating the Bodie manner. Then he would ring the changes with a characteristic twist in the Bodie moustache, the long flowing adornment which the "Electric Spark" affected, not the now world-famous toothbrush variety.

(*Weekly Record* – 10 September 1921)

Harry Charmain (*ibid*) added a little insight into how Charlie practised Bodie's routine of passing many thousands of volts of electricity through his body.

I lost sight of Charlie for some time, but I met him again when he was with Mr. Murray in *Casey's Court* [*sic*]. At the time I am speaking of, Charlie lived in the buildings in Munton-road, off New Kent-road, and I rather fancy he went to Rodney-road school.[3]

He used to practise his caricature of Dr. Walford Bodie (the man who passed many thousands of volts of electricity through his body) in *Casey's Court* on my mother's mangling machine.

(*The Star* – 2 September 1921)

So just who was Bodie, and what was all this talk of 'electricity'? Well, Dr. Walford Bodie, to give him his full billing (although he wasn't a doctor of medicine), was one of the greatest self-publicist of all time in the field of entertainment. An oft used line in mini-biographies of Bodie is; "The big turning point in Bodie's career came in 1904, with his appearance at the Britannia Theatre, Hoxton," the review for which ran as follows:

Considerable interest is being taken here this week in the wonderful feats of Dr. Walford Bodie, who, together with his own combination, is nightly taxing the seating capacity of *The Britannia* to its fullest extent. Dr. Bodie's entertainment, which is distinctly novel in that there is no other show upon the stage like it, should not be missed by those who are at all interested in electricity and its various uses, or the value of hypnotism when medicinally applied. His graphic illustration of the manner in which criminals are electrocuted in America – a man being placed in a chair which, together with its deadly appliances, is an exact replica of those in use – sends a thrill through the audience, while his restoration to activity of the apparently inanimate and paralysed, by means of electricity and hypnotic suggestion, is truly remarkable.

---

[3] It seems highly unlikely that Charlie was still attending school at the age of seventeen.

(*The Stage* – 7 April 1904)

But Bodie had been a massive draw for several years by then. As early as March 1899 he had played to full houses at the London Aquarium for four weeks, and ended his run there only because of commitment to provincial engagements. The one immediately following was at Leicester, where fully six thousand people on one night alone paid to see him, with hundreds more being turned away.

LEICESTER FLORAL HALL

The principal attraction was Dr. Bodie who, without doubt, has no equal as a ventriloquist and hypnotist, whilst as the former he is simply amusing, as the latter he is simply astounding. In his electrical the doctor commences by lighting six incandescent lamps of 2,000 candle power, through the body of a person, and then proceeded to pass an intermittent current of electricity, of from twelve to thousand volts, through his own system. To any person who can accomplish the same experiment he offered a sum of £500. Dr, Bodie also introduced his electrocuted man, with which he has caused such a sensation in London. The experiment was skilfully and successfully accomplished, and fairly staggered the onlookers.

(*Leicester Daily Post* – 25 April 1899)

The secret of passing such enormous voltage through one's body was, of course, that it was very low current, and thus relatively harmless. Some seven years later Bodie's act had advanced from 'staggering the audience' to curing their staggering.

SURREY THEATRE

His cures of paralysis by means of massage, electricity, and hypnotic suggestions have been the wonder of the world, and he has been patronised by clergy, medical men, and the elite of society in every part of the Kingdom. Moreover he has been the means of drawing to our music halls a class of people who have never entered their portals, and who, in all probability, would never have done so had it not been for the fame of his miracles – beg pardon – the Doctor emphatically rejects the idea of anything miraculous. Everything he does, he claims, can be explained by natural scientific means.

(*Variety Theatre Annual* – 1906)

And one review, which though it came some twenty months after Charlie had joined *Casey's Circus,* showed that Bodie's act still contained the business that he mimicked.

WILLESDEN HIPPODROME

Enormous business is being done at the Willesden Hippodrome this week on the occasion of the visit of Doctor Bodie, the famous bloodless surgeon, who causes great interest with electrical experiments amongst the audience. The Doctor then proceeds to attend to his patients, many of whom are children who have been discharged as 'hopeless' from London hospitals. After having their irons, etc. taken off, the Doctor effects his cure, and the children are able to walk off the stage unattended. Several local children during the weeks have, it is said, been successfully cured, and a tremendous reception awaits the Doctor at the final of his marvellous show.

(*Kilburn Times* – 3 January 1908)

Dan Lipton:

"The way that boy burlesqued Dr. Bodie was wonderful," said Dan. "I tell you he had never seen the man. He just put on an old dress suit and bowler hat, and as he marched onto the stage he swelled with dignity.

"He always had the most remarkable nerve," continued Dan; "at the same time, like all real artists he was sensitive and temperamental.

"He could feel his audience, even in those early days – he knew just exactly when and how to tease them. But he just had to have the right sort of part and a sympathetic manager."

(*Daily Graphic* – 1 September 1921)

In his book *My Life in Pictures* Chaplin says of the above photographs:
"Among the vaudeville turns I devised for myself at the age of sixteen was an impersonation of a well-known quack, 'Dr' Walford Bodie (above left). I performed this act with a travelling company called *Casey's Court Circus*. I also liked to imitate the great Beerbohm Tree as 'Fagin' in *Oliver Twist*." (above right).

The attention to detail of Chaplin's costume and make-up are stunning, as can be judged by comparing the photos of the subjects themselves (above), with the impersonator (top). Chaplin's caption, though, is at fault on a few points. Firstly, but as always, he makes himself out to be younger than he actually was. Next he calls the sketch "*Casey's Court Circus*" whereas *Casey's Court* and *Casey's Circus* were two entirely different sketches. In writing of his stage parts Chaplin has never once mentioned playing 'Fagin.' The only Dicken's character he is known to have played is a one night, and one night only, impersonation of Bransby Williams's 'old man' from *The Old Curiosity Shop*, when he was with *The Eight Lancashire Lads:*

> Although I had a large head, the wig was larger; it was a bald-headed wig, fringed with long, grey stringy hair, so that when I appeared on stage bent as an old man, the effect was like a crawling beetle, and the audience endorsed the act with titters. But I went on feebly whispering, all very intimate; so intimate that the audience began to stamp. It was the end of my career as a delineator of Charles Dicken's characters.

Clearly it wasn't the end of Chaplin's impersonation of 'the old man,' as the above photo was obviously taken several years after he had left *The Eight Lancashire Lads*. Weight of photgraphic evidence would suggest it was taken at the same time and studio as the Bodie photo, but nowhere did I find any reviews wherein Chaplin played Fagin in *Casey's Circus,* nor does he himself mention doing so. Just one more thing: The man in the above 'Fagin' photo is *not* Beerbohm Tree, but Bransby Williams.

Will Murray, on one episode during the run of *Casey's Circus.*

> I remember one evening the front row of the stalls was occupied by a party of ladies and gentlemen. I noticed that they were deeply interested in the doings of the young actors, and that when Charlie came on they paid special attention to him. They encored him again and again, and after the show sent round a message, and he was utterly taken aback. In those days callers at the theatre were few and far between, and it was a tremendous honour for anyone – especially among the would-be stars – to have a card sent round. Charlie recounted the conversation he had there to me afterwards.
>
> "You're very young," the lady said to him. "Yes," replied Charlie, giving her his correct age [That'll be a first!]. "Dear me," she went on, "I have never seen anything like your impersonation of Dr. Bodie in all my life. I ought to know, for I have known him all my life."

(Weekly Record – 10 September 1921)

The lady in question was almost certainly Marie Walford, Bodie's sister, who assisted him at the piano during his act. Although complimentary about Charlie's impersonation of Dr. Walford Bodie, it is doubtful if she would have been taken by the change in name given to his character – namely: 'Dr. Awful Bogie.'

Of Charlie's other roles, Will Murray continued:

> In addition, Charlie was the principal in another burlesque, *Dick Turpin.* His first appearance with *Casey's Circus* was at the Olympia, Liverpool [4], and he "got" the audience right away with Dr. Bodie. Then came *Dick Turpin,* that old, invincible ever-green standby at the circus. It all went well, but the climax was the fight after the death of 'Bonnie Black Bess.'

(Weekly Record – 10 September 1921)

If one is to make a spoof version of something, the number-one requirement is that the original is known to the audience – in the same way that the humour in doing an impersonation of someone is lost if one doesn't know the subject. But here, in the *Dick Turpin* spoof, there was no danger of audiences not being familiar with the plot, for it had been playing in one form or another for many a year with, as Murray rightly points out, its origins being in the circus ring. At the time of this tour of *Casey's Circus* there were two 'authentic' versions of *Dick Turpin's Ride to York* also touring the halls: one by R. A. Roberts, who had been playing this sketch for at least three years; and the second by Fred Ginnet's Company, a circus family, who had been playing it for three generations.

BRADFORD, Empire

> Mr. R.A. Roberts, the clever and successful protean actor, is here at present, and provides an enjoyable sketch, *Dick Turpin,* in which his marvellously quick changes and assumptions of character surprise the audience.

(The Stage – 19 October 1903)

In an article reproduced earlier in this chapter, Dan Lipton stated: "'Casey's Circus,' in which Charlie, then about seventeen years of age, played no fewer than seven different parts ..." The figure of 'seven different parts' appears to be excessive. With the two known sketches that Charlie performed, plus the sketches played by the other youngsters, there wouldn't appear to have been enough time during the thirty-minute duration of *Casey's Circus* for Charlie to introduce more characterisations. In the R.A. Roberts' version of *Dick Turpin,* Roberts made four quick-change disguises to evade capture: Jacob Sly (a Bow-street runner); Soft Sally

---

[4] Note that Murray names Liverpool as Chaplin's debut – NOT Bradford.

(Innkeeper and Fortune Teller) Jerry Binks (a Yorkshire Farmer); Lady Maude Romander (the daughter of a nobleman he had previously held up); as well as the eponymous role. Maybe Charlie included these, or similar, in the act, which would put up the number of parts he played to six. To this can be added Charlie's part when he was playing "himself" which was that of 'Billy Baggs.'[5] As with all good spoofs there has to be a new title which, though different from the original, refers back to its source. The *Casey's Circus* spoof was known simply as: *Mick Turpin's Ride to York.*

Will Murray, on Chaplin's 'Turpin':

> You can imagine the position of poor Mr. Turpin. He had to run, hide, do anything to get out of the way of the runners, and yet he had nowhere to go, except around the circus track. Nevertheless, Charlie started to run, and run – and run. He had to turn innumerable corners and, as he rotated one foot and hopped along a little way on the other in getting round a nasty 'bend', the audience simply howled.

> I think it can be justly said that I am the man who taught Charlie to turn corners. Yes, that particular run, and still more weird one leg turning of corners, which seems so simple when you see it carried out in the pictures, is the very same manoeuvre that I taught Chaplin to go through in the burlesque of *Dick Turpin.* It took many, many weary hours of monotonous rehearsals, but I am sure Charlie Chaplin, in looking back over those hours of rehearsals, will thank me for being so persistent in my instructions as to how I wanted the thing done.

> *(Weekly Record* – 10 September 1921)

Sorry to record that not only did Chaplin not thank Will Murray for all the training he gave him, but never so much as mentioned Murray in his autobiography. How soon we forget.

---

[5] There is still a possibility that Charlie had revived his previously unsuccessful role of Bransby Williams's 'old man.' If not, how can one explain the "mystery photograph" highlighted on Page 74.

Chapter 8

CATCH A FALLING STAR

Chaplin's memories of Will Murray may have been quick to disappear but, thankfully, Murray's memories of Chaplin were to reveal yet more of their time together:

> One little incident during Chaplin's stay with me always comes back. It happened when we were appearing at the Empire Theatre, Nottingham, in 1907. The races were on, and Charlie asked if he could come with me. Just before the start of the second, he came up to me and asked if I could loan him 6d.
>
> "What for," I asked. "Well, I've got a sure thing for the race, and I've only got a 'tanner'."[1]
>
> "It'll go down, too," I said.
>
> "Not at all," he replied, "This is bound to win."
>
> "Oh," I queried, "What's its name?"
>
> He said it was 'Babarinsky', I don't know if that is how it's spelt, but that's what it sounded like. In the end he put the bob on.
>
> When the horse came into the straight, Babarinsky was leading by a couple of lengths. Charlie became so excited that he scrambled up the rails shouting "Babarinsky, Babarinsky!" at the pitch of his voice. A lady standing near said to me "How excited the young man is. He must have a lot of money on the horse."
>
> "He has," I replied, "Sixpence of mine and sixpence of his." And Babarinsky didn't win after all.
>
> (*Weekly Record* – 10 September 1921)

The newspapers of the day bear out Murray's recollection, and very accurate they were too, although he was out by one year. For the record, Bobrinski came in seventh out of eight runners.

One particular review for *Casey Circus* opened up a very intriguing possibility. On 8 October 1906 at the Palace Theatre, Sunderland, *Casey's Court* was the featured act, then the following week it was *Casey's Circus:*

---

[1] A 'tanner' is another name for a sixpence coin (6d). A 'bob' is a one shilling coin (1s.).

(w/c 15 October 1906)

SUNDERLAND, Palace – 'CASEY'S CIRCUS'

A Street Urchin's Idea of Producing a Circus Entertainment

The "Casey Court" youngsters remain from last week, but now they are producing a circus, and it is very much more amusing than their music hall. The burlesques of the drilled "street-arab" turns, the bumptious magnetic healer and bloodless surgeon, and Dick Turpin's Ride to York, are all very funny.

(*Sunderland Echo* – 9 October 1906)

The reviewer is claiming that the same company played *both* 'Casey' sketches, but he had fooled himself. The previous week the *Casey's Circus'* company had played in Hanley, so could not have been in Sunderland. Also, there were already two companies touring a version of *Casey's Court,* so having a third company playing it, at the expense of dropping *Casey Circus* for that one week, would not have made any business sense.

Casey's Circus allowed Charlie the greatest freedom he had had to date to show off his natural talents. When with *The Eight Lancashire Lads* there had been no scope for individuality. The whole raison d'être of the clog-dance dance act was to achieve synchronisation, which automatically rules out individuality and improvisation. When playing 'Billy' in *Sherlock Holmes* Charlie had been bound by the role – which again meant no improvisation or the inclusion of anything extra from his repertoire of talents. Because of the considerable number of repeat performances of *Sherlock Holmes* Charlie would have been rendered a virtual automaton; but now, in the latest sketch, most restrictions were gone, and it was purely the talents of Master Charles Chaplin which were on show. Unfortunately, as Charlie's part grew so too did his head, and he began to make demands for an increase in wage. Earlier reviews like the following three would certainly have helped to fuel Charlie's ego:

NOTTINGHAM, Empire

The principal feature in The *Casey Circus,* a somewhat extraordinary production, which purports to show how street boys might give an imitation of a circus entertainment. It was amusing, and there is one performer who, first in the exploits of burlesque of 'bloodless surgery' and later as 'Dick Turpin', displays genuine light comedy ability.

(*Nottingham Evening* Post – 10 July 1906)

SHEPHERDS BUSH, Empire

Mr. Harry Cadle's Company appear in "The Casey's Circus," which is aptly described as "a screamingly funny eccentric act." The item is quaintly conceived, and the sheer absurdity of the business is its chief charm. The burlesque of "bloodless surgery" and the evolutions of "Casey's Guards", attired in all manner of nondescript costumes, are clever and entertaining "turns" in the circus.

(*The Stage* – 13 September 1906)

BURY, Circus of Varieties – *Casey's Circus*

The production is exceedingly amusing, the humour being for the most part in the absurdity of the performance. The repreasentation of "Dick Turpin's Ride to York," and the doings of the 'bloodless surgeon' cause a great deal of laughter.

(*Bury* – 25 February 1907)

Will Murray said of Charlie's last few weeks with *Casey's Circus:*

But others in the profession weren't long in seeing that there was a great future before the lad. Fred Karno was one of them, and he offered Charlie an engagement at 2 pound a week.

WILL MURRAY
as himself, and as
Mrs. Casey

Charlie came and told me; so, desirous of keeping him with me, I said I would give him 3 pound. But Karno was keen on the boy, and the game of increasing the offer went on. One day Charlie told me that Karno had offered him 6 pound. "Well, Chaplin," I said, "I'm afraid I can't afford to pay you that, so you'll better take the chance you're being offered."

(*Weekly Record* – 10 September 1921)

Murray has succumbed to manufacturing a myth, here. There was to be a gap of seven months between Chaplin leaving *Casey's Court* and signing for the Karno Company. Nor do the circumstances or the fee involved concur with other, more-qualified, versions. Other biographers have surmised that Chaplin left because he was too old for what was billed as a 'juvenile troupe,' but that wasn't the case. Will Murray had said in the 1921 article: "To carry out a second edition of the sketch, *Casey's Circus,* I found it necessary to advertise for a number of boys between fourteen and nineteen years of age." Although the 1906 original recruitment advert didn't actually state the top age limit to be 'nineteen', Murray must have had this in mind when auditioning applicants. To bear this out, George Doonan, who was in the same company as Chaplin, was born in 1897 – so was at least fifteen months older than Charlie. (If the name sounds familiar, that's because Doonan went on to become a music hall star in his own right).

A more telling reason for Chaplin leaving *Casey's Circus* came in 1952 when Chaplin was visiting Britain. *The Grand Order of Water Rats* had organised a special dinner, at the Park Lane Hotel, London, to honour Fred Russell's ninetieth birthday. Chaplin, who was in town to promote the release of his film *Limelight,* was a guest. During the after-dinner speeches, Chaplin was reunited with Will Murray and began to speak of his old boss. This prompted one heckler to shout out: "Ask him for a pay rise." Chaplin was quick to answer: "He gave me the sack." It had taken some forty-five years but, finally, Charles Chaplin had admitted the truth.

With the star player gone, *Casey's Circus* was put into mothballs and replaced by *Casey's Army* (subtitled: *The Battle of Casey's Backyard*), which was an extension of Mrs. Casey's drilling of 'The Casey Guards'. So how did the ex-star fare, now that he was free to accept all offers? Well, for starters, he appears not to have received any offers, unless you count the following.

> At seventeen[2] I played a juvenile lead in a sketch called *The Merry Major,* a cheap, depressing affair lasting only a week. The leading lady, my wife, was a woman of fifty. Each night she reeled on to the stage smelling of gin, and I, the enthusiastic, loving husband, would have to take her in my arms and kiss her. That experience weaned me away from any ambition to be a leading man.

> (Chaplin's 1964 autobiography)

Charlie named this play as *The Merry Major,* but the only one at the time which might fit the bill was called "*The Major's Middy* – a new musical comedy sketch." Two of the dates it played during Charlie's 'rest' being w/c 19 August and w/c 7 October 1907, both at the Camberwell Empire.

Next, Charlie tried writing:

> I wrote a comedy sketch called "Twelve Just Men," a slapstick affair about a jury arguing a case of breach of promise. One of the jury was a deaf-mute, another a drunk and another a quack doctor. I sold the idea to Charcoat. He gave me three pounds for my script, providing I directed it. We engaged a cast and rehearsed over the Horns public house club-rooms in the Kennington Road. One disgruntled old actor said that the sketch was not only illiterate but silly.

> The third day, in the middle of rehearsals, I received a note from Charcoate[3] to say he had decided not to produce it.

> (Chaplin's 1964 autobiography)

Charlie goes on to relate how he didn't have the courage to tell the other cast members and, instead, got Syd to break the bad news. As it turned out they were in sympathy and, for once, so am I, for the sketch seems to have been quite good. Testimony comes from a review some two years later which shows that, by a circuitous route, the sketch was eventually produced.

MANCHESTER, Grand

"Twelve Just Men"

The comical and absurd deliberation of a jury in a breach of promise case proved a decidedly humorous episode under the title of *Twelve Just Men.* Perhaps it was a trifle overdrawn, but it convulsed the house. Fred Abbot and company were responsible for the predilection and are to be complimented.

> (*The Stage* – 1 July 1909)

Charlie must now have been worried about whether he would find further acting work while at this awkward age – being too old to be a child actor, and yet too young to play a romantic lead. It would, however, appear that he did spend some time in practising the art. Bert Herbert, one of the boys Charlie had given clog-dancing lesson to some years earlier, informed us.

> I have heard it said that Charlie was always funny as a boy, but, on the contrary, I found him just the reverse, and I think he himself would bear out my statement.

> His one ambition was to be a villain in drama. We often used to act a drama in the kitchen, and Charlie always wanted to be a villain.

> (*The Star* – 3 September 1921)

---

[2] Charlie could not have played in "The Major" as a seventeen year-old. He turned seventeen when he was appearing in Repairs. Five weeks later he switched to playing in Casey's Circus, in which he remained till two months past his eighteenth birthday.

[3] The man's name was 'Charcot,' and the act he played was called 'His Automatic Man.'

Chaplin himself confirmed this:

> As the director I always gave myself the villain parts, knowing instinctively they were more colourful than the hero.

(Chaplin's 1964 autobiography)

From villain Charlie then switched to hero, and decided to be like his idol, John Lawson – actor and champion of the cause to end Jewish persecution.

> Did not Mr. John Lawson in his now world-famous sketch, *Humanity,* prove the depth of the Jew's nature; did he not accurately portray the value of his love – the bitterness of his hate? Mr. Lawson's Jew was not an exaggerated one; he was true to nature-the mirror of art never reflected a more perfect likeness. We recognise in the Jewish community the future legislators of the world. The passion of prejudice is dying – violence is a bad creed. An individual may sin; a nation cannot.
>
> In all circles – politics, art, literature; finance, and society – the power of the Jew is recognised. From the rank of the Hebrew race have come forth the greatest philanthropists of the day – Rothschild, Hirsch, and men of whom Charity is rightly proud. The persecution of the Jews must be a thing of the past; their progress the work of the future. With this in view, a National Jewish Congress assembled at Queen's Hall to discuss the Zionist question; a question which here again Mr. John Lawson has been instrumental in bringing prominently before the public. Mr. Lawson is, it is well known, a prominent Zionist, and when some time ago he first presented his splendid "Mission," this caused no end of discussion, and *The Daily Telegraph* devoted nearly a column to the work. Once more this Jewish champion proved the heroic nature of the children of Palestine, and through a series of beautiful stage pictures endeavoured to vividly paint a moral lesson to those who scoff at the Jew.

(*The Magnet* – 8 September 1900)

But it was Lawson's talents as an actor, rather than his efforts as a Zionist, that Charlie wished to emulate. Bert Herbert further revealed:

> Once, when he and one or two boys and girls were playing *Humanity* in our house, he was short of a wig, and he tore up the carpet rug and made one.

(*The Star* – 3 September 1921)

But the only drama to occur in Charlie's next entry into show business, was a dramatic turn; when he hit upon the idea of re-inventing himself as a solo, stand-up comedian. Charlie was now in a real dilemma. As an actor in Sherlock Holmes he was a small cog, turned by other cogs. A play, amongst its many other attributes, is structured, scripted, paced, produced and directed; and each actor is supported by the other actors in the action, in spirit, and word-wise. But now Charlie was on his own, he could not call upon any of these facilities or factors-of-safety. His clog-dancing skills would be of no use whatsoever, and the experience he had gained from being in *Casey's Circus* would be of little benefit. The acts of comedy troupes, like plays, are structured and scripted, and many even choreographed. Again Chaplin would not have others around him to further the business. Even cross-patter comedy duos can perform, to some extent, without acknowledging the audience: that is, they can get on with their act without needing the audience to 'feed' them. One might compare the double act to ping-pong players. They face each other, one serves the ball, and the other returns it with a bit of a spin on it. And thus the act continues, back and forth between them. But Charlie was now attempting to go solo; so, instead of having a partner who would constantly return the ball to him, he would metaphorically have to turn the table through ninety degrees, and rely on the audience to return every ball he served to them. Here then was a 'whole new ball game' and a whole new art form; one that Charlie had not experienced or practised before.

With the months ticking by, and having to borrow money to live on from his brother Sydney, Charlie began touting himself around the theatres at which he thought he might secure bookings. He found a sympathetic ear with the manager of the Foresters' Music Hall, a Mr. F. Baugh, who remembered Charlie from his week in *Casey's Circus,* in June at his theatre. The Forester's regularly held what were termed "Extra Turn Matinees" where up to thirty amateurs were allowed to test themselves out in front of a representative audience, to see if they had what it takes. Chaplin, though, somehow persuaded Baugh to by-pass the try-out, and give him a full week on the regular bill. It was to prove a very bad decision – for both parties.

The Foresters' was in the heart of what may be called the 'Jewish Quarter' of Bethnal Green. At the beginning of 1907 a second entertainment venue had been built, specially to cater for Jewish audiences:

> The first Yiddish music hall in London was opened on Tuesday last, in Christian-street, Whitechapel, the very heart of the alien quarter. It is called the "Princess." Crowds of Russian, Poles and Germans waited for the opening of the doors on Tuesday.
>
> *(The Stage* – 3 January 1907)

To compete with the opposition in satisfying cultural demands, hand-picked Jewish acts were now being put on the bill at other venues in the East-end. One of these was 'Lowenwirth and Cohan', an American-Jewish double act who, back in October 1906, had been billed simply as the 'Lowenwirth Brothers – Hebrew dialect comedians.' On 3 June 1907, they were at the Paragon Theatre in the Mile End district of London, where their billing had changed to "Lowenwirth and Cohan – The Originators of Hebrew Comedy." They were back in London on 1 July, at the Surrey Theatre of Varieties, Camden, this time billed as "Sam Lowenwirth and Chas Cohan – America's Greatest Comedians," the bill matter having been changed to broaden their appeal outside of the Jewish community.

There is no doubt in my mind that Chaplin saw their act. Being known by all the theatre managers as a performer, he would have had privileged free access to any venue he wished to attend. If I had to choose the venue at which he most likely saw them, it would be the London Music Hall, Shoreditch, as this was his local theatre, and one he was known to frequent. The date would have been 5 November 1907.

Feeling comfortable in the Jewish community, Charlie hit upon the idea of presenting himself as an out-and-out Jewish comedian. He thought he would need a name which instantly identified him as such, but how to choose such a name? Well, what about taking the first name of a known Jewish comedian, say 'Sam Lowenwirth', and the surname of another equally well-known Jewish comedian, say 'Chas Cohan,' and becoming 'Sam Cohan?' (Which became corrupted to 'Cohen'.) Sounds good! Now for the material:

Chaplin claims to have acquired his comedy material from *Madison's Weekly* [4] but why try to work jokes from the written page, when one can steal jokes from comedians who have already done the work? Using another act's material has the advantage that the selecting and polishing of the best jokes, and the dropping of the weaker ones, has already been done. The new 'user' has also had a demonstration of the delivery and timing of the jokes. Charlie would have had no qualms whatsoever in what is euphemistically called 'borrowing' other comedians' material, apart from the fear that someone might connect the origin.

So it was that, on 23 December 1907, Charlie turned up at the Foresters' Music Hall, where he was listed sixth on the bill as: "Sam Cohen – The Jewish Comedian." There's a saying that goes something like: "If it looks like a dog, sounds like a dog; and behaves like a dog – then it must be a dog." So here we had Charlie looking like a Jew, sounding like a Jew, and behaving

---

[4] Numerous attempts were made to track down a publication of *Madison's Weekly,* and variants, such as *Madison's Budget,* and *Weekly Budget,* but not even its name was to be found on record, other than in Chaplin's autobiography.

SAM LOWENWIRTH and CHARLES COHAN
the Hebrew comedy double-act who spawned a solo imitator.

like a Jew. Which prompts the question: "Was he a Jew?"

It has also been said repeatedly that he is a Jew: this, too, is incorrect. Charlie's own attitude is:"If people like to think that I'm a Jew, I'm very proud that they should. The Jews are a very fine people."

(*Picturegoer* – 4 October 1952)

Note that, though the writer of the above takes Chaplin's comment as denial, Chaplin has very cleverly phrased his answer so that it is neither denial nor confirmation of his being a Jew. However, the more relevant question is: "Was Chaplin funny in his guise as Sam Cohen?" Well, I'll let Chaplin himself tell you:

Although I was innocent of it, my comedy was most anti-Semitic, and my jokes were not only old ones but very poor, like my Jewish accent. Moreover I was not funny.

After the first couple of jokes the audience started throwing coins and orange peel, and stamping and booing. At first I was not conscious of what was going on. Then the horror of it filtered into my mind. I began to talk faster as the jeers, the raspberries, and throwing of coins and orange peel increased.

When I came off the stage, I did not wait to hear the verdict from the management; I went straight to the dressing room, took off my make-up, left the theatre and never returned, not even to collect my music books.

In 1968, Chaplin said in a taped interview:

On the stage I was a very good comedian in a way. In shows and things like that. I hadn't got that come-hither business that a comedian should have. Talk to an audience – I could never do that. I was too much of an artist for that. My artistry is a bit austere – it is austere.

(1968 – extract from an interview with Richard Meryman)

At the time of the ill-fated Sam Cohen performance, Charlie was lodging with the Fields family in the Kennington Road. He was thankful that on his return they had all retired to bed.

At breakfast, Mrs. Fields was anxious to know how the show had gone, so Charlie bluffed indifference. Mrs. Fields then mentioned that her daughter Phoebe had been to see Charlie, but had told the rest of the family nothing on her return. When Charlie next met Phoebe she offered no account of her visit. In fact, the subject was never brought up again, and no-one ever questioned Charlie as to why he hadn't completed the week at the Foresters'. Obviously, Phoebe had decided not to cause Charlie further embarrassment by discussing the matter.

But, as the old saying goes: "When one door closes ..... ." Within only six weeks a door was to open for Charlie that was to lead to a vast treasure-house of comic sketches and, eventually, to his being crowned the king of comedy.

Chapter 9

HIS FIRST KICK IN THE PANTS

At the turn of 1908 Charlie Chaplin was at a low. Since leaving *Casey's Circus* the previous July he had earned little-to-nothing, and all opportunities to fulfil the ambitions he had harboured in his formative years – to become a dancer, juggler, acrobat, comedy double-act, solo comedian, or dramatic actor – were now behind closed doors. For him to resume a stage career it was going to take a very special person, one who had complete faith in him as a performer, to get him back in. Just where was such a guardian angel going to come from? Well, the answer is in the question: from his guardian – Sydney.

Back in May 1906 Charlie had left Wal Pink's Company, and run away with *Casey's Circus*. Sydney Chaplin, however, had fared a little better and in July of that year had spring-boarded straight into Fred Karno's Company of Comedians. Karno was a former gymnast who, around 1895, had turned his hand to devising and producing comic sketches. In the eleven years since then he had become a promoter and showman of legendary proportions. He also had a brilliant mind for comic invention. Although he could never adequately put his ideas down on paper, his personal coaching ensured the crafting of hilarious sketches. These sketches filled the halls throughout Britain; but it was *his* name on billboards, rather than those of the players, which led to full theatres. When theatre managers asked of Karno: "Who's your star name?" he would reply: "My name's up there, and that's good enough." And how right he was!

At the time Sydney joined, Karno had companies touring with the following sketches: *Mumming Birds; Moses and Son; Jail Birds; Early Birds; The Thirsty First; The Smoking Concert; Dandy Thieves; Saturday to Monday; and His Majesty's Guests.* Sydney was put into the company playing *Mumming Birds,* and a second sketch – *Jail Birds.* After an apprenticeship of just three weeks, Sydney took up the offer of touring North America with a troupe Karno was specially putting together. The idea was to exchange places with the first troupe Karno had sent out in October 1905. So, on 31 July 1906, after giving up a job at sea to go on the stage, Syd Chaplin was back at sea bound for New York.

But the tour was to be ill-fated. The sketch *Mumming Birds* became a victim of its own success, when other companies saw it as a sure-fire formula and began copying it. But their performances were totally inferior to the highly talented, well-trained Karno comedians'. This resulted in many of the Karno company's bookings being cancelled as the theatre managers and audiences had already seen the sketch and didn't like it. With the copycat companies multiplying, and bookings rapidly decreasing, Karno admitted defeat and, at the end of November 1906, disbanded the company and had the players brought back to England.

Starting in December 1906, Syd did the rounds of the British theatre circuit. Come June 1907, after having his contract renewed, he appeared in the debut of a new sketch, *London Suburbia,* which he toured in, on and off, for the next thirteen months. During this period he also played in *Early Birds, Mumming Birds, The Smoking Concert, and The Casuals.*

When Charlie left *Casey's Circus,* Sydney had to go on a six-week tour of the provinces, so

Charlie was left alone with his woe. Upon his return Sydney spent the full month of September touring London boroughs, so was able to give Charlie moral and financial support. There is small weight of evidence that Sydney next persuaded Karno to give Charlie a part in *London Suburbia,* a sketch which Sydney's company had been running-in, in the provinces. It made its London debut on 2 September 1907, playing both the Hackney Empire and the Stratford Empire each evening. The main piece of evidence comes from a handwritten document by Fred Karno Jnr. which he titled: *Fred Karno – As I Knew Him.*

> It was here [in time] that Syd Chaplin, already working with us, asked the 'guvnor' if he could find a spot for his young brother, and so Charlie Chaplin joined us. It was in *London Suburbia* that the two brothers played together, Syd being principal comedian and Charlie making an entrance as a rag-and-bone man, which eventually stole the show.[1] After this he played various comedy parts in subsequent shows.

Charlie might quite possibly have repeated his role in *London Suburbia* over the five weeks following Stratford, as the company played the Empire theatres in the London boroughs of Holloway, New Cross, Stratford (again), Poplar, and Shepherds Bush; after which Sydney went off on another tour, starting in Wales. With Karno showing no interest in putting Charlie under contract, and with Sydney's influence on Karno being temporarily stemmed, Charlie was left to generate his own work, the result of which was the ill-fated Sam Cohen act.

Sydney returned to London the very week after Charlie had been booed off stage at the Foresters'. He immediately realised what a devastating blow to Charlie's ego this had made, and redoubled his efforts in getting Karno to sign Charlie. Karno eventually relented and gave Charlie a part in *The Football Match,* but it was more because of the value of *Sydney's talent,* rather than *Charlie's potential,* that he did so – as Karno himself admitted:

> One day Syd Chaplin brought his young brother along – a boy named Charlie. He was half-grown and ill-nourished, but he had something – a kind of pathetic stout-heartedness, a take-it-and-come-up-for-more attitude to life that somehow seized my imagination. I hired him at four pound a week[2] – more for Syd's sake than because I felt he was worth the money just then. Syd was getting four pound. I believed in paying them high salaries.
>
> *(Picturegoer Weekly* – 7 December 1935)

So we now have both Fred Karno and his son Freddie giving separate, but similar, accounts of how Charlie came to get into the Karno Company. So what does the man himself say?

> One day Sydney told me that Mr. Karno wanted to see me. When I arrived he received me kindly.
>
> "Sydney's been telling me how good you are," he said. "Do you think you could play opposite Harry Weldon in *The Football Match?"*
>
> "All I need is opportunity," I said confidently.
>
> He smiled. "Seventeen's very young, and you look even younger."
>
> I shrugged off-handedly. "That's a question of make-up."
>
> Karno laughed. That shrug, he told Sydney later, got me the job.

Harry Weldon had made the lead role of 'Stiffy – the Goalkeeper' into a stage character known the length and breadth of Britain. For Charlie, as just a seventeen year-old, to play opposite him would probably make him the youngest second-lead comic Karno engaged, ever. It could have, if it weren't for the fact that Charlie was just two months away from his nineteenth birthday.

Charlie continues:

---

[1] Charlie's further appearances in *London Suburbia* are recorded in the next chapter.
[2] The extant contract shows that Karno hired Charlie at £3-10s per week.

IN TRAINING

HARRY WELDON
The Training Session

"Stiffy wore a suit that hung upon him as loosely and unlovingly as the extemporised garb which is often handed to the refractory pauper whose wicked intentions have culminated in too innocent results. One saw that he had "his old brown hat on," and his accoutrements also included an old clay pipe. Stiffy bowed obsequiously to right and left, and he was quite a striking figure, with his fiery furnace-like thatch."

(*Staffordshire Sentinel*)

IN GOAL

HARRY WELDON
The Match

It was laughable to see Stiffy cordially shake hands with an opponent who had done him a great disservice; to demand that a penalty should be taken over again because he had had the bad fortune to save it; to insist on taking a corner kick against himself as goalkeeper.

(Staffordshire Sentinel)

I had a week to study the part before opening at the London Coliseum. Karno told me to go to Shepherd's Bush Empire, where *The Football Match* was playing, and to watch the man whose part I was to play. I must confess he was dull and self-conscious and, without false modesty, I knew I had him beat. The part needed more burlesque. I made up my mind to play him just that way.

I was given only two rehearsals, as Mr. Weldon was not available for more; in fact, he was rather annoyed at having to show up at all because it broke into his game of golf. At rehearsals I was not very impressive. Being a slow reader, I felt that Weldon had reservations about my competence.

(Chaplin's 1964 autobiography)

Firstly, Charlie says he opened in the part at the London Coliseum. So let's go along with Charlie's claims for a while, and then analyse the situation: Here is a young kid, not yet turned nineteen. He's been taken on only because of his *brother's* talents, and he's had just two rehearsals with the lead-comic, who wasn't very impressed with his competence. Now let's look at the venue: The London Coliseum had a seating capacity of three-thousand, every seat of which the Karno Company, as the top-of-the-bill act, was expected to fill at every performance. Then there was the sketch, *The Football Match,* which had been playing for fourteen months, and had been worked up to one of the funniest and finest sketches ever seen on the stage. Now ask yourself this: "If you were Fred Karno, would you risk giving this kid the second-lead role, in this sketch, at this venue? I hope your answer is "No." It was certainly Karno's.

WILL POLUSKI Jnr.
Who played 'Ratty' in all but one of
Chaplin's appearances in
"The Football Match"

Let's just clear up a minor technicality: The phrase "playing opposite Weldon," the principal comic, would intimate that Chaplin was the second-lead, but this was to be a role he would never fill. The part he describes himself as playing was the third-lead. Second-lead role in the sketch was that of 'Ratty', the forward from the opposing team in the 'Cup-Tie,' played by Will Poluski Jnr. Poluski was a very accomplished comedy performer, from a great pedigree. His father and his uncle were the Poluski Brothers, then still active on the variety circuit as a comedy double-act; and his brother, Sam Poluski Jnr., was also an accomplished comedian. A typical review of Will's contribution ran:

BRADFORD, Empire – 'The Football Match'

A more laughable conception of the duties of a goalkeeper than that of Harry Weldon is hardly imaginable, while Will Poluski Jnr., as the versatile forward, is sublimely ridiculous. These two comedians keep the audience in one round of laughter throughout the production

(*Yorkshire Daily Observer* – 24 March 1908)

The week Charlie was given to study the part would have been at the London Coliseum, week commencing 3 February 1908, where he would have rehearsed during the day, and been an observer, or maybe an extra during the performances. Come the second week Charlie was in the sketch for real, but at the New Cross Empire, not the Coliseum. This is the first time ever that Charlie Chaplin was billed in a Karno production. So Charlie's not given us a very accurate account of events so far. Let's see if we can bring it around.

This current tour of *The Football Match* had commenced just two months earlier, with the third-lead being played by Bob Lewis. This is the man Charlie was to replace, but Karno actually retained Lewis in the company for a further five weeks from when Charlie joined. This leads me to believe that Chaplin was occasionally allowed to stand-in for Lewis until he was considered good enough to take over the role completely. The said part was not given an actual name, but was billed simply as 'The Villain' – a despicable cad who approaches Stiffy with a bribe for him to throw the match.

STRATFORD, Empire

Here this week are Fred Karno's Company in the screamingly funny *Football Match*. The antics of the somnolent 'Stiffy' is humorously developed by Harry Weldon is one followed by intense delight, whilst mention must be made of Will Poluski Jnr. and Bob Lewis, who greatly assist the general movement and fun.

(*The Stage* – 17 February 1908)

Charlie's second week as a performer was at the Stratford Empire where, as can be gleaned from the above review, he still hadn't displaced Bob Lewis. However, on the Thursday night of that week, Charlie was allowed to play the Lewis role as Karno was going to be there to observe him. The arrangement had been for Charlie to do a two-week trial engagement and then, if he proved satisfactory, to be given a one-year contract. In the sketch, after the players have done their training routine, they exit – leaving an empty stage. This was Charlie's cue.

THE FOOTBALL MATCH
"The Cup-Tie Final"
Written by FRED KARNO and FRED KITCHEN
Music by J.H. Cleve
Scene 1 - Training Headquarters at 'The Bull.'
        The Middleton Pie Cans getting fit. Enter 'Stiffy'.
Scene 2 - Exterior of the Football Ground.
        The Pay Boxes - No Change Given
Scene 3 - The Football Field.
        The Cup Final - Middleton Pie-Cans v Midnight
Wanderers. Stiffy the Goalkeeper in Form.

    Stiffy - the Goalkeeper ..... Harry Weldon
    Ratty - the Forward .... Will Poluski Jnr.
    Rabbit - the Detective .... Robert Gilmore
    The Villain .... Bob Lewis

And including the following professional footballers:

    F. Spikesley (late with Sheffield Wednesday); T.
    Arkesden (late with Manchester United); W. Wragg
    (late Nottingham Forest); R. Sharp (late Bristol
    City); and T. Litchett (late Bolton Wanderers).

In Scene 1: the Middleton Pie-Cans get fit for the final. The
players are engaged in walking exercise, skipping rope, dumb
bells, punch ball, cycle, and exercises. The trainer, whip in
hand, puts them through their paces. Attempts are made to bribe
the players. A photographer creates roars of laughter with his
posings. A smart detective is very funny with his watchings.

The scene in the training quarters paves the way for the
appearance of Harry Weldon as 'Stiffy - the Goalkeeper'. We have
the semblance of a good plot in an alleged scheme for nobbling
'Stiffy', the goalkeeper. Stiffy is responsible for many
anomalies, among them a quartet of kiddies, one of them black.

Scene 2: Exterior of the Football Ground. There is a continual
struggle at the entrance to the football ground. More fun is
created where no change is given when payment is made to enter.

Scene 3: The Football Field and the struggle of the Cup-tie
Final. As professional players make their appearance, they are
all received with loud applause.

This is full of excitement; free kicks are claimed, the referee
gets into trouble, goals are secured, victory is decided, and
the principal players carried off the field in triumph. And we
are absolutely dumfounded at the great form displayed at goal by
Stiffy, who saves his side and confounds the villain.

'Ratty' becomes an apostate in the end, and deserts the
'Middleton Pie-Cans' on the eve of their great cup-tie with the
'Midnight Wanderers', but 'Stiffy' gives a wonderful exhibition
in goal. Ratty scores for the Wanderers, and 'Stiffy'
congratulates him upon his success, and when the former fails to
obtain a similar advantage with a penalty, the custodian
replaces the ball so that he may have another shot.

The match is brought to an abrupt end by a thunderstorm in
which stage and company are deluged in a real downpour of rain.

> One either rises to an occasion or succumbs to it. The moment I walked on to the stage I was relieved, everything was clear. I entered with my back to the audience-an idea of my own. From the back I looked immaculate, dressed in a frock-coat, top hat, cane and spats- a typical Edwardian villain. Then I turned, showing my nose. There was a laugh. That ingratiated me with the audience. I shrugged melodramatically, then snapped my fingers and veered across the stage, tripping over a dumb-bell. Then my cane became entangled with an upright punching bag, which rebounded and slapped me in the face. I swaggered and swung, hitting myself with my cane on the side of the head. The audience roared.
>
> Now I was relaxed and full of invention. I could have held the stage for five minutes and kept them laughing without uttering a word.

Well, Chaplin never uttered a truer expression than "I was full of invention." In most comedians' routines they condense the accounts of many comical experiences, gained over a long period of time, into just one short moment. Thus, you will never hear a comedian say "A lot of funny things have happened to me in my many years travelling to theatres," but rather: "A funny thing happened to me on the way to the theatre tonight." Chaplin however practised this form of narration in *real* life. So when he gives the above account of his first night, he is actually including every bit of business he built up throughout the length of the tour. Some of it is such blatant embellishment that I shan't even bother to include it in these pages.

One piece of his business even seems to have been borrowed from Gertrude Lawrence's memoirs. Chaplin claims that during his 'struttings' he lost a button and his trousers started to fall down. When Weldon entered, Chaplin says he ad-libbed the line: "Quick! I'm undone! A pin!" Whereas the Gertrude Lawrence mishap ran:

> Every night, as I ran onto the stage, my dress would appear to snag on the scenery, and fall off. It was done solely so that the men could see my knickers. My line would then be: "I am undone."

Whatever did happen that first night was obviously good enough as Karno invited Chaplin to come to his offices in Camberwell the following morning to sign the contract. Of this life-changing moment Charlie wrote:

> I had not written to Sydney about the first night, but sent him a succinct wire: "Have signed contract for one year at four pounds per week. Love Charlie."

No he hadn't signed a contract for four pound per week. I've got a copy in front of me and, as has already been stated, it's for three pound ten shillings per week. Regarding his earlier rehearsing of the role Charlie said:

> Sydney having played the same part, might have helped had he been in London, but he was playing in the provinces in another sketch.

And of his debut performance:

> That night I walked home to get unwound. I wanted to talk to someone, but Sydney was in the provinces. If only he were here so that I could tell him about tonight, how much it all meant to me, especially after the Foresters'.

But Sydney *was* in London. He was there for the full period 30 December 1907 to 29 February 1908, which meant he was there during Charlie's rehearsal week; there during Charlie's debut week at New Cross; and there during the week at Stratford. So Charlie, if he'd wanted to, could have rehearsed with Sydney; could have talked to Sydney about his debut, and could have told him he'd signed a contract with Karno.

Charlie then says that *The Football Match* stayed in London fourteen weeks, before going on tour; whereas, in actual fact, they went on a twelve-week tour just four weeks from the time that

THE STAGE

(w/c 24 February 1908)
SHEPHERDS BUSH, Empire
Fred Karno's Company "Football Match" team played Shepherds Bush Empire team, at Shepherds Bush, a game of "soccer" on Thursday, in aid of local charities. Mr. Karno's team won by 6 goals to 2 after a well-contested match.

BRISTOL EVENING TIMES

Wednesday 14 April 1909, at the City Ground:
KARNO'S v EVENING TIMES AGENTS
J. Kifford (Goal), Will Poluski and J. Fitchett (backs)
L. Anarto, W. Wragg, and T. Ellis
G. Harper, Harry Weldon (Capt.) W. McOustra,
H. Harper, and H. Winperry (Forwards)
Score: 3-3

HARRY WELDON (with the ball at his feet) and WILL POLUSKI Jnr. on his left, this time playing football for real.
If Chaplin wants to become the top man, he's going to have to displace a man who is not only liked and lauded on-stage, but is respected for his charity performances off-stage.

EXETER GAZETTE

(w/c 31 March 1909)
EXETER, New Hippodrome
On Wednesday March 31st Fred Karno's XI will play Exeter City at St. James's Park. The proceeds to be handed over to local charities.

Thursday's report.
Exeter City beat Fred Karno's XI 5-2. Wragg and Roberts scored for the Pie-Cans

BLACKBURN TIMES

(w/c 9 March 1908)
"THE FOOTBALL MATCH"
On Thursday afternoon Crosshill played a team from members of Mr. Fred Karno's Company, and after a most enjoyable, amusing, and farcical match the honours were made even, the score standing at 3-3. An extra 25 minutes was played to allow the Karno team to convert a penalty.

Chaplin had joined[3]. What chance has a chronologist got when Sydney spends nine weeks in London, and Charlie tells us he's in the provinces; then he himself spends twelve weeks in the provinces, and tells us he's in London? Methinks David Robinson wasn't comparing the known facts against Chaplin's accounts when he wrote in his magnificent biography of Chaplin:

> So regularly is his [Chaplin's] memory vindicated by other evidence that, where there are discrepancies without proof one way or the other, the benefit of the doubt often seems best given to Chaplin.

> *(Chaplin – His Life and Art)*

So what of the tour and, more especially, of Chaplin's relationship with Weldon? Well, if we are to believe Chaplin's account – and we have had no cause to, so far – the words 'cat' and 'dog' instantly spring to mind. Of Weldon's personal *and* stage character Charlie wrote:

> Weldon's comedy character was of the cretinous type, a slow-speaking Lancashire boob. That went very well in the North of England, but in the South he was not too well received. Bristol, Cardiff, Plymouth, Southampton[4] were slump towns for Weldon; during those weeks he was irritable and performed perfunctorily and took his spleen out on me. In the show he had to slap and knock me about a bit. This was called 'taking the nap,' that is: he would pretend to hit me in the face, but someone would slap their hands in the wings to give it a realistic effect. Sometimes he really slapped me, and unnecessarily hard – provoked, I think, by jealousy.

Weldon did have a lot to be jealous of. He was only getting thirty-four-pound a week, compared with Charlie's three-pound ten-shillings. The relationship came to a head, Chaplin says, when the company played Belfast. Charlie claims that the critics gave Weldon a dreadful panning, but praised *his* performance. Charlie goes on to claim that this was intolerable to Weldon who then, on the night the reviews came out, gave Charlie a right-hander which made his nose bleed. Backstage, Charlie told Weldon that if he hit him again he would brain him with one of the dumb-bells on the stage. The reviews must have been pretty savage to send Weldon into such a rage – better have a look at them:

(w/c 27 April 1908)

BELFAST, Palace

> The chief attraction was the appearance of the Fred Karno Company, which included Will Poluski Jun., and Harry Weldon, in a very amusing sketch, entitled *The Football Match*. The piece is well-written and excellently staged.

> *(Belfast Evening Telegraph* – 28 April 1908)

Well nothing there to anger Weldon. Let's look at another review:

> The Palace programme this week includes a rare attraction in the shape of one of Fred Karno's amusing productions entitled: *The Football Match,* the joint work of Fred Karno and the well-known comedian Fred Kitchen, with music by J. H. Cleve. The piece is presented by a first-class company, including Will Poluski Jun., and Harry Weldon as 'Stiffy the Goalkeeper. There were crowded audiences at both houses last night, and the piece went swingingly from beginning to end.

> *(Belfast Morning News* – 28 April 1908)

So nothing went wrong on the Monday night. Maybe Weldon blotted his copybook later in the week. It doesn't look like it though, as he was back in front of Belfast audiences just seven weeks later, and this time he didn't need the support of the Karno Company to make him look good:

---

[3] Chaplin states that Shepherds Bush Empire was where he went to watch *The Football Match,* before debuting at the London Coliseum, whereas he actually played Shepherds Bush during his third week with Karno.

[4] No trace was found of *The Football Match* playing either Plymouth or Southampton in 1908, 1909, or 1910.

(Marriot Collection)

BELFAST, Empire

Harry Weldon, of 'Stiffy the goalkeeper' fame, acquits himself as a laughter provoker, was as great, if not a greater success, when doing a solo turn as he did in the Karno combination.

(*Belfast Morning News* – 22 June 1908)

So Chaplin wasn't mentioned in the reviews, and Weldon wasn't panned. So once again I have to question David Robinson's appraisal of Chaplin, the man, when he says: "Chaplin was an accurate and truthful chronicler of what he had seen."

The night before the Cup-Tie Final, 'the Villain' (Chaplin) offers a bribe to 'Stiffy' (Weldon) to throw the match.
"From the back I looked immaculate, dressed in a frock-coat, top hat, cane and spats-a typical Edwardian villain."

(Chaplin)

(Unique and previously unpublished photograph.)

This particular run of *The Football Match* finished on 30 May 1908. And where did it play during its last week? – why, the London Coliseum. By Chaplin's own testimony, when he played the role of the 'The Villain' at the Coliseum, Syd was in the provinces. Well this was the one and only week of Charlie's involvement with *The Football Match,* so far, where he was in London, and Syd was in the provinces. As for how Chaplin describes the way his performance was received and applauded by the audience, surely that must have greatly impressed any theatre critics who were present. Well, *The Stage* reviewer was there, and what *The Stage* prints is well-known for being extremely kind, so he must have received one heck of a write-up. Let's look:

LONDON, Coliseum – "The Football Match"

Mr. Fred Karno's "Football Match" occupies the principal place in the bill this week. It is proving an immense attraction. The wonderful doings of 'Stiffy' the Goalkeeper, portrayed in an original and highly amusing manner by Mr. Harry Weldon, and the clever work of Will Poluski Jnr. prove a source of great hilarity to the house, which is kept in continual laughter throughout.

(The Stage – 28 May 1908)

Ah well! Maybe the man didn't recognise talent when he saw it. Meanwhile, Sydney Chaplin had recently been promoted from fourth- to first-comic in the sketch Mumming Birds. The day *The Football Match* finished at the London Coliseum was the day Sydney finished his tour of the provinces, and then returned to London. Consequently, on Monday morning, 1 June 1908, Charlie was put back under the protective eye of Sydney and sent along to theatres in both Balham and Camden to be allocated a small role in *Mumming Birds.*

Mumming Birds was, and still is, the most famous sketch ever played on the music-hall/variety stage. From this most-famous of all sketches would shortly emerge the most-famous of all comedians. The potentially fastest-growing comedy organism had found the perfect parent-host.

Chapter 10

WHEN HETTY MET CHARLIE

Mumming Birds ran on-and-off, with numerous cast changes and in various forms, for forty-five years. Whether or not "Don't say a Mumming Bird" ever entered Cockney rhyming-slang for "Don't say a word" I don't know, but it certainly deserved to. 'Mumming' comes from the French verb 'momer' – meaning 'to mime.' As late as 1903 the Karno companies had been billed as "Karno's Speechless Comedians," which was not so much a proud boast but, one must surmise, a very clever ruse by Karno to avoid having to submit his scripts to the Lord Chamberlain's office – where they would have been open to censorship laws.

The premise of *Mumming Birds* is the representation of a musical hall performance, as viewed by a "stage audience," and the humour depends on the frequent interruptions and interferences of the stage audience. The performers who appear are: the audience members; the artists; and the stage attendants. Amongst the audience the principal characters are a boy dressed in an Eton suit, and his guardian, 'Uncle Charlie.' These two sit in the bottom box on the left. The 'swell' in a state of semi-intoxication, dressed in evening suit, occupies the bottom box on the right.

The various 'turns' are announced by a numbered card being placed in a frame immediately prior to the start of the act. A representative bill, of many, is:

1. The Topical Vocalist [male] – recites "*The Trail of the Yukon*"
2. The Swiss Nightingale [lady vocalist] – sings "*Come Birdie Come, and Live with me.*"
3. The Prestidigitateur [Magician/Conjurer]
4. The Rustic Glee Party [quartet of singers]
5. The Saucy Serio [soubrette] – sings "*Naughty, Naughty Men*"
6. 'The Terrible Turkey' [Wrestler] – 'Marconi Ali'

As the curtain rises another stage is discovered, with a proscenium, curtain, etc., and boxes on either side, the occupants of which treat the various artists who appear with a comic lack of courtesy. The mischievous Eton boy devours buns and shoots peas at the performers; and much fun is provoked by an inebriated "masher," whose persistent efforts to 'go behind' are most forcibly opposed by a stalwart attendant. Various performers appear: there is a serio, a lady vocalist, a conjurer, a topical vocalist, and a wrestler, all of whose efforts meet with more or less opposition. Indeed, the wrestler receives severe corporal punishment from the 'masher' for refusing to pay the sum he has lost in a bout; and the scene closes in upon a general and very laughable mêlée.

The piece is acted mainly in pantomime, and the 'fun' consists in the incompetence of the performers; the disgust of the [stage] audience; the pranks of the boy who shoots peas or throws buns at the artistes and members of the audience; and especially the swell, who spoils the conjuring tricks, etc.; the general free fights on the stage in which most of the company take part; and the bye-play between the soubrette, the swell, a female programme attendant, and others.

The attendant, too, snatches time to make himself known to the audience as a performer in his own right. Part of his act ran as follows:

```
Attendant: Ladies and Gentlemen (business) I shall have
           great pleasure in giving you a few
           impersonations of London actors. My first –
           Lewis Waller in "Julius Caesar" (recites)
Audience:  Bravo! Hear hear!
Actor:     My next impersonation will be my last.
Swell:     Hear! Hear!
Boy:       Hooray!_
"Ladies and Gentlemen—Will any members of the audience give
           me a subject, and I shall be pleased to
           extemporise upon it. Any subject, please, if you
           know of any."
```

Whereupon various names such as 'Lord Roberts', 'Deadwood Dick', etc., are suggested, and the extemporising follows, but always in the same way and without reference to the particular subject suggested by the audience.

Other business performed in *Mumming Birds* can be found in the newspaper clippings illustrated in the pages which follow. Additional snippets will be gained as the story progresses. Meanwhile, here are a couple of bits of interesting trivia:

The finalé of the sketch was the spoof wrestling bout with a 'Champion' wrestler who would challenge all-comers to a bout of wrestling. As stated once before, a good spoof has to be based on an act the audience are familiar with. In this instance the wrestler was based on Ahmed Madrali – the Turkish wrestling champion – whose bill matter between 1903 and 1906 varyingly included the lines: 'The Terrible Turk'; 'The Sultan of Turkey's Chief Wrestler'; and 'The World's Champion Catch-as-Catch-Can Wrestler.'

So good a fighter was Ahmed that, during his act, the challenge "£25 to anyone who can throw him within fifteen minutes" would be issued. In May 1904, only a few weeks after the debut of *Mumming Birds,* he took part in the 'World's Catch-as Catch-Can championship for £400' – at the London Alhambra. Meanwhile in the *Mumming Birds* sketch he was being parodied under the thinly disguised name of 'Marconi Ali – The Terrible Turkey.' The poor man. Here he was, trying to make a living as a serious wrestler, but was never able to be taken seriously by any audience who had seen *Mumming Birds* prior to his appearance.

MUMMING BIRDS.

Cast.

Inebriated Swell.
Eton Boy
Uncle.
Usherette
Number Man.

Acts.

No.1   Can Can Girls
No.2   Double Act - 2 men Comedy.
No.3   Lady Vocalist (Comedy)
No.4   Actor - Recitation
No.5   Quartette.   Comedy.
No.6   Soubrette.
No.7   Announcer introduces "Marconi Ali" the
Terrible Turk"   Comedy Wrestling Bout.
No.8   Girl Singer - Olde Tyme Songs.

- MUSIC -

Opening - "Lets all go to the Music Hall".   Double ff.
Segue into Waltz.
Usherette shows Boy and Uncle into Box then brings
Drunk into his Box (Bus to be arranged).
Number man puts No.1 card in bracket (cue for Can
Can music)   Girls enter and go straight into Dance.

No.2.   Two Comics — Song, Dance and Patter — Song a la
"Harry Champion's Tempo. (Interruptions from Boy and
Drunk to be arranged).

No.3.   (Lady Vocalist Comedy) Song "Come Birdie Come
and Live with Me"   (Interruptions from Boy & Drunk)

No.4.   Cord on for Actors entrance.   Recites "The
Track of the Yukon" (Boy and Drunk interfere again).

No.5.   Sustained Cord for Quartette.   Comedy bus. to
be explained.   Drunk gets out of Box and gets them off.

No. 6.   Soubrette.   Song & Dance "You naughty,
naughty Man" (bus from Boy & Drunk).

No. 7.   Girl Singer - "Medley of Old Tyme Songs".

No. 8.   . Announcer enters to introduce Wrestling Bout.

1.

2.

"Ladies & Gents" (bus with Boy & Drunk) eventually
"Plant" in audience accepts challenge. Then Announcer
gives direct for music (Waltz — very Piano) and calls
for mat to be brought on.

Boy gets out of Box and has (bus.) with "Marconi Ali"
and is chased back to Box by Announcer.

Enter Plant, takes his coat off and lays it on Drunk's
Box. (bus with Drunk).

Announcer starts Bout (bus with "Marconi Ali" and Plant
to be arranged, finally Marconi throws Plant.

Announcer: Anyone also care for a bout with Marconi.
Drunk gets out of box and goes after Marconi — bus to
be arranged - finally Drunk gets Marconi on his back and
wins bout - is presented with prize money; and
congratulations.

Announcer. And what would you like now Sir?

Drunk. First bring on the Girls. Everybody on for
Finale, with number to be arranged.

PROPS.

Prop Oranges and Bananas.
Pea Shooter - Buns - Buckram, Bouquet, Trumpet, Pie.

Number Boards 1 to 8.
Small mattress for Drunks Box. Wine Glass, Champagne
Bottle, Cushion, Opera Glasses, Ash Tray, Wrestling Mat,
Nap Sticks.

Reproduction of an original script for a later version of *Mumming Birds,* typed by Fred Karno Jnr.
(Courtesy of the late- Olive Karno.)

Other characters in *Mumming Birds* whose names had comic value were: 'The Sisters Lymjus' [pronounced "lime juice"]; Zbiscuit, Champion of Nantypolonia [as in: 'Take zee biscuit.']; The Inharmonious Blacksmiths; Hermoniki, the Perishing Prestidigitator ['Harmonica' or 'Her Monarchy'??]; and "many other star (and garter) turns."

But it wasn't just *Mumming Birds* which Charlie was to become conversant with. Karno had as many as ten different companies, and sketches, touring the U.K. at any one time, and it was common practice for him to pull out the lead comic from a show which was established, and transfer him to one which needed a boost. A few weeks before the lead comic was due to leave, he would be "shadowed" by the comic who was to take his place. Once deemed capable the new boy would take over the lead role, and the "old boy" would take over a new production – often of the same sketch. Since its inception and up to the Spring of 1908, *Mumming Birds* had had Billie Reeves, Billie Ritchie, Billie Crackles, Jimmy Russell, and Bert Weston, playing the lead role of 'the drunk' – some concurrently. To that list could now be added Sydney Chaplin, who had debuted in the role in March 1908, after a six-month apprenticeship under the tutelage of Jimmy Russell. Three months later Karno transferred Charlie to Syd's company, where his job was to understudy the man holding fifth billing in the cast list – Chas. Sewell.

Charlie had to learn quickly to keep up with the herd. After just one week playing *Mumming Birds* the company performed a brand new sketch – *The Casuals*. Come week three, they played a third sketch – *The Smoking Concert*. Here was a company who didn't lie down on the job. Unbelievably, in week five a fourth sketch was added – *Early Birds*; and then in week nine, just so as not to become complacent, t hey brought their repertoire up to five with the addition of *London Suburbia*.

Charlie must have been well up to the job as, come August 1908, he took over the number five slot and Chas. Sewell, having done his job in training the young apprentice, was moved on to another company. In his autobiographical writings Charlie gives little or no mention to the latter four sketches. Maybe he pinched little bits of comic business from them, which were later used in his films, and didn't want to credit them. Although not from an actual performance on the Chaplins' tour, the following newspaper review will give the reader a good idea of what the second sketch was about:

> *The Casuals* is a great novelty, and the first scene shows a small crowd waiting for the 'casual door' to open. An amusing incident occurs here, as a travelling musician [a banjoist] mistakes the Workhouse for a theatre and plays a well-known ditty and afterwards takes round his hat. On being told it is the entrance to the Workhouse he walks off in disgust.
>
> The interior of the 'house' is next shown where all the casuals are being searched. The broken-down golfer who, while 'tipsy,' also mistakes the Workhouse for the theatre, makes himself well at home. At the finish a warder enters and says that the Chairman of the Board of Guardians is about to pay a visit. On entering, this gentleman asks if there are any complaints to make. The golfer rushes in attired in dressing gown and complains that there is a scarcity of billiard chalk in the billiard room, also that the tooth brushes are moulting and so on. Another inmate asks for a fire in his room and the Chairman tells the warder to order a ton of coals, and in a whisper instructs the man to give the inmate a bucketful, and send the rest round to his house. Humour abounds throughout the sketch.
>
> (*Warrington Examiner* – 18 December 1909)

As for *The Smoking Concert*, more of that will be revealed in good time. *Early Birds*, I am happy to place here although, again, the review is not contemporary with Charlie and Syd's involvement:

> The curtain was raised on the *Early Birds*, a most realistic sketch of London life, invented and arranged by Mr. Karno, and played by a selected company of comedians. The scene

represents a workingman's lodging-house. The principal character is that of a precarious money-loving Jew, a part which Mr. Karno formerly played, and which is now very cleverly represented by George Craig, who caused roars of laughter. The turn incidentally included some very smart acrobatic feats, the hoax played on the police officer being heartily laughed at. The production of the *Early Birds* seems to lose nothing in popularity, and, although it is nine years since it was first staged, it is as fresh and as mirth-provoking to-day as ever it was.

(Oldham Standard – 13 August 1907)

As stated in the above, *Early Birds* had been playing since June 1901, but was still being played in its original format, which was:

PRESTON, New Royal – Jail Birds and Early Birds

In both these sketches there is no word of dialogue spoken, and it is a tribute to the artists concerned that not once is the necessity for any word of illustration apparent.

(The Stage – 18 May 1903)

A third review adds a little extra information:

Early Birds has long been a popular sketch, and it proves as amusing as ever. Particularly good is the scene in the doss-house, the pranks that are played on the wily Jew causing endless amusement.

(Rochdale Observer – 19 January 1910)

Couldn't the doss-house scene be the origin of the scene in *The Kid,* wherein Chaplin tries to smuggle his son into the doss-house, past the attendant, when they wish to sleep the night but can only afford to pay for one occupant? And as for the overall premise of *Early Birds*, author Simon Louvish is adamant that it is the basis of Chaplin's film *Easy Street.*

Then came *London Suburbia* which Sydney had played a year earlier, and in which Charlie may possibly have played a part before officially becoming a Karno comedian. The following review comes from Syd's 1907 appearance:

LONDON, Canterbury

The notable feature in Mr. Fred Miller's programme this week is a new sketch by Mr. Fred Karno and Leonard Durrell, entitled *London Suburbia,* a fantastic production of life in rural London, in two scenes, with characters descriptive of the Irritable Author, The Homely Landlady, The Mischievous Boy, The Faithless Wife, The Forgiving Husband, The Noisy Lodgers, and The Calling Costers. The company include Messrs. Jimmy Russell, Geo Craig, John Doyle, Jack Royal, Syd Chaplin, Fred Whittaker, Miss Amy Forest, and many others.

The scene is a very realistic picture of the front view of three small suburban villas. Servants are cleaning the doorsteps, and are interrupted and stumbled over by various callers, including an author in search of quiet for his work, who is persuaded to take the front parlour of one of the houses. Then follows a perfect pandemonium of street noises, all very naturally rendered, and only out of proportion by their concentration at one time. An interlude takes place in the affectionate departure of the husband and father from one of the houses and the speedy arrival of a lover, followed by the return of the husband and the expulsion of the wife and lover.

The second scene reveals the backs of the same three houses, the author having moved to the back for greater quiet. A similar confusion of the noises incident to the backyards of suburban houses takes place, including a reconciliation scene between the injured husband and his wife, and culminating in a concertina chorus. The inhabitants at length go to bed, affording an opportunity for shadow displays on the various blinds, after which a fire breaks out, and they all make their exits from the windows with acrobatic ability. The plot of the sketch is very slight, but it affords scope for some very amusing knockabout business, and is cleverly carried out. When slightly worked up, London Suburbia should be as successful as many of Mr. Karno's other pieces.

(*The Stage* – 20 June 1907)

One piece of business for the reader to make a mental note of is the reference above to:

The inhabitants at length go to bed, affording an opportunity for shadow displays on the various blinds.

A second review for *London Suburbia* some ten months later, minus Syd, ran:

BLACKBURN, Palace – "London Suburbia"

Two sides of a villa are depicted, the front and the back. The former looking so respectable, and the neighbourhood appearing so quiet, a foreign artist engages the front sitting room. To his sorrow the artist finds the appearance of the villa deceptive for, in the morning, the road is alive with excitement with the quarrels of the servants, the cries of the milkman, the calls of the 'coals', the noise of the street organ, and the chatter of costermongers. He beats a retreat to the back, only to find confusion worse confounded. Throughout, the burlesque is admirably sustained and so diverting are the incidents that it is calculated to make the most grave smile.

(*Blackburn Times* – 14 April 1908)

One must give credit to the Karno company members for their ability to learn and perform these five sketches in such a short time. Surprisingly, though, their knowing five sketches was well below the total number they were expected to master, as Chaplin was to explain in a later interview:

All of the pieces we did, as I remember them, were cruel and boisterous, filled with acrobatic humour and low, knockabout comedy. Each man working for Karno had to have perfect timing, and to know the peculiarities of every one else in the cast so that we could, collectively achieve a tempo.

It took about a year for an actor to get the repertoire of a dozen shows down pat. Karno required us to know a number of parts so that the players could be interchanged. When one left the company it was like taking a screw or a pin out of a very delicate piece of machinery.

(*Variety* – January 1942)

As for the tour itself, the amount of travelling in the first eleven weeks could hardly rate it as 'a tour,' for only three times were they outside of London, and one of those weeks was just down the road in Maidstone, Kent. Week nine involved a bit of a journey, but the cast wouldn't have minded that as it was to the Norfolk seaside town of Great Yarmouth. Charlie had had less than a handful of trips to the seaside during the whole of his nineteen-year life. In the Summer of 1899 he had been to Blackpool and Southport, where his playmates had been the other members of *The Eight Lancashire Lads*. There had been a second visit to Blackpool in the Spring of 1904, with the Sherlock Holmes' company, when he had been a callow youth under the guardianship of his brother Syd; and likewise in the week that followed in the South coast resort of Eastbourne. Here though, in Great Yarmouth, Charlie's situation had a whole new complexion. He was now a virile young men, let loose in a town full of young ladies on holiday; all carefree and determined to enjoy the natural pleasures that life brings. The majority of holidaymakers would have been from London, so Charlie was among his own. He had, however, one big advantage over all the other young men in town who were like-minded in their quest to win over a young lady's favours – he was appearing in a show as one of Fred Karno's London Comedians, a name that every one of them knew, and revered. What power and influence dropping that chat-up line into a conversation would have had for Charlie. But did he?

This whole period must have been a real state of bliss for Charlie: he was in the top comedy troupe in the country – if not the world; he was guaranteed fifty weeks' employment a year, working in the best theatres; and he was learning the art of physical comedy from its top performers. In addition, there was no pressure from having to devise his own act; none from having to generate his own bookings; and none from having to arrange transport. What's more, he had with him at all times his brother Sydney to act as tutor, advisor, business manager, protector, friend and confidante. Then there was the financial benefits that sharing can bring. The boys were now relatively well off with a combined wage of £7 10 shillings per week so, following the old adage 'Two can live as cheaply as one', they rented a four-roomed flat at 16 Glenshaw Mansions, on the Brixton Road, Camberwell.

16 GLENSHAW MANSIONS, Brixton Road
(between South Island Place and Mowll Street).
Flat 16 is the one under the first triangular pinnacle from the right
(the two windows just above the security camera).

Charlie was to say of his new home:

> In the early days of my career, I spent much of my time touring the provinces of England. In those days I loathed travelling. It took me away from my little flat in London.

> (*A Comedian Sees the World* – 1933)

And:

> The flat was our cherished haven. How we looked forward to it after playing in the provinces! We were now prosperous enough to help grandfather and give him ten shillings a week and we were able to engage a maid to come twice a week and clean up the flat, but it was hardly necessary, for we rarely disturbed a thing. We lived in it as though it were a holy temple. Sydney and I would sit in our bulky armchairs with smug satisfaction.

So, with all this new found wealth and smug satisfaction, one would have thought that Charlie would have described the happy times he spent touring with his half-brother Sydney. And yet not one word of indication does Charlie offer, in any piece ever written by or about him, that he ever appeared in the same sketch as Sydney – the man who got him the job, trained him in the various parts, and wet-nursed him both on tour and at home. Kate Mowbray, one of Charlie's aunts, had first made this observation:

> It seems strange to me that anyone can write about Charlie Chaplin without mentioning his brother Sydney. They have been inseparable all their lives, except when fate intervened at intervals. Syd, of quiet manner, clever brain and steady nerve, has been father and mother to Charlie. Charlie's always looked up to Syd, and Sydney would suffer anything to spare Charlie.

> *(Pearson's Magazine Weekly* – 21 September 1921)

A lot of what Charlie omits from his writings are times like this, when he wasn't the star name. As the newest member of the troupe, and being placed low down in the pecking order, Charlie might well have looked upon his minor roles as demeaning. As always his sights were set on the principal role and, until he achieved such a status, he would in this instance – as in many others past, present, and future – fail to mention his participation in the allotted sketches. In fact, of the period August 1908 to December 1909, Chaplin makes no attempt to fill us in on any of his stage appearances. One engagement he was offered was potentially life-changing and yet he has never, ever, put it on record. It was only a chance sighting in the American show business newspaper *Variety* which revealed the hitherto unknown fact that Charlie Chaplin was booked to tour America some TWO years before he actually took up the offer.

> The Karno Comedy will arrive in New York within a week or so. Charlie Chapman, an English man, will replace Billy Reeves as 'The Drunk' in the "Night in an English Music Hall" act.

> *(Variety* – August 8, 1908)

OK! the name's wrong, but that's an editing mistake – the man named is undoubtedly Charlie "Chaplin." To find out just why Charlie chose to remain in England, we need to discover what was occupying his mind at the time. Fortunately, he tells us just that:

> I was almost nineteen and already a successful comedian in the Karno Company, but something was lacking. Spring had come and gone and summer was upon me with an emptiness. I grew melancholy and dissatisfied and took lonely walks on Sundays and listened to park bands. I could support neither my own company nor that of anyone else. And of course the obvious thing happened: I fell in love.

Again I have to ask: "Just what month did Charlie believe he'd been born in? As it was summer, and Charlie's birthday is in April, he could hardly have been "almost nineteen." His account continued:

> I was already a successful comedian in the Karno Company. We were playing at the Streatham Empire. In those days we performed at two or three music halls nightly, travelling from one to the other in a private bus. At Streatham we were on early in order to appear later at the Canterbury Music Hall, and then the Tivoli.

> A song-and-dance troupe preceded us called "Bert Coutts' Yankee Doodle Girls".

At this stage I have to warn you to "Hold on! this is going to be a bumpy ride," as we try to straighten out the many inaccuracies in just this one short paragraph. Firstly, the venue is wrong. In the account he gives in *A Comedian Sees the World* Chaplin doesn't name the theatre where he met his first true love; but then in his 1964 autobiography he volunteers "Streatham." He'd have been better advised to leave the venue blank as, in all the years of Karno dates I researched, not once did a Karno company play the Streatham Empire.

Next Charlie says the Karno company were sharing the bill with the 'Yankee Doodle Girls.' Well, there were only ever two incidences of this. These were 19 October 1908 at the Woolwich Hippodrome, and 26 October 1908 at the Putney Hippodrome, for which, on both occasions, I believe Chaplin was in another Karno troupe, playing in Lancashire. Besides which, October seems to be far too late in the year to fit Chaplin's reminiscence: "Spring had come and gone and summer was upon me with an emptiness." And, thirdly, nor is there any trace of a Karno company playing the three London venues he cites, on the same night.

Chaplin's 1964 account of how he met the young lady he fell in love with continues:

> [A song-and-dance troupe preceded us called "Bert Coutts' Yankee Doodle Girls"]. I was hardly aware of any of them. But the second evening, while I stood in the wings indifferent and apathetic, one of the girls slipped during the dance and the others began to giggle.

The girl Charlie had cast his eye upon turned out to be Hetty Kelly. Hetty had been working in Bert Coote's companies since as far back as 1905, as a child-actress and singer in his production of the play *The Fatal Wedding*, as confirmed in the following review.

LONDON, Pavilion E. – "The Fatal Wedding"

Hetty Kelly contributes an Indian coon song "Cariboo"

(The Stage – 20 November 1905)*

And a second review, some sixteen months later:

PLYMOUTH, Grand

A return visit of *The Fatal Wedding* is the Easter attraction. Miss Hetty Kelly as 'The Little Mother', Master Walter Sidney as 'Frank,' and, indeed, all the children, do their work capitally, and introduce some excellent specialities in act three.

(The Stage – 4 April 1907)*

Another fourteen months on, and she's still there, in the same part.

BELFAST, Royal – THE FATAL WEDDING

Entire Production as played at the Princess's Theatre, London. The Unparalled Musical and Dramatic Success of Two Hemispheres. See the great Children's Scene. The talk of every town visited.

In act 3 the following able juvenile artistes appeared: Marie Wilson, Marie Dupre, Hetty Kelly. The séance concludes with the singing of the Indian song "Caraboo," in which all the children take part.

(Belfast Morning News – 2 June 1908)*

Following the above appearance in Belfast *The Fatal Wedding* played one week in Liverpool, after which the company took a summer break. A new tour then commenced 3 August 1908, in Manchester, then coming to London for the weeks commencing 10 and 17 August. As *The Fatal Wedding* was a drama it played only drama theatres – not variety theatres. It also occupied the whole programme – i.e. no support acts. Thus, Chaplin could not have played the same venue on the same night whilst Hetty was still in it.

As Hetty is confirmed as still being in *The Fatal Wedding* when it played the Royal Theatre, Woolwich on 10 August, then he could not have met her any evening during this week. The following week *The Fatal Wedding* played the New Cross Empire but, in what appear to be comprehensive reviews in two separate newspapers, Hetty's name does not appear. Nor does it appear in any reviews after this date. It is almost certain, therefore, that she had left at the end of the week at Woolwich. So, the following scenario is now a distinct probability:

Hetty starts off in the new tour of *The Fatal Wedding*, to break-in her replacement and then, at the end of the second week, she leaves to become a dancer in 'The Yankee Doodle Girls.' She is allowed join at this moment in time as, by the time the dance troupe start work, she will be fifteen. She attends rehearsals during the day, commencing Monday 10 August, whilst playing at the Theatre Royal, Woolwich, in the evening.

"So what has all this got to do with Charlie meeting Hetty one evening in a theatre?" I hear you asking. Well the thing is, Charlie didn't meet Hetty one evening in a theatre – he met her one AFTERNOON. Confirmation comes in an extract from Fred Karno Junior's memoirs:

> Fred [Karno] could no longer rehearse all his performers at the 'Fun Factory'; but in Walworth, not far away, was the Montpelier Theatre[1], which he now leased by day. It was here young Charlie Chaplin was taught the Karno way with comedy, and here too that Charlie met and fell in love with a pretty little actress named Hetty Kelly.

> (*FRED KARNO – As I Knew Him*, by Fred Karno Junior)

Note that Freddie (Karno Junior) describes Hetty as an "actress" – not a "dancer," which points to Hetty still being associated with *The Fatal Wedding* and not the Yankee Doodle Girls. Charlie mentions playing the Tivoli theatre the week he met Hetty. Well, he played the Tivoli for three weeks – 3rd, 10th, and 17th August, but at no other time that year. So during the weeks of the tenth and seventeenth Charlie would have rehearsed at the Montpelier, before leaving to go firstly to Balham Hippodrome, and then to the Tivoli, which is probably what confused him into thinking he had been playing three theatres each evening.

Charlie also says he was playing the drunk in *Mumming Birds*, but he wasn't – Syd was. Unless, that is, Syd played the part at the Tivoli and Charlie played it at the Balham Hippodrome, the latter being one of Karno's try-out venues. As we now know that, during the first week in August, Charlie had been offered to go and play the drunk in *Mumming Birds* in America, we have the reason why Charlie was rehearsing that very part, in the same premises that Hetty Kelly was training to become a dancer. It also gives us the reason why Charlie turned down the offer of going to America – which was because he didn't want to be parted from Hetty.

Charlie goes on to tell that, on the third 'evening' of waiting for her in the wings:

> I had asked her if I could meet her on Sunday. She laughed. "I don't even know what you look like without the red nose!" – I was playing the comedy drunk in Mumming Birds, dressed in long tails and a white tie. "My nose is not quite this red, I hope, and I'm not quite as decrepit as I look," I said, "and to prove it I'll bring along a photo of myself tomorrow night."

> That was the beginning. Each night we would meet for a few moments. We never saw each other during the day, both being busy with rehearsals, and so we arranged to meet at Kennington Gate Sunday afternoon at four o'clock. I was all dressed up for the occasion; a double-breasted coat pinched at the waist, derby hat, cane and gloves. I rattled my thirty shillings impatiently[2]. The Sunday was a typical one. Discarded tram tickets littered the deserted streets and a news-sheet blew aimlessly in the road.

> A street car slowed up. The occupants were getting off. At last a slender-looking girl, neatly dressed in blue serge and looking radiantly beautiful, alighted and came toward me. I recognized her at once. It was Hetty, more lovely than I had dreamed. What a wonderful day that was!

> (1933 *ibid*)

---

[1] The Montpelier Theatre which Freddie refers to was listed in *The Stage Annual* for 1908 as the 'Montpelier Assembly Hall', 18 Montpelier Street, Walworth SE. and was licensed for music and dancing. Yes, the same venue at which Charlie had done a try-out with Ted prince's Nippers.
[2] In his 1964 autobiography Chaplin has doubled the thirty shillings to three pounds. Must be inflation!

In his 1964 autobiography Chaplin adds on four subsequent encounters, where he meets her at seven o'clock to escort her to her destination:

> Camberwell Road was now touched with magic because Hetty Kelly lived there. Those morning walks with hands clasped all the way to the Underground were bliss mingled with confused longings. Shabby, depressing Camberwell Road, which I used to avoid, now had lure as I walked in its morning mist, thrilled at Hetty's outline in the distance coming towards me.

Chaplin starts off this account by telling us that, on their first morning together, Hetty had to go to the underground tube station in the Westminster Bridge Road, to get to rehearsals in Shaftesbury Avenue. But then, as he often did, he loses focus and makes out that he took her on all four mornings to the underground station, which just isn't right. Hetty lived at 11 Councillor Street, Camberwell, which is located just off Camberwell New Road, about a quarter of the way up from the junction with Camberwell Road. The nearest underground station to Hetty's home is the Oval. The Westminster Bridge Road is miles away. Even had they walked to Westminster Bridge Road, they would have still gone via Kennington Road, as going via Camberwell Road was the long way round. The only reason to go up the Camberwell Road would be to get to the Montpelier.

HETTY'S HOUSE
No.11 Councillor Street, Camberwell, is part of a purpose built, two-storey terrace, consisting of twenty four flats. They were built between 1905-1908 to house workers from the nearby Surrey canal. (N.B. The canal has since been filled in and the area is now known as Burgess Park.)

So the new picture looks like this: On their Sunday day out together, Hetty would have boarded the tram at Camberwell Green, and alighted at Kennington Park Road. Charlie was then living at 16, Glenshaw Mansions, which is due south of the park, down the Brixton Road. He chose to walk, while she took the tram. That girl sure knew how to make an entrance. Then, on their first morning together, Charlie picks up Hetty at her house, and walks her to the tube station. On the following three mornings, Charlie again meets her at her home, but then the two of them walk up Camberwell Road to go to the Montpelier. That's my version, but you can go along with Charlie's if you prefer. You've paid your money!

So what was the background of this mystical nymph who fluttered into Charlie's life, broke his heart, then fluttered out – leaving a life-long impression on him? Of Hetty's earliest origins, David Robinson discovered the following:

> Florence Hetty Kelly was born on 28ᵗʰ August 1893 at 30 Broad Street, Westminster, and registered at birth as 'Florence Etty.' Her father was Arthur Kelly, a journeyman window-frame maker. He and his wife, the former Matilda Davis, had one son and three beautiful daughters, for whom their mother evidently planned stage careers.

(Chaplin – His Life and Art)

Further research turned up additional information, contemporary with Chaplin's first sighting of Hetty: Mrs. Kelly was the mother of one son and *four* daughters: Edith – born 5 March 1888 (aged 20); Arthur William – born circa October 1891 (almost 17); Hetty (fifteen that month); Mabel (aged 12); and Matilda (aged 6). As it was Mrs. Kelly who was listed as the householder, it seems as though the father wasn't living with them – if he indeed he were alive at all.

Come the fourth morning, Chaplin went in too hard on Hetty by pushing the issue of why his love for her was unrequited, which resulted in her ending the relationship. Chaplin himself summed it up as:

> What happened was the inevitable. After all, the episode was but a childish infatuation to her, but to me it was the beginning of a spiritual development, a reaching out for beauty. I suppose I must have burdened her with my unabated attentions, for she tired quickly and we parted.

(ibid 1933)

The following day he went round to Hetty's house, but was met by her mother. After a chat with Mrs. Kelly, over a drink at a local pub, he was allowed access to Hetty back home, but their conversation turned from Charlie's hoped-for reconciliation into a final goodbye. Chaplin said of their parting: "Later she left with the troupe for the Continent and I lost sight of her for two years." But yet again he has things wrong. From their debut on 14 September, *The Yankee Doodle Girls* stayed for fourteen weeks in London before hitting the provinces. It was actually Charlie who went on tour, starting off in Scotland and arriving back in London between the Christmas and New Year weeks.

And what of the reason for Hetty rejecting Charlie? Well, for starters, if the date I place their meeting at is correct, then Hetty was only fourteen. What mother would want their fourteen year-old daughter going out with a nineteen year-old man? Freddie Karno comes up with a totally different theory: "But Hetty would have none of Charlie, preferring, she said, to marry a rich man!" So what could have caused Freddie to make such an inference? Well, it probably had everything to do with what had happened to Hetty's eldest sister Edith, the previous month. On 22 July, Edith had set sail from Liverpool on the *Etruria*, bound for New York. Although the ship's manifest lists her occupation as "actress," Edith was not going there to take up an acting role. No! She had already played her greatest role, to perfection. She was actually going there to meet up with her husband-to-be, Frank J. Gould – an American millionaire. Now *there is* a million reasons why Hetty didn't want to marry Charlie.

Chapter 11

THINGS BECOME SKETCHY

So for Charlie, in August 1908, it was back to reality and back to the music halls. There, it would seem that Charlie stayed with the company he and Syd had been in since 1 June – playing *Mumming Birds*, and *London Suburbia*, plus the occasional performance of *The Casuals* and *Early Birds* – right through until the week ending 14 November; at which point Charlie was given a free transfer to *The Football Match.*

A few preliminary performances of The Football Match had been played during October and the first week in November, probably to break in the new ex-professional footballers who were joining the tour. But then, for the start of the second tour proper, at Her Majesty's Theatre, Walsall, Charlie reprised his role as 'The Villain.' A review from the second week of the tour confirms all:

(w/c 30 November 1908)

HANLEY, Grand

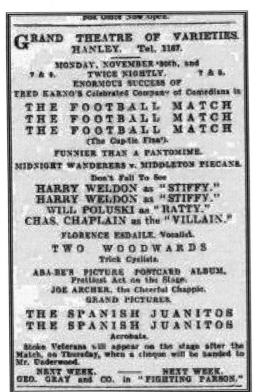

Rare, if not unique, clipping naming Chas. Chaplin as 'The Villain.'

To commence with, the spectators are given an insight into the training methods of the Midnight Club. It may be permitted to say that a certain concoction kept in the 'oil can' takes a prominent place in the medicinal treatment of the Wanderers. During training time the audience were introduced to Stiffy, the goalkeeper, 'a figure of manly beauty.' Stiffy bowed obsequiously to right and left, and he was quite a striking figure- indeed little short of a solar phenomenon-with his fiery furnace-like thatch.

Ratty, the forward, also made his bow to the audience, and one somehow guessed that he must be a first-cousin to Stiffy. At this period a plot came to light, this being none other than a grave and insidious attempt to bribe the Wanderers to lose the Cup [Chaplin's role]. A great deal of fun was witnessed as the crowd assembled outside the Crystal Palace enclosure, the idiosyncrasies of some spectators, and especially of the hanger-on having been well observed and captured. As the representatives of the First League clubs cantered on to the ground the audience were introduced to them one by one, and they were received with flattering plaudits.

At last the whistle blew, and the great match was in progress. The Wanderers wore red shirts and white knickers and the Pie-Cans wore striped shirts and white

108

knickers. Stiffy kept goal for the Wanderers, and the merriment played around him, and also Ratty, the forward. It was laughable to see Stiffy cordially shake hands with an opponent who had done him a great disservice; to demand that a penalty should be taken over again because he had had the bad fortune to save it; to insist on taking a corner kick against himself as goalkeeper; and to give the audience a taste of his quality Ratty came out of a scrimmage looking like a bundle of rags. Incidentally, the referee was put off the field for obstructing the progress of the game, and the cup was won by the Midnight Wanderers.

(Staffordshire Sentinel – 1 December 1908)

Three months into the tour, and the hierarchy within the sketch hadn't changed, as a review from the Newcastle Empire will show:

(w/c 1 March 1909)

NEWCASTLE EMPIRE

Broad farce is the feature of this week's programme, and Fred Karno's production *The Football Match*, is nothing if not hilariously funny. Harry Weldon as 'Stiffy' and Will Poluski. Jun. as 'Ratty' fairly bring down the house with their laughable absurdities.

(The Era – 6 March 1909)

Chaplin continued playing 'The Villain' until, finally, with only three weeks of the tour remaining, he did actually get to play the role of 'Stiffy'. But it is Weldon who tells of the event, and not Chaplin. Just why, we shall discover below:

Charlie had undoubtedly a flair for pantomime, but in a speaking part he was rather out of it. Fred Karno, who always had an eye to new talent, was exceedingly impressed by him, and I know that Fred used to tell all the managers what a great find he had got.

I know on one occasion when we were playing at the Olympia, Liverpool, I did 'Stiffy' at the first house, and Chaplin, on the instructions of Karno, took on the part in the second house. I had the unique experience of sitting in a box and seeing my understudy perform. I cannot say that the audience or myself were very impressed with the show that Charlie made. He did his best, but his slight physique prevented him from looking the part, and the audience were so cold to his 'Stiffy' that he never appeared in goal – at least while I was in the company.

(Pearson's Magazine Weekly)

A search of all the Liverpool papers, and one finally turns up trumps:

(w/c 19 April 1909)

LIVERPOOL, Olympia

The boisterous, rollicking fun of Fred Karno's idea of a football match continues to draw large crowds to the halls. There are, of course, ludicrous situations in *The Football Match*, but they are of that class which produce laughter. Will Poluski. Jun. and Harry Weldon are the leaders, but last night a deputy for Weldon made ample use of his opportunity.

(Liverpool Echo – 20 April 1909)

Well there's a first – a story about Chaplin that checks out. But then it's not Chaplin telling the story – but Weldon. What a pity he didn't tell us more. The only other bit we get was a comment he tagged on to his piece about the Liverpool incident.

Although Karno had such a high opinion of Chaplin, no one else in the company paid him much attention, but regarded him as one of the boys.

Karno must indeed have had a high opinion of Chaplin by letting him stand in on the first night. This has always been the night when the critics attend, and the show then lives or dies the rest of the week on the strength of what they write in their reviews. There would have been far less risk of damaging the week's business had Weldon done the opening night, and Chaplin played one of the mid-week houses, or even a matinee; but Karno must have felt the kid could carry it off – which, indeed, he appears to have done.

But why did Karno let Charlie have a shot at playing 'Stiffy' at all? There were only two further weeks to go before the tour ended and, at the penultimate one, Sheffield, Weldon was still in the lead-part while Chaplin was billed fourth in order of names. But then for the very last week, at Oldham, Chaplin *did* take the lead-role. This is a very surprising change in circumstance. One would think that Weldon would have wanted to end the tour on a high, with his reputation still intact, and with the option of being invited to do another tour. And it wasn't just a case of Chaplin standing in for Weldon at a couple of mid-week performances. Chaplin was actually billed in the local newspaper adverts, and named in reviews, with Weldon's name nowhere to be found. Putting together the adverts, the reviews, and Weldon's comment ".. he [Chaplin] never appeared in goal – at least while I was in the company" and one would have to conclude that Weldon had left the company. Maybe Charlie had hit him with one of the dumbbells.

(w/c 3 May 1909)

OLDHAM, Empire

A football match is splendidly burlesqued, and though we have had the pleasure of seeing the production on two previous occasions-not in Oldham-it was as acceptable and fresh on Monday night as ever. A touch of realism is introduced by the presence of some players who were famous in the football world. Some of the situations are delightfully grotesque, and create uproarious laughter. Charles Chaplin and Will Poluski jun., who take the principal parts, are very droll, and their make-up adds to the enjoyment.

(*Oldham Daily Standard* – 4 May 1909)

Further searching revealed that, with just one week to go before the tour came to its natural end, Weldon had indeed left the Karno company. In a supreme twist of irony Chaplin had stayed on to take over Weldon's role of 'Stiffy,' whilst Weldon had gone off to play in a spoof of 'Dick Turpin.' Normally at the end of a football match players swap shirts, but Weldon and Chaplin must have misread the script and swapped sketches.

With the final whistle having been blown on *The Football Match* we now have no muddy boot-prints by which to follow Charlie's movements. In his autobiography, Chaplin, after saying "Goodbye" to Hetty in August 1908, gives us only: "In 1909 I went to Paris." In doing so he leaves out more than a year of his life, with no reference to his movements. Plotting his stage work has therefore had to be done using the few trace marks he left, inadvertently. One clue comes from the newspaper review of a sketch he was playing in, in July 1910, which revealed:

He [Chaplin] is the youngest principal comedian in the Karno Companies, and has played 'Perkins' in the *G.P.O.* and *The Bailiffs*; 'Stiffy' in The *Football Match*; 'Archibald' in *Skating*; and the 'Inebriated Swell' in *Mumming Birds*.

(*Swansea* – 12 July 1910)

A comment he was to make regarding the sketch he was playing in, in October 1910, further helps the cause, as he reveals the names of two more sketches in which he partook:

We had other much funnier sketches in our repertoire such as *Skating*, *The Dandy Thieves*, *The Post Office*, and *Mr. Perkins, M.P.*[1]

From this we have to assume that Chaplin had played in all of these sketches pre-October 1910. However, the only dates where Chaplin has not been traced to a particular sketch are May

---

[1] *The Post Office*, and *Mr. Perkins, M.P.* were more usually billed as *The G.P.O.* and *Perkins M.P.* respectively.

1909 to October 1909 inclusive. This considerably narrows the time-window in which he could have been in *The G.P.O.*; *The Bailiff*; *The Dandy Thieves*; and *Perkins M.P.* Therefore, all permutations of these sketches, plus a few others he could have been in between these two dates, are listed on [Pages].

Regarding the sketch *The G.P.O.*, it took till 1952 before some form of corroborating evidence was printed confirming Chaplin appearing in it.

> Charlie was given a small part in a sketch called G.P.O. in which Fred Kitchen played the lead. Kitchen was very good at improvising gags. Charlie, confronted by lines that were not in the script, instead of leaving the laugh with the chief comedian, came back with lines of his own that often topped Kitchen's. This caused considerable trouble, and Karno moved Charlie to another sketch, 'The Football Match,' in which Harry Weldon played 'Stiffy' the goalkeeper and Charlie was the villain in a large Inverness cape and a slouch hat.

(Picturegoer – 4 October 1952)

FRED KITCHEN

One of the biggest comedy stars in music-hall history, and the man to whom Chaplin owes so much for his character building. Which is most likely the reason Chaplin doesn't acknowledge him.

The above sparks the question: "Was it in fact Fred Kitchen and *not* Harry Weldon with whom Charlie had clashed?" Charlie had successfully completed two full runs of *The Football Match* with Weldon, whereas his involvement in *The G.P.O.* is short lived and virtually unrecorded. This could be an indication that either Fred Kitchen, or Karno, had Charlie removed from the company to prevent further clashes. Kitchen himself said only of their work together:

> When young Charlie Chaplin joined us he was given the nickname 'Wagger'[2] after the Cockney term 'Charlie Wag' for anyone who is a bit of a comedian. I took a liking to the skinny young lad right away and I could sense he had talent. So I took him under my wing and taught him the rudiments of being a funny man by under- rather than over- playing. I was actually the first comedian to wear oversize boots. Fred Karno came up with this idea to make a bit of business out of my shambling stage walk which was half-way between a shuffle and a hop. I had to smile when Charlie later started to wear a pair of large boots himself.
>
> I also taught him my 'ashtray' kick – throwing a cigarette over my shoulder and kicking it away with my heel before it hit the ground.

This is a disappointing contribution from Kitchen. It gives us no fix in time or sketch. So, let's go back to the 1952 *Picturegoer* article, and the statement that Karno moved Charlie from *The G.P.O.* to *The Football Match*. This does not fit the chronology of the first or second tours of *The Football Match*, but Chaplin was soon to commence a third tour, and so the story may have substance.

The first page of the script of *The G.P.O.*, plus a review from just prior to when Chaplin *could* have joined, reveal much of the business:

_____

[2] It would appear that Charlie had been carrying this nickname for a number of years, as Mrs. Tricks, his alleged former nurse, says she used to call him "Waggie" [see Chapter 1]

G. P. O.

Caste:-

PERKINS
JOLLY
POSTMASTER
CLERK
GIRL CLERK
TOFF
DOCTOR
OLD WOMAN
FRENCHMAN
BUNGAY
CROOK
MOTHER & CHILD
POLICEMAN & DOORMAN

Scene 1 (Out-side the Post-Office).

(When curtain goes up - general action people going in & out of
Post-Office. Poster:- "Hands Wanted" outside Post-Office).
Enter Perkins: out of work, sees sign stops reads it(busies with
cigarette) walks away; stops - goes to read it again, gets all
set nips cigarette, goes to go in but walks past - finally makes
hurried exit through Post-Office door - Black Out -

Scene 2 (Interior of Post-Office).

General Atmosphere.
Perkins enters looking at letters, (begins holding letters to
light).
Enter Postmaster carrying Police reward notice for Crook, hands
this to Clerk, says to him: "Oh, by the way Benson, I have been
watching you very closely in your work and I am more than
satisfied. 1 have just had an urgent message which calls me away
for a few days, this means I must leave someone I can rely on in
charge while I am away, and I think you are just the man."
Benson: "I am very grateful to you Sir, but I am afraid the
responsibility is too much(during this conversation Perkins
gradually works his way over to Postmaster and Benson and listens
to conversation pushing himself forward.) Postmaster looking around
spots Perkins and makes him temporary postmaster during his
absence. - hands over keys of safe and petty cash, then exits.
Perkins (looks at keys)"now we shall be able to back some Winners".
Enter Jolly
Perkins: "Ah, there you are my boy, have you heard the news? - I
have just been made Postmaster. That's what you want to do, climb
the ladder of fame, and when you get to the top, we may let you
clean the windows. Now will you stand by."
Jolly: "Yes Sir"
Perkins: "Now first of all we have got to make this place into a
paying concern, - for instance, in future, we'll send the 8.0 am
mail out at 7.0am."
Jolly: "Whatever for"?
Perkins: "To get there before the other post-offices, you fool".
(Gives Jolly money) - "Here go out and get two nice noodles, a
pennyworth, and a pint, and the late Star". Exit Jolly.
Toff enters: (walks over to Perkins.) "Do you sell stamps here"?
Perkins: Can't say for certain, I'll go and see (walks to counter)
says to girl, "Do we sell stamps here"?

/ .... Girl

NEWCASTLE, Empire – "THE GPO"

Fred Kitchen at the Empire last night drew two crowded houses. This comedian, one of the easy, unctuous order, being a great favourite in the city. He appears with Mr. Karno's Company in the burlesque *The GPO*. This is new to the North, but as it affords fine scope for irresponsible comedy, it is sure to be popular. It is in two scenes, an imposing exterior of a head post office, with posting boxes and notices, including one inviting extra hands to apply for work.

Amongst other loafers Perkins is seen. He enters, and is taken on and put into uniform. He makes himself at home with song and dance, assisted by a bevy of smart postmen, and settles down to work. The postmaster is called away by superiors. He leaves Perkins in charge, the responsibility being declined by the clerk. Perkins, with money, stamps, etc., at his disposal soon has a good time, and allows liberties unheard of in His Majesty's service. Absurdities go on until the time of closing, when the postmaster returns and finds Perkins tampering with the safe, as he thinks. In reality, the latter is securing a blackmailer. On opening the door the miscreant is discovered, and Perkins is complimented. A pathetic note is struck by the discovery, and the adoption by Perkins of the villain's child, found, with label attached, in the sorting office, where it had been left by the mother. Mr. Kitchen and the company scored a decided success.

(Newcastle Daily Journal – 11 February 1909)

To find out the business in another of the sketches Charlie allegedly played in, *The Bailiff,* we need to go back much earlier, when the sketch was still under its working title – *The Hire System:*

BOLTON, Grand

At the Grand, Bolton, is being played Fred Karno's new sketch, recently produced at the Hippodrome, Wigan, entitled The Hire System. The sketch, replete with rollicking fun, is brightly staged and dressed, and should prove one of Mr. Karno's most entertaining productions. It is essentially a one-man play, and Mr. Fred Kitchen, ever smart and resourceful, makes the most of the innumerable humorous situations occurring in the sketch.

There are three scenes. In the first, two broker's men are commissioned by a Jew, the proprietor of a firm who provide furniture on the hire system, to take possession of a house whose inmates have fallen in arrears of payment for their furniture. The Jew is careful to impress on the bailiffs that they will have to exercise a great deal of strategy to secure an entrance into the house. The dialogue between the Jew and the principal bailiff (Mr. Fred Kitchen) is very amusing. The latter by his inane questions rouses the Jew to a pitch of frenzy which renders him almost speechless.

The second scene represents the outside of the house. In order to effect an entrance the bailiff assumes various disguises, all of which prove unsuccessful. Finally his companion takes matters into his own hands. He boldly rings and tells the maid that he has come to sell up the furniture for arrears of payment. To the amazement and disgust of his colleague he is instantly admitted.

In the third scene is enacted the selling by auction of the furniture. Mr Fred Kitchen, as the auctioneer, runs riot in numerous quips and jokes. The scene is rather marred by noise, partly caused by the shifting of furniture and by the would-be buyers at the sale, and which make some of Mr. Kitchen's witticisms inaudible. The sale of the happy home is nearing completion, when the owner of the furniture, just returning from her honeymoon, rushes into the room. Bedlam is then 'out-Bedlamed' and nothing can be heard but inarticulate sounds. It transpires, however, that the bailiffs have made a mistake in the number of the house, and that they have sold up No. 48 instead of No. 43. In the midst of the confusion the Jew appears on the scene, a very picture of despair. His words, which apparently refer to the blunder that has been made by the bailiffs, is however lost in the prevailing hub-bub. The piece caused hearty laughter and applause.

(The Stage – 25 April 1907)

And to discover the contents of the third sketch, *The Dandy Thieves* (which was a shortened version of *His Majesty's Guests*), we turn to a much later review:

ABERDEEN, Palace – 'THE DANDY THIEVES'

Fred Karno's company of clever comedians has now attained a high reputation, and nowhere do these versatile artistes enjoy greater popularity than in Aberdeen. Last night, when they appeared in a new musical farce, *The Dandy Thieves*, they were welcomed by large houses, and the production was pronounced on all hands an unqualified success. The scenery is at once elaborate and tasteful, the dresses exceedingly attractive, and the music bright and pleasing. Of course the acting is marked by the utmost vivacity throughout, and excellent example in this respect being set by Mr. George Hestor who, as 'Sergeant Lightning', has a part affording the most ample scope for his conspicuous ability as a comedian.

The amusing incidents that evoke boisterous merriment take place within, or near, the Emporium of 'Mr. Miffin, universal provider,' and the scene representing the exterior and interior of that colossal establishment are admirably realistic. Shop assistants appear assiduously at work, and the dexterous 'shop-lifter,' arrayed in the height of fashion, is also seen plying her nefarious calling. Burglars and policemen play the familiar game of hide-and-seek, and the pursuit so vigorously maintained is marked by the farcical blundering characteristic of all policemen on the stage-and some of them even in real life. The fun becomes fast and furious as 'Lord Easem;' alias 'Flash Jack,' slips out of one tight place only to flounder into another, and this part is played with unflagging spirit by Mr. Ernest Freshwater. The 'Universal Provider' himself finds a capital representative in Mr. Charles Usher, and 'Lady Maud Easem,' alias 'Maud, the shop-lifter' is dashingly impersonated by Aggie Morris. But the acting is, indeed, remarkably skilful throughout, and the enjoyable effect of the performance is enhanced by the tuneful efforts of an efficient chorus.

(Aberdeen Daily Journal – 12 January 1909)

And for *Perkins M.P.* we have:

(w/c 2 August 1909)

HOLBORN, Empire

Originally produced on July 12 at the Palace Leicester, *Perkins M.P.* the new sketch by Fred Karno, Hickory Wood, and Fred Kitchen made its first bow to a London audience on Monday. Perkins was, of course, the moving spirit of the Karno sketch *G.P.O.*, and in the present instance he is found throwing up his job at the local factory, wither he went after the loss of the Government appointment in order to devote his energies to Parliamentary work. He addresses meeting, obtains the assistance of the women suffragists, and does his own canvassing gorgeously arrayed in motor costume.

The last scene shows the interior of the House of Common, the members being more or less interested in a debate on China. The news of Perkins' success at the poll has hardly been received ere that worthy arrives, and from that moment the comedy introduced is of the broadest kind. Perkins plays havoc with all rules of procedure, points of order and matters of the House's ancient privileges and laws unwritten and written. He breasts upon a division on the questions of 'Votes for Women,' and succeeds in carrying his motion, with the result that the House is stormed by women wearing the familiar 'purple, white and green.'

As Perkins, of course, Fred Kitchen bears the brunt of the work. He is always amusing, and many of his topical allusions are extremely funny. He is capitally assisted by his diminutive friend of other sketches and a good company. Altogether Perkins M.P. should be worked up into a worthy companion to Mr. Karno's other successes.

(The Stage – 5 August 1909)

Reviews from Leicester Palace (12 July) and Cardiff Palace (26 July) give us information on the names of the cast and production staff:

> Fred Kitchen as the Labour candidate is exceedingly diverting. Capital support comes from Herbert Sydney (Nathaniel Grubb); Albert Taylor (Police Constable Gas); Vera Gilda (Mrs. Perkins); Grace Wilson (Hon. Mrs Fitzherbert); and Aggie Morris (Chrissie).
>
> The sketch was produced by Mr. W.H. Morgan, under the personal supervision of Mr. Fred Karno, and the manager and stage director for Mr. Fred Karno is Harold Wellesley.

Although the above information is contemporary with the period in which Chaplin *could have* been in *Perkins M.P.*, it looks as though, as he isn't named in the cast, he was to join sometime later – between 9 August and late October.

There is a possibility that Chaplin, in this "whereabouts unconfirmed" period, did at least one week in *Mumming Birds*. In his autobiography Chaplin gives an account of a meeting with Karno regarding negotiations for a pay rise. He then runs us through a scenario of a meeting in Karno's office, wherein Karno does everything he can to undermine Chaplin's ability. One put-down required getting the manager from the Star Theatre, Bermondsey, on the telephone to tell Chaplin that his recent performance in *Mumming Birds* stank. Just when this supposed meeting took place I dispute. Chaplin places it at the time of his two-year contract running out, which would have been on 21 February 1910. However, Chaplin was not in London between 10 January and 3 April 1910. When he finally returned, it was to play in *Jimmy the Fearless* – not *Mumming Birds*. The only incidence found of *Mumming Birds* playing at the Star Theatre, Bermondsey, was 14 June 1909. Charlie adds:

> Karno's attempt to cut me down was not a success. I told him that if he also felt that way, there was no need to renew my contract. Karno in many ways was a shrewd man, but he was not a psychologist. Even if I did stink, it wasn't good business of Karno to have a man at the other end of the phone tell me so. I was getting five pounds and, although my confidence was low, I demanded six.[3] To my surprise, Karno gave it to me, and I again entered his good graces.

(Chaplin's 1964 autobiography)

Chaplin biographer David Robinson concludes from what Chaplin said about the phone call that the man at the other end of the line was a "plant." i.e. someone whom Karno had put up to playing the part of the theatre manager to ensure that he, Karno, would win the argument. But Chaplin himself makes no such intimation, or harbours any such suspicion. For Karno to have had a plant standing by he would have had to have known in advance what course the conversation was going to take. Besides, Karno would not have been short of anyone to give a critical appraisal of any artiste who had performed at the Star, as it had a terrible reputation for the reception given to acts there. Even the great George Robey did not survive the treatment meted out.

> Many music-hall audiences were rough and rowdy in the early nineties and certain halls in the poorer districts of London had an evil reputation among the profession. One such hall was the Star at Bermondsey and it was Robey's ill-luck to begin a week's engagement there on a bank-holiday.
>
> He was greeted with a storm of jeers and cat-calls and cries expressed in the crudest argot of Bermondsey. He could hardly make himself heard above the din. He got through one song hoping that he would have better luck with his second number, instead of which the tumult was redoubled. As he came off he vowed he would never appear in Bermondsey again. And he never did.

(Prime Minister of Mirth, by A.E. Wilson – a biography of George Robey)

---

[3] The terms, back in 1908 were that Chaplin was to receive £3 10s per week for the first year; £4 for the second year; and the option of third year at the same rate. So where Chaplin got the figures of a raise from £5 to £6 is a mystery.

My own theory is that when Chaplin returned to London at the end of the second run of *The Football Match*, 8 May, he looked to Karno for a pay raise. Karno pointed out that he wasn't worth the extra money, as he hadn't yet proved himself as a principal comic. Chaplin himself admitted:

> But I was haunted by a thought that perhaps I was not equal to taking Weldon's place. And behind it all was the ghost of my failure at the Foresters'. As I had not fully retrieved my confidence, every new sketch in which I played the leading comedy part was a trial of fear. And now the alarming and a most resolute day came to notify Mr Karno that my contract had run out and that I wanted a raise.

Karno had many ways of reducing the ego of any of his acts who were getting a little swell-headed, which prompts me to believe that Karno purposely booked Chaplin into the Star, Bermondsey, knowing full well just what kind of reception he would receive.

So Summer came and went, followed as always by the Autumn, with Chaplin presumed to be alternating in *The G.P.O.*, *Perkins M.P.*, *The Bailiff*, and *The Dandy Thieves*. But then, come the Winter, Charlie was given an offer to reprise his role in *Mumming Birds*, but with a slight catch. No! he didn't have to go back to the Star, but he might have to play in front of equally boisterous audiences, for the venue was the Folies Bergère, in Paris. It was to be a four-week run but, before that, Charlie had a short run of his own. Turning up late at the station, he only managed to catch the train to the Ferry Port by grabbing the handrail of the luggage van as the train pulled away. T. Scott Bell, Karno's secretary for a number of years, described Charlie as follows:

> Charlie took part in one after another of our companies, thus getting himself first-rate schooling. He always showed himself a good, reliable performer. We always thought him a little eccentric, however. He was very untidy in his person. Even when he was leading man, he would often turn up at train-call in a pair of old carpet slippers, his collar only partly buttoned, and his tie hanging loose round his neck! I remember he went to Paris like that!

(Peter Haining – 1915 article – original source unaccredited)

In his autobiography, Chaplin himself admits:

> I began to neglect myself and became desultory in my habits. When travelling with the company, I was always late at the railway station, arriving at the last moment, dishevelled and without a collar, and was continually reprimanded for it.

However, Chaplin's description is from 1905, when he was touring with the 'Sherlock Holmes' Company. The lesson of the ten shilling fine which had been imposed on him then had taught him nothing.

Charlie related being excited to be visiting a foreign country, especially after finishing a week at Woolwich[4], which he described as "a dank, miserable week in a miserable town." The journey to the French capital, however, did nothing to reinforce his optimism. During the ferry sailing the rain came down in torrents and, upon arrival, the coastline was obscured by a mist. The partial view still gave Charlie an unforgettable thrill, and he had to keep reminding himself "It isn't England – it's the Continent! France!"

With the theatre being in a foreign country, and having a cosmopolitan audience, Karno chose the steadfast *Mumming Birds* – being a sketch which, although not totally mime, contained action that could be understood by all nationalities. Another pastime fitting this description is "entertaining ladies of the night," in which Chaplin makes no effort to hide his participation. Indeed, it may be said he fairly boasts of his indulgences with the latter. What a very strange quirk of conscience Chaplin had, in that he would not admit to working with fellow professionals like Dan Leno and George Robey, nor even his own brother or father, and yet is

---

[4] The only Karno company to play Woolwich around that time was eleven weeks prior to the Paris trip. If Charlie's recollection of playing in Woolwich is correct, then he must have been in the Karno sketch *Spring Cleaning*. A second alternative is that he mistakenly quotes Woolwich when he was actually in Rotherithe, playing in *Mumming Birds*. And yet a third alternative is that he played both sketches at both venues.

quite forward in broadcasting his dalliances with ladies in this other profession. Considering the dark side of his family's history, one would have thought that Chaplin would have gone out of his way to avoid such "ladies," but he seems to have regarded it as a conquest, and the yardstick for being a man. Ah well! Let's just do what the audiences did, and judge him purely on his stage performances.

The Folies Bergère engagement began on 1 November 1909, and ended on Sunday 28 November, after which Charlie enjoyed a week's rest to get over the strain of travel and work, or maybe to get over some other physical exertions. Then came rehearsals for a third tour of *The Football Match*, which was to commence with two weeks at the Oxford Music Hall, London. This was great news to Charlie:

> Mr. Karno informed me that I was to take the place of Harry Weldon in the second season of *The Football Match*.

> ..... We were to open at the Oxford, the most important music hall in London. We were to be the main attraction and I was to have my name featured for the first time at the top of the bill.

> .... But at the first rehearsal I had an attack of laryngitis. On the opening night, every vein and cord in my throat was strained to the utmost with a vengeance. But I could not be heard. Karno came round afterwards with an expression of mingled disappointment and contempt. "No one could hear you," he said reprovingly. I assured him that my voice would be better the next night, but it was not. In fact, it was worse. The next night my understudy went on. As a consequence the engagement finished after the first week. All my hopes and dreams of that Oxford engagement had collapsed, and the disappointment of it laid me low with influenza.

> (abridged extracts from Chaplin's 1964 autobiography)

Well! What a heartbreaking story. If only it were true. Again, like any good fabrication, it has its roots in truth, but doesn't stand up to cross-examination. True – Harry Weldon was no longer with the company. True – *The Football Match* did open at the Oxford. To avoid pedantry, we'll forgive Chaplin labelling it the second season of *The Football Match*, when it was the third; and his saying it was the first time he'd been featured as the top-of-the-bill, when he'd already had this distinction at the close of the second tour, in Oldham. Now come the real inconsistencies:

The original programme shows that Chaplin wasn't billed as the headline comic at all. In fact he didn't even play 'Stiffy' – Will Poluski Jun. did. Second-place listing was Gilbert Childs, who was there for a reason. He had played 'Stiffy' before, and was therefore the stand-in. Charlie is listed fifth. However, as only his and Will Poluski's names are in block capitals, it would indicate that Chaplin was still among the principals. In other words: he was still playing 'The Villain.'

So why the story of ultimate glee followed by abject misery, from Chaplin? Well, there are still some more facts to be revealed. The same week *The Football Match* opened at the Oxford, it played nightly at a second theatre, the Willesden Hippodrome. And here Chaplin *did* appear in the lead role of 'Stiffy – the Goalkeeper.' Hurrah! Hurrah!

(w/c 13 December 1909)

WILLESDEN, Hippodrome

Fred Karno's *Football Match* is the leading attraction this week, and the sketch is received with roars of laughter, much being due to the efforts of Charles Chaplin, Gilbert Childs and Will Poluski Jun.

(*The Stage* – 16 December 1909)

MONDAY, DEC. 13th, 1909, Every Evening
AND SATURDAY MATINEE.

SPECIAL NOTICE.—From the opening of the Doors and up to the commencement of the Programme, a series of Novel and Interesting Pictures will be shown by the World's Advertising Co., Ltd., 11 Old Jewry Chambers, E.C.

1 OVERTURE ... "Cleopâtre" ... *Blanchetan*
2 ZAID TRIO, Spanish Moors in an Oriental Act.
3 Mr. TONY BLACK, Scotch Comedian.
4 THE SCHUMANNS, in their Vocal and Instrumental
   Scena—"THE COMPOSER AT HOME."
5 Miss GRACIE GRAHAME, Comedienne.
6 MADAME ELDEE, the Girl in the Golden Frame.
7 Miss DORMA MORGAN, Refined Comedienne.
8 LEE & KINGSTON, Comedy Duo, playing — "A
   RESOURCEFUL LOVER."
9 Miss QUEENIE FINNIS, Comedienne.
10 Mr. JOHN DONALD, the Scottish Baritone.
11 Mr. JULIAN MACK, the Topical Talking Dame.
12 HANVARR & LEE
13 Mr. SAM MAYO, Drowsy Drolleries.
14 KELLY & AGNAS, Australian Comedy Duo.
15 Miss GERTIE GITANA, the Rising Star.
16 Mr. GEO. CHIRGWIN, the great Woe Walloper, with
   White-eyed Witticisms.
17 SELECTION
   Ballet Music from "Faust" ... *Gounod*
18 ALFREDO MARSCHALL,
   "A Dangerous Game in a Naval Port,"
19 Mr. BILLY McCLAIN, in his Original Creation—
   "Down amongst the Sugar Cane and Parson Johnson."
20 Mr. ALBERT TOFT, "Maker of History."
21 LYONS & CULLUM, a Variety of Vaudeville.
22 FRED KARNO'S Colossal Production, entitled—

THE FOOTBALL MATCH

THE CUP-TIE FINAL.
Written by FRED KARNO. Music by J. H. CLEVE.
A Struggle for Supremacy between
MIDNIGHT WANDERERS v MIDDLETON PIE-CANS.
The Cast includes the following Professional Footballers :— George Harper (Birmingham), Harry Harper (Birmingham), Jack West (Birmingham), Jack Fitchett (Fulham), Billy Wragg (Late Brighton and Notts Forest), W. Milson (Millwall), Jack Johnson (Derby), Joe Clark (the Hibernians).
In Addition to
WILL POLUSKI, Jun., R. J. Hamer, Fred Onzella, GILBERT CHILDS, Misses Mary Young and Jessie Grey, Fred Newham and CHARLIE CHAPLIN.

Scene 1—Training Quarters at "The Bull." The Middleton Pie-Cans Getting Fit. Scene 2—Exterior of the Football Ground. The Pay Boxes. No Change Given. Scene 3—The Football Field. "The Match." Stiffy, the Goalkeeper in Form.

23 RUFFELL'S IMPERIAL BIOSCOPE.

The above Programme is Subject to alteration, and the Management disclaim responsibility for the unavoidable absence of any Artiste.

The Piano used on this stage supplied by John Brinsmead & Sons, Ltd., 18, Wigmore Street, W.

Manager ... ... Mr. BLYTH-PRATT
Assistant Manager and Treasurer .. .. Mr. F. C. UPTON
Stage Manager .. .. Mr. GEO. WOMACK
Musical Director.. .. .. .. Mr. LEON A. BASSETT

(a) The Public may leave at the end of the Performance by all exits and entrance doors which must at that time be open.
(b) All gangways, passages and staircases must be kept entirely free from chairs or other obstructions.
(c) The safety curtain is lowered about the middle of the performance to ensure its being in proper working order.

(Marriot Collection)

118

It would appear from the review that Chaplin, Childs, and Poluski had all exchanged roles so that, should any of the three subsequently have to drop out, the two main roles would be adequately filled by an experienced stand-in. Knowing the outcome as we do, it's a good job they did. So when Chaplin says: "The next night my understudy went on. As a consequence the engagement finished after the first week" he can only be referring to the Willesden venue, as it is confirmed that the rest of the Karno players did fulfil the second-week at the Oxford, while Chaplin himself was laid low by influenza.

The Karno company then moved across London to spend the first week of the New Year playing 'Football' at the Metropolitan Theatre, Edgware. So what of Chaplin? Well, according to him:

> Karno put me back into Mumming Birds and, ironically, it was not more than a month before I completely recovered my voice.

> (Chaplin's 1964 autobiography)

This story had been peddled out twelve years earlier, in a magazine article:

> When the sketch was moved to London to open at the Oxford Music Hall, Charlie lost his voice. What a calamity! Charlie saw the doctor, gargled all day, sucked lozenges, but it was no use. He could not produce more than a whisper. The understudy went on and Charlie broke down in the dressing-room.

> Sydney Chaplin, at the time, was playing the lead in another Karno sketch called 'Mumming Birds.' His part, that of the drunk, was purely pantomimic. Not a word had to be spoken. And Karno, to make use of Charlie without his voice, sent him on tour in the same sketch and in the same part.

> (*Picturegoer* – 4 October 1952)

But, and for only the second instance I have found, Chaplin had done himself a disservice, as a contemporary account reveals:

(w/c 3 January 1910)

LONDON, THE METROPOLITAN

"THE FOOTBALL MATCH"

> In the first scene the footers are making themselves fit, and we have the semblance of a good plot in an alleged scheme for nobbling 'Stiffy', the goalkeeper, but it really doesn't count. It is Stiffy whom we watch and at whom we laugh. He is responsible for many anomalies, among them a quartet of kiddies, one of them black. There is a continual struggle at the entrance to the football ground, and when we get there we are absolutely dumfounded at the great form displayed at goal by Stiffy, who saves his side and confounds the villain.

> Mr Charles Chaplin in the character is decidedly droll, and he receives capital support. The whole thing is a screamer from start to finish.

> (*The Era* – 8 January 1910)

So, as he appears to have done all too often, Chaplin has left us with a enigma. He names one venue where he *didn't* play the lead role, and fails to mention two others where he *did*. Whether it was at Willesden where he lost his voice, and was given a second chance when he'd recovered, or whether he lost it during the week at Edgware, we might never know. What we do know is that his football-playing days were now over.

Chapter 12

TWO LOAVES AND SOMETHING FISHY

Back in December 1909, around the time that Chaplin was in danger of losing his place in the Karno Company, another comedian had just gained his. Nineteen-year-old Arthur Stanley Jefferson was the son of Arthur Jefferson, the latter being a very well-known and respected actor, playwright, and theatre lessee and manager. At that time Arthur Jefferson was running the Metropole Theatre, in Glasgow, assisted by Stanley and an older son, Gordon. Meanwhile, Fred Karno was producing the Christmas pantomime *Mother Goose* over at the nearby Glasgow Grand Theatre, where the younger Jefferson went to meet him. Stanley himself tells of just why:

> I presented my card with a request for an interview, and was promptly ushered onto the stage where a gentle-voiced little man came forward to meet me. "Well, Mr Jefferson Junior," he said, "What can I do for you?" I told him I wanted to see Mr Karno. "You're seeing him now," he replied quietly. It was quite a shock and such a relief to find him such a pleasant, friendly man. Briefly I explained that I wanted a job as a comedian. "Are you funny?" he asked. I told him of my youthful experience. He nodded. "Very well," he said, "I'll try you out at two pounds a week. Report to Frank O'Neill, who is running my Mumming Birds company in Manchester. Push yourself forward, and I'll see you in London in a few weeks time."
>
> Bewildered at the suddenness of it all, I blurted out my thanks and staggered into the street in a daze. I had achieved the height of every budding comedian's ambition – I was one of Fred Karno's Comedians.

> (*Tit-Bits* – 14 November 1936)

Stanley Jefferson, who was yet some six years away from changing his name to Stan Laurel, made his debut in *Mumming Birds* on 6 December 1909, at the Hippodrome & Floral Hall, Hulme, Manchester. After the Christmas holiday he played the Wakefield Empire, where he learned a second sketch being played there, *Skating*. Sydney Chaplin was not only the principal comic in *Skating*, but had also co-written it, along with legendary writer J. Hickory Wood. *Skating* had made its debut in May 1909 and played continuously until the end of August. It was then revived and played for two weeks, commencing 20 December 1909, as a "Gigantic Christmas Production" at the Manchester Palace Theatre.

The main character in Skating was 'Archibald Binks' – a name which was to be used in other Karno sketches, for the character billed under the various soubriquets 'the inebriate,' 'the drunk' or the 'drunken swell' and, in North America, 'the souse.' The supporting role was 'Zena Flapper' played by Jimmy Russell – in drag. There were, however, "real" ladies in the company, one of whom was billed as Minnie Chaplin. But the surname "Chaplin" was being used as a name of convenience, as Syd and Minnie Constance had not yet tied the knot.

The following week the company Stan was in travelled the short distance to Liverpool where, at the New Pavilion Theatre, he was back to playing a bit-part in *Mumming Birds*.

> In due course I was given a small part to play, but before I could make my first big appearance, I received a setback. The wardrobe mistress told me, 'There's a new

comedian just joined us from one of the other companies. He's taking over Mr [Frank] O'Neill's part as 'the drunken swell'. I haven't a suit to fit him, except the one you are wearing, so I'm afraid you will have to take that off and hand it over.'

Reluctantly, I removed the suit and took it along to the new comedian's dressing room. I found him to be a pleasant little fellow with dark, curly hair, blue eyes, very white teeth, and a friendly smile. I took to him right away, and in the course of time we became close friends, sharing rooms together on tour. You are quite right; his name was Charlie Chaplin.

(*Tit-Bits* – 14 November 1936)

It might seem that the odds of these two great English comedians coming together, in the same company, are massive, when in actual fact they are remarkably short – by the same reasoning that the best two footballers in the Football League, in any one season, are often playing for the same club.

During their week in Liverpool, Messrs. Chaplin, Laurel and the rest of the company must have held further rehearsals for *Skating* as, the following week, there were two different companies playing this very sketch. One company headed south to play London boroughs, while the one Charlie and Stan were in headed north. After weeks in Lancashire, Yorkshire, and one in Glasgow, they came down to Birmingham, with Charlie continuing in the lead part.

(w/c 21 February 1910)

BIRMINGHAM HIPPODROME

Fred Karno presents an original and screamingly funny sketch at the Hippodrome this week, based upon the latest craze – roller-skating. It is a clever and remarkably humorous but exaggerated representation of how others see us on the rink. Johnny Doyle, as "Zena Flapper", and Charles Chaplin, as "Archibald", present themselves with other strange people at the 'Olympia Rink', and after initial noisy trouble at the door gain admission and join with those who can skate inside to create one continuous outburst of fun. Incidentally some smart skating is introduced, and altogether the sketch is highly diverting.

(*Birmingham Evening Despatch* – 22 February 1910)

And from the following week we get:

(w/c 28 February 1910)

BARRASFORD'S HIPPODROME – SHEFFIELD

FRED KARNO'S Pantomimical Absurdity,

"SKATING"

Including JOHNNY DOYLE as "Zena Flapper"

CHARLIE CHAPLIN as "Archibald"

Fred Karno's sketches always appeal to the frequenters of the *Hippodrome,* and last night's *Skating* – an entirely new and original pantomimical absurdity was typical of all Fred Karno's sketches, with its broad rollicking fun. The large house was kept in continuous laughter from start to finish, and the skating scene in the second act included a clever Quadrille dance. Charlie Chaplin, as "Archibald" was in great form, his tumbling and foolery being extremely funny. With Johnny Doyle as 'Zena Flapper', he was particularly nimble on his skates, and fell with a ludicrous freedom that all learners must have envied. About thirty artistes were included in the cast, the "ladies" providing not the least entertainment.

(*Sheffield Daily Telegraph* – 1 March 1910)

A second review for the show in Sheffield ran:

BURY TIMES

29 JANUARY 1910

(w/c 24 January 1910)
TRAFALGAR RINK
LORD STREET, BURY
THE HOCKEY MATCH OF THE SEASON
THIS (SATURDAY) AFTERNOON
FRED KARNO'S FAMOUS SKATERS
v TRAFALGAR H.C. MIXED TEAM
(two Ladies and three Gents either side)
Bully-off 3-30 p.m. Admission 3d.
Skating before and after as usual.
Don't fail to miss this match.

RINK HOCKEY
TRAFALGAR v FRED KARNO'S COMPANY
The match between members of Mr Fred
Karno's Company of artistes, at the *Trafalgar
Rink*, on Saturday afternoon, and members of
the Ladies and Gentlemen's Hockey Club,
proved a great attraction, there being a
crowded attendance. The teams were:-
Fred Karno's Co.:- Ernie Stone, goal; Miss
M. Schofield, full-back; Gertie Jackson, half-
back; Ted Banks and James Beresford, for-
wards.
Trafalgar:- W.Holt, goal; J.Boardman, full-
back; F.Taylor, half-back; Miss S.Lucas and
Schofield, forwards.
   Trafalgar .... 3 goals
   Karno's Co. ....1 goal
The Trafalgar team deserved their victory,
but the visitors ought not to be downhearted.
It was the first hockey match they had taken
part in and, in view of their performance, was
a good one. The Karno contingent, Banks and
Beresford got in some effective work against a
smart defence. A better knowledge of the
game and more practice should ensure a good
team being made up by the talent to be found
among the visitors.

The Karno Roller-Hockey Team
Standing back left: Stan Jefferson
Seated second from left Charles Chaplin.
Thought to have been taken Saturday 12 March, on the
Saturday of the company's week at the Royal
Hippodrome, Liverpool. The other players are,
probably: Ernie Stone, Ted Banks, Jimmy Beresford,
and Fred Gordon.

WIGAN EXAMINER

1 FEBRUARY 1910

(Wednesday 26 January 1910)
COMEDIANS IN HOCKEY MATCH
On Wednesday afternoon, Fred
Karno's Comedians from the Hippodrome played a rolling skating match
with the King Street Skating Rink team.
The King Street Rockets were far the
superior team, but the comedians gave a
good display considering it was only
their second match. The result was 3—1
for the Rink team, the scorers for the
Rink team being Smith 4, Cubby 2, Topping 1, and Little 1. C. Chaplin scored
for the comedians. The teams were as
follows: Rink: J. Connor; J. E. Little; J.
Topping; J. Smith; and J. Cubby. Comedians: E. Stone, goal; F. Gordon, full-
back; C. Chaplin half-back; and Ted
Banks (captain), Jimmy Beresford, and
J. Doyle, forwards. There was a good
attendance of spectators.

Two typical reports of hockey matches played by
Fred Karno's Hockey Team. Note in the above
review, from Bury, that Chaplin was in this, their
first ever match. Maybe he'd learned from
Weldon that, to become popular with "the
people" you needed to do more than just turn in a
good stage performance. You also had to turn out.

Fred Karno's Company in

SKATING

Cast:
Attendant - (doorkeeper of rink)
Archibald - (a broken down swell)
Percy - (a young swell)
Aunty - Percy's aunt
Herr Polka - (Champion skater)
Miss Flapper - (lady skater)
Lord Dundreary -
Telegraph boys, messengers, etc.

1st scene: Exterior of Olympia Skating Rink
AFTER HERR POLKA HAS LEFT, ENTER ARCHIBALD FROM P.S.

Archie: Has the last train gone for Waterloo?
Attendant: What! Do you take this for - a station?
Archie: What is it?
Attendant: Skating Rink.
Archie: Can you put me up for the night?
Attendant: Certainly not, I don't know you.
Archie: Don't you remember Archibald?
Attendant: Archibald!
Archie: Look at me!
Attendant: Why, it's the Captain, my dear old Captain. Why, I haven't seen you since we were in the army together.
Archie: The dear old Salvation Army.
Attendant: Do you remember when we were in the Sudan surrounded by the enemy on every side?
Archie: Every side, left side, right side, front side, and - all around us.
Attendant: There we stood with our retreat cut off.
Archie: Our what cut off?
Attendant: Retreat cut off.
Archie: Oh! Reggie.
Attendant: Do you remember those 3 days and nights without food or water, think of it, not a drain of water, but what did we do?
Archie: Drink it neat.
Attendant: Well, how's the world been using you?
Archie: Now and then.
Attendant: Where are you working?
Archie: Here and there.
Attendant: What do you work at?
Archie: This and that.
Attendant: Do you have to work hard?
Archie: On and off.

................................/ cont....

(w/c 28 February 1910)

"SKATING" AT THE SHEFFIELD HIPPODROME

You must see 'Archibald' at Barrasford's Hippodrome this week. He is a prominent figure in Karno's latest absurdity Skating, which last night made the audience laugh until they cried. There are two scenes, the exterior and interior of a skating rink, and the fun is fast and furious. Inside the rink 'Archibald' and 'lady' friends provide any amount of good comedy – it is really remarkable how they seem to fall so naturally – and there is also some first-class skating by a talented company.

(*Yorkshire Telegraph* – 1 March 1910)

There are those who like to claim that Chaplin's 1916 film *The Rink* is based upon *Skating* but, if you study the film *The Rink,* and scrutinise the script for *Skating,* you will find that the only similarity between the two is that people are, well er! – skating.

In later life Stan Laurel said of one member of the 'Skating' company:

I feel I'm in a class with old Charlie Griffith, 'Whimmy Walker' & old George Farnley – what characters they were! We don't see those types of personalities any more, what funny comics they were – remember when we played Skating? Farnley could never skate. Before we went on he used to say: "Now, not too boisterous Boy. I can't walk with these bloody wheels on mi plates. If you knock me down you'll bloody well 'ave to drag me orf – so 'elp me, I'll never be able to get up again!"

(Letter from Stan Laurel to Fred Karno Jnr. – 3 July 1959)

In March, Syd Chaplin transferred from the No.1 'Skating' company, and took over the lead in Charlie and Stan's company. This was so that he could train the new actors brought in to fill the gap shortly to be left by the out-going Charlie and Stan. When they did leave – after the week at the Hackney Empire, 9 April 1910 – Syd continued in *Skating,* while Charlie and Stan went into a brand new sketch, *Jimmy the Fearless.* The lead role in this may have been Karno's twenty-first birthday present to Charlie. If so, it turned out to be an unwanted gift, as witnessed by Stan Laurel:

Presently we started rehearsals for a new sketch called *Jimmy the Fearless*, in which Charlie was naturally cast for the leading part, while I was just one of the cowboys in the background. Then, one day, Fred Karno himself dropped in to see how things were shaping and, to tell the truth, said he didn't like Charlie's interpretation of the comedy role. Thereupon Charlie replied that he didn't like the part anyway, and said that he would rather not play it.

(*Tit-Bits* – 14 November 1936)

To Stan's amazement, Frank O'Neill immediately put him up for the part, and Karno nodded his assent. On the opening night the company were appearing at two theatres – Willesden and Ealing – and had to travel between them by one of Karno's private buses.

Stan Laurel:

The show was a terrific hit. I had to take five curtain calls. You can imagine how I felt. I was a 'star' comedian, at last, and a Karno one at that!

Such an enthusiastic response was too much to bear for Chaplin who, after watching the sketch, stated he liked the 'potential' of the part, and decided he would do it after all. Others might prefer to say he took the part after witnessing *Stan's* potential. Stan, however, was more than happy to give praise where praise was due. To biographer John McCabe he opined:

I never quite understood why Charlie didn't take the part in *Jimmy the Fearless.* I thought it was a wonderful sketch, so I jumped at the chance to play 'Jimmy.'

Charlie was out front the opening night and right after the show he told Karno he had made a mistake. He wanted to play Jimmy. And he did. I didn't feel bitter about

"JIMMY THE FEARLESS"

Written by:- Fred Karno and - Charles Baldwin

SCENE 2. ENTER JIMMY.
Hands up. I've got the drop on yer.
Business - Ike put hands up.

(Omnes) ------ the Fearless
Ay - Jimmy the Fearless. So, Ike, you thought when you shot
my mustang and I fell over the cliff - that you had done for
me. Now go.

----- did you escape?
When I went over the cliff - I dropped on to a grissly -
that broke my fall - hastily I mounted a buffalo and
followed your tracks and got here in time to save you.

----- brave of you.
It's nothing. But you must rest. Go into yonder room while I
catch a couple of bronchos. We must leave this place by
daybreak. Good night dear one. One chaste salute.   (kisses
her and sees her off - business)
So Alkali Ike has crossed my path again.
Indian mouth rattle heard off.
'Tis Wampum na Washti the Indian Chief.
Does Indian mouth rattle.
ENTER - Wampum na Washti a typical Red Indian
in War paint - feathers etc.

----- is sad.
Ay - I am not myself to-night.

----- fourteen of his enemies.
Yes - curse it - but my greatest enemy has again escaped me.
Umpuni na Umpini sackety way long.

------ Nerper na muni no.
Nanty munjari sculpa thi letty.

------ Uti language fluently.
Does Man-afraid-of-soap imagine that Jimmy the Fearless has
spent years on the Prairie without keeping his lugs open.
I long for the day when I shall meet my enemy

......................../ cont....

(Reproduction of original script – courtesy of Associated Chaplin)

Anyone reading the above script will immediately realise just why Chaplin turned down the part of
'Jimmy.' There just doesn't seem to be anything in it which sounds in the remotest bit funny. But then
it has already been said of Karno: "Although he could never adequately put his ideas down on paper,
his personal coaching ensured the crafting of hilarious sketches." The man must have been a
miracle-worker.

it. For me, Charlie was, is, and always will be, the greatest comedian in the world. I thought he should have had the part to begin with. But after that I used to kid him – always very proudly – that for once in my life Charlie Chaplin was my replacement.

Well Stan may have been kidding, but Chaplin wasn't going to risk anyone else saying that Stan Laurel had bested him, and so omitted the whole of his involvement with this long-running sketch from his memoirs. So the mystery remains: "Just why did Chaplin turn down the part of 'Jimmy'?" Stan didn't know, and Chaplin chose not to enlighten us, but I believe it stemmed from his losing face during the time he had played 'Stiffy.' To repeat a quote used earlier in this book, in which Chaplin confessed:

> Great as my disappointment was about *The Football Match*, I tried not to dwell on it. But I was haunted by a thought that perhaps I was not equal to taking Weldon's place. As I had had not fully retrieved my confidence, every new sketch in which I played the leading comedy part was a trial of fear.

But Chaplin had adapted magnificently to the role of every character to date whose shoes he had stepped into. And there, I believe is the whole kernel of the matter. From 'Billy – the Page' in *Sherlock Holmes*, to Walford Bodie, and Dick Turpin in *Casey Circus*, and through all the parts he had played in the Karno sketches, Charlie had never had to invent a character. Chaplin's gift was for mimicry and, in every case so far, he had seen the actual person he was about to impersonate, or had seen the role being played by an actor whose place he was about to take. But 'Jimmy' was a completely new character, a character that he would have to find, to develop, to make likeable, and to make funny. And that, I believe, is what frightened the hell out of him. His one and only previous comic creation had been Sam Cohen, which had been a totally misplaced and mischosen invention. However, once Chaplin had seen Laurel as 'Jimmy,' all the unknown elements had been revealed. Laurel had created the character, made him likeable and, most importantly of all, had shown Chaplin how to translate the words and action from the written word, and make them funny ON STAGE. Now Chaplin had nothing to fear. All he needed do was mimic the character that Stan Jefferson had brought to life.

So, with Chaplin in the eponymous role of 'The Boy 'Ero', and Jefferson back to being a lowly cowboy, *Jimmy the Fearless* toured the U.K. In omitting 'Jimmy' from his memoirs Chaplin denied himself the opportunity to reveal some flattering reviews; reviews which actually give more praise to Chaplin than to the sketch itself, which is a considerable achievement considering the reputation attached to Karno productions. The review at the Stratford Empire ran:

> As it stands at present, *Jimmy the Fearless*, is hardly likely to emulate the success of its predecessors. The best work is done by Chas. Chaplin in the name part.

> (25 April 1910)

And from the Swansea Empire review:

> Fred Karno's latest production causes much laughter. The name part is cleverly acted by Charles Chaplin.

> (11 July 1910)

For his appearance at Leeds Empire, Chaplin was singled out for high praise indeed:

> To assume roles made famous by Fred Kitchen is no small task for a stripling of twenty-one, yet Mr. Chas. Chaplin, who has caused so much laughter this week as "Jimmy the Fearless," has done so with vast credit to himself. Mr. Chaplin has not been more that three years with Mr. Karno, yet he has played all the principal parts, and he fully realizes the responsibility of following so consummate an artiste as Fred Kitchen. He is ambitious and painstaking, and is bound to get on. Young as he is, he has done some good work on the stage, and his entrance alone in "Jimmy the Fearless" sets the house in a roar and stamps him as a born comedian.

> (*Yorkshire Evening Post* – 23 July 1910)

THE STAGE

28 APRIL 1910

THE STRATFORD EMPIRE

On Monday 25 April, was produced here a sketch, in four scenes, entitled:-

'Jimmy, the Fearless'

Jimmy	Mr. Chas. Chaplin
Alkali Ike	Mr. Bert Williams
Jimmy's Father	Mr. Arthur Dandoe
Mike	Mr. Mike Asher
Jimmy's Mother	Miss Emily Seaman
Bartender	Mr. Ernest Stone
Washti Wampa	Mr. Albert Austin
Chinaman	Mr. Harry Daniels
Gwendolen	Mrs. B. Williams

Scene 1:   A Hearty Supper and its After-Effects - The Nightmare;

Scene 2:   'The Dog's Nose' Drinking Saloon, Deadman's Gulch.

Scene 3:   The Rocky Mountains - The Attack - The Hand-to-Hand Fight - Saving the Girl - The Rescue - Jimmy Triumphs;

Scene 4:   Then He Awoke!

The name of Fred Karno has so long been a household word in the music hall world, and the popularity of his enterprises so indisputable, that the success of a new production associated with his name is invariably looked upon as assured. It is therefore surprising that *Jimmy, the Fearless*, which is being presented here after a preliminary run at Willesden should prove such a feeble affair. Of course, one hardly looks for a plot in sketches of this class, but rather humorous situations and individual cleverness: these features, however, which often redeem a weak show from mediocrity, are strangely absent. In the 'big' scene there is a quite unnecessary display of six-shooters, and indiscriminate firing is maintained. This is neither skilful, funny, or necessary. The theme is somewhat reminiscent of *When Knights Were Bold*. Jimmy, the son of a raucous-voiced collier, has a penchant for blood-curdling literature. His parents naturally do not approve of this, and during supper Jimmy is treated to a dissertation on the manifold troubles that are bound to follow should he persist in ignoring their advice. Jimmy is not convinced, however, and, when his parents have retired, seats him

self comfortably in front of the fire and voraciously devours his latest weekly - "The Boy Avenger of the Plains" in which the boy avenger comes up against 'Alkali Ike' - the bad man of Deadman's Gulch. This done, he sinks into the arms of Morpheus, and shortly (in his dream) finds himself at the Dog's Nose Drinking Saloon, Deadman's Gulch, where his 'tart' as he touchingly calls her, has been kidnapped by Alkali Ike. This worthy is drinking and making merry in company with a dozen mates to the accompaniment of deafening pistol reports when Jimmy, the Fearless, stalks in. He quickly clears the saloon, and flies to the Rocky Mountains where he engages in a fight with the notorious Ike. Next he confronts a pirate band, to whom he demonstrates his prowess with the cutlass, before returning home in triumph with his fairy princess and a hoard of treasure and gold coins, only to find his parents turned into the street for debt. This affords an opportunity for the introduction of the note of comedy-pathos, without which these shows would appear to be incomplete. Jim clears off the arrears and the family decide to enter the portals of the workhouse together. This marks the conclusion of the penultimate scene, and, incidentally, the dream. The next morning Jim's father, prior to starting his day's work, discovers his progeny noisily snoring in the kitchen armchair, gripping in his hand one of the banned tales. This is the last straw, and his anger rising he roughly pulls the unhappy Jim out of the chair. The last view we have of the Fearless one is as he is ignominiously chastised by his father. The performance calls for little comment. The best work is done by Chas. Chaplin in the name part, and Arthur Dandoe as Jimmy's father. As it stands at present, *Jimmy the Fearless*, is hardly likely to emulate the success of its predecessors. The scenery and dressing are adequate without being in any way pretentious. The show is produced by Fred Karno in conjunction with Charles Baldwin and Frank O'Neill.

Facsimilie of a review for *Jimmy the Fearless*, at the Stratford Empire, taken from different sources so as to include as much as the business as possible.

A fourth, from the Ardwick Green Empire read:

> Somehow the performance is not so amusing as it ought to be, but the swank of the invincible hero makes one laugh fitfully.

(15 August 1910)

A little of Chaplin's movements during his week at the Ardwick Green Empire, Manchester, came to light some eleven years later. He had stayed in digs at 226 Brunswick-street, just a few hundred yards from the theatre, where the landlady was a Mrs. Rome. In September 1921 she told a reporter from the *Manchester Evening Chronicle.*

> "Oh, yes," replied Mrs. Rome, "he was always full of fun. He stayed with us during the week ending August 21, 1910."

> It was then that Mrs. Rome produced a visitors' book, with no little amount of pride, turned the pages over until, familiar to me, were the words at the head of this article.

BARON ALSO SIGNS

The full text was:-

> "Have been most comfortable with Mrs. Rome.
>
> Shall always be pleased to return.
>
> Best wishes to you, Ma,
>
> also to my little 'Sarah.' – Yours,
>
> SIR CHARLES CHAPLIN,
>
> BARON ROTHSCHILD REEVES."

"You will notice," said Mrs. Rome, "that Charlie mentions he would be pleased to return.

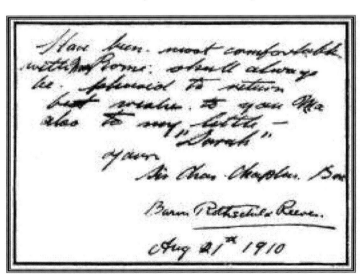

Chaplin's handwritten entry in Mrs. Rome's Guest Book, during his stay in digs in Manchester.

"Charlie was always so pleasing and jolly. In fact, he was always full of fun," added Mrs Rome.

"Did he wear that well-known moustache in this sketch, or on the other hand did he have his notorious baggy trousers?"

"No. He wore a red brown costume, and looked more like a cowboy."

"Baron Rothschild Reeves was Alf Reeves, the actor-manager of the company," stated Mrs. Rome.

Mrs. Rome added that Charlie was very popular with all the rest of the household. He was fond of a game of cards, and played regularly with Mr. Rome and Mr. Reeves, amongst others.

Alf Reeves, Karno's top manager, remembered one outstanding bit of business which Charlie performed in the kitchen scene of *Jimmy the Fearless:*

> His father in the skit was ordering him to drop his novel and eat his supper. 'Get on with it now, m'lad,' and jabbing a loaf of bread at him. Charlie, I noticed, cut the bread without once taking his eyes off his [comic] book. But what particularly attracted my attention was

that while he absentmindedly kept cutting the bread, he held the knife in his left hand. Charlie's left-handed, but I didn't know it then. The next thing I knew, he had carved that loaf into the shape of a concertina.

(Photoplay – August 1934)

Well no-one can deny that Chaplin had a flair for comic invention, but had he in fact invented this piece of business? Here is what Stan Laurel had to say of *his* recollections of the night *he* debuted as 'Jimmy,' before Charlie took the role:

> It was winter and, according to custom, the principals sat inside [the Karno buses] and the lesser lights sat on top. Not yet having earned my spurs, I had an outside seat and, as usual, carried a hot potato to keep my hands warm, as well as to provide a little supper after the show.

> But my hands were warm enough that night. In fact, I was hot all over. One of my bits of business was to cut myself a slice of bread, but I was so nervous that I cut the loaf into a sort of spiral. To cover my embarrassment I picked up the loaf and pulled it in and out, as if it were a concertina. That made the audience laugh, and gave me confidence.

(Tit-Bits – 14 November 1936)

Laurel tagged onto his reminiscences:

> Jimmy, and the memory of that role and of that production stayed with him [Charlie] all his life, I think. You can see *Jimmy the Fearless* all over some of his pictures-dream sequences for instance. He was fond of them, especially in his early pictures. And when it comes right down to it, I've always thought that poor, brave, dreamy Jimmy one day grew up to be Charlie the Tramp.

And therein lies the problem. Chaplin wants everyone to believe that 'The Tramp' was conceived and fathered by him, and him alone. Anyone contesting parentage is eliminated from his records; but, as we have already seen, there are others who have claim to fathering 'The Tramp,' and more to come.

Charlie and Stan toured in *Jimmy the Fearless* till the end of August, then switched to a brand new sketch entitled *The Wow-Wows*, a sketch satirising an initiation into a secret society. After playing this sketch in London for just two weeks, they moved slightly farther afield – America.

So just *how* had Chaplin made this quantum leap, from London to New York? An article in a 1934 edition of *Photoplay*, written following an interview with Alf Reeves, purports to provide the answer. Back in 1910, following a return to England with the Karno troupe he had taken to the U.S. in September 1909, Reeves began recruiting for the next tour, which was to commence September 1910:

> Amy Minister helpfully suggested: "Al, there's a clever boy in the Karno troupe at the Holloway Empire. His name's Charlie Chaplin. He's a wonderful kid and a marvellous actor."

> "I'll have to look at him," decided Reeves. You see, Amy's word went a long way with Al. [1] So, climbing to the top of a bus, he swayed and rumbled through the fog to North London. There, swinging down at Holloway, he pushed through the doors of the murky Empire, with his weather eye out for the lad Amy liked. On the stage, living up to his high recommendation, was a youngster acting away for dear life.

Chaplin gives a totally separate account of this meeting but, with his usual flair for inaccuracy, cites a different sketch, in a different theatre, in a different city.

---

[1] There was an "AL" REEVES (real name, Alfred H. Reeves), comedian and burlesque actor and entertainer, working in American vaudeville in the 1910s. By his use of "Al" throughout this piece it would seem as though the journalist was unable to distinguish between the two.

Alf Reeves, the manager of Karno's American company, returned to England and rumour had it that he was looking for a principal comedian to take back with him to the states.

Since my major setback at the Oxford Music Hall, I was full of the idea of going to America, not alone for the thrill and adventure of it, but because it would mean renewed hope, a new beginning in a new world. Fortunately *Skating*, one of our new sketches in which I was the leading comedian, was going over with great success in Birmingham and when Mr. Reeves joined our company there, I pinned on him as much charm as I could; with the result that Reeves wired Karno that he had found his comedian for the states.

(Chaplin's 1964 autobiography)

Well at least Chaplin got Alf Reeves' name right. Chaplin did play in *Skating* at the Birmingham Hippodrome, but that was much earlier in the year, week commencing 21 February 1910, probably before Alf Reeves had even returned to England. But then, w/c 2 May 1910, Chaplin played in *Jimmy the Fearless*, at the Holloway Empire. So, which one is correct? Well, Reeves goes on to describe the sketch Charlie was in:

"What sort of part was he playing?" I asked Reeves in his office at the Hollywood studio, where he was busy with plans for the forthcoming Chaplin picture.

"A dime-novel-struck London errand boy, forever reading Wild West blood-and-thunder thrillers," he recalled.

"And what was the first thing you heard him say?"

"You'll never believe it," he grinned, "but just as I popped in he was putting great dramatic fire into the good old speech, "Another shot rang out, and another redskin bit the dust!""

"How was he dressed?" Somehow, I never can imagine Charlie Chaplin in anything but the inspired outfit which has become part and parcel of him.

"He looked," Reeves described, "the typical London street urchin who knows every inch of the town as he darts through hurrying throngs and dodges in and out of rushing traffic, managing by some miracle to escape with his life. He had a cap on the back of his head and wore a shabby old suit, short in the sleeves and frayed at the cuffs-a suit he had long since outgrown."

"Do you remember the name of the piece he was in?"

"I'll never forget it!" he laughed. "It was 'Jimmy the Fearless.' a right-enough name so far as that goes. He had the leading part."

"Then he had got on, even at that time?"

"Indeed he had," Reeves proudly agreed, "though only in his teens."[2]

(*Photoplay* – August 1934)

So that's clear enough – Chaplin was obviously playing in *Jimmy the Fearless*, which rules out Birmingham Hippodrome, week commencing 21 February, where *Skating* was the sketch. However, the latter date does have a special significance. It was exactly two years, to the day, since Chaplin had signed his first contract with Karno. This meant that both sides would have to come together to agree if they were going to go ahead with the third year option. But was it Reeves who went along to arrange terms? I don't believe it was. February would seem to be far too early in the year for Reeves to have returned to England.

So Reeves' version is correct. His account of recruiting Chaplin continues:

---

[2] Reeves must have used Chaplin's method of working out his age. Charlie was TWENTY-ONE when he appeared in Jimmy the Fearless.

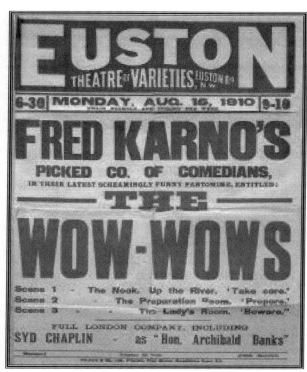

Two posters advertising "SKATING" and "THE WOW-WOWS."

(By kind permission of Associated Chaplin)

Directly after the performance Charlie Chaplin had an unexpected visitor and a most unexpected offer.

"Will I go to America?" he cried. "Only too gladly, if you'll take me!"

"I told him," related Reeves, "I'd have a talk with Karno." At hearing this, he wiped the smudge of make-up off his face to give his smile full play, and I saw he was a very good-looking boy. I had made up my mind about him before leaving his dressing room.

"Well," considered Karno, "you can have him for the American company if you think he's old enough for the parts." "He's old enough," I told Karno, "and big enough and clever enough for anything." We were then giving "A Night in an English Music Hall," "A Night in a London Club," and "A Night in a London Secret Society."

That settled it. Al lost no time in carrying the news to Amy.

"You're a good judge of talent, my girl" he assured her. "What about a bite of dinner together?" A little celebration was in order, for, thanks to a woman, Charlie Chaplin had been "discovered" for America.

(*Photoplay* – August, 1934)

So why does Chaplin cite Birmingham, and Reeves cite *Jimmy the Fearless*, when they don't match up? Well they do, if one rolls forward, for Chaplin played in *Jimmy the Fearless*, at the Birmingham Empire Palace, w/c 25 July. But what has this got to do with their meeting? Well, it was simply that Reeves went to see Chaplin again, to confirm that he was going to America. Following on from their first meeting, Chaplin himself explains

[..... with the result that Reeves wired Karno that he had found his comedian for the states.] But Karno had other plans for me. This sickening fact left me in doubt for several weeks until he became interested in a sketch called The Wow-Wows. It was a burlesque on initiating a member into a secret society. Reeves and I thought the show silly, fatuous and without merit. But Karno was obsessed with the idea and insisted that America was full of secret societies and that a burlesque on them would be a great success there, so to my happy relief and excitement, Karno chose me to play the principal part in The Wow-Wows for America.

But there is still something wrong in Reeves' account. Reeves is making out that this was just a one-off visit, whereas Chaplin says Reeves actually joined the company there. Reeves is also giving the impression that Chaplin was totally unknown to him before the visit, and that he only went to see Chaplin on Amy Minister's say-so. But there is a prior history between the three of them. Amy Minister had already been on three U.S. Karno tours – 1906-7; 1907-8; and 1909-10. In 1908, between the American tours, she had toured London and the suburbs with different Karno companies, six weeks of which was as a member of the Karno Company headed by Syd Chaplin. And who else was in that company? Why, Charlie Chaplin of course. And who joined that company in August, as acting manager? – None other than Alf Reeves.

Using several pieces, instead of just the two supplied by Chaplin and Reeves, we *may* now have the correct sequence of events:

21 February 1910 BIRMINGHAM, Hippodrome *Skating*
Charlie is principal comic in *Skating*. Someone from the Karno management team goes to see him about the third year option on his contract. It seems as though one of the parties didn't sign immediately, as the next-but-one contract was to begin on 11 March 1911, which may indicate that the 1910 contract was signed on 11 March 1910.

02 May HOLLOWAY, Empire *Jimmy the Fearless*
Charlie is principal comic. Reeves offers him the chance of going to America. Reeves informs Karno, but Karno keeps him waiting for the answer.

25 July BIRMINGHAM, Empire Palace *Jimmy the Fearless*
Charlie is principal comic. Reeves confirms that Karno says he can go to America, but it will be in *The Wow-Wows*.

08 August LIVERPOOL, Empire *Jimmy the Fearless* – should have played, but was withdrawn and comedian Mike S. Wallen stood in. This could well have been so that the members who were about to go to America could shoot down to London to rehearse *The Wow-Wows*, during its debut week at both East Ham Palace and Tottenham Palace, with Syd in the lead role.

29 August BRADFORD, Empire *Jimmy the Fearless* – finishes its run at the end of this week.

05 September WOOLWICH, Hippodrome *The Wow-Wows* – Charlie is able to play a try-out week, after having previously rehearsed the sketch with Syd during it's London debut.

12 September ILFORD, Hippodrome *The Wow-Wows*
doubling with SHOREDITCH, Olympia *The Wow-Wows*
Syd Chaplin is almost certainly playing the lead at one venue, while Charlie is playing the lead at the other, as this was a common arrangement made by Karno. Stan Jefferson and the rest of those about to go to New York would also have been in the company.

19 September ISLINGTON, Empire *The Wow-Wows*
Syd Chaplin continues in The Wow-Wows on the English circuit while, later in the week, Charlie Chaplin and Stan Jefferson go off to America with the second company.

The nineteenth of September was also the day Chaplin signed a new, three-year, contract with

Karno. Because the old agreement still had till February 1911 to run, the new one would start in March. However, there was a rider clause appended:

> It is understood that should the Manager require the said Artiste to perform in the United States of America prior to or during the period of this Contract, He shall pay the said Artiste the Salary of Ten pounds per week for the first year and Twelve pounds per week for the second year and Fifteen pounds per week for the third year – inclusive of all performances at all times.

> (From original contract – courtesy of Associated Chaplin)

David Robinson records that the new agreement was for £6, £8, and £10 per week in those three years but, as I have a copy of the contract in front of me, I can assure you it is for the above figures. Perhaps the lower figures are what Chaplin would have received had he remained in England. As to why Chaplin wanted to go to America, just when he was nearing the top rung of the Karno ladder, he told:

> This chance to go to the United States was what I needed. In England I felt I had reached the limit of my prospects; besides, my opportunities there were circumscribed. With scant educational background, if I failed as a music-hall comedian I would have little chance but to do menial work. In the States the prospects were brighter.

> The night before sailing, I walked about the West End of London, pausing at Leicester Square, Coventry Street, the Mall and Piccadilly, with the wistful feeling that it would be the last time I would see London, for I had made up my mind to settle permanently in America.

> I loathed saying goodbye. I was up at six in the morning. Therefore I did not bother to wake Sydney, but left a note on the table stating: "Off to America. Will keep you posted. Love, Charlie."

What better way to end a chapter!

Chapter 13

VARIETY TO VAUDEVILLE

The full Karno company setting off to play New York was: Alfred Reeves, Amy Minister, Charles Chaplin, Albert Austin, Albert Williams, George Henry Seaman, Emily Seaman, Frank Melroyd, Fred Westcott (aka: Fred Karno Jnr.), Stanley Jefferson, Arthur Dandoe, Fred Palmer, Muriel Palmer, Mike Asher, and Charlie Griffiths – totalling twelve men and three women.

After missing the *SS Lusitania*, which left Liverpool on 17 September, our intrepid travellers ended up on the British steamer the *Cairnrona*. This had two major drawbacks: it was a converted cattle-boat and, instead of going to New York, was going to Montreal. How they were to rue missing the *Lusitania*, and the comfort it would have afforded them. From leaving Southampton on 22 September 1910, the passengers on the *Cairnrona* had to endure bad weather and rough seas. This not only incapacitated the passengers but also the ship, for which there was a three-day delay while the broken rudder was repaired. Consequently, during the eleven days between departure and arrival, rehearsals were infrequent.

The Karno Company aboard the *SS Cairnrona*, bound for Quebec, 22 September 1910.
Back Row L-R: Albert Austin, Fred Palmer, Bert Williams, George Seaman, Frank Melroyd.
Middle Row: Stan Jefferson, Fred Karno Jnr., Charles Chaplin, Arthur Dandoe.
Front Row: Muriel Palmer, Mike Asher, Amy Minister, the Captain.
(Missing from picture: Emily Seaman, Charles Griffiths, Alf Reeves.)

After finally disembarking on Sunday 2 October, and taking a train ride via Toronto, the weary and travel-stained company arrived with a little over twenty-four hours to spare before the opening curtain at the Colonial Theatre, New York[1]. Walking around in daylight hours, Chaplin found the city to be bewildering, and a little frightening. Of his inner feelings he said he felt 'inadequate'; 'uncomfortable'; 'lone'; and 'isolated'. However, in the evening, the city took on a new dimension, for which Chaplin had more of an affinity:

> As I walked along Broadway with the crowd dressed in their summer clothes, I became reassured. We had left England in the middle of a bitter cold September and arrived in New York in an Indian summer with a temperature of eighty degrees; and as I walked along Broadway it began to light up with myriads of coloured electric bulbs and sparkled like a brilliant jewel. And in the warm night my attitude changed and the meaning of America came to me: the tall skyscrapers, the brilliant gay lights, the thrilling display of advertisements stirred me with hope and a sense of adventure. "This is it!" I said to myself. "This is were I belong!"

Sad to say, this feeling of belonging was to last less then twenty-four hours. To be exact, until the review for the first evening's show came out. The chosen sketch was the one they had most recently played back in London – *The Wow-Wows* (subtitled: *A Night in a London Secret Society*). Karno thought that America was full of secret societies, and so a burlesque on them would be a great success. Stan Laurel said of this:

> Karno was dead wrong. *The Wow-Wows* was awful. Everybody in the company said so during all those dreary days of rehearsal [back in England].
>
> (*CHARLIE CHAPLIN* – John McCabe)

Chaplin too thought it a bad choice:

> Reeves and I thought the show silly, fatuous, and without merit.
>
> ..... and I had advised Karno not to open with it.
>
> (*My Autobiography*, Charles Chaplin – 1964)

The fears the latter two had held were to be borne out in the review printed in the show business newspaper *Variety*:

(w/c Monday October 3, 1910)

NEW YORK, Colonial Theater

A Karno company that talks seemed to hit the Colonial audience as a bit queer. Having seen the 'Music Hall,' 'Slums' and 'Dandy Thieves' [performed by previous companies], it is but natural that American audiences should expect only pantomime from a Karno group. Anyone familiar with London music halls at all will not be surprised, for most of the Karno productions over there depend to some extent upon dialog. *The Wow Wows* is the real English type of Karno act, with the red nose comic in the fore, and the proceedings built around him.

Laid in three scenes, the act consists merely of a burlesque on a secret society initiation. To 'get even' on the 'tightwad' of a summer camp, the rest of the bunch frame up a phony secret society into which they initiate M. Neverloosen[2].

Charles Chaplin is the 'mark' and chief comedian. Chaplin is typically English, the sort of comedian that the American audiences seem to like, although unaccustomed to. His manner is quiet and easy and he goes about his work in a devil-may-care manner, in direct contrast to the twenty-minutes-from-a-cemetery make-up he employs.

---

[1] In his autobiography, Chaplin states that they took a rehearsal room and spent a week rehearsing *The Wow-Wows*. He also says that Whimsical Walker was in the cast. Both these statements are incorrect when applied to the 1910 tour, but do fit the tour the company were to make in 1912.
[2] Chaplin's role was 'Archibald Binks' – 'M. Neverloosen' is merely a term to reflect that he was a 'tightwad.'

The make-up and the manner in themselves are funny. That is what will have to carry *The Wow-Wows* over, if it goes that way. Chaplin will do all right for America, but it is too bad that he didn't first appear in New York with something more in it than this piece. The company amounts to little, because there is little for them to do. Dialog in the opening doesn't amount to anything and at intervals during the piece there are talky places which drags the time when Chaplin does not occupy the center[3] of the stage.

In the last scene-initiating chamber-there are one or two funny bits of business. Three women in the act are not needed. One has a scene with the comedian; the others simply walk on and off a couple of times. The genuine fun in *The Wow-Wows* is not quite enough to stand off the half-hour of running time. The act can be fixed by interjecting more speed, and cutting the unnecessary talk.

The Colonial audience laughed at the show Monday night, but not enough. An act of this sort, erected solely for comedy, should register a bigger percentage of laughs.

(*Variety* – October 8, 1910)

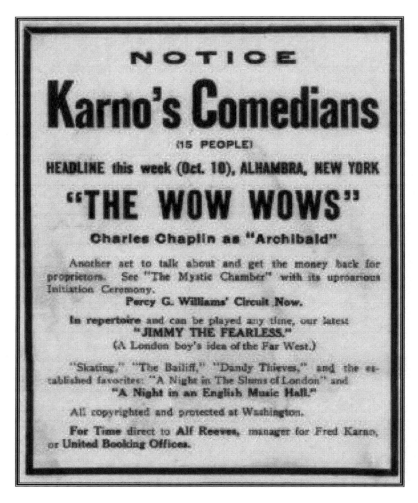

The Wow-Wows, written by Herbert Sydney, owes much of its premise to the sketch *A Night in a Chamber of Horrors*, which Charles Baldwin produced in November 1909. In the latter, as part of an initiation ceremony, a group of wags make one of their members spend a night alone in the Chamber of Horrors in 'Baxter's Famous Waxworks.'. Somewhere between then and August 1910 the idea had been "borrowed" by Karno, and the setting moved to that of a campsite by the river. I would surmise that Herbert Sydney didn't write the additional scene, as

---

[3] U.S. variant spellings have been left in, in all reviews quoted from American newspaper sources.

it differed greatly from his usual style of work. Sydney wrote 'business' (a term for physical/visual gags) not verbal humour. He was to write at least three subsequent sketches for Karno, but let it be put on record that his greatest creation was *Mumming Birds*, which relies little, if at all, on verbal dexterities. The first scene of *The Wow-Wows*, however, is just a succession of terrible puns, enough to make even the most receptive of audiences groan. Consider having to endure the following:

Jimmy:	There's two eggs for you, but they're both rotten.
Archie:	What, that one bad and that one bad?
Jimmy:	Yes.
Archie:	Oh that's too bad. I am a devil when I crack these little jokes.
Lydia:	Oh, how dreadful, I say dear, have you been in for your morning dip?
Archie:	Yes, I've had my usual river plunge.
Lydia:	And was the water up to your expectations?
Archie:	No, only up to my knees.

If you can stand any more of this, read the extract from the script reproduced on the next page. The audience certainly couldn't. At the following week's venue, the Alhambra on 7th Avenue, one reviewer branded the cast: ".. a collection of blithering, blathering Englishmen," and with material like the above, who could question him?

(w/c Monday October 10,1910)

A Night in a Secret Society

Now, in Charles Chaplin, is so arriving a comedian that Mr Karno will be forgiven for whatever else the act may lack. The most enthusiastic Karno-ite will surely admit, too, the act lacks a great deal that might help to make it vastly more entertaining. Still, Mr. Chaplin heads the cast, so the people laughed and were content.

He plays Archibald, a chappie with one end of his moustache turned up and the other turned down, a chappie with spots on his face betokening many a bad night, a chappie who declared himself in on everything though never paying his or any share. [hence: 'Mr. Neverloosen'].

His first appearance is made from a tent, one of several occupied by a camping party. He looks more than seedy, despite his dress being immaculate.

'How are you, Archie?' inquires a woman visitor, decidedly attractive, and of whom Archie appears to be enamoured.

'Not well,' he responds. 'I just had a terrible dream.'

'Very terrible?' she asks solicitously.

'Oh, frightful!' says Archie. 'I dreamed I was being chased by a caterpillar.'

Archie makes such remarks as this in an exceedingly droll, ludicrous fashion. Outside Archie the company is composed of the most remarkable collection of blithering, blathering Englishmen New York has seen in many a day.

(*New York Clipper* – October 1910)

Karno had allowed the first three rules of comedy to be broken: 'No puns; no puns; no puns.' Even worse, the sketch had been stripped of nearly all its comedic business by relocating it from a Chamber of Horrors to what was merely a darkened room, in 'Brown's Lodge' on the campsite. Here, the only 'horror' Archibald had to endure was sitting on an electrified magic-carpet. Oooo! – scary! This obvious omission didn't seem to have occurred to whomsoever was responsible

THE WOW WOWS

A Farcical Sketch in 3 Scenes.
Scene 1 – Up the River
Scene 2 – Corridor at Brown's Club House
Scene 3 – the "Lodge" at Brown's

Characters:
Hon. Archibald Binks   Who won't pay his share
Charlie Blazer
Jimmy Bottles
Freddy Brunton
Billie Brindle   His friends are determined to make him pay
Miss Lydia Flopp   Archie's sweetheart
Florrie & Vi   Up River girls

Tom. Dick. Harry. Alf. Charlie. Frank. Jack. Etc - Up River
men on their holidays.

Scene 1 – Blazer is shaving, Brunton on stool reading paper.
Bottles cooking breakfast at table. Up river men cross left
to right, with boat oars over shoulder. 2nd man knocks up
against Blazer.
Blazer: Confound you, man, can't you see I'm shaving.
2nd Man: Sorry old man, an accident.
Blazer: Sorry, so am I. I'll have no face left shortly.
(more bus. with oars)
Brunton: Its going to be a glorious day, Blazer!
(talk about rain, and being tired of standing Archibald
drinks without him ever paying.
Archie enters):
[Archie: Good morning Brunton. Do you mind giving me a
little water?
Brunton: Certainly. What do you want if for?]
Archie: I'm going to have a bath. I say, Jimmy, what have
you for breakfast?
Jimmy: There's two eggs for you, but they're both rotten.
Archie: What, that one bad and that one bad?
Jimmy: Yes.
Archie: Oh that's too bad. I am a devil when I crack these
little jokes. (to Blazer) I say, Blazer, where are you going
tonight?
Brunton: Well I'll tell you, Archie, tonight we are going
to Brown's Club House to have a lovely supper.
Archie: Ha! That just reminds me, you might tell old Brown
I can't come tonight.
Brunton: My dear old chap, you're not invited.
Archie: No, that's why I can't come. (leaves)
Brunton: (rising): Blazer, he's impossible.
Blazer: He's incorrigible.
Jimmy: He's sickening.

(Reproduction of original script – courtesy of the late – Olive Karno)

for the programme notes, as Scenes 2 and 3 are billed as the 'exterior' and 'interior of the Chamber of Horrors,' respectively. A more accurate description would have been 'the exterior' and 'interior of the Initiation Room.' No wonder the audiences were unimpressed.

Chaplin was particularly affected by the poor reception the sketch received. He had come to conquer America, not run home with his tail between his legs. He reflected:

> Although I hated the sketch, I naturally tried to make the best of it. I will not describe the nerves, agony and suspense that preceded my entrance the first night, or my embarrassment as the American artists stood in the wings watching us. My first joke was considered a big laugh in England and a barometer for how the rest of the comedy would go over. It was a camping scene. I entered from a tent with a cup of tea.
>
> | Archie (me): | Good morning Hudson. Do you mind giving me a little water? |
> | Hudson: | Certainly, what do you want it for? |
> | Archie: | I want to take a bath. |
>
> (A faint snicker, then cold silence from the audience.)
>
> | Hudson: | How did you sleep last night, Archie? |
> | Archie: | Oh! Terribly. I dreamt I was being chased by a caterpillar. |

Still deadly silence. And so we droned on, with faces of the Americans in the wings growing longer and longer. But they were gone before we had finished our act.

To say the least, failure in a foreign country is distressing. Appearing each night before a cold and silent audience as they listened to our effusive, jovial English comedy was a grim affair. We entered and exited from the theatre like fugitives. For six weeks we endured the ignominy. The other performers quarantined us as if we had the plague. When we gathered in the wings to go on, crushed and humiliated, it was as though we were about to be lined up and shot.

Chaplin's only comfort came from the quote in *Variety*: "Chaplin will do all right for America," And it was in America where Chaplin felt his future lay, but not necessarily in his present capacity, as he himself confirms:

> Paradoxically enough, as a result of our failure I began to feel light and unhampered. There were many other opportunities in America. Why should I stick to show business? I was not dedicated to art. Get into another racket! I began to regain confidence. Whatever happened I was determined to stay in America.

(*My Autobiography*, Charles Chaplin – 1964)

So just why had Karno decided not to tour the trusty *Mumming Birds* sketch (re-titled for American audiences: *A Night in an English Music Hall*)? One reason may be found in its earlier history in the U.S. Firstly, there were the incidents in 1906, when the actions of copycat companies had led to Karno disbanding his company. But then in the Autumn-Winter seasons of 1907, 1908, and 1909 Karno had again sent over companies to the States, all of which performed *Mumming Birds*. Now, come the 1910 tour, maybe Karno believed that *Mumming Birds* was too well-known to have any impact.

So with *The Wows-Wows* as the chosen sketch, the morale of the company began to sink lower and lower. But then, in week three, a little ray of hope shone through. Chaplin tells:

> By now we had resigned ourselves to pack up and return to England after six weeks. But the third week we played at the Fifth Avenue Theatre, to an audience composed largely of English butlers and valets. To my surprise on the opening Monday night we went over with a bang. They laughed at every joke. Everyone in the company was surprised, including myself, for I had expected the usual indifferent reception.

(*My Autobiography*, Charles Chaplin – 1964)

A newspaper review sheds further light on just who the audience was composed of:

(w/c October 17, 1910)

Orpheum Theater, Fifth Avenue, Brooklyn

Charles Chaplin, leading comedian of Karno's Comedians, which are playing at the Orpheum Theatre, this week, is being extensively entertained by the British residents of Brooklyn. The members of the St. George Society and the Usonas[4] are among those who have arranged affairs for Mr. Chaplin and his confrères.

(Brooklyn Eagle – October 18, 1910)

The following week they were at the Bronx Theater, at 149th Street and Bergen Avenue, in the area of New York City known as 'the Bronx.' The booking was obtained almost by chance, as this new 2,800-seater theatre had opened only the previous week. This is, and always has been, a tough area, but the audiences inside the theatre seem to have been remarkably kind:

(w/c 24 October)

BRONX, Bronx Theatre

Another act that made its first appearance over the Harlem River side was Karno's *Wow-Wows*, replete with laughter provoking situation. Charles Chaplin, the star of the aggregation, received a wave of applause almost continually after he got started.

(Variety – October 29, 1910)

The following week the troupe were at the Greenpoint Theatre, a theatre so far down the newspaper listings that it often fell off the page. New York theatres then shut their doors on the Karno Company, and they found themselves out-of-town in Fall River, Massachusetts.

Karno's Company, presenting *A Night in a London Music Hall*, is to be the feature attraction of the Loew bill at the Savoy, Fall River (Mass.) next week. This is the inauguration of the full week policy at the house.

(Variety – November 5, 1910)

Their initial six week run with the Percy Williams Agency had now finished, and wasn't about to be extended. And that should have been the end of that. The English entertainers had come, been seen, and been conquered. It was time for Karno's London Comedians to pack up and go back to where they worked best – London.

But then, at the eleventh hour, they were given a reprieve. Chaplin states that owing to a favourable report by an agency representative, on their performance at the Orpheum Theater in Brooklyn, they were given a twenty-two week tour on the Sullivan and Considine circuit of theatres. This is unlikely. For an agent to go into a theatre owned by Orpheum, which had its own huge circuit of theatres, and try to poach an act for the rival Sullivan and Considine circuit could have caused a major battle. Chaplin's statement is inaccurate on a second point, as they weren't booked for the Sullivan and Considine at all.

Marcus Loew was the booker for numerous vaudeville houses in and around New York, including Hammerstein's and the National. He offered to give the Karno Company a try-out week at the latter, but with the proviso that they play *A Night in an English Music Hall*. If the National week were to prove successful, then Lowe would give them a further three weeks work at the American Music Hall, in New York. Week six, in Fall River, had therefore been deliberately set up so that the company could rehearse and work-up 'Music Hall.' And so, on week seven, commencing 14 November, they duly played at the National:

---

[4] USONAS is an acronym for United States Overseas Nannys and Servants – I think!

(w/c November 14, 1910)

BRONX – Loew's National Theatre

A play within a play is "A Night in a English Music Hall." now filling Marcus Loew's fine new National Theatre in the Bronx by its drawing powers as the head-liner. In this comedy skit it's the box-holders having fun with the actors that makes fun for the onlookers. On one side is the schoolboy with his stock of buns and "banawnas," some for eating, more for human target ammunition; on the other side is the real "toff" in a state of real spifflication, and between them the audience are kept in a state of laughable uproar. A burlesque wrestling match brings the act to a climax.

The change of sketch had obviously fixed the problem as, come the Saturday of their week at the National, *Variety* announced:

November 28th the Karno act opens at the American, New York, in 'The Wow-Wows,' remaining there three weeks, playing a different sketch each one. 'Jimmy the Fearless,' and 'The Music Hall' will be the other two.

(*Variety* – November 19, 1910)

Although it was Marcus Loew who had extended the Karno Company's stay in the U.S., it was their very own tour manager, Alf Reeves, who should be given the credit for negotiating the deal. His qualities have rarely, if ever, been acknowledged, and certainly never praised. He didn't just book the hotels and the transport; get the company on and off stage, and on and off trains – he was far more than that. He was the man who had to 'sell' the company to the agencies. Whenever the Karno Company faced rejection, or had bad reviews written about them, he would go into the agency offices, disperse all the negative comments and come out of the meeting with more bookings. The situation in 1910 was very delicate as the Karno Company had been placed on a blacklist. I surmise this was because they broke the rule which states that when an act returns to the States within a year of leaving, they have to do so through the same agency which had last booked them. Somehow, Reeves had managed to get the Karno Company name off the blacklist, and they were able to tour the States once again.

Reeves next secured an additional two weeks at the American Music Hall, making a total of five. This may not seem a lot, but it would at least ensure that Christmas was not spent aboard a ship bound for England. As Reeves well knew, it would also act as a great showcase. The terms of the extended engagement stipulated that the company play their full working repertoire of sketches. For some reason Jimmy the Fearless was sidelined, and so *A Night in an English Music Hall* played week one; *The Wow-Wows* – week two; *A Night in a London Club* – week three; *A Night in London Slums* – week four; and for week five *A Night in an English Music Hall* was repeated. If Reeves thought the cast members might baulk at this schedule, and demand to be allowed to keep *The Wow-Wows* throughout the run, he couldn't have been more wrong. To them, it was like being told to drop one piece of red-hot coal and pick up three cold ones. It may have been extra work, but it was certainly less painful.

The company's fortunes now appeared to be turning. The earlier booking at Fall River, had materialised because the theatre had changed its policy to staying open for the full week, thus causing an unforeseen last-minute demand for acts. For the week commencing 21 November 1910 they were also asked to fill a vacuum. The Nixon-Nirdlinger Agency, who ran a rapidly expanding circuit of theatres, was opening a brand new venue in Philadelphia; simply named 'The Nixon,' and hired the Karno Company for its first week. To perform the actual 'Opening Ceremony' the bookers decided to use a star of the legit stage, rather than one from vaudeville. Chaplin had met this lady before, when she had rendered him a speechless quivering wreck. And the lady's name? Marie Doro.

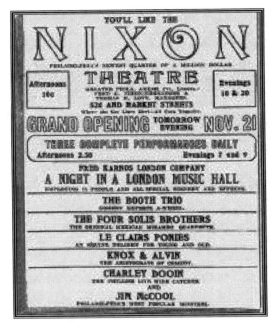

PHILADELPHIA INQUIRER

NOVEMBER 22, 1910

(w/c November 21, 1910)
PHILADELPHIA, Nixon
CROWDS ATTEND
NIXON THEATRE

**Marie Doro Makes Speech at
Opening Night of New Playhouse**

With every seat in the house occupied and the sidewalk outside black with hundreds who could not be accommodated for the first performance, the new Nixon Theatre on Fifty-second street, below Market, was formally opened last night at 7.30 o'clock.

Miss Marie Doro, who is playing at the Broad Street Theater, made the dedicatory address. The performance opened with Le Clair's Ponies, a collection of trained equines, which did stunts little short of marvelous. Charlie Dooin, captain and manager of the Philadelphia baseball team, and a favorite athlete among the fans of his city, was there with his partner Jim McCool. They presented an act which certainly made a hit with the crowd. The Four Solis Brothers, a famous Mexican quartet, pleased all lovers of music, by their selections on the marimbophone. Knox and Alvin kept the audience amused with a very funny sketch. The Booth Trio of trick bicycle riders thrilled every spectator present by their daring feats awheel. The performance ended with the screamingly funny farce entitled *A Night in a London Music Hall*, with Alf Reeves as the star. This sketch employs fifteen persons in its presentation, and has made use of the biggest successes in modern vaudeville. As the intoxicated box-holder, Reeves kept the large audience in paroxisms of laughter.

When he had first met Ms. Doro, in *Sherlock Holmes*, at the Duke of York's Theatre, he had been just a young boy playing a bit part; but now he was a mature man and, what is more, the star performer in his company. So! what did Charlie do to make up for all those lost years since then? Fortunately, he does tell us:

Two or three years later[5] in Philadelphia, I saw her again. She dedicated the opening of a new theatre in which I was playing in Karno's Comedy Company. She was still as beautiful as ever. I stood in the wings watching her in my comedy make-up while she made a speech, but I was too shy to make myself known to her.

Chaplin *did* eventually introduce himself to Marie Doro, and even had dinner with her in the privacy of her hotel suite; but no points for guessing that, by then, he was a huge film star. That boy sure needed a lot of status to overcome his insecurities.

Having broken-in "Music Hall" out-of-town, the act was now ready to bring into New York to start its run at the American Music Hall. The first two weeks passed off with little press attention:

(w/c Monday December 5, 1910)

AMERICAN MUSIC HALL (Hammerstein's)

The Karno Comedians, for their second week here, are offering *The Wow-Wows*. The act has been changed for the better since seen in the United houses, and scored a laughing hit.

(*Variety* – December 10, 1910)

[5] Charlie's "Two or three years later in Philadelphia" should read "SIX years later in Philadelphia,"

SIXTH CONSECUTIVE XMAS IN NEW YORK   **SIXTH CONSECUTIVE XMAS IN NEW YORK**

Fred Karno's Comedians

ESTABLISHED HEADLINERS
"A NIGHT IN AN ENGLISH MUSIC HALL"

"SLUMS OF LONDON"   "DANDY THIEVES"   "WOW WOWS"   "NIGHT IN CLUB," Etc

The Company that is always working and always gets the money back for the proprietor

A Sure Draw   Always a Hit   Always a Great Big Act

Presented in the United States for the Sixth Consecutive Christmas by ALF. REEVES, to whom all communications should be addressed. (En route with the Show.)

COMPLIMENTS OF THE SEASON TO ALL   American Music Hall, New York, Next Week (Dec. 12)

But then, in week three, came the worst review Chaplin could have hoped for; and it had nothing to do with the bad reception many of the acts were given – far from it:

(w/c Monday December 12, 1910)

AMERICAN MUSIC HALL

The show on the stage at the American this week could not have been recognized from the program Monday evening. The bill was all chopped up, many names listed in the billing not appearing on the indicators. The show started rapidly because they died fast. They were dying all evening. But a few successes came out of the eighteen acts. The faster they died the better the show seemed, for that gave speed through speedy exits.

In the second half, Karno's Company in *A Night in a London Club*, a revival over here, made the laughing hit of the bill. Though full of rough slapstick, and the usual Karno ingredients, it looks like the best of all the Karno acts, not excepting 'The Music Hall.' The hit with S. Jefferson as 'the dude' was really very funny. Mr. Jefferson, Chas. Chaplin, Arthur Dandoe, Muriel Palmer and Frank Melroyd all did famously.

(*Variety* – December 17, 1910)

Ho! Ho! – "The hit with S. Jefferson as 'the dude' was really very funny." That's not what Chaplin wanted to hear. In Philadelphia, when Alf Reeves had been credited as keeping the large audience in "paroxisms" (U.S. spelling) of laughter, that was a mistake, but this wasn't. The reviewer genuinely felt that Stan Jefferson as 'Percy Swoffles – the Dude' was the funniest thing in the sketch. Chaplin now had two courses of action to choose from: he could suppress Stan's role, or he could improve his own performance. Having the seen the reviews to come, I can happily inform you that he chose the latter.

For week four the company were to play *A Night in the Slums*, which they had played back in England in January 1910, under its then title – *Early Birds*, but the burden in reviving this sketch was made easier by their having to perform only the second scene: "The Lodging House."

(w/c December 19, 1910)

AMERICAN MUSIC HALL

The Karno Company, for the fourth week, presented the last half of *A Night in the Slums*, and scored easily.

(*Variety* – December 24, 1910)

For week five, commencing Boxing Day, 1910, the company repeated *A Night in an English Music Hall*. Making its debut that same week, at the same venue, was a sketch billed as 'Harlequinade – an old fashioned English pantomime.' The latter term might make one think of such pantomimes as *Cinderella*; *Puss in Boots*; or *Aladdin*; but this one was a 'shadow mime,' i.e. a playlet performed behind a back-lit white screen.

(w/c December 26, 1910)

AMERICAN MUSIC HALL

"A Harlequinade in Black and White" – Shadowgraph Pantomime

The entire action takes place behind the moving-picture sheet. The characters are Clown, Pantaloon, Harlequin, Columbine, Policeman, Nursemaid, and Strolling Musician. The figures are shadowed onto the sheet by means of light placed upon the stage, the entire effect being a motion picture in black and white. The finish, the illusion of the artists leaping out over the heads of the audience, received quite a bit of laughter. It is an expensive little novelty that just filled the mood of the holiday theatregoers and was applauded. As a good filler in at the holiday period it answers.

(*Variety* – December 31, 1910)

Chaplin was very taken by this sketch, and saved the following contemporary newspaper review, in which more of the business was revealed:

It brought forth our old friends: Clown, Pantaloon, Harlequin, Columbine. The pantomime was much more interesting than one would imagine it to be by merely hearing about it, for the pantomimists were funny in their extravagant make-up and actions. There was plenty of action to it, a diversity of ideas shown, and much pleasure derived by the audience, judging by the way they received it.

First the characters indulged in a little general knockabout fooling, then they had fun with a stolen bottle, after which the policeman was relieved of his clothes, and another 'cop' was knocked out and laid upon a table to be dissected, his internal organs being brought forth one-by-one. The baby was stolen from the carriage of the nurse-maid, and all the characters had a 'rough-house' experience while seeking lodgings. A droll duel brought forth two characters who grew and diminished in size rapidly as they fought, the phantom army appeared and paraded, and all the characters leaped 'up to the moon,' the silhouettes showing them apparently jumping up into the air and out of sight. They all jumped back again, and the act closed. It was quite a happy little idea for the holiday season, occupying about eleven minutes.

(Cutting found by David Robinson in the Chaplin Archives – original source unidentified)

The advanced publicity proclaimed *Harlequinade* as "Especially for the Children" and that "it will have the important place on the program." So just why was Chaplin smitten by this presentation? Well, the surprising answer is that *A Harlequinade in Black and White* was actually performed by the Karno Company. From this evidence, David Robinson presumed that *Harlequinade* was a newly created sketch, devised on the spot, in which Chaplin had most likely played the major role in its creation. But, surely, there is no way that Marcus Loew would have dared to risk presenting a hastily improvised, untried and unseen act to the largest and most-demanding audiences of the year – and certainly not as top-of-the-bill.

There are other factors, too, which may rule out Robinson's theory. First of all, why would the Karno Company feel a need to devise a new act, when they still had other sketches in their repertoire? Then there was the time factor. In the last five weeks the Karno members had been performing '3 Shows Daily.' They had also staged *four* different sketches, which meant that all spare time must have been spent in run-throughs – to refresh the memories of the members who had played them back in England, and to break-in those members who hadn't. This must have left little or no time at all for devising and rehearsing a new sketch.

Thirdly, *Harlequinade* ran for ten to eleven minutes which, taking in the breathtaking speed at which it was played; the split-second timing; and the performance skills involved; would have taken weeks, if not months, to perfect. Fifth drawback was how would they have acquired or had made, in such a short time, all the necessary equipment, props and costumes needed to stage it?

"A Night in a London Secret Society"

FRED KARNO presents his Latest and Greatest Laughable Production, entitled:

"THE WOW-WOWS"

In Three Scenes. The sign of the three flaps or Pom-tiddle-om-Pom-Pompom

Written by Fred Karno and Herbert Sydney

The Cast Includes

Chas. Chaplin, as .... Archibald Binks
Arthur Dandoe, as .... Charlie Blazer
Albert Williams, as .... Fred Brunton
Frank Melroyd, as .... Jack Denton
Mike Asher, as .... Jimmie Bottles
Fred Palmer, as .... Percy
Muriel Palmer, as .... Lady Binks
Amy Minister, as .... Lydia Scotch

Albert Austin, Stan Jefferson, Fred Westcott, Geo. Seaman, etc.

Supported by the renowned Karno Troupe of picked London performers.

Scene I. "The Nook." Depicting River Life with its beauty and gayety.
PREPARE: "What man hath joined together, let no man put asunder."
Scene II: Entrance to Secret Society's Chamber of Horrors. The password, "Kiss me, Good Night! "Nurse!" TAKE CARE.
Scene III. Interior of Chamber of Horrors. The Initiation. Archibald on the Magic Carpet. BEWARE.

Manager for Fred Karno's Company: ALF REEVES.

FRED KARNO'S COMEDIANS

"A NIGHT IN THE SLUMS OF LONDON"

A Pantomimic Comedy, in Two Scenes

Scene 1: A Street in Whitechapel   Scene II: The Lodging House

CAST:

Bill, an East Side bully .... Charles Chaplin
Bobbie, a newspaper boy .... Arthur Dandoe
Dennie, a bootblack .... Albert Williams
Jack Manly, a sailor ashore .... Fred Palmer
Bung, landlord of "Seven Dials Saloon" .... Stanley Jefferson
Sergeant A.Z., a London policeman .... Mike Asher
Blowhard, a wondering musician .... Charles Griffiths
McBooser, his companion .... Frank Melroyd
Jane Makebread, a police nuisance .... Emily Seaman
Furpence, keeper of lodging house .... Fred Westcott
Harold Hardup, a broken-down swell .... Fred Westcott
Piecan, lunch wagon proprietor .... Albert Austin
Isaacstein, a glazier .... Will Stanley
Nancy, an East End Belle .... Maude Crewe
'Liza, her pal .... Muriel Palmer
Virginia, a flower girl .... Amy Minister

Produced under the direction of Alf Reeves, manager Fred Karno's Companies in the United States

---

THE 1910 FRED KARNO COMPANY

By comparing the two cast lists one can see that when the Karno company staged *A Night in the Slums of London* they had two additional members – Will Stanley and Maude Crewe. So we know the latter two were there come week commencing 19 December, as this was the only time "Slums" was played, but they might well have joined at the start of the run at the American Music Hall, New York. Could these two have brought with them the props and costumes necessary to stage *A Harlequinade in Black & White?*

And, last of all, from where had Chaplin learned and developed the knowledge and techniques needed to stage a back-lit projection presentation? He makes no mention of any previous performance of this art. And it was then, whilst I was pondering this question, that something led me back to my notes on *London Suburbia*. There, in one review, I found the following mention:

> The second scene reveals the backs of the same three houses. ..... The inhabitants at length
> go to bed, affording an opportunity for shadow displays on the various blinds.
>
> *(Blackburn Times – 14 April 1908)*

Further searching in my records revealed that, from among the Karno players on the current U.S. tour, Bert Williams, Fred Westcott, George Seaman, Muriel Palmer, Amy Minister, Frank Melroyd, and Chaplin himself, had all played in *London Suburbia* back in England. So here then were the players with the experience, the knowledge, the skill, and the timing to execute *Harlequinade*. This may give us the source of the sketch, but still doesn't tell us why they would go to all the time, trouble, and expense involved to perfect *Harlequinade*, when they could have simply inserted another working sketch.

For the first show of the New Year the company moved over to the Plaza, on 59th Street and Madison Avenue. Here they reverted to playing *The Wow-Wows*, but retained Harlequinade.

(w/c Monday January 2, 1911)

NEW YORK, Plaza

> The Karno Company gave two shows, *The Wow-Wows* and the shadowgraph thing [*sic*]. *The Wow-Wows* closing the interval was a big laughing success. The act has been cut some since first shown at the Colonial, and is now a fast moving laughing number of the best sort. The Shadowgraph was interesting and amusing and should be a corking number for the matinee audiences.
>
> *(Variety – January 7, 1911)*

Chaplin intimates that they played *A Harlequinade in Black and White* for six weeks at the American Music Hall, New York, but I can assure you that it was performed there solely during the fifth of their five weeks there, and for just one week more, here at the Plaza. After that, there is no sign of it being staged ever again.

With New York venues now spent, the company moved on to Philadelphia, for a three-week engagement at Nixon-Nirdlinger theatres commencing January 9, 1911. For the first two weeks they were at the Park Theater and then, for the third, returned to the 'Nixon' – the theatre they had appeared at on its opening week back in November. The sketches played were: *A Night in a London Club*, *A Night in an English Music Hall*, and *The Wow-Wows* – in successive weeks.

The recent run at the New York American Music Hall did, as had been hoped for, prove to be a great showcase. Chaplin tells that Max Sennett saw him there one night and said: "If ever I become a big shot, there's a guy Ill sign up." At the time, Sennett was working as an actor and part-time director of comedies for D.W. Griffiths, at the Biograph company, based in Manhattan. It would be two more years before he went on to help form the Keystone Film Company. There are several versions of Sennett's sighting of Chaplin, with various theatres and years being offered. But if these accounts donut cite one of the theatres the Karno company had played between October 3, 1910 and January 7, 1911, then they can be dismissed; for when Chaplin left New York at the end of this period he never played New York again.

A more immediate benefit of the December run in New York was that, from it, the company had secured a twenty-two week tour on the Sullivan and Considine circuit. This is the tour Chaplin refers to, but he wrongly places it *before* the run at the American Music Hall. The tour was to run from January 30 to June 24, 1911, travelling East to West. Everything was on the up-and-up.

Chapter 14

WAY OUT WEST

First stop-over on the Sullivan-Considine circuit was in Chicago, for three weeks at the American Music Hall, where they had a similar arrangement to the one in Philadelphia.

(w/c January 30, 1911)

CHICAGO, American Music Hall

Fred Karno's London Comedians began a three weeks' stay at the Music Hall with *A Night in a London Club*, or: *The Amateur Entertainers*. The plan is to produce a different farce each week. There are ten men and three women in the company[1]. The offering somehow suggest Dickens. Seeing it, one is reminded of the gatherings of the Pickwick Club. The caricatures of the individual members of the club are with a graveness that makes the comedy stand out. The comedy is rough, but the characters are well drawn.

Various members of the Club are called upon to entertain. There is a woman singer who gets her key repeatedly, but cannot strike it when she begins to sing, a precocious daughter of one of them, who offers a childish selection to the plaudits of admiring friends and among others an ambitious tragedian who, after reminding the Master of Ceremonies several times, is at length permitted to start a scene of a play, only to be interrupted by 'the drunk' (played by Charles Chaplin) which has come to be recognized as the leading comedy character of the Karno offerings. As seen Monday afternoon the only shortcoming of the farce was the lack of a big laugh at the finish.

(*Show World* – February 4, 1911)

David Robinson says of *A Night in a London Club*:

Some mystery surrounds this presentation, since it was apparently not repeated, and only briefly figured in Karno publicity. The most likely explanation was that, with the resourcefulness in which Karno players were trained, they had simply improvised a completely new act, using the club set from *The Wow-Wows*. It was related to an old Karno sketch, *The Smoking Concert*, but with elements taken from *Mumming Birds* and *The Wow-Wows*.

But there is no mystery, just a lack of information left by Chaplin in his personal archives. Thankfully, other sources have helped to fill in the missing records and solve "the mystery." Firstly, *A Night in a London Club* was in no way a newly improvised sketch. It was simply *The Smoking Concert*, under a new title. In all the bill matter and publicity for the U.S. tours, Karno was keen to reflect that this was an *English* company, playing sketches containing *English* humour: Hence we get 'Karno's *London* Comedians;' 'A Night in an *English* Music Hall;' 'A Night in a *London* Club;' 'A Night in *London Slums*;' and 'A Night in a *London* Secret Society,' replacing the titles the sketches were known by over in the U.K. This is confirmed in an article written from an interview with T. Scott-Bell (*ibid*) who, in writing of the sketches Chaplin

---

[1] There were still twelve men in the company, but Albert Austin and George Seaman weren't listed in the programme.

"CLUB NIGHT".

Scene: CONCERT ROOM - CHAIRMAN'S TABLE,
        GUESTS TABLE. SMALL ROSTRUM WITH PIANO.

Cast.

        CHAIRMAN
        STEWARD
        ARCHIE BINKS (Semi-intoxicated)
        MRS. MEEK
        MR. MEEK.
        PERCY SWOFFLES
        LITTLE AGGIE
        PIANIST
        HERBERT TAYLOR
        HARRY CLARK
        MR. BASIL KEENE (ACTOR)
        MISS PARKER etc (GUESTS)

The idea of the sketch is that the members of the Club have got
together on this special occasion to receive their prizes which
they won at their "ANNUAL SPORTS" and followed by a Concert
given by members of the Club.

The Scene opens - Everyone standing with raised glasses toasting
the "Chairman" and singing "For he's a Jolly Good Fellow".

Chairman raps on table and everyone takes their seats.

Chairman - Now Ladies & Gents you all know why we are here this
evening - it is to present the prizes that were won at our
"Annual Sports" which we held last Saturday, so while the
Steward is putting things in order "Liberty All" (Chairman moves
among Members and Guests introducing one to the other). While
this is going on Waltz is being played (very piano) then a
special introduction is given to Archie Binks and Mrs. Meek (comedy
business) with Binks
eventually finishing with his arms around Mrs. Meek. Mr. Meek
in the back ground very much annoyed with this and starts to
take off his coat to fight Binks.
Chairman brings things to order goes back to his table and then
starts to present the prizes.
Now, the first prize was won for the Hurdle race by Mr. Harry
Clark. (Everybody applauds - Bravo Clarkie).
Clark gets up and goes to Chairman's table to receive prize.
Chairman: Now Mr. Clark it gives me great pleasure to present
you with this very handsome alarm clock and I hopes as how it
will be always like you - Keep good time and never go on strike.
Chairman takes a bow for his own joke and Clark gets a hand from
the members.

(Reproduction of original script – courtesy of the late – Olive Karno)

played on the U.S. tours, names three of them only by their English titles:

> At last we decided to send him [Chaplin] on tour in America. The repertoire included three sketches, into which Charlie had put a good deal of his amusing personality – though, mind you, the business in all of them was of Mr. Karno's creating. The most popular of these three was the *Mumming Birds*, Charlie playing the part of a drunken swell. Another of the sketches was *The Wow-Wows*, a skit on secret societies. The third piece was *The Smoking Concert* in which various people were called upon to entertain and the proceedings were interrupted by an inebriated Charlie.

> (1915 article in *Charlie Chaplin*, by Peter Haining – source unaccredited)

Secondly, *A Night in a London Club* bears no similarity whatsoever to *The Wow-Wows*, and was a fully-formed working sketch some four years before the debut of the latter[2]. There *is* a cross-over of business from *Mumming Birds*, in that we see a variety of bad artists being paraded on stage, but the premise for *A Night in a London Club* is a Ladies' Evening. Charlie would have been well-versed in playing *The Smoking Concert* as he and his brother Syd had toured with it between July and October 1908, over in the U.K. The premise then had been a 'Prize Presentation Evening' at the 'Semolina Cycling Club'; but other than that it was pretty much the same sketch.

Thirdly, this was not a one-off performance of *A Night in a London Club*. They had already played this sketch at the American Music Hall in New York, and the Park Theater in Philadelphia, and were to do so many more times on the tours to come.

There were good reasons why *A Night in a London Club* was often staged in preference to "Music Hall": The first, and simplest, was as a change of programme when they stayed more than one week at the same venue. The second was as a change of programme when they went back to a particular venue. The third is more involved. The volume of props and scenery carried by the Karno Company necessitated them having their own railway box-car to transport it from town-to-town. On the occasions when they did Monday to Wednesday in one town, then

ALF REEVES Presents
FRED KARNO'S LONDON COMEDIANS
In a New Pantomime Farce
"A NIGHT IN A LONDON CLUB"
or "The Amateur Entertainers"
CHARACTERS:

Archibald Binks (Inebriated)	Chas. Chaplin
Mr. Meek (Henpecked)	Arthur Dandoe
Mrs. Meek (The Pecker)	Muriel Palmer
Martin Harvey Dustbin (An Actor)	Albert Williams
Percy Swoffles (A Dude)	Stan Jefferson
Miss Taylor (A Guest)	Amy Minster
Agnes (The Infant Prodigy)	Emily Seaman
Mr. Taylor (Member of the Club)	Mike Asher
Mr. Clark (Member of the Club)	Albert Austin
Mr. Jenkins (Member of the Club)	Charles Griffiths
Mr. Wilkins (Member of the Club)	Albert Seaman
Mr. Lothario (At the Piano)	Fred Westcott
The Steward of the Club	Fred Palmer
The Chairman of the Club	Frank Melroyd

Manager for Fred Karno's Company: Alf Reeves.

Repertoire: "Night in a London Music Hall," "Night in Slums," "Wow-Wows," etc.

INTERMISSION

---

[2] The Smoking Concert made its debut at the Argyle Theatre, Birkenhead, England, in April 1906

A NIGHT IN A LONDON CLUB

Mr. Jenkins
CHARLES GRIFFITHS

Miss Taylor
AMY MINISTER

Percy Swoffles
STAN JEFFERSON

Archibald Binks
CHARLES CHAPLIN

Mr. Lothario
FRED WESTCOTT

The Chairman
FRANK MELROYD

Martin Harvey Dustbin
ALBERT WILLIAMS

Mr. Taylor
MIKE ASHER

Agnes
EMILY SEAMAN

Mr. Wilkins
ALBERT SEAMAN

Mrs. Meek
MURIEL PALMER

Mr. Meek
ARTHUR DANDOE

The Steward
FRED PALMER

Mr. Clark
ALBERT AUSTIN

Unique and previously unpublished photograph showing the cast and the set of "A Night in a London Club" (Names in **BOLD** are confirmed).

Thursday to Saturday at another, it would be have been almost impossible to strike the "Music Hall" set at one theatre, get it to the rail yard, load it, travel to the next town, unload the box car, transport it from the rail yard to the next theatre, and then erect it in time for the first performance. The "London Club" set however, was basically a layout of tables and chairs, most of which could, if so required, be supplied by the resident stage manager. The huge backcloth could have been sent on ahead. The fourth is that some venues simply didn't have enough headroom on stage to install the massive two-storey theatre boxes used in "Music Hall." And then, on the rare occasions when they were doing two different theatres on the same night, they would have to put the set up for "Music Hall" at one venue, and "London Club" at the other; although the latter situation applied almost exclusively in the U.K.

The second and third weeks in Chicago seemed to have hit a happy-medium, and nothing more:

(w/c February 6, 1911)

CHICAGO, American Music Hall

Before intermission very little of moment happened, save the appearance of the Karnos in *The Wow-Wows.* Chas. Chaplin, as Archie, won a personal success, to which the others contributed as support.

(*Variety* – February 11, 1911)

(w/c February 13, 1911)

CHICAGO, American Music Hall

"A Night in An English Music Hall" ended the show joyfully

(*Variety* – February 18, 1911)

Chaplin was well aware of the lack of impact the company were making:

Although on that Sullivan and Considine first tour we were not a roaring success, we passed muster by comparison with the other acts.

Of Chicago, itself, he revealed:

We lived up-town on Wabash Avenue in a small hotel; although grim and seedy, it had romantic appeal, for most of the burlesque girls lived there. In each town we always made a bee-line for the hotel where the show girls stayed, with a libidinous hope that never materialised. The elevated trains swept by at night and flickered on my bedroom wall like an old-fashioned bioscope. Yet I loved that hotel, though nothing adventurous ever happened there.

(*My Autobiography*, Charles Chaplin – 1964)

After Chicago, the company stayed in the mid-west for several weeks:

MINNEAPOLIS, Unique Theater (w/c March 20)

Broad English humor is very broad indeed. It smacks even more of the slapstick than our old friend, the burlesque comedian. Yet there are always moments of unexpectedness. Where the American would do the obvious thing, the Englishman does the unusual. Fred Karno's *Night in an English Music Hall*, now headlining at the Unique, is one of the funniest of all the skits. It is elaborately staged, showing several boxes and a miniature stage, with all the habitues of that place of entertainment. There is the inebriated swell, the fresh young chap from Eton, his dignified uncle, and then the typical turns – the topical extemporist, the ballad vocalist, the magician, the village choir singers, the saucy soubrette, and, finally, 'The Terrible Turk', the whole ending with a wild rough-and-tumble burlesque wrestling match. There is just enough of truth in the whole to make it entertaining, despite some far-fetched comedy and the fact that the company is not especially strong.

(*Minneapolis* – March 21, 1911)

Newspaper advertisement from the Winnipeg Telegram
w/c April 3, 1911
Showing the giant set for
"A NIGHT IN AN ENGLISH MUSIC HALL"
In the bottom L/H box is the 'Eton Boy' with his 'Uncle Charlie'
In the bottom R/H box is 'the souse' (Chaplin)
The top two boxes are filled by other members of the cast,
when they are not performing as an act.

Duluth followed Minneapolis, then the troupe headed North, and crossed the border into Canada, to spend just one week in Winnipeg.

(w/c April 3, 1911)

WINNIPEG, Empress

A more delightful audience than was found at the conclusion of yesterday's bill at the Empress would be indeed hard too find, and they had good reason to be satisfied for the bill was unquestionably one of the best that has been seen in this theatre this year. It is headed by the Karno Company in their burlesque *A Night In An English Music Hall*. It is purely slapstick, but very funny slapstick. Charlie Chaplin, the drunken swell, is decidedly clever, and supplies the greater part of the fun throughout the entire act, which is exceptionally well-staged.

(*Winnipeg Telegram* – April 4, 1911)

From Canada, the company re-crossed the border and journeyed on into the Western state of Montana, of which Chaplin reflected:

The further west we went, the better I liked it. Looking out of the train at the vast stretches of wild land, though it was drear and sombre, filled me with promise. Space is good for the soul. It is broadening. My outlook was larger. Such cities as Cleveland, St. Louis, Minneapolis, St. Paul, Kansas City, Butte, Billings, throbbed with the dynamism of the future, and I was imbued with it.

(Chaplin's 1964 Autobiography)

Although the troupe *would* eventually visit all the places Chaplin mentions, this tour took in only Cleveland [unconfirmed], Cincinnati, Chicago (repeat visit), Milwaukee, Minneapolis and Duluth. A few years earlier the extensive tour the Karno company were engaged upon would not have been possible. The railway had developed in the form of a squid, with New York at its head, and the tentacles spreading outwards East to West, but only for a few hundred miles. Now, in 1911 the lines reached coast to coast, and North to South, although not *every* town was easily accessible. Still, the "Golden Age of Railways" had spawned the "Golden Age of Vaudeville."

From Winnipeg the troupe would have most likely broken their journey, for a couple of nights each in Miles City and Billings, before moving on to the major town of Butte.

(w/c Saturday April 15, 1911)

BUTTE, Majestic

The art of pantomime is recognized in theaterdom as one of the most difficult known to the profession. It means that the actor must make known his intentions solely by signs and his general actions.

The great act known as Fred Karno's *A Night in an English Music Hall*, is in considerable part pantomime and it therefore is essential that each member of the cast should be a pantomime artists of much ability.

The act shows the stage and the boxes of an English music hall. Seated in one of the music boxes is a decidedly hilarious person who evidently is suffering from too many exciting libations and consequently he insists on participating in each and every act in a manner that is so funny that the audience out front can't help laughing enthusiastically. He scarcely says more than three words during the entire course of the act, yet so funny are his actions that he proves himself one of the best pantomime artists ever seen here.

There are many others in the cast who provide all manner of fun, and the act from start to finish is one of the greatest novelties as well as thoroughly entertaining creations ever brought to this part of the country.

Mike Asher, Stan Jefferson, Charles Chaplin, Arthur Dandoe, and Fred Westcott (seated).

(Taken during the company's stay in Butte, w/c April 15, 1911)
The Western slope of Colorado's Rocky Mountains begins at the Continental Divide, the apex of the high peaks. Rivers east of the Divide flow eastward to the Gulf of Mexico; while rivers west of the Divide flow into the Pacific Ocean.

The graffiti on the standing stones behind our subjects is an advert for "The Red Boot Shoe Co. N. Main St." Let's hope this doesn't encourage some major company to put a huge red "M" on top of the Great Pyramid, in Gisa.

Not only are various members of the cast excellent pantomime artists, but they are high class athletes and acrobats as well, for they have to take many falls and go through various stunts that only well qualified athletes could hope to successfully attempt.

The act has become the talk of Butte. Everywhere the great importation is spoken of and those who have seen it are urging their friends to see it before it concludes its Butte engagement.

Twenty people are required for its presentation and much special scenery. The act is one of the biggest sent on tour this season and testifies to the enterprise and up-to-date methods of the Sullivan and Considine organisation.

(*Butte Inter Mountain* – April 18, 1911)

Inside the theatre the audiences were civilised and friendly but, outside, the townsfolk seemed a little different. Chaplin:

In 1910 Butte, Montana, was still a 'Nick Carter' town, with miners wearing top-boots and two-gallon hats and red neckerchiefs. I actually saw gun-play in the street, a fat old sheriff shooting at the heels of an escaped prisoner, who was eventually cornered in a blind alley, without harm, fortunately.

Chaplin also painted a picture of the more colourful part of town.

The red-light district consisted of a long street and several by-streets containing a hundred cribs in which young girls were installed ranging in age from sixteen up, for one dollar. Butte boasted having the prettiest women of any red-light district in the Middle-West, and it was true.

He also confessed:

We made friends with the members of other vaudeville companies. In each town we would get together in the red-light district, six or more of us. Sometimes we won the affection of the madam of a bordel and she would close up the 'joint' for the night and we would take over.

(*My Autobiography*, Charles Chaplin – 1964)

Boy! Had he had some sexual awakening! Just eleven weeks earlier Chaplin had been staying in a hotel in Chicago where the show girls stayed with, in his own words, "a libidinous hope that never materialised," and at a hotel where "nothing adventurous ever happened." Now he was taking over brothels for whole nights. That thin air at high altitude might well make you a bit dizzy in the head, but it sure compensates in other areas.

In the next state, Washington, they first spent a week in Spokane, before moving on to Seattle, in the Pacific Northwest.

(w/c Monday May 1, 1911)

SEATTLE, Majestic

No act that has ever played the Sullivan & Considine circuit has made the hit that has been made this week by Fred Karno's Comedians in *A Night in an English Music Hall*. For a matter of fact, it is the biggest comedy act that has ever come into Northwestern vaudeville. The act is all comedy, every minute, but the biggest fun in it centers in the intoxicated chappie who sits in one of the stage boxes and makes evident his poor opinion of the numerous turns that are brought on.

(*Seattle Post Intelligencer* – May 6, 1911)

Armed with the above review, Alf Reeves went along to the Sullivan-Considine Building in Seattle to start negotiations for a second tour. By luck, or arrangement, John W. Considine was visiting there that week, so Reeves had no middleman to go through. The current tour was scheduled to end in eight weeks time, so Reeves needed to use all his negotiation skills to ensure that further work was secured. He again proved himself to be the man for the job, and came away with the desired second tour. However, there was one proviso, which was that *A Night in an English Music Hall* be replaced by *A Night in a London Club*. This is rather a surprising requirement especially considering that, that very week in that very town, the theatre reviewer had opined: "*A Night in an English Music Hall* is the biggest comedy act that has ever come into Northwestern vaudeville." However, Reeves was up for it, and immediately commissioned new scenery to be made in readiness for the twenty-week run of *A Night in a London Club* to begin in August, 1911.

Of the eight weeks left on this tour, the next one was to be spent in Vancouver, British Columbia. Of his visit to this region Chaplin revealed:

My heart grew lighter as we travelled west: cities looked cleaner. Our route was Winnipeg, Tacoma, Seattle, Vancouver Portland. In Winnipeg and Vancouver, audiences were essentially English and, in spite of my pro-American leanings, it was pleasant to play before them.

(Chaplin's 1964 Autobiography)

Again Chaplin's accounts are enough to frustrate anyone intent on tracing his movements, as their actual route was: Winnipeg, Miles City, Billings, Butte, Spokane, Seattle, Vancouver, Tacoma, and Portland. However, he was correct in his summary of the reception given by audiences in Winnipeg (see w/c April 3) and Vancouver:

(w/c Monday May 8, 1911)

VANCOUVER, Orpheum

The much-heralded *A Night in an English Music Hall* was the reason of the crowded houses at the Orpheum Theatre yesterday. The chief cause of their amusement, and the one to whom all the honors go, is Charles Champlin[3] [*sic*] who plays the part of the inebriated swell. During the whole action he does not say a single word, but expresses himself in pantomime. His gestures, his facial expression as the various artistes appeared in their turns, and his approval or disapproval of the same, all are inimitable, and evokes roars and roars of laughter. The wrestling bout at the finish, in which he bests the "Terrible Turk," is the best of all, and he brings the offering to an enjoyable conclusion. Mike Asher,

---

[3] I have already informed you of the problem that one reviewer had in differentiating between Al Reeves and Alf Reeves: well here we have another unbelievable coincidence of names. There was actually an American entertainer working the vaudeville stage, by the name of CHARLES K. CHAMPLIN. Once again, it would appear that the reviewer had reverted to the name more familiar to him, instead of being able to accept there were two individuals with similar names. This was not to be the last time this would happened.

as the "bad boy", is also very clever, and he causes a lot of fun also. The Englishmusic hall turns are, of course, all caricatured and of the comedy kind, and the artistes who take part are all excellent. *A Night in an English Music Hall* is an act that should be seen by every one. All attendance records will undoubtedly be broken this week.

(*Vancouver Daily* News advertiser – May 9, 1911)

Rare, if not unique, picture of the culmination of the wrestling bout, which ends the sketch *A Night in an English Music Hall.*

The people pictured are believed to be:
L to R: Fred Palmer (Stage Manager); Emily Seaman (Mary – the attendant); Mike Asher (Eton Boy); Charles Griffiths (Uncle Charley); Charles Chaplin (The Swell); and, possibly, Albert Austin. Lying on the floor is Bert Williams (The Terrible Turk).

Interesting to note the line: "The wrestling bout at the finish, in which he bests the 'Terrible Turk,' is the best of all." Just where did Chaplin get his ideas from for the wrestling match? Well obviously from Karno and previous 'drunks', but an event which happened when Chaplin was with Wal Pink's company in 1906 would also have helped:

BELFAST, Palace

A funny turn was that supplied by "Wal Pink's Workmen," who appear in an amusing rough and tumble acrobatic sketch entitled *Repairs* The production is well set, and evoked hearty laughter from crowded audiences at both performances.

Ahmed Madrali, the terrible Turk, is appearing with a troupe of three exponents of the "catch-as-catch-can" style. This will be his last appearance before his meeting with Hackenschmidt at the Olympia, London, 28 April. Madrali fights two of his own troupe, then a volunteer for £25.

(*Belfast Morning News* – 17 April 1906)

From Vancouver, the troupe headed back North, on the same railway line they had come down on from Spokane, but disembarked a couple of stops earlier in Tacoma. One week later they headed South again, to hit Portland, just over the border, in Oregon:

(w/c May 22, 1911)

PORTLAND, Grand

Fun runs riot at the Grand this week when Fred Karno's "*A Night in a London Music Hall*" is presented by a company of good English comedians. The acting of Charlie Chaplin as the 'inebriated swell' and Mike Asher, the bad boy from Eton school, is especially praiseworthy, though all turn out a series of screamingly funny stunts.

(*Morning Oregonian* – May 23, 1991)

No venue was traced for the week following Portland, but then the trail picks up in San Francisco, of which Chaplin informs us:

At last California! – a paradise of sunshine, orange groves, vineyards and palm-trees stretching along the Pacific coast for a thousand miles. San Francisco, the gateway to the Orient, was a city of good food and cheap prices. We arrived in 1910, after the city had risen from the earthquake of 1906, or 'the fire,' as they prefer to call it. There were still one or two cracks in the hilly streets, but little remnant of damage was left. Everything was new and bright, including my small hotel.

```
┌─────────────────────────────────────────────────────────────────┐
│  FRED KARNO'S Original London Pantomime Company                    │
│      Presenting "A NIGHT IN AN ENGLISH MUSIC HALL"                  │
│                        CAST:                                        │
│  The Inebriated Swell ........................ Chas. Chaplin}        │
│  The Bad Boy ................................. Mike Asher}  In the Boxes │
│  Uncle Charley ............................... Chas. Griffiths}      │
│                      The Turns                                      │
│  1  The Topical Extemporist ................... Frank Melroyd       │
│  2  The Ballad Vocalist ....................... Muriel Palmer       │
│  3  Bunco the Magician ........................ Arthur Dandoe       │
│  4  The Village Choir Singers .......... J. Westcott, A. Austin     │
│  ....................................... S. Jefferson, and G. Seaman │
│  5  The Saucy Soubrette ....................... Amy Minister        │
│  6  The Terrible Turk ......................... Albert Williams     │
│  7  The Stage Manager ......................... Fred Palmer         │
│  8  Mary the Attendant ........................ Emily Seaman        │
│           Manager for Fred Karno, Alf Reeves                        │
│  The Comany's repertoire includes: "Wow Wows," "A Night in the Slums of London," │
│  "Early Birds" and "Dandy Thieves," all of which will be seen on the Sullivan & │
│  Considine Tour and at this Theatre at dates to be announced later. All productions under │
│  copyright in London, England.                                      │
└─────────────────────────────────────────────────────────────────┘
```

We played at the Empress, owned by Sid Grauman and his father, friendly gregarious people. It was the first time I was featured alone on a poster with no mention of Karno

(Chaplin's 1964 Autobiography)

Time to untangle a few more knots: The Karno company arrived in June 1911, not 1910, but Chaplin does at least get the year of the earthquake correct. The quake stuck on April 18, 1906, but caused a fire that burned for four days. Chaplin again quotes the wrong date, when he talks of the Karno poster. His landmark event is yet six months away. Of the present show, Chaplin recalled:

And the audience, what a delight! In spite of "The Wow-wows" being a dull show, there were packed houses every performance and screams of laughter. Grauman said enthusiastically: 'Any time you're through with the Karno outfit, come back here and we'll put on shows together.' This enthusiasm was new to me. In San Francisco one felt the spirit of optimism and enterprise.

The reviews confirm the laughter, but Chaplin is again pre-empting the next time they would visit San Francisco, and so he has named the wrong sketch:

(w/c Sunday June 4, 1911)

SAN FRANCISCO, Empress

Shows at: 1.30 – 3.30 – 6.30 – 8.30

A crowded house enjoyed a splendid bill at the Empress yesterday afternoon. Beginning with the headliner, Fred Karno's *A Night in an English Music Hall* kept the audience in continual roars of laughter. This sketch is almost a whole show itself.

(*San Francisco Chronicle* – June 5, 1911)

And a second:

Without a doubt the week of 4 June was the record week at the Empress Theatre: even with three shows daily and a big capacity, turnaways were the rule at many of the performances.

The big draw was Fred Karno's London Pantomime Company, in *A Night in an English Music Hall*, which was one continuous scream of laughter. In addition to this strong attraction were Barrows-Lancaster Company, in "Tactics;" Lohse and Sterling rapid mid-air performers; Jack Goldie a clever monologist and whistler; Nellie Sherman, a fascinating soubrette.

(Billboard – June 24, 1911)

In Sacramento, the following week, Chaplin was singled out as the reason for the success of the sketch:

(w/c Sunday June 11, 1911)

SACRAMENTO, Grand

The much-heralded *A Night in an English Music Hall* is with us this week at the Grand. It is good and in every way acceptable, but does not outclass other things on the bill. The fact is that the show is made up, with a slight exception, of about as good material as the public has a right to demand from a vaudeville house.

There are a dozen or more characters and participants in the act, but its success depends entirely upon one man, Charles Chaplin, who enacts the role of the inebriated swell occupying a box at the music hall show. As a bit of character work his acting is perfect. He is the whole show. The act commends itself because it is different and is a success on account of Chaplin.

(Sacramento Bee – June 12, 1911)

However, one reviewer from around this time actually reserves his praise for an unaccredited and unseen member of the company:

EMPRESS:- It might not be generally realized by those playgoers who witness *A Night in an English Music Hall* at the Empress this week, but one of the highest priced men with the company is the performer who stands off stage and operates the noise machine with which the illusions are carried out in the performance of the sketch. Charles Chaplin, who plays "the souse," is constantly thrashing around in his miniature stage box, that forms a portion of the scenic set in *A Night in an English Music Hall*, and every time he bumps his face or some other part of his head or tumbles backward into his box, the man in the wings, who operates the noise apparatus, must work the latter with a great deal of finesse.

(Cutting from Chaplin's personal scrapbook – undated.)

For their third week in the state of California, the company moved on to Oakland:

(w/c Sunday June 18, 1911)

OAKLAND, Bell

A record-breaking week just concluded. The cleanest pantomime stunt that ever graced a vaudeville stage was given unanimous support and patronage this week at the Bell theater. Fred Karno's *A Night in an English Music Hall* was the pacemaker for fun and laughter.

(Oakland Tribune – June 25, 1911)

The fourth week was spent in Los Angeles, which Chaplin didn't exactly find to be a 'City of Angels.'

Los Angeles was an ugly city, hot and oppressive, and the people looked sallow and anaemic. It was a much warmer climate but had not the freshness of San Francisco; nature has endowed the north of California with resources that will endure and flourish when Hollywood has disappeared into the prehistoric tar-pits of Wilshire Boulevard.

(Chaplin's 1964 Autobiography)

He was probably grateful that the locals thought more of him, then he of them.

(w/c Sunday June 25, 1911)

EMPRESS THEATER

"A NIGHT IN AN ENGLISH MUSIC HALL"

One Charles Chaplin playing Billy Reeves' original role of the polite drunk, is the best member of the boisterous crew. Large laughs still result from these oft-done and well-remembered antics.

Lohse and Stirling furnish the sensations with aerial performance that is second to none.

(*Los Angeles Times* – June 27, 1911)

The Karno company were now regularly sharing the bill with the male trapeze duo 'Lohse and Sterling.' Ralph Lohse came from Texan farm stock, and told Chaplin of life on the farm. Chaplin befriended him, and revealed:

Soon we were talking ourselves into leaving showbusiness and going into partnership, raising hogs. Travelling on the train, we would look out of the window and see hog farms and go into paroxysms of excitement. We ate slept and dreamed hogs.

Chaplin speaks of Lohse as if he were a constant companion throughout the U.S. tours; whereas they only appeared on the same bill during May to July, 1911. As for the hog farm it was, as were most of Charlie's dreams, forgotten before even being attempted.

Newspaper adverts from the
Los Angeles Herald
and the *Kansas City Star*

It is thought that the people in the above photograph are as follows:
Arthur Dandoe, Stan Jefferson, George Seaman, Charlie Griffiths, Charles Chaplin, Fred Wescott, Albert Austin,
Emily Seaman, Amy Minster, Muriel Palmer,
Mike Asher, and Fred Palmer
(Missing from the picture: Frank Melroyd, Bert Williams)

Next on the tour was a trip South, almost to California's border with Mexico, to San Diego:

(July 3, 1911)

SAN DIEGO, Garrick

"Really, it's a shame; such a nice looking young fellow, too." That's what a woman, who had been at the Empress theater yesterday afternoon, said when she had got a glimpse after the show of the real Chaplin, who plays the inebriated swell in *A Night in an English Music Hall*. He was easily the star of the production, which is saying much, for every one of the twenty performers helped sustain the chorus of laughter that ran through the audience from the minute after the curtain went up. Chaplin is one of the most artistic inebriates that has ever appeared on any stage. He is loaded to the limit of capacity and yet there is no exuberance in the jag-no staggering, no horseplay. He is just simply soaked to the cracking of his skin; and it is this condition of being "soused" that makes more than half of the fun of the performance.

(*San Diego Union* – July 4, 1911)

Of the next four weeks, no engagement was traced for week one. Week two was spent in Denver, Colorado; week three in Colorado Springs; and week four in Kansas City, Missouri; where the tour ended on August 5, 1911. However, thanks to the good business they had done, the troupe were about to start a new tour. But take a good look at the photograph above, for two of the members pictured would not be going with them. These two had found the ten months of touring more than enough, and were returning to Blighty.

Chapter 15

ONE GOOD TOUR DESERVES ANOTHER

Stan Jefferson was grateful for the experience he had been gaining whilst with the Karno Company, but considered the lack of a decent living-wage too high a price to pay and so, along with Arthur Dandoe, he quit. Stan explained:

> The idea of touring the states was thrilling enough, but when I learned that it meant double salary – four pounds a week! – I jibbered with joy. I didn't know then that the cost of living in America was so high that I should be no better off, that the long journeys from state to state, with sometimes twenty-five shows a week in between, would makes us all so heartily homesick.

> (*Tit-Bits* – 14 November 1936)

And later, in the same serialised article:

> I actually visited Los Angeles with the Karno Company, but I wasn't interested in films, and never thought of going to Hollywood. To tell the truth, my only desire was to get out of America. I was so sick of travelling from coast to coast and back again, so terribly anxious to get another glimpse of the old country, that I was scraping and saving every dollar I could to pay my fare home.

Stan says he and Dandoe left at the end of the week in Colorado Springs but, as there was only one more week before the end of the tour proper, it is far more likely that this is where he only handed in his notice. Plus, on 6 August 1911, when the two home-sick Brits were making their way by train to New York, before sailing home 'steerage' on the *Lusitania*, their two replacements, Ted Banks and Charles Cardon, where simultaneous making their way over from England.[1]

Laurel's "lack of a decent living wage" contrasted sharply with Charlie's accountancy:

> There were fifteen or more in our troupe and yet every member saved at least half of his wages, even after paying his own sleeping berth on the train. My salary was seventy-five dollars a week and fifty of it went regularly and resolutely into the Bank of Manhattan.

Of just how cheap it was to obtain food, Chaplin told of the following:

> Living was cheap. At a small hotel one could get a room and board for seven dollars a week, with three meals a day. Food was remarkably cheap. The saloon free lunch counter was the mainstay of our troupe. For a nickel one could get a glass of beer and the pick of a whole delicatessen counter. Some of our members took advantage of this and piled up their plates until the barman would intervene: 'Hey! Where the hell are you tracking with that load – to the Klondike?'

The above can be taken with a pinch of salt and a free pumpernickle. Firstly Chaplin contradicts himself by saying: "one could get a room and board for seven dollars a week, with three meals a day," then goes on to say: "The saloon free lunch counter was the mainstay of our troupe." Why

---

[1] For an account of what Stan did next, read my book: *LAUREL & HARDY – The British Tours.*

would it be their mainstay if they were getting three meals a day at their lodgings? And if lodgings were only seven dollars a week, how come he was managing to spend a further eighteen dollars – this, one of the most frugal men that ever lived. For him to say "living was cheap" is also a very naive statement, as he does not take into account the other cast-members' wages. Chaplin's own figures show that his weekly expenditure was $25 per week, whereas Stan's weekly wage was just $20. This means that, had Stan's expenditure been the same as Charlie's, Stan would have been spending $5 per week more than he was earning.

So now two players down, the company could have been caught ill-prepared for the start of the next tour but, mercifully, there was a nine day gap before then. This gave Alf Reeves time to plan ahead for transport and accommodation, and to get the new scenery made for *A Night in a London Club*. It also allowed time for the two replacement players to make their way over. So just how would audiences, who had come to the opinion that *A Night in an English Music Hall* was the funniest sketch of all time, react to its successor – *A Night in a London Club*? A Minneapolis newspaper, in reviewing the opening night of the tour, provides the answer:

(w/c Sunday August 14, 1911)

MINNEAPOLIS, Unique

Heading one of the best bills of the season at the Unique is Karno's *A Night at a London Club*. Without a doubt this is one of the greatest laugh producing pieces before the public. To attempt to describe it would be folly, but those who miss seeing these clever comedians will miss a treat of a lifetime.

(*Duluth Tribune* – August 1911)

This review speaks volumes for the skill and talents of the Karno comedians. They had now had rave reviews for *The Wow-Wows*; *A Night in an English Music Hall*; *A Night in (London) Slums*; and for the shadowgraph presentation *Harlequinade*. But their fifth production, *A Night in a London Club*, had topped them all. This really was some achievement. Many acts have tried to get through their whole career just playing the one act, but these players could, it seems, make everything funny at will.

But, one review does not a summary make. Would it last? Well, of the appearance in St. Paul we were told little, but were given an advert featuring a cartoon of Chaplin as "Archie." Unfortunately it bears no resemblance to Chaplin facially, or costume wise:

St. Paul Daily News – August 20, 1911   *Duluth Herald* – August 27, 1911

Duluth gave us:

(w/c Sunday August 27, 1911)

DULUTH, Empress

Fred Karno's London comedians, presenting *A Night in a London Club*, are a fitting climax to the excellent entertainment. This company is composed of a dozen people and they keep things moving every minute. They kept the spectators laughing and they deserved the generous applause given them yesterday.

(*Duluth Herald* – August 28, 1911)

Followed by Winnipeg:

(w/c Monday September 4, 1911)

WINNIPEG, Empress (Portage Avenue East)

There can be no question as to how the audience enjoyed Fred Karno's *A Night in a London Club*. The slapstick comedy kept the audience in a scream from the opening to the close of the burlesque. A great deal of merriment was caused by a very "boozy" individual who, like many a person off a stage, would persist in removing his coat to fight any- and everybody, and when he finally did get it off was himself severely trounced.

The Empress was packed to the aisles, and some hundreds of disappointed patrons were turned away at each performance.

(*Winnipeg Telegram* – September 5, 1911)

Chaplin was now making a name for himself, and threatening to become even more highly-rated than his predecessor, Billy Reeves. For the last four seasons Billy Reeves, Alf's brother, had himself been in America, but not on tour. Instead he had opted for the easier life, in a Revue Show at the American Music Hall Roof Gardens. Maybe Reeves sensed a need to defend his title as, after informing Marcus Loew that he would not be renewing his contract, he went into negotiations to head a second company touring with *A Night in an English Music Hall*. In July 1911, Billy had made a trip back to England to alleviate a bout of home-sickness then, in mid-August, had successfully negotiated with Fred Karno to lease *A Night in an English Music Hall* on royalty payments. On August 19 he had sailed back to New York, from Glasgow, on the *California*, bringing with him with a company of fourteen hand-picked comedians, for a twenty-five week tour.

Billy opened in New York – w/c September 11, 1911 – at the Colonial Theatre, just like Alf's company had. It had been five years since Billy had last appeared in *A Night in an English Music Hall*, and so he billed himself as 'The Original Drunk,' whilst obviously wanting to be known as 'the best.' However, a head-to-head never occurred as the two companies never so much as came within a thousand miles of each other. All that Billy achieved in the billings' stakes was to confuse some historians.

And, taking advantage of a cheap link, two nights in "Billings" was where they are believed to have spent part of the following week, after two similar nights in Miles City, before playing a full week in Butte, opening on a Saturday.

(w/c Saturday September 16, 1911)

BUTTE EMPRESS (formerly the Majestic)

Fred Karno's London comedians presenting *A Night in a London Club*, certainly are laugh creators. It's a very funny act and really can be regarded as one continuous laugh. A large company is required for its presentation and the principals are genuine comedians.

(*Butte Miner* – September 17, 1911)

Cast members of "A Night in a London Club"

(Believed to have been taken during their week of appearances at the Empress Theater, Butte. Below is what is thought to be the correct line-up although the names in [ ] are not confirmed.)

[George Seaman]; Fred Palmer; Albert Austin; [Bert Williams]

Chas. Chaplin; Mike Asher; Muriel Palmer; Amy Minister; [Ted Banks] Emily Seaman

Fred Westcott

This photo has appeared in at least one other book, but with Stan Jefferson being identified as the man standing against the wall under the high window on the left. However, Stan had returned to England well before this picture was taken. His replacement, as 'Percy Swoffles,' is correctly identified by Muriel Palmer, who sent home this picture postcard with the following note written on the back:

> Fred [Palmer] has a X above him. The little man on my right is MR. MEEK my husband. The funny looking fellow stooping in front like a monkey is Fred Karno, son of THE Fred Karno, our manager.

Further confirmation of the change in roles since Stan Jefferson and Arthur Dandoe's departure can be found in the review below:

> Charles Chaplin, who, as Archibald Binks will not stand for any interference of any sort: Mike Asher, as Mr. Meek: Muriel Palmer, as Mrs. Meek: Albert Williams, as Martin Harvey Dustbin: F. Palmer, as Percy Swoffles: Emily Seaman, as Agnes: F. Wescott, as Mr. Lothario: E. Banks, as the Steward: and Frank Melroyd, as the chairman, as well as the rest of the big cast, are thoroughly competent. The act made a most pronounced hit at yesterday's initial matinee and is certain to duplicate that success at every succeeding performance.
>
> (*Butte Miner* – September 17, 1911)

The run continued through Spokane, Seattle, and into Vancouver B.C., where Chaplin had praised the audiences on their last visit. For an act, the hardest act to follow is the act itself. So: "Would the Karno comedians be able to follow themselves?" must have been a question on Chaplin's mind. He needn't have worried.

(w/c Monday October 9. 1911)

VANCOUVER, Orpheum

All those who saw the Karno Pantomime Co. at the Orpheum theatre last spring were there again yesterday when it reappeared in the pantomime farce *A Night in a London Club*. Laugh, some of the people were on the verge of hysterics, and they laughed until they could do so no longer. Chas. Chaplin, who played the part of the "inebriated one" in *A Night in an English Music Hall*, is still with the company and in a similar role in the present offering, and he is inimitable. He does not speak one word, but his actions, his facial expression and his gestures place him in a class by himself, and as a pantomimist he has no equals in his line. All the other members of the company fit their parts, and put plenty of life into their work. The whole act is full of broad comedy, but it does not border on the offensive, and it certainly makes the audience laugh their heartiest. The Orpheum is practically sold out for the entire week and that shows the drawing power of this famous English act.

The rest of the show is unusually good and makes capital entertainment. Marie Dore was another one of the big song hits and she scored unmistakably.

(Vancouver Daily News Advertiser – October 10, 1911)

For sharp-eyed readers who spotted Marie Dore on the bill, you can sit down again. It's Marie D o r e – not Doro. Can you imagine if Charles Champlin, Al Reeves, and Marie Dore had ever been on the same bill? That would have thrown a few researchers.

Far from playing the last tour in reverse, the Karnos were pretty well duplicating it in the same order – Vancouver, Tacoma, Portland, San Francisco, and Los Angeles. The reviewer in Portland wasn't too impressed.

(w/c Monday October 23, 1911)

PORTLAND, Empress (formerly Grand)

A much lower order of entertainment is the farce given by Fred Karno's London Comedians, called *A Night in a London Club*. It consist of a dozen or more low-class English comedians attempting to give an amateur performance. Some of it is funny and a good deal of it is vulgar. There is a lot of old slapstick work.

(Morning Oregonian – October 24, 1911)

Come Sacramento, however, the troupe were back to receiving one of their usual great reviews:

(w/c Sunday November 12, 1911)

SACRAMENTO, Grand

These clever entertainers have brought across the water a new pantomimic farce supposedly satirizing club life. It borders on the rough-house order much of the time, and keeps the audience in a continual scream of laughter from start to finish. Charles Chaplin as 'Archibald Binks,' the inebriated, was the chief manufacturer of merriment, at which business he is the past master. He speaks little, but the merest wave of his hand is enough to get the crowd started, and every time he takes off his coat the act throws the audience into paroxysms of laughter. When the club's dinner breaks up the excitement is something fierce.

The good reviews continued through Los Angeles:

(w/c Monday November 27, 1911)

LOS ANGELES, Empress

The new Karno act is *A Night in a London Club*, and while neither so keen or clever as the first study – seconds never are so good – it is nevertheless full of lively and boisterous sort of amusement, which keeps the average American audience in a state of mirth, but which before an audience of Englishmen would super-induce convulsions. Some of the best characters are repeats from the other act, notably the "gag," and besides there are about a dozen others, making in all one of the largest single turns which ever played Sullivan-Considine time. The occasion is evidently "Ladies Night," if ladies these energetic and entertaining butters-in can be called, and there is every sort of number on the programme, from the recital of a lugubrious poem by a large girl in short skirts, to the "impersonations" of an extremely lady-like young man in all of which, of course, the inebriate and others mingle plentifully and ad-lib. Charles Chaplin plays the drunk, and is at least the most perniciously active of all the participants.

(*Los Angeles Times* – November 28, 1911)

Following a week in Denver, Colorado, it was on to Salt Lake City, a place deliberately manufactured to inspire the feeling of God all around you. The only thing Chaplin felt all around him was desert.

We finished our first tour in Salt Lake City, the home of the Mormons, which made me think of Moses leading the children of Israel. It is a gaping wide city, that seems to waver in the heat of the sun like a mirage, with wide streets that only a people who had traversed vast plains would conceive. Like the Mormons, the city is aloof and austere-and so was the audience.

(*My Autobiography*, Charles Chaplin – 1964)

Chaplin is incorrect when he states, above, that the tour ended here – as there were still another three weeks to go. I can forgive him that, but not his next statement: "We returned to England at the end of 1911," (Chaplin – *My Life in Pictures*) as they were not to return for another six months. The second tour was due to end on January 6, 1912, following a second week in Kansas. However, this arrangement was changed at late notice, and the troupe had to scurry the considerable distance to Chicago to spend the first week of the New Year at the Hamlin Theater. The tour was then extended by a further week when they were retained at the Hamlin.

(w/c Monday January 8, 1912)

CHICAGO, Hamlin

The bill at the Hamlin Theatre this week is very good, but hardly up to the high standard of last week's offering. Karno's Comedians were held over for the second week and presented *A Night at the London Club*. This act offers more good hearty laughs than the offering of the company for last week when they presented *A Night in an English Music Hall*. Archibald Binks, the drunk, is a riot, played by that excellent comedian Charles Chaplin.

Karno's London Comedians close the show in their riotous success, *A Night at the London Club*. There is very little plot in the piece. Of course it was not written for the plot; it was written and staged for the express purpose of forcing laughs, and it fulfills its mission. Charlie Chaplin scores heavily as the drunk, and in fact, the entire company are cast to the very best advantage for their respective talents. There is not a moment during the entire act when some one is not laughing in the audience and there are moments when the act had to be stopped completely until the laughs subsided.

(*Billboard* – January 20, 1912)

Finally, the company were able to breath a big sigh, and take a week out. They would need it, for Alf Reeves had done yet again what he did so well, and secured a third tour on the Sullivan and Considine circuit, this one to last a little over six-months. For the first week's engagement, the company hooked up their personal box-car and boarded the train to Cincinnati, Ohio, where they played only one week before coming right back to play yet another week in Chicago.

The Principal Members of the Karno Company aboard the Box Car which carried them, and their props and scenery, everywhere they went on the U.S. Tours.
Amy Minister, Emily Seaman, Muriel Palmer
Albert Austin, Fred Westcott, [Bert Williams], Charles Chaplin
[George Seaman]

The company had now switched back to playing "Music Hall" as the principal sketch, as they were about to return to most of the venues they had so recently played. February saw them playing a week in Milwaukee, one in Minneapolis, then St. Paul, and rounded off by a week in Waterloo, in the state of Iowa. March then found them in Winnipeg

(w/c Monday March 4, 1912)

WINNIPEG, Empress

FRED KARNO'S COMPANY of Twenty-Five Players in

"A Night in an English Music Hall"

If the Empress patrons were not satisfied with the show that was put on yesterday, then they would not be satisfied with anything. Fred Karno's *A Night in an English Music Hall* is the feature, and while it is purely an act of slap-stick comedy, it is one of the best "slap-sticks" that has been seen here since its own performance last year. Charles Chaplin, in theatrical parlance, "hogs the show." He is the funniest person who has been at this theatre in some time.

(*Winnipeg Telegram* – March 5, 1912)

Once again, providing a break on the Winnipeg to Butte line, was a couple of nights each in Miles City and Billings, before playing Butte itself:

(Sat-Fri March 16-22, 1912)

BUTTE, Empress

The headline attraction this week is Karno's famous production of *A Night in an English Music Hall*. The offering is better than ever this season and is just as full of life and ginger.

167

The production is one continuous laugh and for genuine amusement would be hard to equal. Charles Chaplin as the inebriated swell, is immense. The other members of the company are capable performers and give a high-class entertainment. The scene represents the interior of an English music hall during an entertainment. All the details have been carefully brought out and this English production is well worth going miles to see.

(*Butte Miner* – March 17, 1912)

Chaplin reveals how happy he was to be returning to Butte, where he could meet up again with the barman he had befriended on his last visit. The barman worked at Mack and Carey's Orpheum bar, the place where stage and vaudeville artistes would congregate for a drink and to discuss how their show was playing. The majority of the population of Butte were miners so, when they were working, the rest of Butte became a virtual ghost town. To generate lunchtime custom the management of Mack and Carey's bar ran a free buffet bar to attract in whomsoever was left, this being mainly the vaudeville acts, and the legit actors. Chaplin describes the contents of the buffet at length but, as was a common trait of his, makes the exception the rule, and gives us the picture that such buffets were commonplace in *all* the towns they visited. Hence his earlier told "living was cheap" story.

Spokane followed Butte, and then came Seattle, Vancouver, Tacoma, Portland, San Francisco, and Los Angeles:

(w/c Monday April 1, 1912)

SEATTLE, Empress

With the return of the famous Fred Karno's London Comedians in *A Night in an English Music Hall* as top-notchers, and every other act of usual merit, the Empress offers a Class A program this week. The music hall performers, with Charles Chaplin as the man with a terrible souse are even better than before, and it was plainly evident that a big part of the audience had come for another taste of their rare, hilariously crazy act.

(*Seattle Star* – April 2, 1912)

(w/c April 8, 1912)

VANCOUVER, Orpheum

The Karno Company are back in town again, and at the Orpheum yesterday they made the biggest kind of a hit in their old stand-by, *A Night in an English Music Hall*. Everybody who was there came especially to see their old favorites, and while the other acts on the bill are more than good, it was for the British act that they waited, and they certainly laughed their heartiest at them. Charlie Chaplin is still playing the part of "the drunk." He improves with each appearance, and he has made the role his own. The rest of the company is uniformly good and it goes without saying that the Orpheum will be taxed to the doors at every one of the performances this week.

(*Daily News Advertiser* – April 9, 1912)

Whenever and wherever the Karno Company opened at a theatre, buying the following day's newspaper was always exciting, as they would look to see how the reviewer had rated their act. But reading the newspapers for Tuesday April 16, 1912 would have been an unforgettable experience. It was Charlie's twenty-third birthday, and he may well have intended to go straight to the 'Star Signs' to see if his horoscope was favourable. But the thought would have been immediately wiped from his mind after reading the banner headline, for it read:

TITANIC FOUNDERED YESTERDAY
1800 SOULS GO DOWN TO DEATH

Knowing that in a few months time they were about to do the very same route the *Titanic* took, but in the reverse direction, would have been rather unsettling, for they must have thought: "There but for the grace of God go we." But all thoughts of the tragedy had to be put aside, as there were still thousands of theatregoers who wanted to be made to laugh.

(w/c 22 April 1912)

PORTLAND, Empress

An amusing entertainment of the slap-stick kind is Fred Karno's *A Night in an English Music Hall.* The rear of the stage represents two tiers of boxes. As each performer comes in, he is greeted with a fusillade of soft oranges and bananas. There is an "inebriated swell," two bad boys and some other trouble-makers who bring on a general rough-house. The concluding scene, a mock wrestling match between the swell and "Marconi Ali," a "terrible Turk," is uproariously funny.

(*Morning Oregonian* – April 23, 1912)

(w/c Sunday May 5, 1912)

SAN FRANCISCO, Empress

A Night in an English Music Hall, presented by Fred Karno's London Comedians, closed the show and carried off the honors This company carries 12 people and a special stage setting. Charles Chaplin is the hit of the act, in the role of the souse. The cast also includes: Mike Asher, Charles Griffiths, Emily Seaman, Frank Melroyd, Muriel Palmer, Albert Austin, Fred Westcott, George Seaman, Ted Banks, Amy Minster, and Albert Williams.

(*Billboard* – May 15, 1912)

Interesting to note that the bill matter in Winnipeg, the first week in March, proclaimed: "Fred Karno's Company of Twenty-Five Players," while here is San Francisco, just eight weeks later the review announced that the company carried only twelve people." As we have already seen, the odd one or two additional players were sometimes drafted in, but the numbers had certainly never attained twenty five. It would seem as though Karno's publicity machine had turned out a few extra copies, but to what benefit I can't understand.

(w/c Sunday May 12, 1912)

SACRAMENTO, Empress

With *A Night in an English Music Hall* as the feature, and the Kinemacolour pictures as the attraction, containing the greatest interest, the Empress this week has a bill that holds a little of everything. Charles Chaplin, as the inebriate swell, is screechingly funny in the comedy. The music hall scene is a bit dull in spots but, on the whole, the silent work of Chaplin keeps the fun sizzing all the time.

(*Sacramento Bee* – May 13, 1912)

(w/c Monday May 20, 1912)

LOS ANGELES, Empress

"A Night in an English Music Hall"

If you never saw Charles Chaplin as "The Souse" don't let your opportunity slip now. He's the subtlest of actors and the most agile of tumblers. The beautiful gravity of his gestures and features drives his audience into convulsions. The London company is big-thirteen in all-and some of them are almost as clever as Chaplin himself, especially at rough tumbling.

(*Los Angeles Times* – May 21, 1912)

Los Angeles Daily Times
Monday May 20, 1912

Kansas City Star
June 15, 1912

And a second review:

(w/c Monday May 20, 1912)

LOS ANGELES, Empress

The final number, "A Night in an English Music Hall," is on its third visit at the Empress and in every way lives up to its reputation as a scream getter. Horseplay and an inebriated "swell" are the combination that keep the audience in one long uproar. Charles Chaplin, the "swell," thoroughly proves that "actions speak louder than words," for whether waving off one of the "bum actors" or hitting the floor with a dull thud, he never fails to draw a laugh, and that without the use of words.

(*Los Angeles Express* – May 22, 1912)

Confirmation of the company's whereabouts in the next three weeks proved elusive, but it is believed to be Salt Lake City, Denver, then Colorado Springs, before finally arriving in Kansas City, where the tour ended on 22 June.

So this talented bunch of comedians and acrobats had done it. Within less than a week of first arriving in the States they had had their bags packed, ready to come home as complete failures. But now, some twenty months later, they were returning to England as one of the finest acts ever to have hit the American Vaudeville circuit. That's talent!

Chapter 16

A ENGLISH SUMMER

Of his feelings as the tour was coming to a close Chaplin had reminisced: "I felt sad as we drew near to the end of our second tour." But then, when it finally ended, he was a little more philosophical about the situation:

> I was not too upset at leaving the States, for I had made up my mind to return; how or when I did not know. Nevertheless, I looked forward to returning to London and our comfortable little flat. Since I had toured the States it had become a sort of shrine.

However, his feelings and happy memories of the home he was returning to were all too quickly to evaporate

> On my arrival in London, Sydney met me at the station and told me that he had given up the flat, that he had married and was living in furnished rooms along the Brixton Road. This was a severe blow to me. ... I was homeless. I rented a back room in the Brixton Road. It was so dismal that I resolved to return to the United States as soon as possible.

> Each day I felt more of a nondescript and completely uprooted. I suppose had I returned to our little flat, my feelings might have been different.

Followed by:

> Our American troupe was put to work and for fourteen weeks we played the halls around London. The show was received well and all the audiences were wonderful, but all the time I was wondering if we'd ever get back to the States again.

> (*My Autobiography*, Charles Chaplin – 1964)

Few, if any, clues here to tell us what Chaplin did next. He does say ".. for fourteen weeks we played the halls around London," which makes it an absolute stone-wall guarantee that they didn't play fourteen weeks around London, so we'll have to proceed one stepping stone at a time:

Back on June 12, while the Karno company were still in the States, *Variety* had announced:

KARNO'S "HYDRO" NEXT

> Fred Karno's London Comedians, with Charles Chaplin as Nick Sharp will present "The Hydro" in New York before the wane of another vaudeville season. "The Hydro" is in two scenes, the first showing the pump room at the Hydro-Merranbad, France, and the other the interior of Bathe de Luxe at the same place.

And then a few weeks later:

> ALF REEVES mgr. of the Karno Comedy Company will sail for England tomorrow. The company also goes back. Mr. Reeves will return with the new Karno act, *The Hydro*, in October.

> (*Variety* – July 5, 1912)

THE ASTORIA
On his return to England Chaplin was invited to spend a day with Karno,
on his houseboat moored at Taggs Island, in the Thames.
(Unique photograph, courtesy of the late- Olive Karno)

The Hydro had made its debut as recently as 1 April 1912, at the Oxford Music Hall, London. It was in two scenes, written by Frank Calvert, Fred Karno, and Syd Chaplin. Little seems to have been written about the actual content other than this tiny review:

(London, April 1, 1912)

KARNO'S LAUGHING HIT

Fred Karno's new show, "The Hydro" at the Oxford, is very ingenious, showing a scene in a Pump Room, with a real bath and bathing girls. It is a dramatic story, with comedy predominating. A big laughing hit.

(*Variety* – 6 April 1912)

As none of the company newly returned from the States had seen *The Hydro*, it is a near-certainty that their first 'job' was to go and watch it. This would have caused no great hardship as, for three weeks starting from 15 July, it played following London venues: the Euston, the Hackney Empire, and the Kingston Empire. There is even a very good chance that many, if not all, of the company took part in the sketch, to learn the parts. One member of the US company was definitely there. Bolton ventriloquist Bert Williams was billed as one of the support acts.

However, the results of their reconnaissance was that *The Hydro* was dropped as a potential sketch to take to the U.S., and the company were set to work playing the ever trusty *Mumming Birds*. To make the sketch seem a bigger attraction to the potential audiences at the London Metropolitan, and the Tivoli, which it played in successive weeks, it was billed as: "Fred Karno introduces his American Company of Comedians in 'Mumming Birds'."

For reasons we are unlikely ever to discover, Karno next sent the company to play Jersey and Guernsey in the Channel Islands, which are situated between England and France. Monday to Thursday was spent at the Opera House in Jersey, followed by the Friday night at the St. Julian's theatre on the island of Guernsey.

(12 August 1912 – Monday to Thursday only)

THE OPERA HOUSE, ST. HELIER, JERSEY

Variety is the salt of life, and the decision of the management of the *Opera House* to introduce variety into their summer season's programme by the inclusion of a week, or rather four nights, of vaudeville was a wise one. At any rate, that is the conclusion that the public came to, if we may judge by the attendance at the *Opera House*, last evening. The whole building was filled to overflowing, and not only was the audience a large one, but it was also enthusiastic, and accorded a capital reception to each of the artistes in the company of star performers presented in two of Mr Fred Karno's sketches. One of these, *Mumming Birds*, is a skit on the modern-day music hall, the setting representing the stage and boxes of a music hall, and amusing dialogue takes place between the stage, audience, and performers. The turns presented were five in number, and were typical of the music hall stage, the last one, 'The Terrible Turk,' who offers to wrestle against all-comers, and does so, too, to the amusement of the audience, being undoubtedly one of the funniest things we've seen.

The company presented still another sketch of Mr. Karno – *The Wow Wows* – this being a most laughable little playlet showing how a party of men-about-town, in other words "Knutts" imposed upon one of their number by getting him to imagine he was being initiated into the mysteries of a secret society.

(Jersey Evening Post – 13 August 1912)

How Karno could have benefitted from sending such a huge company all that way, I can't begin to understand. It wasn't just a matter of sticking them and the enormous amount of props and scenery they carried onto a train, as had been the routine in the U.S., as in this instance there was the little problem of negotiating the waters of the English Channel.

A well-documented incident occurred during the troupe's Thursday afternoon day out on Jersey, although many reports have often been far from accurate. The occasion was the annual "Battle of the Flowers" pageant. The first "Battle of Flowers" took place on 9th August 1902, as a celebration for the coronation of Edward VII. During this, the tenth, the flotilla of flower-bedecked floats was being filmed. A 1957 magazine article purports to tell part of what happened, from information given in an interview with legendary Karno comedian Fred Kitchen:

I don't think many people know that Charlie actually first appeared on film before he left Britain. It happened in August 1912 when we were on tour with Mumming Birds in Jersey, one of the Channel Islands. We were playing the St. Helier Opera House. It was the time of the famous Jersey Carnival of Flowers, and a film cameraman had been sent down to film the procession for the cinema newsreels. After some difficulty in setting up his camera, the man managed to get in a good spot on the racecourse and, with his eye glued to the 'finder' started cranking the handle at the moment a particularly fine floral float came into his line of vision.

Suddenly he was roused from his preoccupation by a yell of delight from the crowd. A slender little man had emerged unobserved from somewhere and had been entertaining them for some minutes by performing a variety of curious shambling steps just in front of the camera. A particularly funny bit of business had broken the silence and the on-lookers had given him a round of applause. It was then that the cameraman discovered his machine had taken several dozen feet of the procession as well as the comic performance by the little man. That man was of course Charlie Chaplin. Charlie later told me that the thing he remembered best about the incident was the voice of a little boy protesting afterwards, "Oh! Mummy, why has the funny man gone away?" Charlie said it did his confidence no end of good – and it seems now like a kind of omen, doesn't it?"

(1950s article in *Charlie Chaplin*, by Peter Haining – source unaccredited)

Doesn't seem like an omen to me, more like a load of old tosh. This story was even a load tosh the first time it was peddled out, which was in the May 1917 edition of *Pearson's Magazine Weekly.* The 1957 'writer,' if one can call him that, had simply rehashed the forty year-old article, and inserted the name of Fred Kitchen to try to give the story some substance. But Fred Kitchen wasn't qualified to act as an eye-witness to the event, as he wasn't in Jersey at the time. In fact, Fred Kitchen wasn't in *any* Karno company at that time. He was with Herbert Darnley's Company, playing the lead character in the sketch *Potts in Port*, up in Yorkshire

The article also wrongly identifies the little man who had been entertaining the crowd, in front of the camera. This was not Chaplin at all. Alf Reeves, who *was* an eye-witness, gives us a much more accurate account:

> While playing the theatre on the island of Jersey, there was a street parade and carnival in progress, and a news weekly cameraman recorded the event. He was here, there, and everywhere, but wherever he went a very pompous gentleman, who was apparently in charge of affairs would always be found in front of the camera lens. He would shake hands with the local dignitaries and always turn away from them and face the camera as he did so. He might be termed the first 'camera hog.' Always would he bow and register his greetings to the camera while guests stood in the background, or off to one side.
>
> Charlie was completely fascinated by this bit of business and told me that some day he would put it in a picture. In an early picture of his – *Kid's Auto Races* you will find the fulfilment of his resolve.

(Photoplay – July 1921)

So what Karno may have lost in sending the company to Jersey, Chaplin surely gained. After playing Guernsey on the Friday night only, the company were able to return to London, in time to stage *Mumming Birds* at the Shepherds Bush Empire, on the following Monday. They doubled with *Mumming Birds* at the Hackney Empire and the Middlesex, the week after that, but then at the beginning of September came a complete change of sketch.

Having dropped the plan to take play the sketch *The Hydro* on their forthcoming tour of the U.S., the troupe switched their attentions to the possibility of taking another new sketch, *The Village Sports.* This was yet another variation of *The Smoking Concert*, with the premise this time around being the Prize-Giving Evening for the village sportsday.

The U.S company made their debut with *The Village Sports* in Colchester, Essex, Monday 2 September 1912.

COLCHESTER. Hippodrome

> Fred Karno's Company in the *Mumming Birds* head the bill, and in addition are playing *Village Sports*, with Charles Chaplin as the leading character in each.

In successive weeks, they then took it to Birmingham, and Liverpool, doubling with Warrington at the latter. So much for Chaplin's "fourteen weeks in London" claim. September had turned to October, when the following announcement was made:

> ALF REEVES is due in New York, Monday next, on the *Oceanic*, which sailed Tuesday from Liverpool. He brings with him two vaudeville offerings. One of them is *The Village Sports*, which has never been seen on this side. The other is *The Wow-Wows.* Alf will arrive in time to "catch" his brother BILLIE REEVES in his new act, opening at Fifth Avenue, Monday.

(Variety – October 4, 1912)

However, *The Village Sports* never made it onto the ship. What was even more scary was that the company very nearly didn't make it onto the ship. If we back-peddle a little bit, we will find

Alf Reeves desperately scouring London for suitable comedians to make up the numbers. In one chance encounter he bumped into Stan Jefferson in Leicester Square.

"What are you doing nowadays? enquired Reeves of Stan. "Starring in the West-end?"

"Starving in the West-end, more like it," Stan riposted.

"Do you want your old job back? "

"Sure! When do we leave? "

"Next week. "

"How much?"

"How much do you want? "

"Well I'll need $25 just to live on."

"How does $30 sound?"

"Alright."

"See you next week."

Luckily for Reeves, Chaplin had made his mind up long ago, of which he said:

> I loved England, but it was impossible for me to live there; because of my background I had a disquieting feeling of sinking back into a depressing commonplaceness. So that when news came that we were booked for another tour in the States I was elated.

But with less than twenty-four hours to go before the troupe left for the U.S., they still didn't have their full complement of players, as Mike Asher, Arthur Dandoe, and Fred and Muriel Palmer had decided not to make the return. Alf Reeves hadn't given up, however, and got a contact to invite over the well-known, former Drury Lane clown 'Whimsical' Walker, whom they knew to be down on his luck. Walker himself takes up the story:

> It was on my ninth visit to America that I went out with Charlie Chaplin. It came about in this way. I was on my beam ends – nothing to do – just lost my savings in a bad speculation, and absolutely broke to the world. I was in London looking for work and I met a friend who invited me to have some refreshment with him, so we went into an hotel, where we found Charlie Chaplin, Arthur Reeves [*sic*], Charlie Baldwin, and two or three others.

> One of the party hailed me. "Whimmy," said he, "we were just talking about you. How would you like to go to America? We sail tomorrow morning." "What's the business?" I asked. "Fred Karno's sending *The Wow-Wows* (one of Karno's burlesque companies) with Charlie Chaplin. Will you come with us and play a part?"

> "What about the salary?" was my natural query. We discussed this important matter and eventually settled terms, but it was absolutely the lowest salary I ever had for forty years. Still, I was glad to take it, and went into the billiard room and signed the contract. We left Waterloo station early next morning and we were off to America.

> (*From Sawdust to Windsor Castle*, by Whimsical Walker)

So finally they could go, of which Chaplin's final thoughts were:

> On my last night in London, emotionally confused, sad and embittered, I again walked about the West End, thinking to myself: "This is the last time I shall ever see these streets."

Stan Jefferson expected his stay in America to be for one season only, but he was to take up residency there till the end of his days. Whimsical Walker expected it be for one season only, but didn't even get that far. For Chaplin, however, the final outcome would be far beyond what anyone expected.

Chapter 17

ANYBODY HERE SEEN KELLY?
(A Second Interlude)

On 2 October 1912, after a short unhappy return to England, Chaplin set sail for America for the second time. So what of his love life? Of his October 1909 stay in Paris and his 1911 visit to Butte he writes openly of his sexual exploits with ladies of the night, but in none of his writings ever makes mention of any relationship. And what of Hetty Kelly? Where is she? Did Charlie see her in America on the first tour, or during his brief stay in London, or is he about to look her up in New York this time around? Now that he is one of the biggest stars in American vaudeville, maybe he feels better suited to win her favour.

Charlie's brief time with Hetty had been in the Autumn of 1908. His next record of seeing her was of an accidental meeting:

> I had not seen Hetty in over a year. In a state of weakness and melancholy after the 'flu, I thought of her again and wandered late one night towards her home in Camberwell. But the house was empty with a sign: 'To Let.' I continued wandering the streets with no special objective. Suddenly, out of the night a figure appeared, crossing the road and coming towards me. "Charlie! What are you doing up this way?" It was Hetty. She was dressed in a black sealskin coat with a round sealskin hat.
>
> "I came to meet you," I said, jokingly.
>
> She smiled. "You're very thin."
>
> I told her I had just recovered from flu. She was seventeen now, quite pretty and smartly dressed.
>
> "But the thing is, what are you doing up this way?" I asked.
>
> "I've been visiting a friend and now I'm going to my brother's house. Would you like to come along?" she answered.
>
> On the way, she told me that her sister had married an American millionaire, Frank J. Gould, and that they lived in Nice, and that she was leaving London in the morning to join them.

This account comes from Chaplin's 1964 autobiography but, yet again, in his 1933 article he gives a varying account. Just why, when Chaplin wrote his autobiography, he did not use the original text from the earlier articles, I fail to understand. If it were only that the later account had bits left out it would be almost forgivable; but for Chaplin to actually re-write events, with so many inconsistencies, is not the mark of an honest chronicler. See how many variations from the 1964 version, above, you can spot in the 1933 account, below:

> Later she left with the troupe for the Continent and I lost sight of her for two years, but the next time we met it was in a curious way.

I was crossing Piccadilly when the screech of an automobile made me turn in the direction of a black limousine which had stopped abruptly. A small gloved hand waved from the window. There must be some mistake, I thought, when a voice unmistakably called, "Charlie!"

As I approached, the door of the car opened and there was Hetty beckoning me to get in. She had left the troupe and had been living on the Continent with her sister. Oh yes, her sister had married an American multimillionaire. All this as we drove along.

"Now tell me something about yourself," she said eyeing me kindly.

"There is very little to tell," I answered. "I am still doing the same old grind- trying to be funny. I think I shall try my luck in America."

"Then I shall see you there," she interposed.

"Oh, yes, I'll fix that up with my secretary," I laughed ironically.

"But I mean it," she insisted. "You know I've thought of you a good deal since the old days."

Again I was lifted into paradise, yet in the back of my mind I knew it was more hopeless than ever now.

That evening we spent visiting her brother and mother; Hetty was to leave the following day for Paris.

(*A Comedian Sees the World*, September 1933)

So, from the two accounts we now know that: It was one year after he'd last met her – no, two. He was walking along Camberwell Road – no, sorry – crossing Piccadilly, which is about two miles away, on the other side of the Thames; when he met Hetty who was walking across the road towards him, – no, she was in a car. The first thing he saw was a gloved hand waving to him – no, she was dressed in a black sealskin coat with a round sealskin hat. They immediately walked down to her brother's house – no, sorry – later that evening they went to her mother's house.

Let's now follow Chaplin's wishes and bring the blurred past into focus. We can safely take it that Charlie's melancholy mood led him to Camberwell Road, not Piccadilly. After turning away from the Kellys' former home at 11 Councillor Street and bumping into Hetty, the two of them would have walked down to Hetty's mother's latest residence, at 79 Holmewood Gardens, off Brixton Hill, where her brother Arthur was also residing. On the way Hetty would have informed Charlie that she was leaving London the following morning to go to Nice, not Paris, as that is where her sister Edith and husband Frank J. Gould had their holiday home, not residence.

Charlie was pleased to note, after witnessing Hetty's behaviour in her mother's house, that his ardour for her had greatly diminished, and that he didn't really want to marry anyone.

We said good-bye and she promised to write. But after one letter she ceased corresponding. Later I left for America.

(*A Comedian Sees the World*, September 1933)

If Hetty had indeed turned seventeen, then the meeting must have come after 28 August 1910. But Charlie sailed for America on 22 September, which would hardly allow time for Hetty to write one letter then cease corresponding. The bout of flu Charlie mentions recovering from would seem to be the one that incapacitated him during Christmas 1909 and New Year 1910, when he had to drop out of *The Football Match*, and provides a more acceptable time frame. Whenever it was, Charlie tells us it was the last he saw of her. He does however give an account of how he later contrived to effect a meeting when she came over to New York whilst he was touring America:

> Soon after, I read of her arrival there with her sister. The thought of meeting her now embarrassed me. The affluence of her position added to my sense of inferiority complex. Yet I would often walk by the house on Fifth Avenue where she lived, hoping to meet her accidentally, but nothing ever came of it. Eventually I gave up the idea of ever seeing her again.

Shipping records show that Hetty arrived in New York on 15 December 1911, fourteen months into Chaplin's first tour. However, Chaplin didn't get within a 500-mile radius of New York during the ten months following Hetty's arrival so, even though she is confirmed as staying at her sister's home at 834 Fifth Avenue, there was to be no chance meeting on this occasion. However, Hetty did return to New York, 4 October 1912, and Chaplin arrived with the Karno Company just a few days later, on 10 October. The company's first engagement was to be 20 October, which allowed them a over a week's free-time in New York. So, up till now, this is the only window of opportunity that Charlie would have had to stake out Hetty's address. But, as he says above "nothing ever came of it. Eventually I gave up the idea of ever seeing her again."

So, from joint information in my records and Chaplin's accounts, we can safely assume that Charlie never met Hetty during his time in the States. Or can we? Is all the evidence in? I myself thought so, but then I was given a newspaper article from 1912, which puts the most dramatic twist on the situation. You are now about to read an article, the contents of which have never been reproduced since the date of publication.

FOLLOWED HERE BY NEW YORK HEIRESS

> It is bad enough to be spurned by the girl you love, especially if she happens to be a millionaire's daughter, but to be chased all over the country by the same girl after you had wiped her name off your memory slate, and after becoming betrothed to another fair damsel, is a predicament that is calculated to get on one's nerves.
>
> Yet that is the entangling web that has enmeshed Charles Chaplin, the noted actor who plays the role of "the inebriated dude" in *A Night in an English Music Hall* at the Empress this week.
>
> The story leaked out by accident. Chaplin had retired to his dressing room after a particularly successful performance last night, and seating himself wearily in a chair exclaimed in eloquent disgust the one word "D – !"
>
> #### Girl in the Case
>
> One of his fellow players looked up sympathetically and said, in a tone of alarm: "What! Is she here?"
>
> For answer Chaplin merely nodded his head and gave vent to a tragical wearisome sigh – not the stage kind, but the real thing.
>
> "Pretty little love story, eh?" chirped a reporter who was standing unnoticed nearby and who, smirking amiably, scented a "story."
>
> Charlie looked up, and then repeated the same cuss-word that had preceded the conversation, but this time with added emphasis.
>
> "Goodness, you are shockingly profane," said the reporter with mock modesty. "Especially for a young man," he added.
>
> #### Bares His Secret
>
> Chaplin laughed. "Well," he said, his proverbial good nature bubbling to the surface, "I suppose I may as well tell you the story. But you must promise not to breathe a word of it!"

"I promise," said the scribe. But he didn't promise not to WRITE a word of it, so here is the tale.

Chaplin is an Englishman-one of the well-bred and democratic kind. He fell heels over head in love with the daughter of a New York millionaire who was spending a holiday in London with her dear papa. The heiress reciprocated his affections and Cupid was dancing a turkey trot when the glooms hove in sight. Papa was blithely informed of the engagement and was furious, for at that time Chaplin was just a rising young man with his future before him, though both he and the girl were convinced that he would eventually climb to the highest rung of the thespian ladder-whatever that is. At that time Chaplin hadn't achieved fame as a stage inebriate.

She Turned Him Cold

Soon he forgot her, but later met a girl whose parents, though high in the social scale, didn't possess such well-defined ideas on "social stations," or if they did, they adjudged Chaplin to be an equal plane. And Chaplin will marry this girl when he returns to England, if all goes well.

T'other Girl Tagging Him.

But when he reached New York, to start the present American tour, the millionaire's daughter attended the theatre where he was playing, and when her austere parent realized that Chaplin had reached a class by himself he relented. At least, so the girl intimated in a pretty little note she dispatched to Chaplin in a dainty lavender-scented envelope. Chaplin ignored the missive. But he often got a glimpse of a familiar, wistful face in a box on the left.

At the next city he visited, Chaplin, while playing the "drunk" as usual, was almost startled into soberness when glancing beerily out of half-closed orbs towards the audience, he saw the same face in the box on the left.

And the same thing has happened at each subsequent city in which he has played.

Won't Give Up Hope.

Now he refuses to look up at the audience, but last night felt impelled to glance at one of the boxes on the left. And there she was!

"You should at least be grateful to her," said the reporter; "she is indirectly responsible for your success."

"That's right, too," said Chaplin. She was looking awful pale tonight, and if she dies of a broken heart I will feel directly responsible. But what can I do? I'd gladly take her back, but I'm engaged to Dol – to another affinity in London. I wish you'd ask your women readers to send along some advice. They can generally solve these problems much more readily than men."

(U.S. newspaper cutting – title and date not identified)

And where is the source of this cutting? Why, in Chaplin's very own scrapbook – a book which he carried on the U.S. tours, and into which he cut and pasted newspaper articles which took his fancy. And what a strange article it is. Chaplin is a big star, and has the opportunity to feed the press with stories of his present and future aims, with the added bonus that some of what he says might actually *benefit* his future. So why does his engineer this situation: i.e. lure at least two journalists backstage and feed them a work of pure fiction?

They say a good lie has to be based as near to the truth as possible, and this one certainly was. The girl being used as the basis of the story is obviously Hetty, for there can't have been another girl who fits the description: "He fell heels over head in love with the daughter of a New York millionaire who was spending a holiday in London with her dear papa." Up till this moment in time, Hetty is the only girl who Chaplin has recounted as falling in love with. Admittedly, she wasn't the daughter of a New York millionaire, but she *was* the sister-in-law of one, and that is what gave the lie substance.

But why switch the 'stalker' roles? Chaplin admits to staking out Hetty's London address in 1910; then to staking out her New York address in 1912; and even *years later* he was still at:

> Then came my adventure into motion pictures – my sudden rise to popularity.
>
> I had arrived in New York to sign million-dollar contracts. Now is my opportunity to meet her, I thought, but somehow I cannot do it normally. I couldn't go to her house or send a letter. I am not shy. However, I stayed on in New York hoping to meet her accidentally.
>
> A New York paper had a headline: "Chaplin in Hiding – Nowhere to be Found." Nothing of the kind. If they had noticed a taxi waiting on the opposite side of a certain house on Fifth Avenue they would have found the culprit.

This is probably around late-1920 early 1921, and still she wasn't out of his system:

> At last I ran across her brother. I invited him to dinner. He was always aware of my devotion to his sister and was a little shy about discussing her. So during the meal we talked of my affairs.
>
> Eventually I broached the subject. "By the bye, how's your sister?"
>
> "Oh, she's quite well. Of course you know she's married and living in England."

So what did Charlie do next? Well, he planned to go to London and seek her out, which demonstrates more than sufficiently that Charlie never got over Hetty, and would do anything just to catch a fleeting glimpse of her. But here in the 1912 newspaper article he projects himself as being totally devoid of all feelings for her, and cites Hetty as being the one who is actively stalking him. To further "prove" he is over Hetty, he conjures up a fictitious fiancée whose name begins with 'Dol.' Why break off after the first syllable? She can only be named 'Dolly' or 'Dolores.'

Well, it looks like we're never going to know what led Chaplin to conjure up such a story, but it does strengthen my resolve not to accept the claim that Chaplin was "an honest and truthful biographer." Unless, that is, you want to believe Charlie's account that he fell in and out of love with a millionaire's daughter, and then got engaged to an English socialite but, outside of this article, chose never to mention any of it.

As for the two sisters, Hetty and Edith Kelly, stories of both of them had an unhappy outcome. During the time of Chaplin's visit to London, September 1921, Edith was there too, appearing in *Pins and Needles* at the Gaiety Theatre. Meanwhile, Frank Gould was in France awaiting the outcome of an attempt to sue Edith for divorce on the grounds of desertion, so that he could marry Paris beauty Florence Lacaze. News of Hetty was far more tragic: she died just before Chaplin reached England.

Chapter 18

NEVER GO BACK

The members of the 1912 Karno company sailing to America were: Alf Reeves, Amy Reeve,[1] Charles Chaplin, Albert[2] Westcott, George Seaman, Emily Seaman, Edward Banks, and Stanley Jefferson; plus new members: Edgar Hurley, Ethel Hurley, Amy Forrest and, of course, 'Whimsical' Walker, who was listed as 'Tom' Walker – totalling eight men and four ladies. This time the trip was from Liverpool direct to New York and, being on the British White Star passenger ship the *Oceanic*, was a much more comfortable crossing than the one back in 1910. It took less time, too – Wednesday 2 to Wednesday 9 October. This was a day longer than the trans-Atlantic record but, since the tragedy of her sister ship the *Titanic*, on that very route, the policy of "full-steam ahead and damn the consequences" had been revised.

With ten days to go before their opening night, the Karno Company were given some evenings off to explore the sights and sounds of New York. One of the first things Charlie did was to go with Alf Reeves to see Alf's brother, Billie Reeves, who by sheer coincidence had opened in his own show on Monday of that very week. Although both brothers had been in the States for the last two years, this was the first time they had had a chance to get together and compare notes.

Since last having toured with *A Night in an English Music Hall* – September 1911 to April 1912 – Billie had turned down all offers to head another Karno company and, instead, was playing in a single act titled *A Lesson in Temperance*. Although Chaplin was now himself a recognised vaudeville star he must have felt some reserve in meeting Billie, who was far more established; which is probably why, in his writings, Chaplin makes no mention of this meeting. In fact, he makes no mention of Billie Reeves ever having set foot in America. So we'll never know what Chaplin thought of Reeves' act. Fortunately, we do have a review:

(w/c October 7, 1912)

Proctor's Fifth Avenue Theater

Billie Reeves – "A Lesson in Temperance" (Comedy) – 17 Mins.

The opening scene shows the exit of a booze parlor and the entrance of the drunk's home. Reeves appeared at the exit and was immediately recognised by the audience, although wearing a gray moustache as part of his makeup. In high hat and evening clothes covered by a top coat, from the pocket of which protrudes the head of a duck, he staggers across the stage to his residence. He breathes upon a lamppost and it immediately moves away. The duck keeps up a constant squawking, Every attempt of the drunk to hit it with his cane carries him off his balance. A funny bit is the moving about of the keyhole, all over the door when the drunk attempts to let himself in. Once on the inside everything turns about. The pictures move, the bed is a revolving table, the telephone and clock have concealed springs. There are a hundred and one laughable props. It is a very difficult act to handle

---

[1] Amy Minister had married Alf Reeves on 4 January 1911, at the City Hall, New York.
[2] The ship's manifest records Albert Westcott as "Age: 27. Occupation: Actor. Nearest Relative: F. Westcott (Brother) 28 Vaughn Rd. Camberwell." Other than being Fred Karno Senior's brother, there seems to be little documentary evidence about him.

and must require the services of at least three men behind the scenes. Billie Reeves, of course, goes a long way toward making the offering a success. He is always in the role of "The Drunk," and although not falling about as much as formerly, his work is as effective. Closing the show at the Fifth Avenue, the act did not lose a customer.

(*Variety* – October 12, 1912)

Well! what a great idea for a sketch: a drunk returning home only to find that everyday objects in his house have taken on a life of their own, and do all they can to frustrate, and even menace, him. I can't see why Chaplin didn't use this idea. He could have changed a few things: like the revolving bed becoming a revolving table; and built up the business with the clock, and later made a film of it. He could have called it, say: *1 a.m.* But then Chaplin wouldn't deliberately make out he had never seen someone, just so he couldn't be accused of plagiarism – would he? Oh! Wait a minute. Didn't Chaplin say he'd never seen Leno work? Naw, but he wouldn't do that to a second person – especially his manager's brother. Forget it.

Of the second arrival in New York, Chaplin recalled: "This time I felt at home in the States-a foreigner among foreigners, allied with the rest." The company too would have felt more at ease. Upon their 1910 arrival they had been unrehearsed and unprepared but, for the latest tour, were familiar with the main sketch they were performing, and the audiences they would be performing to. Chaplin, however, wasn't happy with the contribution made by Whimsical Walker, of whom he gave the opinion:

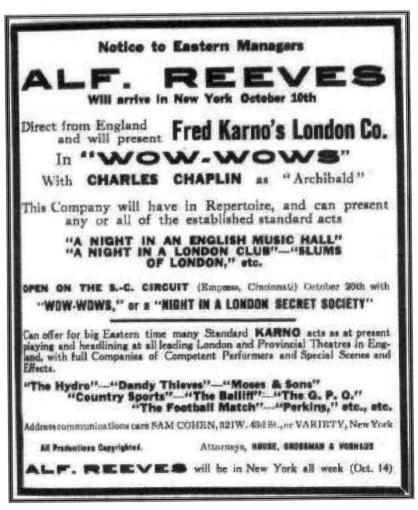

Did you spot the private joke in the above advert from *Variety*? No! Well have another look. Reeves and Chaplin have given their contact address as care of "Sam Cohen."

We took a rehearsal room and had a week of rehearsing *The Wow-Wows*. In the cast was old Whimsical Walker, the famous Drury Lane clown. He was over seventy[1], with a deep, resonant voice, but had no diction, as we discovered at rehearsals, and he had the major part of explaining the plot. Such a line as: "The fun will be furious, ad libitum," he could not say and never did. The first night he spluttered 'ablib-blum,' and eventually it became 'ablibum,' but never the correct word.

(Chaplin's 1964 Autobiography)

Chaplin singling out this minor affliction as a major flaw was totally uncalled for. Walker himself had bigger worries than his stumbling over two Latin words, and astutely pointed out:

We arrived at New York to find that New York had greatly altered. In fact it was a new America. I had been there eight previous times, but it was a new world to me, everybody and everything had altered so much.

We found we were up against great opposition. The caterers for amusement had increased and multiplied since my previous visit. The taste had changed and novelties had been introduced to suit the jaded palates of the excitement-seeking Americans. We were on the Sullivan circuit and at each town we had opposition at the other theatres – Sarah Bernhardt at one theatre and Mrs (Lily) Langtry at the other – until we got right up to San Francisco.

(*From Sawdust to Windsor Castle*, by Whimsical Walker)

The company opened on 20 October, in Cincinnati, where the critics were a lot less critical of the Karno company than was Chaplin.

(w/c Sunday October 20, 1912)

CINCINNATI, Empress

The Empress offered an interesting bill last week. One of the best things ever seen at this house was Fred Karno's London Comedy Company in *The Wow-Wows*, presented by Alf Reeves. Charles Chaplin, who assumes the role of the souse, is exceedingly funny.

(*Billboard* – November 2, 1912)

Followed by a week in Chicago:

(w/c Monday October 28, 1912)

CHICAGO, Empress

Fred Karno's comedy company appearing in the "Kow-Wows" [*sic*] close the show. Charles Champlin [*sic*] as Archibald is fine and is practically the whole show, assuming all of the comedy parts and doing it in a very capable manner. His part is that of a "willie-boy" and he carries it out from the manner of his walk to the way he tips his "at," meaning hat. The whole thing is a burlesque on secret societies and the initiation ceremonies of which Archibald is the "goat" are extremely ridiculous.

(*Billboard* – November 9, 1912)

The advert for the Cincinnati Empress proclaimed that the Karno company was fifteen-strong whilst, the following week, the advert for the Chicago Empress stated sixteen. Only twelve had come over on the *Oceanic*, so could these previews be wrong? Well, no! An extant cast list shows that the company had been joined by Charles Griffiths, Charles Cardon, Fred Westcott, and Bert Howard. The sixteen-strong company then moved on through Milwaukee, Minneapolis and St. Paul, before arriving in Winnipeg:

---

[1] Chaplin wrongly places Whimsical Walker in his account of the 1910 tour. His estimate of Walker's age is also wildly inaccurate. Walker was born 1 April 1856, making him fifty-six – which is somewhat short of "over-seventy."

Alf Reeves Presents

Fred Karno's London Comedy Co.
in
"THE WOW-WOWS"
With Charles Chaplin as
"Archibald."
(First Time in America)

Chas. Chaplin	Archibald Binks
Charles Cardon	Charlie Blazer
Tom Walker	Freddy Brunton
Stan Jefferson	Jack Denton
Edgar Hurley	Jimmie Bottles
Charles Griffiths	Billy Brindle

Up the River Boys:

Fred Westcott	Bert Howard
Ted Banks	George Seaman

Amy Forrest	Lydia Scotch
Ethel Hurley	Mary
Emily Seaman	Selina
Amy Minister	Flossie

Stage Director, Alf Reeves.

Scene 1. "The Nook on the Thames" River Life with its beauty and gaiety
PREPARE!
Scene 2. Entrance to Secret Society's Chamber of Horrors. The sign and password.
"Kiss Me Good Night! 'Nurse!'"
TAKE CARE!
Scene 3. Interior of Chamber of Horrors. The Initiation.
Archibald on the Magic Carpet.
BEWARE!

(w/c November 25, 1912)

WINNIPEG, Empress

Every time Fred Karno's London Company of Comedians comes to Winnipeg it brings with it an act that taxes the house at every performance. This week on his third visit Charles Chaplin, in *The Wow-Wows*, keeps the audience in roars of laughter and the act promises to outdo his previous skits in popularity. In the leading part he takes the role of that peculiar type of English whose cheek and freshness is the source of great amusement. At all the performances yesterday the Empress was jammed to the doors to see the Englishmen in their new act.

(*Winnipeg Telegram* – Tuesday November 26, 1912)

After just a two-night play-over in Billings, and two in Miles City (unconfirmed) it was on to Butte, the mining town for which Chaplin had a fondness. The townspeople reciprocated the feeling:

(w/c Saturday December 7, 1911)

BUTTE, Empress

Archie is here. His coming to the Empress theater is a most interesting event for Archie's presence there means a thoroughly good time for all patrons, a good time made all the more so and in fact strongly emphasised by all other attractions on the delightful, sparkling bill.

'Archie' is really Charles Chaplin and he is the leading comedian in the big act produced by Fred Karno and known as *The Wow Wows*, or "*A Night in a Secret Society.*" The latter part of the title begins to throw some light on Archie and what he does. Many patrons immediately will recall on reading it that Mr. Chaplin made a tremendous hit here as Archie in *A Night in a London Music Hall*, and Archie in *A Night in an English Club*. The way he used to fall out of the box in that London Music hall sketch and the funny pantomime work he did in the other production-well Archie certainly was one great big scream.

This time Mr. Chaplin has a new departure. Instead of pantomime work he has a speaking part as well and thus the question that often was asked as to what kind of a speaking actor he would be has been answered and most satisfactory at that.

As for the act, it is an elaborate affair in three big scenes with a big company of artists supporting Mr. Chaplin. The act is presented by Alf Reeves.

(Butte Miner – December 8, 1911)

Whimsical Walker, however, had totally different feelings, and memories, of the week in Butte:

We then went on to Butte, 2,000 feet above the sea, and when we arrived there we found out that the theatre at which we had arranged to appear had been burnt down[1]. Ill-luck seemed bent upon pursuing us. However, our manager engaged a large hall and we opened. Most of the population were miners, diggers, etc., and a very rough lot too. It was the roughest place I have ever been into. The climate, the hard travelling and the living didn't suit any of us, and the company began to feel very bad. The ladies lost their voices – the gentlemen could hardly work, and some of them, including myself, began bleeding at the nose. This rather frightened some of us, and to make matters worse we could not get any quinine at the drug stores. Possibly we had influenza very badly. We were glad enough to be free from the town.

(From Sawdust to Windsor Castle, by Whimsical Walker)

Chaplin's earlier criticism of "Old Whimmy" pales into insignificance when one considers the illness and discomfort that he, among other members of the troupe, was suffering. Just how the correct pronunciation of "ad libitum" would have alleviated all this begs to be questioned.

A Good Luck note to Stan Jefferson, by Chaplin,.
It reads:

May your path be a "rosy one."
Your Old Pal
Chas. Chaplin
Fred Karno Co.
Seattle
Wash. U.S.A.
Dec. 25ᵗʰ
[another hand has written "1912"]

Chaplin also drew the cartoon of himself as 'Archie' in *The Wow-Wows* (left).
The phrase "rosy one" is in parenthesis and has a small arrow leading to Stan's cheek. One can only assume this is a private joke.
Above is a picture of Stan in his role of 'Jack Denton' in *The Wow-Wows*. No other photographs from this sketch are known to exist.

[1] In the week's newspapers for Butte, there weren't any accounts of a fire. The most-likely explanation is that the fire had been in Billings, or Miles City, immediately prior to the Butte engagement, for which no cuttings were forthcoming.

From Montana the troupe headed into Washington state. A week in Spokane, was followed by a week in Seattle, where we pick up Whimsical Walker's account:

> We travelled on to Seattle, the starting point for the Klondyke region. It was a very long journey and raining hard all the while. I became so bad that I thought my time had come. I went up to my hotel, but could not sleep or rest a bit.

> (*ibid*)

The following day, Christmas Eve, Walker was sent to hospital, where he was diagnosed as having erysipelas – a streptococcal infectious disease of the skin, characterized by fever, headache, vomiting, and purplish raised lesions on the face. Poor chap! His hospitalisation lasted fully three months, after which he was happy to accept the advice that he would be better off going home, and went without waiting for a second opinion. Back in October 1912 an insert in *Variety* had proclaimed: "One of England's greatest clown comedians, Whimsical Walker, has started on a tour round the world." Now, five months later, he was returning to England with his health, his finances, and his reputation all diminished.

Minus their narrator, the troupe moved on to British Columbia, to ring in the New Year in Vancouver:

> (w/c Monday December 30, 1912)
>
> ### VANCOUVER, Orpheum
>
> The programme at the Orpheum Theatre this week has the correct expression when it announces the "welcome" return of Karno's Comedians, for this well-known company was given one of the heartiest of welcomes at the opening performance yesterday, and they deserved it too for their offering this trip is even better than their last and it was considered excellent. These fourteen talented people offer a screamingly funny farce in three scenes, entitled *The Wow Wows*, and to say that it took the house by storm is putting it mildly indeed. The story concerns the efforts of a party of campers to get even with one of their number for various abuses by initiating him into a secret order and the situations can easily be imagined. Charles Chaplin, who has hitherto been a silent comedian, has a speaking part in this sketch and is very funny. He is well supported by other members of the company

> (*Daily News Advertiser* – December 31, 1912)

The above description "These fourteen talented people offer a screamingly funny farce," is somewhat of a different turn of phrase to the one they received back in New York in October 1910, when they were branded: "a collection of blithering, blathering Englishmen." Then, they were almost deported – now, they were "given one of the heartiest of welcomes." So what had brought about this complete turnaround. We do know that Chaplin was credited as having added more comic business to *The Wow-Wows*, most notably to his own role, by making Archie 'a souse.' But was Chaplin deserving of all the praise? Stan Laurel seemed to think so. He commented in later life: "*The Wow-Wows* had been developed into a ruddy good show, which Charlie really built up out of nothing,"

The first week of 1913 found the Karno Company back in Washington, this time in Tacoma.

> (w/c January 6, 1913)
>
> ### TACOMA, Empress – "THE WOW-WOWS"
>
> Chaplin has more to do than in previous sketches which is just what his audiences will like, for he is undeniably funny in everything he does and says.

> (*Daily Ledger* – January 7, 1913)

And the following week in Portland, Oregon:

(Stan Laurel Collection)

(Stan Laurel Collection)
(Los Angeles Natural History Museum)

"THE WOW-WOWS"

I had never come across any photographs or cartoons showing the set or cast from *The Wow-Wows*, until these stunning cartoons from the 1912-1913 tour surfaced just before I went to press. These depict some of the new business in the revised sketch. When first aired, the 'Initiation Ceremony' consisted almost solely of 'Archie' being made to suffer electrical shocks from a "magic carpet." Here though we have a much more elaborate ceremony, with hooded figures leading 'Archie' through a decidedly darker ritual. If the cartoon is a true depiction, then the Karno company were either extremely brave or extremely foolish in their choice of costume, for it seems to be a direct satire on the Ku Klux Klan with, instead of white men in white garb, black-face men in black garb. Good job they didn't play Georgia, I say.

(w/c January 13, 1913)

PORTLAND, Empress

Charles Chaplin as Archibald Binks, at the Empress this week, makes "a hit" and incidentally is hit several times while being initiated into the order of *"The Wow Wows."* He is a clever chap and is supported by an excellent company, who present the little three-scene comedy depicting "A Night in an English Secret Society." The scenery is realistic, representing a camp on the Thames and, later, the interior of the clubroom of "The Wow Wows." Among those supporting Chaplin are Charles Cardon, Tom Walker, Stan Jefferson, Amy Forrest, Ethel Hurley and Charles Griffiths.

(*Morning Oregonian* – January 14, 1913)

We have already covered how the original twelve passengers aboard the *Oceanic* became a cast of sixteen, but round about this time came some other changes. Firstly, Arthur Dandoe crept in by the back door, and rejoined the company – probably as a replacement for Whimsical Walker. Walker's name appears on the Portland programme, though by his own account he had left a few weeks earlier, in Seattle. Another later inclusion in the cast was Billy Crackles, a veteran of the Karno Company, and a returnee to the U.S. Maybe the illness mentioned by Walker had also laid out another member of the troupe, for whom he had been brought in as a replacement.

From the state of Oregon the troupe took the train to California to play one week in San Francisco, one in Sacramento, and then Los Angeles, a city that Chaplin had been disparaging about last time around.

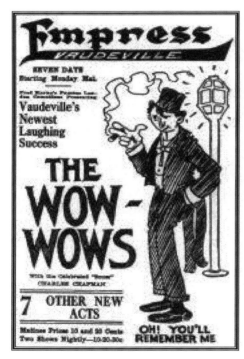

A cartoon which depicts nothing whatsoever of the costume, character or the set of *The Wow-Wows*. Its most likely origins is Billie Reeves' character in *A Lesson in Temperance*, in which is he has some interplay with a lamppost on his way home after a drunken binge.

(w/c Monday February 10, 1913)

LOS ANGELES, Empress

One act on the bill which opened yesterday afternoon is worth double the price of admission if one compares the money paid out with the number of laughs received in return. And this happy state of affairs is all due to *The Wow Wows* – whatever they are. The act might just as well have been called by any other name, but it isn't the name that counts – it's the act itself. You snicker at the absurd costumes, you holler at the antics of the players, and you almost scream your head off when you hear them talk. If the old saying, "Laugh and grow fat," has a grain of truth in it, some six hundred or more persons at yesterday's matinee have taken on weight.

(*Los Angeles Herald* – February 11, 1913)

A second review ran:

"The Wow Wows" is composed of a small troupe of performers, featuring Charles Chaplin as Binks, an inebriate. Binks is one of a camping party. His companions decide to put him through the mysteries of "The Wow Wows," and the broad comedy and horseplay that takes place in the initiation scene is more than worth the money.

(*Los Angeles Express* – February 11, 1913)

One more week in California found them in San Diego:

(w/c February 17, 1913)

SAN DIEGO, Empress

Charles Chaplin, who made a reputation as a comedian in "A Night in an English Music Hall," which appeared at the Empress two years ago, proved last night as much of a hit in his performance of the part of "Archibald Birke" in *The Wow Wows*. "The Wow Wows" is a burlesque secret society, and that the comedy consists mainly in action is indicated when it is said that the initiation of Archibald into the mysteries of the order furnishes the theme for most of the fun.

Chaplin has an off hand, indifferent way of "taking his medicine," which adds more to the comic effect by far than if he affected to undergo the most excruciating agonies. The company is a large one, but Chaplin, as always, outshines the rest.

(San Diego Union – February 18, 1913)

San Diego was followed by a week in Salt Lake, Utah, from where they pushed on through Colorado, playing Denver, Pueblo, and Colorado Springs on the way, and ended the tour in Kansas City, Missouri. However, Reeves had secured them a twelve-week contract to tour part of the Nixon-Nirdlinger circuit, commencing in one week's time in Philadelphia. The break was very welcome, as the whole troupe was beginning to tire of the repetitiveness of their schedule. But for Chaplin, at least, there was one consolation. On 6 March 1913 he had entered into the third year of his three-year contract, which meant his pay had now been increased from £12 per week to £15 – which was then the equivalent of $75. This obviously gave him a feeling of affluence as, for one fleeting moment, he totally abandoned his usual thrifty ways:

We had been working the 'sticks' continuously for five months and the weariness of it had left me discouraged, so that when we had a week's lay-off in Philadelphia, I welcomed it. I needed a change, another environment – to lose my identity and become someone else. I was fed up with the drab routine of tenth-rate vaudeville and decided that for one week I would indulge in the romance of graceful living. I had saved a considerable sum of money and, in sheer desperation, I decided to go on a spending spree. Now I would go to New York and shed myself of tenth-rate vaudeville and its whole drab existence.

Chaplin then goes on to describe how he spent a whole week's wages on just a dressing-gown and a smart over-night case. The specification of the latter proved apt, as Chaplin's proposed week of indulgence in graceful living turned out to be for one night only. The experience of being fussed over by hotel staff in the New York Astor, and an uncontrollable bout of sobbing, brought about by watching *Tannhäuser* at the Metropolitan Opera House, had left him emotionally drained. It also affected his feelings towards his fellow man, as he himself disclosed:

The following day I decided to return to Philadelphia. Although that one day had been the change I needed, it had been an emotional and a lonely one. Now I wanted company. I looked forward to our Monday morning performance and meeting members of the troupe. No matter how irksome it was returning to the old grind, that one day of graceful living had sufficed me.

Well there's an admission:- Charles Chaplin wanting company. And not the company of writers, film stars, or state leaders, but his own workmates. If only he had had regular nights away he might have appreciated them a whole lot more, and a whole lot sooner. But then maybe he had done this kind of thing before, but just not mentioned it. Stan Laurel said of him:

I was Charlie's roommate on that tour and he was fascinating to watch. People through the years have talked about how eccentric he became. He was very eccentric even then. He was very moody and often very shabby in appearance. Then suddenly he would astonish us all by getting dressed to kill. It seemed that every once in a while he would get an urge to look very smart. At these times he would wear a derby hat, an expensive one, gloves, smart suit, fancy vest, two-tone side-button shoes, and carry a cane.

The accuracy of Laurel's memories is, as usual, outstanding, and his accounts can be relied on about ninety-five per cent of the time; whereas Chaplin's come in at less than fifty per cent – and I think I'm being generous at that figure. However, in this instance, Chaplin's version tallies: "I wore" he says, "my smart cut-away coat and derby hat and cane." However, he lets himself down badly when he claims: "As usual I lived alone." Why does Chaplin makes this claim, when it so obviously isn't true? There is much documentation of the incidence of Stan and Charlie rooming together, stories that just wouldn't work had they not been sharing. The following two, from interviews Stan Laurel gave, should make the point:

> It was on that tour that I shared rooms with Charlie Chaplin. To save spending money in restaurants we used to cook our food over the gas flame in our bedroom. One night, with my usual clumsiness, I tried to cook some tinned beans without first puncturing the lid. The tin bursts with a loud report and splattered its contents all over the wall. After that, the landlady issued a stern edict that cooking in the bedrooms was strictly forbidden. But I'm afraid we disregarded it.
>
> One night while we were frying some chops, we heard her coming along the corridor. With characteristic resourcefulness, Charlie promptly snatched up his violin and played a lively air to drown the sound of the sizzling, whilst I snatched the chops from the gas jet and held the pan out of the window to get rid of the smell!

> (*Tit-Bits* – 21 November 1936)

Stan had narrated this story some seven years earlier than the latter:

> Charlie was the featured comedian in the troupe, while I was billed as second in importance and his understudy. He was earning twelve pounds a week, while I was only getting five – a mere pittance, in view of American costs – but we had fun in those days, with Charlie always the life and soul of the party.
>
> Charlie and I lived together, sharing the same room, for more than two years, and many's the time we've cooked our dinners in our room. I fried the chops, while Charlie sat close to the door, playing his mandolin[1] to keep the landlady from hearing the sizzling of the meat over the gas – which was put there for lighting purposes only and not with any idea of cooking!
>
> Charlie was the ringleader in everything. Even then we all felt there was something in him which was different from other men. We didn't know what he was; we couldn't put our fingers on it; but it *was* there.

> (*Film Weekly* – 23 September 1929)

Two very telling additional comments are contained in the above. Firstly Stan says: ".. with Charlie always the life and soul of the party," and then: "Charlie was the ringleader in everything." These give an entirely different picture to the one Charlie paints, wherein he is uncomfortable in the company of the rest of the troupe. Fred Karno added his thoughts on Chaplin's social skills:

> He [Chaplin] could also be very unlikeable. I've known him to go whole weeks without saying a word to anyone in the company. Occasionally he would be quite chatty but, on the whole, he was dour and unsociable.

---

[1] The interviewer is probably at fault here. It should say "violin." He may have either misheard Stan, or couldn't read his own notes.

And here lies the ambivalence within Chaplin. He would join in fun and games with the company, but only if he were the leader. The best analogy I can think of to describe this relationship is to compare it with that between a sheepdog and sheep. The sheepdog will not run with the flock. Nor will it play with the flock, nor lie down with it. The only time it spends with the sheep is when it is controlling all the action. Were it asked to relinquish its dominant role, and let one of the sheep have a turn, it would not acquiesce. When the fun is over the sheep stay together, whereas the sheepdog removes itself and becomes a solitary figure.

Now returned to Philadelphia, after his one night sojourn to New York, Chaplin was made to wish he had stayed where he was by the contents of a telegram that was awaiting him.

> We were playing somewhere in the 'smalls' of Philadelphia. The wire read: 'Are you the man who played the drunk at the American Music Hall three years ago? If so, will you get in touch with Kessel and Bauman, Longacre Building, New York?'

> I hadn't the faintest idea who Kessel and Bauman were. Perhaps it was a firm of lawyers and some rich relative of mine had died and left me a fortune. I was a little let down when I discovered it was a motion picture concern, nevertheless I was elated.

(A Comedian Sees the World – 1933)

So he immediately returned to New York, to see what they wanted:

> Mr. Kessel informed me that Mack Sennett had instructed him to get in touch with me. I remember how well I played my cards at that interview with Charlie Kessel; how I boosted my salary, I was getting seventy-five dollars a week at that time. I assured Kessel that my only interest in motion pictures was the consideration of my health. The work would be in the open air and the outdoor life appealed to me. It was for this reason only that I would consider pictures. Of course, I went on, I got two hundred and fifty dollars a week in vaudeville, but on account of the nature of the work, I would make a sacrifice. We eventually compromised for one hundred and fifty dollars, and I left the office firm in the belief that I was an embezzler.

The agreement was left open-ended, with Kessel and Baumann informing Chaplin that the final decision rested with Mr. Sennett. Chaplin was currently almost as far away from Sennett as it was possible to be within U.S. limits, as his studios were in Los Angeles, on the West coast. However, in five months time the company was due in California, so Chaplin would be able to meet up with his potential new boss then. As to why he had been summoned, Chaplin related:

> Mr. Charles Kessel, one of the owners of the Keystone Comedy Film Company, said that Mr Mack Sennett had seen me playing the drunk in the American Music Hall on Forty-second Street and if I were the same man he would like to engage me to take the place of Mr Ford Sterling.

So just how accurate is Chaplin's account? Well, he continually names Adam Kessel as "Charles," which was Baumann's first name; but, for the first time in this book, I am delighted to say that Chaplin got the year, month, week, and even days correct. The Karno company's week-off after finishing on the S&C circuit in Kansas was Monday March 31 to Sunday April 6, 1913. *Tannhäuser* played at the New York Metropolitan on Thursday April 3, for one night only, which makes it the one-and-only night Chaplin could have attended. The following day Chaplin returns to Philadelphia. Saturday morning, with telegram in hand, he returns to New York for the meeting with Kessel and Baumann. By Sunday he is back in Philadelphia and then, on Monday morning April 7, rejoins the rest of the cast for a run through with the stage staff.

The first six weeks of the Nixon engagement were all at theatres in Philadelphia, so the company rotated three different sketches; "*Music Hall*," "*London Club*," and *The Wow-Wows*.

(w/c April 21, 1913)

PHILADELPHIA, Nixon

Karno's London Co. appeared in the uproariously funny sketch *A Night in a London Music Hall*, with Charles Chaplin enacting the part of the drunk. He was a scream.

(w/c May 5, 1913)

PHILADELPHIA, Nixon

For the third week of their sparkling engagement at the Nixon, the Karno Komedy Company yesterday presented *The Wow-Wows*, a lively sketch, in which Chas. Chaplin made a decided hit as the silly bounder, who is the butt of much of the fun.

(*Philadelphia Inquirer* – May 6, 1913)

Above and below are newspaper ads. for the three different sketches the Karno company played during their extended stay in Philadelphia. The billing for *The Wow-Wows* is a sign of just how much this sketch had been improved upon, as it is described as: "Their Comedy Masterpiece."

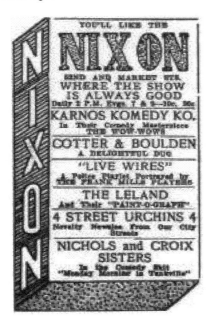

Rare, if not unique, photo of Alf Reeves (right) and Chaplin standing in front of the poster advertising their presence at the Metropolitan Opera House, Philadelphia.

A Night in an English Music Hall was played only four times on the October 1912 to November 1913 U.S. tours. Happily, we have three different items of ephemera to mark the events. Above is a cartoon showing 'Archie' doing one of his famous tumbles out of the box, whilst being peppered with ammunition from a pea-shooter being used by the Eton boy, left.

'The Saucy Soubrette' sings "You Naughty, Naughty Men," whilst being leered at by Archie.

FRED KARNO'S Original London Pantomime Company
Presenting "A NIGHT IN AN ENGLISH MUSIC HALL"
CAST:

The Inebriated Swell	CHARLES CHAPLIN
The Bad Boy	Edgar Hurley
Uncle William	Charles Griffiths

THE VAUDEVILLE ACTS

1	The Red Nose Comic	Stanley Jefferson
2	The Ballad Vocalist	Amy Forrest
3	Professor Bunco, Magician	Chas. Gordon
4	The Village Glee Singers	Fred Westcott, Albert Austin, Bert Howard, Frank Williams
5	The Saucy Soubrette	Amy Minister
6	The Terrible Turk	Ted Banks

Manager for Fred Karno's Company in America, Alf Reeves.

The cast from *A Night in an English Music Hall* reveals additional members
Charles Griffiths, Chas. Gordon, Bert Howard, and Frank Williams.
Also of note is that Stan Jefferson has now gained a solo part as "The Red-Nose Comic."
And what of the character played by Chas. Gordon? Makes you wonder where Chaplin
got the idea from for "Prof. Bosco, Magician" as seen in his film *The Circus*.

For their sixth, and final, week in Philadelphia, our unhappy band played the Metropolitan, formerly the home of opera, which had opened as a vaudeville venue just two weeks earlier. Here they changed the sketch in mid-week.

w/c May 19, 1913

PHILADELPHIA, Metropolitan

For the third week at the Metropolitan under the new management of Marcus Loew and Nixon-Nirdlinger, the headliner for the first half of the week will be Karno's Komedy Kompany in *A Night in a London Music Hall*, and, for the second half, *A Night at the Club*.

(Philadelphia Inquirer – Sunday May 18, 1913)

From Philadelphia the troupe moved on for two, two-week stays in Baltimore and Washington DC, where "Music Hall" was again presented the first week, and "London Club" the second. June 21 then signalled the end of their run on the Nixon-Nirdlinger circuit, which came as a relief to the whole company. Working these second-rate, ten-cent theatres had taken its toll on them. Chaplin himself admitted:

> These cheap vaudeville circuits were bleak and depressing, and hopes about my future in America disappeared in the grind of doing three and sometimes four shows a day, seven days a week. Vaudeville in England was paradise by comparison. At least we only worked there six days a week and only gave two shows a night.

(Chaplin's 1964 Autobiography)

The thrill of the chase had obviously run its course for Chaplin. The first challenge had been to become one of Fred Karno's Comedians; the second was to become the lead-comic; and the third – to become famous. Having passed all three challenges, there was nothing else within the Karno Company for Chaplin to achieve. All he had now was the tedium of returning to the same towns and venues, and repeating the same sketches. For the first six months of this tour they had played almost solely *The Wow-Wows*, and for the next five months, the only sketch would be *A Night in a London Club*. This must have been soul destroying. These players were masters of comedy. They thrived on comic invention and working-up new sketches but, on this tour, they were just going through the motions.

Before coming back to the States, the plan had been for them to play two new sketches: *The Hydro*, and *The Village Sports*. The latter had similarities to *A Night in a London Club*, in that the premise was a sport's presentation evening in a village hall. But at least it would have given the company something new and challenging to perform. As for *The Hydro*, which was all about guests "taking the waters" at a health spa, maybe Chaplin could salvage some of that for a later film – say: *The Cure*.

Even the excitement of working and socialising with new acts had been denied them as, following a week off, it was back to the Sullivan & Considine circuit, where all the acts in their show were now touring as one complete package. Morale was at an all-time low. It was inevitable that, shortly, someone was about to make a break for it and, when they did, the whole "House That Karno Built" would come tumbling down.

Chapter 19

THE FINAL STAGE

With *A Night In a London Club* as the main sketch, the next tour started in Detroit, Michigan, after which came Chicago.

> (w/c Sunday July 6, 1913)
>
> ## CHICAGO, Halstead Empress
>
> The Karno Company is playing a burlesque-pantomime called *A Night In a London Club*. Full of slap-stick humor, it is diverting, and Sunday afternoon the act had the house in an uproar of laughter. Charles Chaplin tumbles about in a surprising style and is the principal funmaker, although several others perform lively stunts and bring out numerous laughs. The character make-up of the people is excellent, and there are several moments in the sketch where laughter is at a high point.
>
> (*Variety* – July 11, 1913)

Four weeks later, two of which had been spent in the "Twin Cities" of Minneapolis and St. Paul, the company paid their third visit to Winnipeg

> (w/c Monday August 4, 1913)
>
> ## WINNIPEG, Empress – "A Night in a London Club"
>
> Karno's English Comedy Company, headed by Charles Chaplin, is the headline attraction at the Empress this week and well deserves the reputation as a merriment producer. Charles Chaplin, known as the only comedian who can act the part of a drunk realistically, without at any time approaching the vulgar, is the leading spirit of the sketch, and keeps the audience in an uproar from the rise of the curtain. Mr. Chaplin is remarkably supported, especially by Edgar Hurley and Amy Forest. The act itself is a farce of the extreme order, but it is so well carried out that the idea proves a fun maker – so "nuff said."
>
> (*Winnipeg Telegram* – August 5, 1913)

The vast majority of reviews credit only Chaplin by name, but the above gives a very rare mention to two of the other featured players. Although the reviewer excuses himself from divulging more about the act itself, a couple of days earlier he had written a preview, using the advance publicity notes, which gives an insight into the premise of the sketch:

> Charles Chaplin, who always portrays the very funny role of the inebriated gentleman of the productions, has a personal following that is always effusive and warm in its greeting, and in this elaborate and best of the Karno successes he is better-if such a thing is possible-than in any other of the comedies.
>
> The scene depicts "ladies night" at the Bumblers' Angling Society, with "Archibald" (Charles Chaplin) in a hopelessly maudlin condition, while the other members have their "company manners," and are trying their unsuccessful best to squelch the pugnacious Archie. The antics and dialogue of the amateur entertainers to secure the attention of their

Archie removes his jacket in readiness for a
punch-up with Mr. Meek.
Washington Post
Cosmos Theater, Washington

fellow members while they add their
songs and recitations to the enjoyment of
"ladies night" are screamingly funny.

(*Winnipeg Telegram* – August 3, 1913)

Whilst in Winnipeg, Chaplin stayed at the *Le
Claire Hotel*, where he wrote a letter to his brother
Syd. David Robinson later found this letter in the
Chaplin Archives. One paragraph revealed:

> Right here in Winnipeg I met one of the
> old boys who use to be in the Eight
> Lancashire Lads. I dont know wether you
> would know him or not – Tommy Bristol
> – he use to be my biggest pal – now he's
> working the Orpheum turns with a
> partner.

(Chaplin Archive – w/c August 4, 1913)

Of those acts appearing at the Orpheum that
week, "Handers & Milliss – Dancing Pianists"
seems to be the likeliest bet for the one Tommy
Bristol was in. The act was described as follows:

Two clever entertainers from England, where they are famous favourites, are Handers and
Milliss, known as "Eccentric Dancing Pianists." The chief distinction of their work lies in
the fact that they do these things – and also sing – all at the same time, and have given the
turn real finish as well.

(*Winnipeg Telegram* – August 2, 1913)

On the last night of the week in Winnipeg, Chaplin met and befriended one of four brothers
from a touring sketch titled: *Mrs Green's Reception Room*. Maybe you've heard of him –
Groucho Marx. In his memoirs, Groucho was relaxed enough to divulge:

I was on the Pantages Circuit, the last act on the bill, doing four shows a day, rain or shine.
There was a three-hour layover in Winnipeg before jumping to the Coast. As a rule, I made
a bee-line for the pool room. It was generally warmer! This particular night I decided on
the spur of the moment to take in a show.

Well, sir, at this show, the audience was roaring with laughter. I looked at the stage and saw
Chaplin for the first time. I had never heard people laugh like that. I began to laugh, too.
His act was called A Night at the Club. It was supposed to be an English social club.
Chaplin sat at a small table and ate soda crackers one after another. A woman up front was
singing all the while, but nobody heard a note, I'm sure. They were intent on Chaplin's
every move. A fine stream of cracker dust was slowly coming out of his mouth. He kept
that up for exactly fifteen minutes.

At the table was a large basket of oranges. Finally, he started to pick up the oranges, one
by one, and throw them at the woman. One of the oranges knocked the pianist off his chair.
People became hysterical. There never was such continuous laughter. I thought he was the
greatest fellow I had ever seen on the stage.

I was so impressed by Chaplin that I sought him out after the show and we became friends.
The two circuits that we were on made the same towns, and when we were on stage at the
same times we would visit each other between shows.

(*Photoplay Magazine* – 1936)

On the bill with the Karno Company between June and September 1913 was a sketch called "*The Tamer*" played by Mabel Florence and Beresford Lovett. Chaplin signed one of his publicity photos to Mabel, but then, for some unknown reason, kept it. He then forgot just who Mabel was.

(see *Chaplin – My Life in Pictures.*)

The Marx Brothers weren't yet actually on the Pantages circuit, but were on their way through to Edmonton, Alberta, Canada, where their tour was to commence on August 11. So what Groucho actually means when he says: "There was a three-hour layover in Winnipeg before jumping to the coasts," is simply that they had to wait for the connecting train.

Of the show itself, the relevant part of the script, as below, will show us just how accurate Groucho's recollection was:

```
               A NIGHT IN A LONDON CLUB
Chairman calls for order and then on comes Percy Swoffles¹ for
the next song.
Percy obliges with song and dance and finishes with being
bombarded with prop oranges from the members, finally he falls
off rostrum and Steward helps him to his feet.
Mr. Binks goes to him and presents him with a red ribbon, kisses
him on the forehead then pushes him and he finally lands
knocking over Taylor and Clark.
Chairman again regains order, then announces item - calling on
the Steward's daughter little Aggie for a recitation "The
Collier's Dying Child".
Steward escorts Aggie to the rostrum.
Aggie "The Cottage was a thatched one" etc., the guests get very
sad and one or two start to shed a tear.
Mr. Binks starts eating crackers and blows them over Taylor and
Clark.
               ------------------------
```

It's interesting to note that Groucho was happy to speak of this, and subsequent, meetings with Chaplin, whilst Chaplin never wrote a single word about meeting Groucho. But, as we have witnessed many times, Chaplin was wont to omit from his records anyone who went on to be famous.

Through Montana, with stopovers in Miles City and Butte; on through Washington state, to play Spokane and Seattle, the company arrived in Vancouver:

(w/c September 8, 1913)

VANCOUVER B.C., Orpheum

The Fred Karno Company, with Charles Chaplin featured, are back once more in the city in *A Night In A London Club*, and were heartily welcomed by the many friends at the Orpheum yesterday. Chaplin's conception of the "inebriate" could not be improved upon, and he has made the part his own. While he is the star of the company, the rest of the members all do their part to amuse and they surely do make the audience laugh.

(Daily News Advertiser – September 9, 1913)

Groucho Marx, back in Winnipeg, may have found the "cracker spitting" hilarious, but the reviewer for the show in Tacoma could not have had a more opposing view:

(w/c September 15, 1913)

TACOMA, Empress

Save for the idea of comedy which consists of spitting water or chewed crackers into another's face, the *Night in an English Club* is still the funny slap-stick farce as on its former visit. It seems odd that this revolting feature of a successful act cannot be eliminated. Charles Chaplin is inimitable in his characterization of the drunk and the farce is reaping its usual harvest of laughs.

(Daily Ledger – September 16, 1913)

However the following week the theatre critic found all the business to be "hilariously funny."

(w/c September 22, 1913)

PORTLAND, Empress

Archibald, Mr. Meek, the henpecked, Mrs. Meek, his better-half; the Chairman; Steward; a long-haired musician; and a would-be actor; and several other comical characters are to be seen in *A Night in a London Club*, which is presented this week at the Empress by a troupe of clever English character actors. The playlet is a satire on the organizations that are made up of supposed-to-be Bohemians and think-they-can-sing musicians.

There are eighteen in the company and stellar place is filled by Charles Chaplin who is noted for his comic portrayal of Archibald, the "souse." The latest act of *A Night in a London Club* is crowded with hilariously funny situations and the comedians are kept on the jump throughout the half-hour they hold the stage.

(Morning Oregonian – September 23, 1913)

It was while in Portland that Chaplin's contract to join the Keystone Company arrived, which he duly signed and returned. Now that Chaplin knew his time with the Karno company was limited, the remaining weeks would have been agony. He would have just wanted to quit and start a new challenge. Knowing he was leaving almost certainly also had a negative effect on the rest of the cast, and maybe it began to show.

(w/c Sunday, October 5, 1913)

SAN FRANCISCO, Empress – "A NIGHT IN A LONDON CLUB"

Fred Karno's Company with Charlie Chaplin, had the closing spot, but the offering only proved ordinarily entertaining to the Empress regulars.

(Variety – October 10, 1913)

This disappointing review was followed, in Sacramento, by one even more damaging:

(w/c Sunday, October 12, 1913)

SACRAMENTO, Empress – "A NIGHT IN A LONDON CLUB"

Karno's Comedians comprised fifteen people, a number of whom could be dispensed with so far as the humor of the act. Their funmaking was of the slapstick variety, laughable in its ridiculousness but lacking in high-class comedy. None of the dialogue was distinguishable in the rough-house methods used to snatch the giggles from the audience and possibly it was just as well. The best part of the act was the way in which Charles Chaplin impersonated a stolid Englishman inebriated.

(Sacramento Bee – October 13, 1913)

These reviews would have had Charlie desperately worried. The troupe were about to revisit Los Angeles, where Chaplin was to meet Sennett, and he certainly didn't want bad reviews preceding him. Even more importantly, when they got there, he didn't want a bad reception from any of the Los Angeles' audiences, especially on the night Sennett would be in the house. So how was he received?

(w/c October 20, 1913)

LOS ANGELES, Empress

Charlie Chaplin is back with his amusing characterisation of a "souse." This time he appears in *A Night in a London Club*, a social affair where everybody has a good time and does exactly what he likes. Chaplin does his usual stunts at tumbling and knocking everybody down, he himself remaining preternaturally solemn all the time. There are no less than fifteen people in the cast, bright men and women, who know how to keep the ball of fun rolling.

(*Los Angeles Times* – October 21, 1913)

A second review ran:

Mr. Chaplin is known from coast to coast as the original "souse." The word is not pretty, but neither is Mr. Chaplin. As the original dyed in the wool, dead in the face drunkard, Mr. Chaplin is immense. At this point the house slipped and stripped its gears, and went stark staring crazy with joy. Mr. Chaplin slammed and was slammed about the stage in a manner most miraculous. He inflicted falls upon others, but took a number himself. Everyone on the stage did weird topplings. The piano player stood on his ear and spun about – the woman – oh well, what's the use? See it yourself, but don't tear up the benches.

(*Los Angeles Herald* – October 22, 1913)

Chaplin adds a personal insight from which one can feel his obvious relief at the turnaround in audience reaction from the ones in San Francisco and Sacramento:

When we played the Empress in Los Angeles, we were a howling success, thank God. It was a comedy called *A Night at the Club*. I played a decrepit old drunk and I looked at least fifty years old. Mr. Sennett came round after the performance and congratulated me. But I wondered how sympathetic he would be in our future relationship. All through the interview I was extremely nervous and was not sure whether he was pleased with me or not.

(Chaplin's 1964 Autobiography)

There was one particular item on the bill which Sennett would undoubtedly have asked Chaplin his opinion on, namely:

Exclusive of the new acts will be the Keystone comedies in which the popular comedian Ford Sterling figures as the star.

(*Los Angeles Times* – October 21, 1913)

And there is no doubt that members of the company did watch the films they shared the bill with, as Stan Laurel testifies in a letter to a fan, dated June 2, 1958:

Dear Earl:-

Most of my picture viewing was done in my Vaudeville days when they used to run films on the same show, so to fill time between shows I'd go out front to watch them – I guess I got pretty fed up with them.

(Stan Laurel letter – Marriot Collection)

And Chaplin's confirmation, which came out at the first meeting with Kessel and Baumann.

"Had I seen a Keystone Comedy?" Asked Mr Kessel. Of course I had seen several, I did not tell him that I thought they were a crude mélange of rough and tumble. However, a pretty dark-eyed girl named Mabel Normand, who was quite charming, weaved in and out of them and justified their existence. I was not terribly enthusiastic about the Keystone type of comedy, but I realised their publicity value.

(Chaplin's 1964 Autobiography)

Obviously Chaplin did not reveal his thoughts to Sennett, but there is a very real probability that Sennett would have detected a coldness within Chaplin, hence his showing no outward liking for Chaplin, the man.

Chaplin:

He [Sennett] asked me casually when I would join them. I told him that I could start the first week in September, which would be the termination of my contract with the Karno Company.

(Chaplin's 1964 Autobiography)

When Chaplin went to the New York offices of Kessel and Baumann, back in April, he may well have said he could join Keystone in September, but he certainly didn't say it here in Los Angeles, for it was now the end of October. So why was Chaplin still with Karno when his contract had finished over eleven weeks ago? The simple answer is that it *hadn't* finished. The last contract Chaplin had signed with Karno was back on 19 September 1910, just before he first sailed for America. Chaplin must have therefore convinced himself that the contract was up on 19 September 1913. But he had forgotten one thing: although the contract *had* been signed in September 1910, it was an amendment to an existing contract, but with the date of commencement being 6 March 1911, meaning it would terminate in March 1914.

It would appear, however, that Kessel and Baumann had taken Chaplin's word at face-value and, in July 1913, had drafted a contract wherein Chaplin would commence work as a "moving picture actor" on November 1, 1913. Chaplin never signed it. A second contract was then drawn up with the date of commencement changed to December 16, 1913, which is the one he signed in Portland, during the last week in September.

David Robinson, who later found both contracts in the Chaplin Archives, surmises that the reason Chaplin did not sign the first contract was because: "Chaplin, at this stage of his career, was not prepared to throw up security with Karno to run the risk of unforeseen employment within the year." But Chaplin's staying an extra six weeks with Karno was hardly providing him with security or long-term employment. No! Something has been overlooked here. These dates must have relevance. The negotiating parties were not just plucking them out of the air at random.

One must realise that Chaplin was not a free agent, and was therefore not at liberty to call all the shots. First and foremost, he still had six months of his contract with Karno to run. If Karno didn't wish to release him, and Chaplin chose to walk, he could be severely financially penalised, or even blacklisted.

Conversely, Karno didn't have all the rights to agree to a mutual termination, as he was not the only party wanting to keep hold of the star performer. Sullivan and Considine wanted their theatres filling thirteen to twenty times a week but, without the star attraction of Chaplin, there was a very real likelihood that this wouldn't be achieved. And this one tour was only a fraction of the big picture, for Sullivan & Considine had by now given Karno a five year contract, which meant both parties had an investment of hundreds of thousands of pounds to protect.

Fred Karno, the owner of "A Night in a London Club" is one of England's largest producers and has fifteen or twenty pantomime companies on the road. Sullivan & Considine have succeeded in securing contracts with Mr. Karno whereby they will present the different Karno acts at their theaters for the company for five years. Considering what a power Mr. Karno is in the theatrical world, he paid the Sullivan & Considine circuit a very high compliment when he entered into such a contract with them. Mr. Karno considers "A Night in a London Club" as being one of the best pieces he has on the road and judging from its wonderful success, he is justified in this belief.

One must conclude that Karno sent instructions saying he would release Chaplin from the contract between the two of them, but on condition that Chaplin satisfactorily saw out the current tour on the Sullivan and Considine contract, a point which Chaplin himself makes:

> I did not exist while waiting to hear from Kessel. Perhaps I had asked too much? At last the letter came, stating that they were willing to sign a year's contract for one hundred and fifty dollars the first three months and one hundred and seventy-five dollars for the remaining nine, more money than I had ever been offered in my life. It was to start with the termination of our Sullivan and Considine tour.

> (Chaplin's 1964 Autobiography)

Chaplin makes a second reference to this clause, in the letter he wrote to Syd, back in August, which makes me wonder why it has previously been overlooked:

> Of course I told them I would not leave this company until we finished the SC circuit, so I will join them about the beginning of Dec that will be about the time we get through.

> (*ibid*)

The Sullivan and Considine tour was due to terminate on November 29, and that is why a second contract was drawn up wherein Chaplin was to begin work for Sennett on December 16, and with no "out" clause before the earlier date. So, as we have seen, Chaplin was allowed to end his contract with Karno fifteen weeks early but, throughout the rest of his life, he remained convinced had seen it out. The story below is from just one journalist of many who accepted his version.

> When Ford Sterling, the star of Keystone, wanted more money, they thought again of Charlie, but could not remember his name. They located him at last, offered him £25 a week, and Charlie, feeling that he might as well take the money while films were able to pay it, accepted, but only on condition that they waited until the end of his tour, which had another forty weeks to run. He didn't want to let the "Guv'nor" down.

> (*Picturegoer* – 4 October 1952)

So just who was Sennett, and what was his association with Kessel and Baumann? Already among industry's most active film producers by 1912, Kessel and Baumann were persuaded by Sennett to form another company, this one to specialise in comedies. Based on the reputation he had earned as a comic actor and director at Biograph, Sennett was given a one-third interest in the new company, Keystone. Sennett had then defected from Biograph with several key performers, including Mabel Normand, Ford Sterling and Henry "Pathé" Lehrman, and moved the studios to Los Angeles, where he continued to build his roster of comedy performers. By the time Sennett instructed Kessel and Baumann to find Chaplin, Keystone had developed into Hollywood's pre-eminent fun factory of slapstick comedy.

After his meeting with Sennett, one of the first people Chaplin contacted was Groucho Marx:

> Finally, we both landed in Los Angeles. One day Charlie called me up. He said he had been offered $100 a week to go with Keystone. What's the matter?" I said, "isn't that enough?" Chaplin was then getting about $35 a week. "It's too much. I can't be worth $100 a week!"

> (*Photoplay Magazine* – 1936)

Original poster from the
Empress, Salt Lake City
w/c Wednesday November 5

Although Groucho has misquoted the figures involved he has at least got the location right. The Marx Brothers were in Los Angeles the last week in October. However, the bigger mystery here is not why Chaplin never mentioned Groucho in his later writings, but why he was so euphoric with the pay he would be getting at Keystone. Admittedly it was double what he was getting with Karno, but even so it wasn't the outlandish amount he made it out to be. For example, in the letter Charlie wrote to Syd from Winnipeg, he revealed that his former colleague Tommy Bristol and his partner were paid three hundred dollars a week – this for just a run-of-the-mill support act, in vaudeville. And the fees two other former Karno stars were getting made Chaplin's look like pocket-money. In March 1912 Fred Kitchen had been given a three-year contract to play the Moss Empire houses, in the U.K., at a weekly salary starting at the sterling equivalent of $1,250 and rising to $1,500. And Billy Reeves, who as late April 1912 had been touring the U.S. in *A Night in an English Music Hall*, was announced in that same month as about to sign a contract for $1,500 – $2,000 per week for another tour (article in *Variety* – April 6, 1912). It would seem that, though Chaplin could now match both Reeves and Kitchen as a stage performer and box-office draw, he couldn't touch them as a business man. Not yet, anyway.

But, for Chaplin, there was still the matter of more vaudeville dates to be fulfilled. From Los Angeles the company headed south, and stopped just short of the Mexico border, in San Diego, where, following the good reviews in Los Angeles, Chaplin would seem to have had an adrenalin boost.

(w/c October 27, 1913)

SAN DIEGO, Empress – "A NIGHT IN A LONDON CLUB"

Fred Karno's London comedians, in a sketch showing London music hall life, are as funny as ever. They have appeared in San Diego many times, but "bigger, brighter and better than ever" describes them. Charles Chaplin as "Archibald" seems to improve with every appearance.

(*San Diego Union* – October 28, 1913)

The weeks were now going slower and slower for Chaplin. He had to endure another week in Salt Lake City, followed by two in Colorado, before they finally reached Kansas City where the tour was to end.

(w/c November 23, 1913)

KANSAS CITY, Empress

The Empress had its top-liner *A Night in a London Club*, with Karno's English company presenting the act. The usual big crowds were in attendance.

(*New York Dramatic Mirror* – December 3, 1913)

And that was the end of that. Despite having captured numerous headlines, having had euphoric reviews written about him, and having had countless numbers of cartoons of his stage characters printed in newspapers, Chaplin left the stage with only a whimper. The following is the only newspaper article found which mentioned the subject:

> Charlie Chaplin, who numbers his friends by the thousands, is going to desert the stage to become a movie actor and play the chief comedy roles with the Keystone Company. As a film actor Charlie should surely make good for, during the five years he has been with the Karno Company, and on all his visits to this city, he has not spoken a dozen lines, and has depended on facial expression and pan-drama, to gain him the laughs. We shall all be anxiously awaiting the Keystone films in which he appears, and it goes without saying they will be just as funny as he has been in his Karno offerings.

> (Chaplin's scrapbook – cutting not identified)

The only other two known accounts of his departure were given by Chaplin himself, and Stan Laurel, and these didn't exactly conform to the back-slapping, bear-hugging, handshaking, tear-jerking reactions we may have imagined from a troupe that had been together for nigh on four years.

Chaplin first:

> A member of our troupe, Arthur Dando, who for some reason disliked me, thought he would play a joke a joke and conveyed whispered innuendos that I was to receive a small gift from the company. I must confess I was touched by the thought. However, nothing happened. When everyone had left the dressing-room, Fred Karno Junior confessed that Dando had arranged to make a speech and present me with the gift, but after I had bought drinks for everyone he had not had the courage to go through with it and had left the so-called 'present' behind the dressing-table mirror. It was an empty tobacco-box, wrapped in tin-foil, containing small ends of old pieces of greasepaint.

> (Chaplin's 1964 Autobiography)

Chaplin had totally misunderstood the significance of the pieces of greasepaint. If only he'd asked his roommate, Stan Jefferson, he would have received an honest, but hurtful, answer. Instead it was some fifty years later before Stan revealed the secret:

> Arthur didn't like Charlie because he considered him haughty and cold. So in Kansas, on our last night with Charlie, he announced that he was going to present a special goodbye present. He told me what it was – about five pieces of old brown Leichner grease paint, looking just like turds, all of this wrapped up in a very fancy box. "Some shit for a shit" is the way Arthur put it. This was Arthur's idea of a joke. I tried to argue him out of it but all Arthur said was, "It'll serve the superior bastard right."

> The so-called presentation never took place, however, and later Arthur told me why. First of all, Charlie stood the entire company drinks after the show. That fazed Arthur a bit but the thing that really shamed him into not going through with the so-called gag was this: just after his final curtain with us, Charlie hurried off to a deserted spot backstage. Curious, Arthur followed, and he saw haughty, cold, unsentimental Charlie crying.

> (*Charlie Chaplin*, by John McCabe)

So then came the parting of the waves. Not so very long ago before this, whenever Fred Karno had been asked, "Who's your star name?" he would retort: "My name's up there, and that's enough." But circumstances had changed. The student had become bigger than the master.

Chapter 20

FROM STAGE TO SCREEN

Chaplin said of his departing:

> I had qualms about leaving the troupe in Kansas City. The company was returning to England, and I to Los Angeles, where I would be on my own, and the feeling was not too reassuring.

Chaplin is incorrect when he states that the company were returning to England, for they still had a twelve-week contract to complete on the Nixon-Nirdlinger circuit. The problem with this was that the terms were for Chaplin to be in the lead role. Alf Reeves tried to reassure the bookers that Chaplin's understudy, Stan Jefferson, was every bit as good, but they wouldn't consider this option. Stan himself related:

> As I was the understudy, Charlie had taken a lot of trouble to rehearse me in his various parts, and I fondly imagined that I should take his place. But I was doomed to disappointment. Charlie had made quite a name for himself by this time, and the managers refused to accept a substitute. Our bookings dwindled, then petered out altogether.
>
> (*Tit-Bits* – 21 November 1936)

Adding, in another interview:

> It ended up, however, with their agreeing to accept the contract if Karno would bring over from England the principal comedian from the London Karno Company named Dan Raynor. We laid off three weeks waiting for him.[1] He came, we opened, but the show was a terrible flop and, after we played a couple of weeks, the contract was cancelled and the troupe disbanded. Those who wanted to return to England were given tickets, while those who didn't want to go could stay.
>
> (*The Comedy World of Stan Laurel* – John McCabe)

And of Chaplin's decision to leave, Laurel offered:

> Then came the day when Charlie listened to the lure of the movies. We all prophesied, blindly, that he was making a great mistake, that he should remain true to the stage. But he passed off his departure with his usual clowning, and made a grand gesture of farewell. Still there was a trembling in his handclasp. After all, we had been trouping together for more than seven years.[2] We all wished him well from the bottom of our hearts, but we secretly congratulated ourselves on possessing a superior wisdom.
>
> (*Film Weekly* – September 1929)

And what did Chaplin himself think of his pathway to stardom?

---

[1] Stan's memory is again impeccable. Dan Raynor arrived at New York, on the *Lusitania*, on 19 December 1913.

[2] Stan is known to have quoted this figure of 'seven years' in other instances. Why this figure stuck in his head is hard to fathom. He had, of course, been with the Karno company for only FOUR years.

In the ordinary sense of the word I did not choose my own career. I just drifted into it. I did not set out in life with any carefully prepared plans, but was content to take opportunities as they arose, always feeling that if I did my best, in the sphere in which I happened to find myself at the moment, it would carry me to something better.

Had I been free to choose my occupation, in the light of what I know now, it would have been different. Not even the measure of success I have achieved, with its promise of being taken out of the squalid surroundings against which my whole being revolted, would have induced me to enter on the career into which Fate forced me.

(Weekly Record – 10 September 1921)

Even when he had signed the film contract with Keystone his thoughts were:

A year at that racket and I could return to vaudeville an international star.

(Chaplin's 1964 Autobiography)

But after three years in "that racket" Chaplin's views would change. He told the actor Fred Goodwin, whom he was to work with at the Essanay Studios:

Back to the stage! I'll never go back to the stage again as long as I live. No. Unless my money leaves me, not ten thousand dollars would tempt me back behind the footlights again.

(1915 *Pearson's Weekly* – Fred Goodwin article)

For Chaplin it was, literally "the last stage." So how would he fare now he was going into films? Well, if you want to rule the world, all you need is to have all the ammunition, and Chaplin had certainly amassed more than anyone. Let's have a recap of Chaplin's career to date:

At his first-ever stage appearance he had mimicked his mother. In *The Eight Lancashire Lads*, he had mimicked the other seven, plus Bransby Williams. In *Sherlock Holmes* he had portrayed the well-established character of 'Billy,' in the way it was shown to him. In *Casey's Circus* he had mimicked Dr. Walford Bodie and the character 'Dick Turpin.' In the Karno Company he had mimicked Bob Lewis; Chas. Sewell; Harry Weldon; Fred Kitchen; Stan Laurel; and several of Syd Chaplin's original comic creations – including "the drunk" in "*Music Hall*," *Skating* and *The Wow-Wows*. Not once, in all that time had he created a single, original character. So why change the habit of a lifetime time? Now that he was going into film, all he need do was mimic the people he had worked with along the way, and others he had observed in passing, both on stage and in real life. For material he could call upon the numerous Karno sketches he had played in, plus all the other sketches he had observed during his years in variety and vaudeville. It couldn't have been easier. Mind you, it did help that he was a brilliant comedian.

BIBLIOGRAPHY

To help you to further enjoy reading "CHAPLIN – Stage by Stage" I would strongly advise you to first read the early life of Chaplin in the following two major works, as these are constantly cross-referenced in the narrative.

Charles Chaplin   CHAPLIN – MY AUTOBIOGRAPHY (Bodley Head 1964)

David Robinson   CHAPLIN – His Life and Art (Collins 1985) ISBN 0-00-216387-X

Other works referenced were:

Fred Karno Jnr.   FRED KARNO – As I Knew Him (unpublished handwritten work)

Charles Chaplin   MY LIFE IN PICTURES (Peerage Books 1985)

Adeler and West   REMEMBER FRED KARNO (John Long 1939)

J.P. Gallagher   FRED KARNO – Master of Mirth & Tears (Hale 1971)

John McCabe   CHARLIE CHAPLIN (Magnum 1979)

John McCabe   The Comedy World of STAN LAUREL (Doubleday 1974)

Simon Louvish   STAN and OLLIE – The Roots of Comedy (Faber and Faber 2001)

Ben Abramson   THE PAINFUL PREDICAMENT of SHERLOCK HOLMES (1955)

David Haining   CHARLIE CHAPLIN – a Centenary Celebration (W. Foulsham 1989)

A.E. Wilson   PRIME MINISTER of MIRTH – Sir George Robey (Odhams Press 1956)

Whimsical Walker   FROM SAWDUST TO WINDSOR CASTLE

Reference works:

STAGE YEARBOOK 1908 and 1911

VARIETY THEATRE ANNUAL – 1906

Magazine and Newspaper articles

Women's Home Companion   September 1933 and on (serialised)

Tit-Bits   14 November 1936 (serialised)

Picturegoer   7 December 1935; and 4 October 1952

Photoplay   July 1921; August 1934; and 1936

Film Weekly   23 September 1929

Other magazine and newspaper articles referred to are acknowledged in the text.

PHOTOGRAPHS and ILLUSTRATIONS

Every effort was made to trace the present copyright holders of the photographs and illustrations contained within these pages. Not all were successful. Therefore, if anyone has claim to the copyright of any of those featured, please make representation to the publishers, who will be only too pleased to give appropriate acknowledgement in any subsequent edition(s).

DATE-SHEETS

Chaplin's stage appearances in the

United Kingdom

On the following pages are "Date-Sheets" containing every known stage appearance which Chaplin made before going to America – starting with *The Eight Lancashire Lads* in 1899, and ending with the Karno Company in 1912.[1]

The standard "week" for theatre engagements is six days – Monday to Saturday. One exception to the "six-day rule" is when touring companies played split-weeks in the smaller towns, where there just wasn't sufficient numbers of people to fill the theatre for a full week. These have been listed as "Mon-Fri" or "Thu-Sat." Another exception is "one-off" performances at Benefit Shows, which have been identified as such. But, *no performances* were ever played on a Sunday. God would have struck the theatre with a bolt of fire if they had ever dared.

HOW TO READ THE TABLES.

The date on the left is what is termed as "Week Commencing" (often abbreviated to w/c) which in all cases is a Monday – unless otherwise stated.

The next entry is the "Town or City" where the theatre was located. Space did not permit the inclusion of the "County," so apologies to those readers whose geographical knowledge of the U.K. does not extend to the limits imposed.

Then comes the name of the actual "Theatre." Where the same theatre was played on two or more consecutive weeks by the same company, this has been highlighted in brackets, on the extreme right of the column.

On the second line of each entry: Text in [brackets] is the "Author's Comments." Text in *italics* is, in most instances, one of two items: The first is "One-line Reviews" from contemporary sources." The second is the name of the "Sketch."

Where space permits, some larger reviews have been inserted to complement the date-sheets and, in other instances, lists of the cast members and/or photographs are featured.

Some of Chaplin's date-sheets are cross-referenced with those of his father's, and others with his brother Sydney's. Instructions regarding these can be found on the appropriate pages.

❦

It has taken over six years to find and collate all these dates, so the publishers are keen to point out that, just because they are now in print, this does gives someone the right to take them and use them for their own publication. So, please note that:

THESE DATE-SHEETS ARE COPYRIGHTED

THE PUBLISHERS WILL NOT HESITATE TO TAKE LEGAL ACTION AGAINST ANYONE WHO REPRODUCES THEM BY WAY OF PRINTED MATTER; WEB-SITES; ELECTRONIC DATA or IMAGE FILES; PRESENTATIONS; OR ANY OTHER FORM; WITHOUT PRIOR WRITTEN CONSENT.

❦

---

[1] Acknowledgement is given to David Robinson's pioneering work in laying down many of the dates for *The Eight Lancashire Lads*; *Sherlock Holmes*, and *Casey Circus*; but all the dates listed here were found by independent means, using *several* sources. A quick comparison between the Robinson and the Marriot listings will suffice to show that the former was not plagiarised by the latter.

"THE EIGHT LANCASHIRE LADS"

Date Sheet – matched with:

CHARLES CHAPLIN Snr.

Read across the columns, on this page, to see where Charles Chaplin Snr.'s movements have an influence on Charlie's .

"EIGHT LANCASHIRE LADS"

DATE SHEET

1898

"BABES IN THE WOODS"

26 December   MANCHESTER, Royal   (week 1)
Opens Boxing Day.

.. a remarkably smart and clever clog dance by The Eight Lancashire Lads fairly brought the house down.

1899

2 January   MANCHESTER, Royal   (week 2)

9 January   MANCHESTER, Royal   (week 3)
[Charlie enrolled at Armitage Street School.]

16 January   MANCHESTER, Royal   (week 4)
"Babes in the Woods" – brilliantly successful

23 January   MANCHESTER, Royal   (week 5)
because of success, matinees will continue till 28 Jan

30 January   MANCHESTER, Royal   (week 6)
Babes in the Woods is the most successful pantomime of all time, at the Royal.

6 February   MANCHESTER, Royal   (week 7)
.. now with new songs, new dances, new jokes.

13 February   MANCHESTER, Royal   (week 8)
20 February   MANCHESTER, Royal   (week 9)
27 February   MANCHESTER, Grand   (week 1)
The Eight Lancashire Lads – clever clog dancing act.

6 March   MANCHESTER, Grand   (week 2)
The Lancashire Lads are still a powerful attraction.

(continued in left-hand column on next page)

MANCHESTER, Royal

At the *Royal*, the gorgeous and elaborate nature of *Babes in the Wood*, the original treatment of the theme, and the unusual strength of the company, were early recognised. The pantomime has now developed into one of the funniest ever seen at the principal house, and the humours of Mr. Murray and Miss Freear, the 'go' and dash of Miss. Duggan, and the grace and charm of Miss Maidie Hope and Miss Ethel Hayden, have countless admirers. The pantomime is crammed with good things, of which the *The Eight Lancashire* clog dancers , and the Orchid Ballet are not the least noteworthy.

CHARLES CHAPLIN Snr's

DATE SHEET

1898

26 September   HULL, Alhambra   (top-of-the bill)
24 October   MILE END, Paragon   (14th on the bill)
14 November   BRISTOL, Tivoli
5 December   LONDON, Canterbury   (week 1)
12 December   LONDON, Canterbury   (week 2)
19 December   no trace
26 December   MANCHESTER, Tivoli   (week 1)
Charles Chaplin – descriptive Comedian.
[Chaplin Senior has a meeting with William Jackson to discuss enrolling Charlie in the troupe.]

1899

2 January   MANCHESTER, Tivoli   (week 2)
Charles Chaplin – is a successful comedian

9 January   PORTSMOUTH, Empire
.. introduces some stirring songs

16 January   LEICESTER, Empire
.. after rendering four songs is compelled to sing more

23 January   LEICESTER, Empire
.. still finds form with the large audience

30 January   HULL, Alhambra
Mr. Charles Chaplin is premier among "stars" and makes his usual success with a strong vocal repertory.

6 February   CAMDEN, Bedford
[Grand Re-Opening of this Theatre]

13 February   CAMDEN, Bedford
20 February   CAMDEN, Bedford
27 February   CAMDEN, Bedford
[CC Snr. NOT in review. Has he been sacked?]

6 March   CAMDEN, Bedford
[again NOT mentioned in Music Hall review.]

(doubling at)   LONDON, Oxford

3 July   CLAPHAM, Grand
10 July   CLAPHAM, Grand
17 July   PIMLICO, Royal Standard

(doubling at)   CROYDON, Palace
Charles Chaplin's ditties are capital – ERA

24 July   PIMLICO, Royal Standard
No trace of further bookings until:

26 December   WALHAM GREEN, Granville
Charles Chaplin, who is something of an unconscious humorist. Plus Leo Dryden

1900

1 January   WALHAM GREEN, Granville
No trace of further bookings until:

5 February   MANCHESTER, Tivoli
No trace of further bookings until

6 August   CLAPHAM, Grand

(continued in right-hand column on Page 203)

EIGHT LANCASHIRE LADS
1899 (continued)

13 March   no trace
[Charlie is in rehearsal.]
20 March   PORTSMOUTH, Empire
The Eight Lancashire Lads won hearty approval with
their smart clog dancing. [Charlie's first appearance]
27 March   no trace

3 April   LONDON, Oxford Music Hall
The Lancashire Lads danced themselves into favour;
they can dance these little fellows, and no mistake
20 May   LONDON, Oxford
[End of 7 week run at the Oxford]
22 May   MIDDLESBROUGH, Oxford

29 May   CARDIFF, Empire
plus Wal Pink & Company
5 June   SWANSEA, Empire
.. Singers and Champion Clog-Dancers.
Plus Wal Pink & Company.
12 June   no trace

19 June   BLACKPOOL, Pavilion   (week 1)
.. speciality dancers and vocalists
26 June   BLACKPOOL, Pavilion   (week 2)
The Eight Lancashire Lads are great favourites.
3 July   LIVERPOOL, Parthenon   (week 1)
.. whose talents lie in the direction of clog-dancing
and characteristic vocalism. – ERA
10 July   SOUTHPORT, Pavilion
.. give an excellent exhibition of clog-dancing and prove
that they have musical voices in a well-rendered glee.
(doubling at)   LIVERPOOL, Parthenon   (week 2)
17 July   NOTTINGHAM, Empire
An attractive turn is provided by vocalists and dancers
'The Eight Lancashire Lads'; and a performance by
the Fred Karno Company in 'Jail Birds' is a rich treat.
24 July   BIRMINGHAM, Gaiety

31 July   WOLVERHAMPTON, Empire Palace
.. vocalists and dancers
7 August   NEW CROSS, Empire

14 August   BRADFORD, Empire
.. in a clog-dancing entertainment.
21 August   DUNDEE, People's Palace
.. a popular and clever clog-dancing turn
28 August   ABERDEEN, Palace
.. dance with grace and precision.
4 September   HULL, Alhambra
The greatest turn is undoubtedly The Eight Lancashire
Lads, a really first-rate combination of dancers.
11 September   no trace

18 September   no trace
25 September   CHATHAM, Barnard's Palace
The Eight Lancashire Lads hold their first position,
their smart clog dancing being loudly applauded.

(continued in right-hand column on this page)

2 October   LONDON, Canterbury   (week 1)
(doubling at)   MILE END, Paragon   (week 1)
plus George Robey [at both venues]
9 October   LONDON, Canterbury   (week 2)
plus George Robey
(doubling at)   MILE END Paragon   (week 2)
16 October   LONDON, Canterbury   (week 3)

(doubling at)   MILE END, Paragon   (week 3)

23 October   LONDON, Canterbury   (week 4)

(doubling at)   MILE END, Paragon   (week 4)

24 October   LONDON, Cambridge   (1 perf. only)
[Tuesday Night – First Anniversary Benefit Show]
24 October   CLAPHAM, Grand   (1 perf. only)
Tuesday Night – Fifth Anniversary Benefit Show
30 October   BOLTON, Grand
The Lancashire Lads have met with a hearty
reception.
6 November   LONDON, Oxford Music Hall   (week 1)
The Eight Lancashire Lads make music with their
clogs.
13 November   LONDON, Oxford Music Hall   (week 2)

20 November   LONDON, Oxford Music Hall   (week 3)

23 November   LONDON, Middlesex Music Hall
[28th Anniversary Benefit]   (1 perf. only)
27 November   LONDON, Oxford Music Hall   (week 4)

4 December   LONDON, Oxford Music Hall   (week 5)

11 December   LONDON, Oxford Music Hall   (week 6)

(continued in left-hand column on next page)

SINBAD the SAILOR

STOKE NEWINGTON, New Alexandra

1899

18 December   rehearsals for panto

26 December   Christmas Day fell on Monday 25th. so panto opened Tuesday afternoon.
A capital clog-dance by The Eight Lancashire Lads is admirably done and highly appreciated.

1900

1 January   STOKE NEWINGTON, New Alexandra
[*Sinbad the Sailor* runs for seven weeks in total.]
10 Feb   PANTO CLOSES (Saturday)

(continued in right-hand column on this page)

NEW ALEXANDRA THEATRE
STOKE NEWINGTON, N.

SOLE OWNER AND MANAGER F. W. PURCELL

Opening on BOXING DAY at 1.30 and 7.30 with F. W. Purcell's Third Christmas Pantomime,

SINBAD THE SAILOR

The cast will include: -

Miss Lola Hawthorne . . . . Mr. Fred Eastman
Miss Lydia Flopp . . . . Mr. E. W. Colman
Miss Ada Binning . . . . Mr. Charles Bignell
Miss Lillian Lee . . . . Mr. Harry Walsh
Mdlle. Lucretia . . . . Mr Herbert Cathcart
Miss Isable Dillon . . . . Burns and Evans
The Eight Lancashire Lads . . . . The Kellinos
The Ashley Team
The Entire Production under the Personal Supervision of F. W. Purcell.

THE TIVOLI

A bright and early start is made by Kitty Beresford, who is brimful of vivacity and good spirits. She can sing a good song, and foots it in the merriest of fashions. Warm applause greets this young lady's efforts. Joe Archer, with song, "Matrimonial Bliss," scores well, and Alice Leamar with a coon song and dance is much liked. Dan Leno has the warmest of welcomes, and never has been in better form. His two latest songs, "I'll Fit You," and "Man is Not Complete," wildly extravagant as is their humour, are decidedly entertaining. The last-mentioned song is particularly good, and Mr. Leno's blackboard illustrations of man, simply bring down the house. The Sisters Levey work their "Saucy 7th Hussars" for all it is worth, and score well, and a notable success is achieved by handsomely-clad Lil Hawthorne in a tuneful song entitled "Kitty Mahone." A pretty, lithesome young lady is Ada Willoughby, graceful, and with a charmingly-coquettish style. In both song and dance she is seen to advantage, and well-merited applause rewards her. The Countess Russell continues her engagement for one week longer, and her "Bravo Volunteers" song takes as well as ever it did. George Robey has a couple of humorous songs, "Without a Word," and "What She Ought to Be" and, given in his unctuous style, they are very successful. Harry Randall is also well-suited, and is the cause of much amusement. A lively ten minutes is spent with those merry eccentrics, Drew and Alders, and Will Evans with his whimsicalities, tumbling, and clever musical abilities entertains in capital style. Austen Rudd, Constance Moxon, Bransby Williams, the Glinserettis troupe of Acrobats, Albert Christian, the Gotham Comedy Quartet and The Eight Lancashire Lads make up the programme.

EIGHT LANCASHIRE LADS
1900

(continued from left-hand column)

12 February   MIDDLESBROUGH, Empire
plus The Karno Trio
19 February   no trace

26 February   NEWCASTLE, Empire

5 March   SOUTH SHIELDS, Empire

12 March   GLASGOW, Empire   (week 1)
plus: Bransby Williams in his celebrated characters from Charles Dickens.
19 March   GLASGOW, Empire   (week 2)
plus G. H. Chirgwin.
26 March   EDINBURGH, Empire Palace
.. we predict a revival of this style of dancing when these lads have to do something for themselves.
2 April   BIRMINGHAM Empire   (week 1)

9 April   BIRMINGHAM Empire   (week 2)

16 April   LONDON, Tivoli Music Hall   (week 1)
plus DAN LENO, George Robey
23 April   LONDON, Tivoli Music Hall   (week 2)
plus DAN LENO, George Robey, Bransby Williams
30 April   LONDON, Tivoli Music Hall   (week 3)
[*The Eight Lancashire Lads* on at 11:15 p.m.]
plus DAN LENO, and Bransby Williams
7 May   LONDON, Tivoli Music Hall   (week 4)
[DAN LENO 9:20-9:35, George Robey 10:00-10:25, The Eight Lancashire Lads 11:00-11:15 p.m]

(continued in left-hand column on next page)

1900 (continued)

14 May	LONDON, Tivoli Music Hall	(week 5)

[*Eight Lancashire Lads* on at 11:15 p.m.] plus
DAN LENO, George Robey, Bransby Williams

(doubling at)	LONDON, Metropolitan	(week 1)

plus George Robey, and Eugene Stratton.

21 May	LONDON, Tivoli Music Hall	(week 6)

plus DAN LENO, Bransby Williams, George Robey,

(doubling at)	LONDON, Metropolitan	(week 2)

*.. we have seen nothing more delightfuly novel and
attractive for a long time.* Plus George Robey

28 May	LONDON, Tivoli Music Hall	(week 7)
(trebling at)	LONDON, Metropolitan	(week 3)

plus George Robey, MARIE LLOYD

(trebling at)	PIMLICO, Royal Standard	(week 1)
4 June	LONDON, Canterbury	(week 1)

plus DAN LENO, G. H. Chirgwin.

(trebling at)	MILE END, Paragon	(week 1)

plus G. H. Chirgwin.

(trebling at)	PIMLICO, Royal Standard	(week 2)
11 June	LONDON, Canterbury	(week 2)

plus DAN LENO

(trebling at)	MILE END, Paragon	(week 2)

plus G. H. Chirgwin.

(trebling at)	PIMLICO, Royal Standard	(week 3)
18 June	LONDON, Canterbury	(week 3)

plus DAN LENO, Joe Elvin & Co.

25 June	LONDON, Canterbury	(week 4)

plus DAN LENO

2 July	PLYMOUTH, Empire	

plus the Jackson Family (musicians)

9 July	WOOLWICH, Royal	(week 1)
16 July	WOOLWICH, Royal	(week 2)
23 July	no trace	

Summer Holidays.

30 July	BARROW, Star Palace	

The Eight Lancashire Lads are a big draw this week.

6 August	LONDON, Oxford Music Hall	(week 1)

[*The Eight Lancashire Lads* on at 8:10 p.m.]
plus DAN LENO

(trebling at)	CAMBERWELL, Palace of Varieties	
(trebling at)	CLAPHAM, Grand	(week 1)

The Eight Lancashire Lads, plus **Charles Chaplin Snr.**

13 August	LONDON, Oxford Music Hall	(week 2)

[*The Eight Lancashire Lads* on at 8:10 p.m.]
plus DAN LENO

(doubling at)	CLAPHAM, Grand	(week 2)

The Eight Lancashire Lads, plus **Charles Chaplin Snr.**

20 August	LONDON, Oxford Music Hall	(week 3)

plus DAN LENO

(doubling at)	WALHAM GREEN, Granville	

(continued in left-hand column on next page)

THE TIVOLI

The current programme is particularly strong in its lady turns, nine out of twenty-three turns being contributed to by the fair sex. Priority of notice belongs to Vesta Tilley. Miss Tilley has a thorough command of the minutiae of her art, and in voice, style, dress, and gesture she "takes off" her subjects to perfection. Particularly good is Miss Tilley when holding up the ways and manners of the "swell" youth, and just now she is giving an excellent study of the kind in "Burlington Bertie"; it may be ranked as one of the best things that this clever artist has done. Soon after Miss Tilley appears the Baroness Christina Valmar, a lady of charming personality and pleasing style and nice voice. Quite early appears that clever and favourite artist Bransby Williams, whose Dickens impersonations have so often been the theme of our praise. An acquisition to any bill is Bransby Williams. Ernest Shand, a comedian of resource and strong personality, is well applauded for his efforts to please; and another early successful comer is George Mozart, musical eccentric. Looking very fresh and nice in her nurse's costume, Ada Willoughby gains the favour of her audience at once. Her nurse's song is a good one, but the second song, "I'll try to do Better in the Future," is what catches on most. Mr. Albert Christian still pins his faith to "Soldier of the Queen," and wisely so. Minnie Palmer, in *Rose Pompon*, holds a prominent place in the bill, and makes a hit. Dan Leno, with his "Incomplete Man," now given with fresh and excruciatingly funny "diagrams," as he puts it, and his "Bootshop" song goes "immense."

Other scorers in the comedy line are Harry Randall, Will Evans, George Robey, Joe Archer and Austen Rudd. A pleasing and much-liked artist is Annette Fengler. Miss Fengler has a full, clear, tuneful voice, and she renders her catchy ditties with piquancy and point. Leo Tell and Mdlle. Linda, Alice Leamar, Constance Moxon, the Glinserettis troupe of Acrobats, the Gotham Comedy Quartet and *The Eight Lancashire Lads* complete the entertainment.

CHARLES CHAPLIN Snr.'s

DATE SHEET

1900

6 August	CLAPHAM, Grand	

Charles Chaplin Snr., plus The Eight Lancashire Lads

13 August	CLAPHAM, Grand	

Plus Rezene and Robini.

Charles Chaplin Snr., plus The Eight Lancashire Lads

20 August	CAMBERWELL, Palace	

(continued in right-hand column on next page)

EIGHT LANCASHIRE LADS
1900 (continued)

27 August   LONDON, Oxford Music Hall   (week 4)
[*The Eight Lancashire Lads* 8:20 to 8:25 only]
plus DAN LENO
(doubling at)   CROYDON, Palace

3 September   LONDON, Oxford Music Hall   (week 5)
George Robey replaced DAN LENO;

10 September   LONDON, Oxford Music Hall   (week 6)
[DAN LENO returns; George Robey stays on]
(doubling at)   SHOREDITCH, London Music Hall
plus George Robey, Rezene and Robini.

17 September   HULL, Palace
*.. win unlimited applause by their talented and striking
performances.* Plus Bransby Williams

24 September   SHEFFIELD, Empire Palace
The Eight Lancashire Lads are expert clog dancers.

1 October   LEEDS, Empire Palace
*.. lovers of the 'clogs' have been appreciating the turn of
The Eight Lancashire Lads. A fine turn this.*

8 October   BRADFORD, Empire
.. clog dancers without rivals.

15 October   MANCHESTER, Palace
The Eight Lancashire Lads are expert clog-dancers.

22 October   MANCHESTER, Palace
The Eight Lancashire Lads, plus Fred Karno's Company
in Jail Birds and The New Woman's Club

29 October   LIVERPOOL, Empire   (week 1)

5 November   LIVERPOOL, Empire   (week 2)
plus Gus Elen

12 November   DUBLIN, Empire   (week 1)

19 November   DUBLIN, Empire   (week 2)

26 November   BELFAST, Empire

3 December   NEW CROSS, Empire
plus T.E. Dunville

8 December   I believe that Charlie left the company
here.

List of known Members of
EIGHT LANCASHIRE LADS

20 March 1899 – 8 December 1900
Herbert (aka: Albert) Jackson,
[John Jackson], Alfred Jackson,
Tommy Bristol, Billy Caryll
Charles Chaplin.

CHARLES CHAPLIN Snr.
1900 (continued)

27 August   CAMBERWELL, Palace
*CHARLES CHAPLIN as a descriptive vocalist is less
well suited in his serious selection than in his humorous
one, the latter making a hit.*

3 September   CAMBERWELL, Palace
CHARLES CHAPLIN [well down the bill]

10 September   WALHAM GREEN, Granville

17 September   WALHAM GREEN, Granville

24 September   WALHAM GREEN, Granville
CHARLES CHAPLIN, plus LEO DRYDEN
No trace of further bookings until:

31 December   PORTSMOUTH, Empire
[Chaplin's appearance here is confirmed in the review in
The Stage, and is almost certainly his last.]

THE STAGE

(w/c 22 October 1900)
MANCHESTER, Palace
There is plenty of fun and variety in this
week's bill, and good business is being done.
Fred Karno and his Co. arouse laughter with
the pantomime sketch *Jail Birds*, and also
with the farcical pantomime burlesque
sketch, *The New Woman's Club*.

A very popular turn is that of the Selbinis, in
a remarkably clever cycle act. W.E. Bates, a
talented cornet solo player, is vociferously
encored. Novelties are also given by Walter
King, an amusing and capable comedian and
dancer; and Fred Hallam, eccentric comedian. Fred Russell, ventriloquial humourist,
with his automaton "Coster Joe," is as great a
favourite as last week. *The Eight Lancashire
Lads*, expert and well-trained clog-dancers,
also continue to be popular.

Others remaining are the Sister Oliver
(vocalists and dancers), and the Brothers
Onda, in the nautical comedy act, *On Deck*.

I believe that Charlie left the company on 8 December 1900. In the event that history might prove me wrong I have listed, below, *The Eight Lancashire Lads'* schedule for the four months that followed. The pantomime *Cinderella* is also listed, just to illustrate the clash with the tour dates. By reading across the two columns you can match the dates.

CINDERELLA

London Hippodrome

1900

10 December	panto rehearsals?
17 December	panto rehearsals
26 December	"Cinderella" – OPENS
31 December	*"Cinderella"*

1901

7 January	*"Cinderella"*
14 January	*"Cinderella"*
21 January	*"Cinderella"*
28 January	*"Cinderella"*
4 February	*"Cinderella"*
11 February	*"Cinderella"*
18 February	*"Cinderella"*
25 February	*"Cinderella"*
4 March	*"Cinderella"*
11 March	*"Cinderella"*
18 March	*"Cinderella"*
25 March	*"Cinderella"*
31 March	Charlie is listed in the Census as living at the house of John Jackson (age 17) at 92 Ferndale Road.
1 April	*"Cinderella"*
8 April	*"Cinderella"*
13 April	*"Cinderella"* – CLOSES

EIGHT LANCASHIRE LADS

(Tour Post-Chaplin)

1900

10 December	no trace
17 December	no trace
24 December	no trace
31 December	no trace

1901

7 January	no trace
14 January	no trace
21 January	no trace
28 January	no trace
4 February	no trace

(Tour continues after 9 week gap)

11 February	SHEFFIELD, Empire	
18 February	GLASGOW, Empire	
25 February	EDINBURGH, Empire	
4 March	HULL, Palace	
11 March	LEEDS, Empire	
18 March	HOLBORN, Royal	(week 1)
(doubling at)	CAMBERWELL,	
25 March	HOLBORN, Royal	(week 2)
(trebling at)	CLAPHAM JUNCTION, Grand	
(trebling at)	PIMLICO, Royal Standard	
1 April	HOLBORN, Royal	(week 3)
(doubling at)	WALHAM GREEN, Granville	
8 April	LONDON, Canterbury	(week 1)
(doubling at)	MILE END, Paragon	(week 1)
15 April	LONDON, Canterbury	(week 2)
(doubling at)	MILE END, Paragon	(week 2)

The tour continues almost without a break until:

21 December   TOUR ENDS

Over subsequent tours in 1903, 1904, 1905, 1907 and 1908, among others, The Eight Lancashire Lads were to lose their top-of-the-bill status and slip further and further down the billing. All the latter tours were, of course, without Charles Chaplin.

THE STAGE

LONDON HIPPODROME

The 'Amphibious Burletta' called "Giddy Ostend" or "The Absent-Minded Millionaire" is an exceedingly lively affair, that engages not only the stage but the lake, which is supposed to represent the sea. Mr. S. Asher makes a donkey of himself for the diversion of the boys and girls who look for amusement on the sands.

"JIM – A Romance of Cockayne"
A play by H.A. Saintsbury
1903

6 July   KINGSTON-upon-THAMES,
                     Royal County Theatre
Master Charles Chaplin shows decided promise as 'Sam'
a newspaper boy.

13 July   FULHAM, Grand
'Sam' was made vastly amusing by Master Charles
Chaplin.

18 July   Jim – CLOSES

"SHERLOCK HOLMES"
Charles Frohman's Northern Company
H.A. Saintsbury as 'Sherlock Holmes'

20 July   rehearsals

27 July   LONDON, Pavilion E
A faithful portrait of 'Billy' is given by Master Charles
Chaplin, who shows considerable ability, and bids fair to
develop into a capable and clever actor.

3 August   BURTON-on-TRENT, Opera House

10 August   NEWCASTLE, Royal

17 August   SHEFFIELD, Lyceum
Charles Chaplin plays 'Billy' the office boy.

24 August   MANCHESTER, Queen's
Master Charles Chaplin is an excellent 'Billy'.

31 August   READING, Royal County
.. there is a slight alteration in the cast. [cast not given]

7 September   NORTHAMPTON, Opera House
Mr. Charles Chaplin, a very smart page-boy 'Billy', gains
well-earned applause.

14 September   WOLVERHAMPTON, Grand
The rapidity of speech and actions of Master Charles
Chaplin, as 'Billy', interested the audience greatly.

21 September   COVENTRY, Opera House
We almost omitted to mention the very smart performance
of Master Charles Chaplin.

28 September   no trace

5 October   BIRKENHEAD, Metropole

12 October   BLACKBURN, Royal
[Charlie buys a rabbit and a dog – allegedly.]

19 October   HUDDERSFIELD, Royal
Master Charles Chaplin makes a smart 'Billy'.

26 October   BOLTON, Royal
Master Charles Chaplin is a cute 'Billy'.

2 November   WIGAN, Royal Court
Master Charles Chaplin is a clever 'Billy'.

9 November   ASHTON-under-LYNE, Royal
'Billy' is played well by Mr. Charles Chaplin.

16 November   STOCKPORT Royal & Opera

23 November   BURNLEY, Gaiety

(continued in left-hand column on next page)

THE STAGE

Royal County - KINGSTON

On Monday evening, July 6, 1903, was produced here a play, in four acts, by H.A. Saintsbury, entitled:-

Jim

Role	Actor
Roydon Carstairs	H. A. Saintsbury
James Seton Gatlock	James C. Aubrey
Walter Jenifer	Mr. Blake Adams
Inspector Grint	Mr. Caleb Porter
Inspector Bradstreet	Mr. Harry Payne
Bill Caffle	Mr. Charles Rock.
Snarpe	Mr. Graham Herington
Sam	Master Charles Chaplin
Alma Treherne	Miss Beatrix de Burgh
'Jim'	Miss Dorothea Desmond

Act one - No. 7a, Devreux Court, Temple
Act two - The Top Front Floor at Mrs. Putherby's Lodging House in Drury Lane.
Acts three and four - At the Savoy Hotel.

*   *   *

(w/c 21 December 1903)
DEWSBURY, Royal

Deserved success attends the engagement here this week of Mr. Charles Frohman's Company in Gillette's *Sherlock Holmes*. Mr. H.A. Saintsbury in the title part is most effective; his assumption of an arduous part is highly meritorious. He is highly supported by a strong cast as follows: -

Role	Actor
Doctor Watson	Mr. Charles Musset
John Forman	Mr. F. Clive Ross
Sir Edward Leighton	Mr. Harold Broughton
Count Von Stahlberg	Mr. Sydney Chaplin
Professor Moriarty	Mr. Robert Forsyth
James Larrabee	Mr. Ernest Ruston
Sydney Prince	Mr. Pelham Rayner
Alfred Bassick	Mr H. S. Davis
Jim Craigin	Mr. W. F. Stirling
Thomas Leary	Mr. James F. Anson
"Lightfoot" McTague	Mr. M. M. Loomie
John	Mr E. H Fairburn
Parson	Mr. George Henry
Billy	Mr. Charles Chaplin
Alice Faulkner	Miss Grete Hahn
Mrs. Faulkener	Miss Mariette Hyde
Madge Larrabee	Miss Theodora Diehl
Thérèse	Miss Lilla Nordon
Mrs. Smeedley	Miss Alice Farquar

To celebrate the 500th performance, a souvenir in colours on rich paper was presented to each attendant at a full-house on Monday.

30 November   ROCHDALE, Royal and Opera
Master Charles Chaplin shows promise as 'Billy'.
7 December   BROUGHTON, Victoria
[Syd Chaplin joins around this time]
14 December   BURY, Royal and Palace
Master Charles Chaplin is a capital 'Billy'.
21 December   DEWSBURY, Royal
[500th performance.]
28 December   BARROW in FURNESS,
Royalty and Opera House

1904

4 January   WAKEFIELD, Opera House

11 January   LEEDS, Queen's

18 January   HALIFAX, Grand
A sprightly and clever impersonation of the sharp, bright, faithful page-boy 'Billy' is the outcome of Charles Chaplin's performance. Syd Chaplin (Count von Stahlberg) acquits himself creditably.
25 January   GATESHEAD, Metropole

1 February   YORK, Grand Opera House   (Mon-Wed)

4 February   HARROGATE, Grand Opera House
(Thu to Sat.) The cast includes Sydney Chaplin as Count von Stahlberg; and his brother Charlie as 'Billy'.
8 February   JARROW, Royal

15 February   MIDDLESBROUGH, Royal

22 February   SUNDERLAND, Avenue Theatre

29 February   BIRMINGHAM, Prince of Wales
[H.A. Saintsbury is ill. Dalziel Heron understudies.]
7 March   SCARBOROUGH, Londesborough
[Saintsbury is still out – Charlie is still in.]
14 March   ABERDEEN, Her Majesty's
[Dalziel Heron as 'Holmes']
Mr. Charles Chaplin as the pageboy 'Billy' deserves a mention as a clever juvenile actor.
21 March   DUNDEE, Her Majesty's
[Dalziel Heron as 'Holmes']
Mr. Charles Chaplin is unusually bright and natural as 'Billy'.
28 March   PAISLEY, Paisley
[Dalziel Heron as 'Holmes']
Master Charles Chaplin makes a first-rate 'Billy'.
4 April   CARLISLE, Her Majesty's
[Dalziel Heron as 'Holmes']
11 April   HANLEY, Royal
[Dalziel Heron as 'Holmes']
As 'Billy,' the boy, Master Chas. Chaplin is decidedly clever.

(continued in right-hand column on this page)

18 April   HULL, Royal
[H.A. Saintsbury back as 'Holmes' after illness.]
A very smart 'Billy' is found in Master Charles Chaplin
25 April   HARTLEPOOL WEST, Grand
As 'Billy' Mr. Charles Chaplin is excellent.
2 May   NOTTINGHAM, Grand
A special word should be devoted to Master Charles Chaplin who makes a perfect study of the part of 'Billy'.
9 May   ALDERSHOT, Royal and Hippodrome
.. little Charles Chaplin, who is a smart 'Billy'
[Sydney Chaplin named in review]
16 May   BRADFORD, Royal
.. the juvenile part of 'Billy' is very cleverly presented by Master Charles Chaplin.
23 May   BLACKPOOL, Opera House

30 May   EASTBOURNE, Pier Theatre
Master Charles Chaplin adds his share to the merriment as the youngster 'Billy'. [Sydney Chaplin named]
6 June   LONDON, West London
.. the boy 'Billy' is acted with rare ability by Master Charles Chaplin.
11 June   TOUR ENDS (Saturday)

1904 (continued)
Charlie is 'resting'.

13 June
20 June
26 June
27 June
4 July
11 July
18 July
25 July
1 August
8 August   "RAGS TO RICHES"
Advert appears in The Stage for first time, and states: "Spring tour starting Boxing Day."
15 August   Advert for RAGS TO RICHES
Master Charles Chaplin as 'Ned Nimble'
15 August
22 August
29 August
5 September
12 September
19 September
26 September
3 October
10 October
17 October
24 October   Chaplin goes into rehearsal for next tour.

SHERLOCK HOLMES"
Charles Frohman Company
Kenneth Rivington as 'Sherlock Holmes'
1904
[Chaplin's second tour)]

31 October	KING'S LYNN, Royal	(Mon-Wed)
3 November	READING, County	[Thu-Sat unconf.]

[Is this where Charlie's mother joined him?]
[*Rags to Riches* advert has been discontinued.]

7 November	SHREWSBURY, Royal & Hippodrome	
14 November	WARRINGTON, Royal Court	

'Billy' has a first-class representation in Mr. Charles. Chaplin.

21 November   ILKESTON, Royal
Mr. Charles Chaplin is notably smart as 'Billy'.

28 November   MEXBOROUGH, Prince of Wales
Master Charles Chaplin is a smart 'Billy'.

5 December   SHEFFIELD, Lyceum

12 December   BARNSLEY, Royal,

19 December   no trace

26 December   no trace

1905

2 January   DARLINGTON, Royal

9-11 January	DUMFRIES, Royal	(Mon-Wed)?
12-14 January	no trace	(Thu-Sat)
16 January	KIRKCALDY, King's	(Mon-Wed)

Master Charles Chaplin plays 'Billy' cleverly.

19 January   DUNFERMLINE, Royal   (Thu-Sat)

23 January   PERTH, Opera House
Mr. Charles Chaplin is exceedingly smart as 'Billy'

30 January   MOTHERWELL, New Century

6 February   GREENOCK, Royal

13 February   no trace

20 February   BOOTLE, Royal Muncaster
Mr. Charles Chaplin is well-placed as 'Billy'

27 February   ACCRINGTON, Prince's
Mr. Charles Chaplin is very smart as 'Billy'

6 March   HYDE, Royal

13-15 March   STAFFORD, Lyceum   (Mon-Wed)

16-18 March   no trace

(continued in right-hand column on this page)

SHERLOCK HOLMES
Charles Frohman Company
List of Players

Sherlock Holmes	Kenneth Rivington
Professor Moriarty	Arthur B. Murray
Dr. Watson	Fred Inwood
James Larrabee	Ernest Gray
Madge Larrabee	Miss Carrie Lacey
Sydney Prince	Harry Stafford
John Forman	Charles E. Scutt
Billy	Mr. Charles Chaplin
Sir Edward Leighton	Howard E. Laing
Count von Stahlberg	William Wilson
Alice Faulkner	Florence Radcliffe
Mrs. Faulkner	Miss Ethel Gordon
Thérèse	Majorie Murray
Mrs. Smeedley	Hettie Newcombe
Alfred Bassick	Harry Mann

The rest of the cast is made up of:
Mr. George Fairburn, Mr. T. Williams,
Harry G. Wright, and Mr. F. Clive Ross.

---

20 March   MERTHYR TYDFIL, Royal

27 March   no trace

3-5 April   TONYPANDY, Royal   (Mon-Wed)
Mr. Charles Chaplin as 'Billy' is distinctly good.

6-8 April   EBBW VALE,   (Thu-Sat)
[Unconfirmed. Mentioned by Chaplin but not traced.]

10-12 April   no trace   (Mon-Wed)

13-15 April   TREHEBERT, Opera House   (Thu-Sat)
Master Charles Chaplin as 'Billy' was well placed.

17 April   PERTH, Poole's Opera House

24 April   no trace

1 May   EALING, New Theatre
Mr. Chas. Chaplin as 'Billy' is good, but overdoes the part a little.

5 May   TOUR ENDS

Charlie is resting

6 May – 6 August
7 August   Chaplin goes into rehearsal for next tour.

"SHERLOCK HOLMES"

Harry Yorke's Touring Company

H. Lawrence Leyton as 'Sherlock Holmes'

1905

[Chaplin's third tour]

14 August   BLACKBURN, Royal
Mr. Charles Chaplin as 'Billy' also acts well.
21 August   HULL, Royal

28 August   DEWSBURY, Royal

4 September   HUDDERSFIELD, Royal

11 September   MANCHESTER, Queen's

18 September   LIVERPOOL, Rotunda

25 September   WARRINGTON, Royal Court
Mr. Charles Chaplin is excellent as 'Billy'.
[Chaplin leaves the tour Saturday 30 September.]
*[2 October   NEWCASTLE, Palace]
[Charlie has left. Ernest Hollom is the new 'Billy']
----
3 October   LONDON, Duke of York's   [Tuesday]
"Clarice" and
"The Painful Predicament of Sherlock Holmes"
Master Charles Chaplin was duly boisterous as the
harmless, necessary page.
9 October   LONDON, Duke of York's
The Painful Predicament of Sherlock Holmes
       [Ends Saturday 14 October]
17 October   LONDON, Duke of York's   (Tuesday)
William C. Gillette's *Sherlock Holmes* – OPENS
Charles Chaplin is capital as the faithful page 'Billy'
23 October   LONDON, Duke of York's

30 October   LONDON, Duke of York's

6 November   LONDON, Duke of York's

13 November   LONDON, Duke of York's

20 November   LONDON, Duke of York's
Royal Gala Performance.
27 November   LONDON, Duke of York's
Clarice – CLOSES. Saturday 2 December
Sherlock Holmes – CLOSES
4 December   Charlie is resting
11 December   Charlie is resting
19 December   LONDON, Duke of York's
(Tuesday)   *Peter Pan* – OPENS
[Charlie denies playing the part of a wolf.]
[25 December LONDON, Duke of York's]
[*Peter Pan* continues well into January. However, from 1
January on, Chaplin is touring in *Sherlock Holmes*]

(continued across right)

"SHERLOCK HOLMES"

Harry Yorke's Touring Company

H. Lawrence Leyton as 'Sherlock Holmes'

1906

[Charlie re-joins the tour here]

1 January   DONCASTER, Grand

8 January   SHEFFIELD, Lyceum
Master Charles Chaplin is a nimble 'Billy'.
15 January   CAMBRIDGE, New
[Sidney Chaplin is named in cast list.]
22 January   LONDON, Pavilion E.
Master Charles Chaplin as 'Billy' proves himself a clever
youth, Holmes's remark "Billy, you're a smart boy!" aptly
describing his characterisation.
[Sydney named in the review in *The Era.*]
29 January   DALSTON, Dalston N.E.
'Billy' is briskly played by Master Charles Chaplin.
5 February   GREENWICH, Charlton

12 February   PECKHAM, Crown
Master Charles Chaplin proved an excellent 'Billy'.
19 February   CREWE, Lyceum
Master Charles Chaplin makes 'Billy' exceedingly smart.
26 February   ROCHDALE, New Royal
Sherlock Holmes – TOUR ENDS. Saturday 3 March

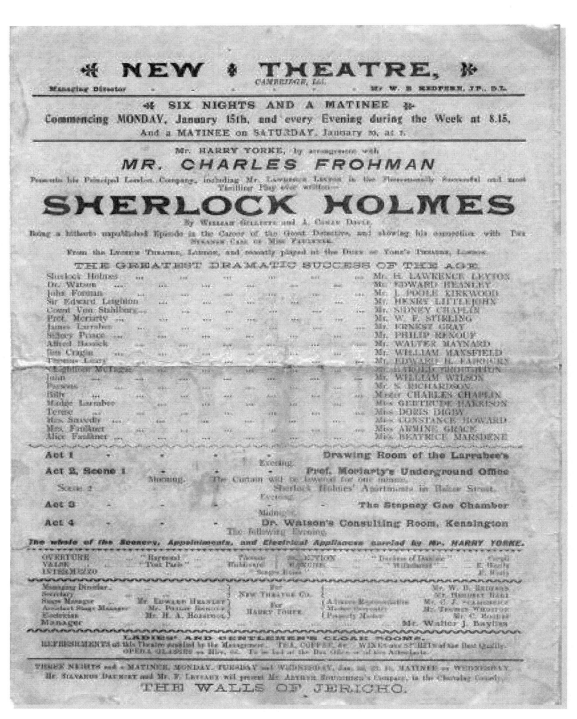

Programme page from the New Theatre, Cambridge, for "Sherlock Holmes," showing the names of Sidney and Charles Chaplin in the cast.

Information is vague regarding Charlie and Syd's appearances with Wal Pink's Company in *Repairs*. Even fewer clues are given by Chaplin as to his involvement with 'The Ten Loonies' in *Dotty* – if indeed there was any. The full facts might never be known but, whatever Syd and Charlie's Chaplin's movements, they would have been within the dates listed below.

Wal Pink's Workmen in "REPAIRS" 1906

19 February

26 February
[Charlie disengages from *Sherlock Holmes* 3 March]
5 March

12 March

19 March   SOUTHAMPTON, Hippodrome
DEBUT .. *a clever example of the low comedy school of humour.* [Sydney and Charlie]
26 March   PORTSMOUTH [not traced]
         BOSCOMBE [not traced]
2 April   BALHAM, Duchesse

9 April   GLASGOW, Zoo & Hippodrome

16 April   BELFAST,
.. *an amusing rough and tumble acrobatic sketch.*
[Charlie's 17th Birthday]
23 April   MANCHESTER, Palace
.. *created loud laughter in their absurdities of how not to do it.*
30 April   HAMMERSMITH, Palace
.. *the acrobatic actors are as smart a crowd as can be found around Variety Land.*
7 May   CLAPHAM, Grand
[Charlie quits the company here. Syd stays on.]
14 May   LIVERPOOL,
Syd Chaplin only
*[14 May   BRADFORD, Empire]
[*Casey's Court*]
*[14 May   WOOLWICH, Hippodrome
Casey's Circus [production try-out]
21 May   WOLVERHAMPTON, Hippodrome
'Repairs' is a capital knockabout, pantomimical sketch after the manner, in scenic effects, of 'The Jerry Builder
*[21 May   LIVERPOOL, Olympia]
[Chaplin makes his first appearance proper in *Casey's Circus.*]
28 May   LEEDS, City Palace,
Repairs – a skit on the house decorator, and shows how it should not be done.

END of this LISTING

The Ten Loonies in "DOTTY" 1906

19 February   LONDON, Coliseum
'The Ten Loonies' in Dotty
26 February   LONDON, Coliseum
[Charlie disengages from *Sherlock Holmes* 3 March]
5 March   LONDON, Coliseum
[Did Charlie play with them? Here?]
12 March   LONDON, Coliseum
[Did Charlie play with them? Here?]
19 March   LONDON, Coliseum

26 March   LONDON, Coliseum

2 April   LONDON, Coliseum
[last week at this venue]

END of this LISTING

Harry Cadle's Company of Juvenile Performers in

"CASEY'S COURT"
1906

5 March	RICHMOND, Richmond Theatre	
12 March	PRESTON, Royal Hippodrome	
19 March	BURY, Hippodrome	
26 March	SALFORD, Royal Hippodrome	
2 April	PRESTON, Royal Hippodrome	
9 April	LONGSIGHT, Kings'	

.. Bob King with his Midget Mimics

16 April	HULME, Hippodrome	
16 April	OLDHAM, Gaiety	
23 April	GLASGOW, Coliseum	(No.1 Co.)
23 April	WALTHAMSTOW, Palace	(No.2 Co.)

[There are now 2 companies.]

30 April	EDINBURGH, Empire Palace	(No.1)
30 April	BATH, Palace	(No.2)
*[30 April	NOTTINGHAM, Empire]	

[R.A. Roberts in his clever sketch Dick Turpin, with its
many quick changes.]

7 May	MIDDLESBROUGH, Palace	
14 May	BOLTON, Grand	
14 May	BRADFORD, Empire	

'Casey's Court' – by 30 clever boys and girls.

Harry Cadle's Company of Juvenile Performers in:

"CASEY'S CIRCUS"
1906

14 May	WOOLWICH, Royal

[Production try-out.]

21 May	LIVERPOOL, Olympia

*'Casey's Circus' conjures up tumultuous laughter during
its all too short run.*

28 May	GLASGOW, Coliseum

'Casey's Circus' is even better than 'Casey's Court'.

4 June	NEWCASTLE, Empire

11 June	LEEDS, Empire Palace

*.. is most ingenious, cleverly acted, and full of smartness
and humour.*

18 June	no trace

25 June	SHEFFIELD, Empire Palace

2 July	ARDWICK GREEN, Empire

*Casey's Circus causes much amusement, being a fine
piece of tomfoolery.*

9 July	NOTTINGHAM, Empire

Very diverting is the Casey Circus.

[Will Murray takes Charlie to the races.]

16 July	LEICESTER, Palace

23 July	BIRMINGHAM, Bordesley Palace

*The Casey's Circus, a most diverting entertainment, is
contributed by some smart youngsters.*

30 July	HALIFAX, Palace

Casey's Circus is a boisterously funny burlesque.

(continued in left-hand column on next page)

(w/c 28 May 1906)
GLASGOW, Coliseum

At the Coliseum this week the chief item in the bill of fare is the laughable sketch *Casey's Circus*. Recently we had *Casey's Court*, but the circus is much better, and last night was productive of much genuine laughter. Amusing skits on bloodless surgery, bloodless bull-fights &c., . are given, and Mrs. Casey and her troublesome kids are due a mead of praise.

MAGNET

(w/c 11 June 1906)
LEEDS, Empire

"Casey's Court" Circus is the top item of the bill and shows a troupe of "slummers" giving their idea of the up-to-date music-hall performance, and right well do the youngsters carry out the idea; the "Bodie" skit and the absurdly funny "Mick Turpin's Ride to York," seems to be the two big features of the turn. Really a novel and entertaining act.

Read across the columns to compare Charlie and Syd's whereabouts.

SYD CHAPLIN
Early Karno Dates
1906

9 July – SYD CHAPLIN signs first contract with the Fred Karno Company.

9 July 1906	CAMBERWELL, Palace

Mumming Birds

(Syd's first engagement as a Karno Comedian)

16 July	CHATHAM, Barnard's Palace

Jail Birds and *Mumming Birds*

----

31 July	Karno's U.S. company sails for New York

Sydney Chaplin, Frederick Bendon, Jack Osborne,
Ernie Stone, Harry Royston, George Welch, Ethel Welch,
Jack Lloyd, William Fern, Amy Minister.

"CASEY'S CIRCUS"
1906 (continued)

6 August   RICHMOND, Richmond Theatre
Casey's Circus is another attractive item from the Casey children.

13 August   HACKNEY, Empire

20 August   HOLLOWAY, Empire

27 August   NEW CROSS, Empire
.. the show is full of quaint business and clever touches.

3 September   BRIGHTON, Empire and Hippodrome

10 September   SHEPHERDS BUSH, Empire
.. the sheer absurdity of the business is its chief charm.

17 September   STRATFORD, Empire
plus George Formby, and Fred Russell

24 September   CAMDEN, Surrey Varieties

1 October   CARDIFF, Empire
plus George Formby, and Fred Russell

8 October   HANLEY, Grand
..the piece occupies the best part of the second division of the entertainment, and while its humour is in progress of development everybody is highly entertained.

15 October   SUNDERLAND, Palace
Caseys' Circus is very much more amusing than their music hall. [there the previous week]

22 October   PRESTON, Royal Hippodrome
The best bill lately seen here is filling two houses nightly

29 October   SOUTHAMPTON, Palace
.. best bill for many weeks

5 November   PLYMOUTH, Palace

12 November   BOLTON, Grand

19 November   no trace

26 November   BIRKENHEAD, Argyle

3 December   BLACKBURN, Palace
.. their imitations of well-known music hall turns are extremely apt.

10 December   BATH, Palace
[unconfirmed]

17 December   FINSBURY, Sadler's Wells

24 December   SOUTH SHIELDS, Empire Palace

31 December   GREENOCK, Empire
1907

7 January   ABERDEEN, Palace of Varieties
.. in which Will Murray takes a prominent part, forms a diverting and mirth-provoking item.

14 January   no trace

21 January   BELFAST, Empire

(continued in right-hand column on this page)

28 January   DUBLIN, Empire

4 February   LIVERPOOL, Olympia

11 February   no trace

18 February   no trace

25 February   BURY, Circus of Varieties
.. the production is exceedingly amusing.

4 March   HARTLEPOOL WEST, Palace

11 March   DUNDEE, Palace

18 March   GLASGOW, Zoo and Hippodrome

25 March   EDINBURGH, Empire Palace

1 April   NEWCASTLE, Empire Palace

8 April   MANCHESTER, Hippodrome
.. a street-boy's idea of producing a circus.

15 April   ROCHDALE, Circus of Varieties
The Casey's Circus is about the most uproariously funny absurdity we have had here.
[Watched by Walford Bodie's sister??]
[Tuesday: Charlie's 18th Birthday]

22 April   LEEDS, Empire Palace
Casey's Circus is still on the road and proves as diverting as on its first visit.

29 April   BIRMINGHAM, Empire Palace
Will Murray is welcomed back after his serious illness and his tour abroad.

6 May   NOTTINGHAM, Empire
Casey's Circus heads the bill and provides a great amount of knockabout fun.
[Charlie allegedly wins a 20 mile walking race!!]

13 May   HACKNEY, Empire

20 May   HOLLOWAY, Empire

27 May   NEW CROSS, Empire

3 June   STRATFORD, Empire
Casey's Circus is a screamingly funny eccentric act.

10 June   SHEPHERDS BUSH, Empire

(continued in left-hand column on next page)

List of Known Players in CASEY'S CIRCUS
2 July 1906 – 15 June 1907

Mrs. Casey . . . . Will Murray
Billy Baggs . . . . Charles Chaplin
Dr. Awful Bogie . . . . Charles Chaplin
Mick Turpin . . . . Charles Chaplin
plus George Doonan

Read down the left-hand column to trace Charlie's tour in *Casey's Circus*. Read down the right-hand column to trace Sydney's tour with the Karno Company.

Read ACROSS the columns to find whenever they were simultaneously in London.

Also included are some dates for Sam Lowenwirth and Chas. Cohan, as I firmly believe Chaplin went to see them just before his own appearance as 'Sam Cohen'; plus *The Major's Middy"* as this is almost certainly what Chaplin referred to as *"The Major"* in which he played the romantic lead for just one week.

CHARLIE CHAPLIN "Casey's Circus" 1907 (continued)		SYD CHAPLIN Karno Company 1907	
17 June	LEICESTER, Palace	17 June	LONDON, Canterbury *London Suburbia* (debut)
24 June plus Tom Foy	BETHNAL GREEN, Foresters'	24 June	MILE END, Paragon *London Suburbia* [Syd Chaplin signs second contract with Karno]
1 July	CAMDEN, Surrey Varieties	1 July	SOUTHPORT, Pier Pavilion
8 July	BOW, Palace	8 July	BRIGHTON, Hippodrome *London Suburbia*
15 July 20 July	FINSBURY, Sadler's Wells [CHAPLIN LEAVES HERE]	15 July	LONDON, Canterbury *London Suburbia* [*unconfirmed* – see 17 June]
22 July	Charlie is 'resting'	22 July	no trace
29 July	[Syd goes off on a tour of the provinces.]	29 July	HARTLEPOOL WEST, Palace *Early Birds,* and *Mumming Birds*
[5 August	LONDON, Royal Cambridge Sam Lowenwirth and Chas. Cohan, plus *Dick Turpin's Ride to York* – Claude Ginnet's Company	5 August	no trace
12 August		12 August	OLDHAM, Empire *Early Birds, London Suburbia,* and *Mumming Birds*
[19 August	CAMBERWELL, Empire] *The Major's Middy* [Could this be the play Chaplin refers to as *The Major?*]	19 August	BURTON on TRENT, Opera House *Early Birds,* and *Mumming Birds*
26 August		26 August	MARGATE, Hippodrome *Mumming Birds*
2 September *London Suburbia* [Did Charlie have a part??] 9 September	STRATFORD, Empire	2 September (doubling at)	HACKNEY, Empire STRATFORD, Empire *London Suburbia* [Did Charlie have a part??]
		9 September	HOLLOWAY, Empire *London Suburbia*
16 September		16 September	NEW CROSS, Empire
23 September *London Suburbia* [Did Charlie have a part??]	STRATFORD, Empire	23 September *London Suburbia* [Did Charlie have a part??]	STRATFORD, Empire
30 September (doubling at) *London Suburbia*	POPLAR, Prince's SHEPHERDS BUSH, Empire	30 September (doubling at) *London Suburbia*	POPLAR, Prince's SHEPHERDS BUSH, Empire
7 October *The Major's Middy* – New musical comedy sketch.	CAMBERWELL, Empire	7 October *London Suburbia*	CARDIFF, Empire
14 October		14 October *London Suburbia*	SWANSEA, Empire
(continued in left-hand column on next page)		*(continued in right-hand column on next page)*	

Read down the left-hand column to trace Charlie's tour in *Casey's Circus*. Read down the right-hand column to trace Sydney's tour with the Karno Company.
Read ACROSS the columns to find whenever they were simultaneously in London.

CHARLIE CHAPLIN "Casey's Circus" 1907 (continued)	SYD CHAPLIN Karno Company 1907 (continued)
21 October	21 October NEWPORT, Empire *London Suburbia*
28 October	28 October NOTTINGHAM, Empire *London Suburbia*
4 November	4 November LEICESTER, Palace *London Suburbia*
11 November	11 November ARDWICK GREEN, Empire *London Suburbia*
18 November	18 November ARDWICK GREEN, Empire *Mumming Birds*

[25 November   SHOREDITCH, London Music Hall]
  Sam Lowenwirth and Chas. Cohan.
  [The most likely date when Charlie saw them perform.]
	25 November LAMBETH, South London Palace
	London Suburbia
	
	plus Harry Weldon – solo

2 December	2 December SOUTH SHIELDS, Empire Palace *Mumming Birds*
9 December	9 December IPSWICH, Hippodrome *Mumming Birds*
16 December	16 December PLYMOUTH, Palace *London Suburbia*
23 December BETHNAL GREEN, Foresters' Charlie appears as 'SAM COHEN'	23 December BRISTOL, People's Palace *London Suburbia*
30 December [Charlie may well have started accompanying Syd to the Karno shows, commencing here, and for the next four weeks.]	30 December SHOREDITCH, Hippodrome *Early Birds* plus Leo Dryden. (doubling at) CROYDON, Palace *Mumming Birds* – "The artist who plays the inebriated dude is particularly good."* [Jimmy Russell]

**List of Artists at
The Foresters', BETHNAL GREEN
Monday 23 December 1907**

Brothers Ashley; Raymond; Grossmith and Grant; Burg, Hand, and Wise; Horace White, Cora Corina; Fred Southern and Company; **SAM COHEN**; Winona and King, La Bello Maie; Lack and Ford.
Theatre Manager: F. BAUGH

**List of Players for
Mumming Birds and London Suburbia
as @ 30 December 1907**

Jimmy Russell, John E. Doyle, Arthur Forrest, Sydney Chaplin, George Craig, Jack Royal, Sam Leo, Frank Melroyd, Billy Moran, John Charters, Victor Knight, Amy Forrest, Louie Dean, Rosie Mayville, Lillie Craig, Maud Montague, Dolly Baker, Violet Vaughn, Lilac Hemp.
Tour Manager: ARTHUR FORREST

Read down the left-hand column to trace Charlie's tour in *The Football Match*. Read down the right-hand column to trace Sydney's tour with the Karno Company. Read ACROSS the columns to find whenever there were simultaneously in London

CHARLIE CHAPLIN
THE FOOTBALL MATCH
1908 (1st Tour)

27 January   HACKNEY, Empire
Harry Weldon, Will Poluski Jun., Bob Lewis
'Stiffy,' played by Harry Weldon, is in his best form.

3 February   LONDON, London Coliseum
Harry Weldon, Will Poluski Jun., Bob Lewis
[Charlie sent to watch and rehearse]

10 February   NEW CROSS, Empire
Harry Weldon, Will Poluski Jun., Chas. Chaplin,
Bob Lewis.
[Chaplin is billed for first time as a Karno comedian.]

17 February   STRATFORD, Empire
Harry Weldon, Will Poluski Jun., Chas. Chaplin,
Bob Lewis.
[21st Feb. Chaplin signs his first contract with Karno.]

24 February   SHEPHERDS BUSH, Empire
Harry Weldon, Will Poluski Jun., Chas. Chaplin,
Bob Lewis. Will Poluski has no small share in the success of the sketch.

2 March   NEWCASTLE, Empire Palace

9 March   BLACKBURN, Palace
Harry Weldon, Will Poluski Jun., Chas. Chaplin,
Bob Lewis

16 March   EDINBURGH, Empire Palace
Harry Weldon, Will Poluski Jun., Chas. Chaplin,
Bob Lewis.

23 March   BRADFORD, Empire
Harry Weldon, Will Poluski Jun., Chas. Chaplin
[Bob Lewis has been transferred to another Karno Co.]
.. the operations of 'Stiffy' (Harry Weldon) in goal are simply convulsing.

30 March   GLASGOW, Palace
Harry Weldon, Will Poluski Jun., Chas. Chaplin

(continued in left-hand column on next page)

SYDNEY CHAPLIN
Karno Company
1908

6 January   HAMMERSMITH, Palace
London Suburbia
(doubling at) MILE END, Paragon
Mumming Birds   Jimmy Russell (1st) Sydney (4th)

13 January   BALHAM, Duchess
Mumming Birds
(doubling at) SHOREDITCH, Hippodrome
Jail Birds

20 January   CLAPHAM, Grand Palace
London Suburbia and *Mumming Birds*
(doubling at) ROTHERITHE, Hippodrome
The Smoking Concert

27 January   BALHAM, Duchess
The Smoking Concert
(doubling at) CROYDON, Empire
London Suburbia

3 February   ISLINGTON, Empire
The Smoking Concert
(doubling at) WALHAM GREEN, Granville
Mumming Birds

10 February   EALING, Hippodrome
Mumming Birds
(doubling at) PUTNEY, Hippodrome
Mumming Birds

17 February   POPLAR, Hippodrome
The Smoking Concert
(doubling at) WOOLWICH, Hippodrome
London Suburbia

24 February   HAMMERSMITH, Palace
Mumming Birds
(doubling at) WILLESDEN, Hippodrome
London Suburbia

2 March   SHEERNESS, Hippodrome
Mumming Birds

9 March   TUNBRIDGE WELLS, Opera House
Mumming Bird and *The Outcasts*
(1) Jimmy Russell, Sydney Chaplin

16 March   PETERBOROUGH, Hippodrome
Early Birds and *Mumming Birds*

23 March   LAMBETH, South London Palace
The Smoking Concert
(doubling at) LONDON, Oxford Music Hall
Mumming Birds [Syd Chaplin is promoted from fourth in the cast listing, to principal comedian.

30 March   LONDON, Oxford Music Hall
Mumming Birds Sydney Chaplin, Muriel Palmer.
(doubling at) STOKE NEWINGTON, Palace
The Casuals (DEBUT)

(continued in right-hand column on next page)

CHARLIE CHAPLIN

6 April   LIVERPOOL, Empire
Harry Weldon, Will Letters, Will Poluski Jnr.,
Chas. Chaplin.

13 April   SUNDERLAND, Empire
Harry Weldon, Will Poluski Jun., Chas. Chaplin

[Charlie's 19th Birthday]

20 April   DUNDEE, Gaiety
Harry Weldon, Will Poluski Jun., Chas. Chaplin

27 April   BELFAST, Palace
Harry Weldon, Will Poluski Jun., Chas. Chaplin
The piece is presented by a first-class company, including
Will Poluski Jun., and Harry Weldon.

4 May   LEEDS, Empire Palace
Harry Weldon, Will Poluski Jun., Chas. Chaplin

11 May   BIRKENHEAD, Argyle
Harry Weldon, Will Poluski Jun., Chas. Chaplin
Stiffy is a host in himself for pure drollery and fun.

18 May   BURNLEY, Palace and Hippodrome
Harry Weldon, Will Poluski Jun., Chas. Chaplin

25 May   LONDON, London Coliseum
Harry Weldon, Will Poluski Jun., Chas. Chaplin

SYDNEY CHAPLIN

6 April   EAST HAM, Palace
The Smoking Concert
(doubling at) LONDON, Oxford Music Hall
Mumming Birds Sydney Chaplin.

13 April   CLAPHAM, Grand Palace
The Casuals
(trebling at)   LONDON, Oxford Music Hall
Mumming Birds Sydney Chaplin as 'the Drunk'.
(trebling at)   STRAND, Tivoli Music Hall
Mumming Birds – Sydney Chaplin as 'the Drunk'.

20 April   EDGWARE, Metropolitan
Mumming Birds – Sydney Chaplin as 'the Drunk'.
(doubling at) ISLINGTON, Collins's Music Hall
Early Birds   Sydney Chaplin.

27 April   ISLINGTON, Empire
The Casuals
(doubling at) SHOREDITCH, Empire/Olympia
Early Birds   Sydney Chaplin

4 May   BRIGHTON, Alhambra
Early Birds and *Mumming Birds* Syd Chaplin,
Jimmy Russell, Johnny Doyle, Sam Poluski

11 May   LONDON, London Coliseum
The Smoking Concert – Syd Chaplin, Jimmy Russell,
Johnny Doyle, Sam Poluski.

18 May   WOLVERHAMPTON, Empire
Mumming Birds

25 May   WIGAN, Grand Hippodrome
The Casuals, *Early Birds*, *The Smoking Concert*, and
Karno's Variety Company. Sydney Chaplin

THE FOOTBALL MATCH

List of Players

LONDON, London Coliseum

25 May 1908

Harry Weldon, Will Poluski jun., Chas. Chaplin,
Clifford Walton, R.J. Hamer, Bert Harrington,
Bert Royston Frank Haytor jun., Fred Newham,
Fred Onzella, C. Turner, J. Thure, Harry Ferguson,
Ted Banks, Harry Douglas, Jock Roberts,
H. Jackson, Jack Melville, J. Fitchett, S. Arkesden,
Chas. Price, Chas. Donaghy, W. Wragg,
Vi Morella, Victoria Wright, Lucy Waldon.
Manager: FRANK GALLAGHER
Stage manager: T. ELLIS BUXTON

Mumming Birds and London Suburbia
30 December 1907 – 16 March 1908

Jimmy Russell, John E. Doyle, Arthur Forrest,
Sydney Chaplin, George Craig, Jack Royal, Sam Leo,
Frank Melroyd, Billy Moran, John Charters,
Victor Knight, Amy Forrest, Louie Dean,
Rosie Mayville, Lillie Craig, Maud Montague,
Dolly Baker, Violet Vaughn, Lila Kemp

Tour Manager: ARTHUR FORREST.

Mumming Birds, The Casuals,
Early Birds, London Suburbia
The Smoking Concert
23 March – 25 May 1908

Sydney Chaplin, Jimmy Russell, Johnny Doyle,
Sam Poluski Jnr., Chas. Sewell, George Craig,
Jack Royal, Freddy Palmer, Frank Melroyd, Billy
Moran, John Hoare, Sara Dudley, Louie Dean,
Rosie Mayville, Lillie Craig, Maud Montague,
Dolly Baker, Muriel Palmer, Lila Kemp, Vere Neale,
Dorothy Ashton, Vallerie Neale.

Tour Manager: CHAS. SEWELL
Stage Manager. GEO CRAIG

CHARLIE and SYD CHAPLIN
Karno Company
[JOINT DATES]
1908

1 June   BALHAM, Hippodrome
Mumming Birds
(doubling at)   CAMDEN, Hippodrome
Mumming Birds
8 June   POPLAR, Hippodrome
The Casuals and *Mumming Birds*
(doubling at)   SHOREDITCH, Olympia
The Casuals, and *Mumming Birds*
15 June   ROTHERITHE, Hippodrome
The Casuals, and *The Smoking Concert*
(doubling at)   SHOREDITCH, Empire
The Casuals, and *The Smoking Concert*
22 June   BRADFORD, Palace
The Casuals and *The Smoking Concert*
29 June   CLAPHAM, Grand Palace
The Casuals and *Early Birds*
(doubling at)   POPLAR, Hippodrome
The Casuals and *Early Birds*
6 July   SHOREDITCH, Olympia
The Casuals and *Mumming Birds*
(doubling at)   WOOLWICH, Hippodrome
The Casuals and *Mumming Birds*
Sydney Chaplin and Charles Chaplin
13 July   HOLBORN, Empire
The Casuals and *Mumming Birds*
(doubling at)   WILLESDEN, Hippodrome
The Casuals and *Mumming Birds*
20 July   MAIDSTONE, Palace
The Casuals and *London Suburbia*
27 July   GREAT YARMOUTH, Royal
The Casuals, *London Suburbia*, and *Mumming Birds*
3 August   BALHAM, Hippodrome
Mumming Birds and *The Smoking Concert*
(doubling at)   LONDON, Tivoli Music Hall
Mumming Birds and *The Smoking Concert*.
10 August   BALHAM, Hippodrome
Mumming Birds and *The Smoking Concert*
(doubling at)   LONDON, Tivoli Music Hall
Mumming Birds and *The Smoking Concert*.
17 August   SHOREDITCH, Olympia
London Suburbia
(doubling at)   LONDON, Tivoli Music Hall
Mumming Birds. Plus Marie Lloyd
24 August   ABERDEEN, Palace
London Suburbia and *Mumming Birds*
31 August   GREENOCK, Hippodrome
London Suburbia and *Mumming Birds*
7 September   GLASGOW, Zoo Hippodrome
London Suburbia
14 September   no trace
21 September   SOUTHPORT, Pier Pavilion
London Suburbia and *Mumming Birds*
28 September   BLACKBURN, Palace
The Casuals, and *Mumming Birds*
               (continued in right-hand column on this page)

5 October   HARTLEPOOL, Palace
London Suburbia and *Mumming Birds*
12 October   MIDDLESBROUGH, Empire
The Casuals
19 October   ARDWICK, Empire
Mumming Birds
(doubling at)   WARRINGTON, Palace & Hippodrome
Mumming Birds
26 October   BURNLEY, Palace & Hippodrome
Mumming Birds
2 November   BIRKENHEAD, Argyle
Mumming Birds
9 November   BIRKENHEAD, Argyle
Early Birds [Chaplin leaves at end of week here.]

List of Players for
Mumming Birds; London Suburbia; and The Casuals as @ 10 August 1908

Sydney Chaplin, Jimmy Russell, Johnny Doyle, Albert Darnley, **Charles Chaplin**, **Chas. Sewell**, George Craig, Jack Royal, Frank Melroyd, Billy Moran, John Hoare, Will Amstell, E. Piddock, Sara Dudley, Louie Dean, Rosie Mayville, Lillie Craig, Dolly Baker, Amy Minister. Stage Manager: GEO. CRAIG.

HETTY KELLY
Bert Coote's Company
"FATAL WEDDING"
1908

3 August   MANCHESTER, Queen's
[New tour commences here.]

10 August   WOOLWICH, Royal
[Hetty Kelly confirmed as still being with the *Fatal Wedding* company.]
[Hetty rehearses during the day at the Montpelier]
17 August   NEW CROSS, Broadway
[This week and the previous week are the only two weeks that Charlie could have met Hetty.]
[Hetty rehearses during the day at the Montpelier]
24 August   WAKEFIELD, Empire
[*Fatal Wedding* goes on a tour of the provinces.]
28th August   HETTY KELLY'S 15th BIRTHDAY
[Which means she was just fourteen during the time the nineteen year-old Charlie was seeing her.]

14 September   HOLBORN, Empire
The Yankee Doodle Girls [DEBUT performance]
(doubling at)   London Pavilion
Bert Coote's Yankee Doodle Girls (nine in number) are a very smart troop of vocalists and dancers. They wear costumes of Union Jacks and Stars & Stripe pattern, full of vivacity, and gain well-earned applause.

Although, between 5 October and 2 November, there were three performances of *The Football Match*, I believe that Chaplin remained in the provinces with the company playing *London Suburbia* and *Mumming Birds*, and then joined at the commencement of the tour proper, in Walsall, 23 November 1908.

1908
Karno Company

5 October   EAST HAM, Palace
The Football Match (pre-tour try-out)
Will Poluski jun., Harry Weldon
(doubling at)   WALTHAMSTOW, Palace
2 November   CLAPHAM, Grand
The Football Match (pre-tour try-out)
(doubling at)   TOTTENHAM, Palace
The Football Match]
16 November   [no trace of Chaplin's company. Probably rehearsing.]

The Football Match

[Charlie's second tour]

23 November   WALSALL, Her Majesty's
The Football Match [start of tour proper. Chaplin is thought to have re-joined here, and not before.]
30 November   HANLEY, Grand
The Football Match
[Charles Chaplin confirmed as playing 'The Villain']
7 December   CARDIFF, Empire
The Football Match
14 December   MANCHESTER, Hippodrome
The Football Match
Harry Weldon, Will Poluski
21 December   LEICESTER, Palace
The Football Match. Harry Weldon is responsible for most of the humour, but he is admirably helped by a most capable company.
28 December   SHEPHERDS BUSH, Empire
The Football Match

1909
The Football Match

4 January   NOTTINGHAM, Empire
The Football Match
11 January   BIRMINGHAM, Grand
The Football Match
18 January   HULL, Palace
The Football Match
25 January   HACKNEY, Empire
The Football Match
1 February   HOLLOWAY, Empire
The Football Match
8 February   NEW CROSS, Empire
The Football Match
15 February   BRADFORD, Empire
The Football Match
22 February   WARRINGTON, Palace & Hippodrome
The Football Match
1 March   NEWCASTLE, Empire Palace
The Football Match

(continued in right-hand column on this page)

8 March   GLASGOW, Empire Palace
The Football Match
15 March   LEEDS, Empire Palace
The Football Match
22 March   STRATFORD, Empire Palace
The Football Match
29 March   EXETER, New Hippodrome
The Football Match
5 April   BLACKBURN, Hippodrome
The Football Match
12 April   BRISTOL, People's Palace
The Football Match
19 April   LIVERPOOL, Olympia
Will Poluski Jun. and Harry Weldon are the leaders, but last night a deputy for Weldon made ample use of his opportunity. [CHAPLIN]
26 April   SHEFFIELD, Empire Palace
The Football Match
3 May   OLDHAM, Empire
Charles Chaplin and Will Poluski jun., who take the principal parts, are very droll, and their make-up adds to the enjoyment.

[Second tour ends here – 8 May 1909]

Poster showing the first time Chaplin displaced Weldon as 'Stiffy'.

Posters for two of Karno's most famous sketches.

(Marriot Collection)

It has proved impossible to track Chaplin's movements within the Karno Company during certain periods. This is because he was being moved around playing different sketches and, as he was playing only small parts, wasn't billed.

To misquote a classic line from a Morecambe & Wise sketch: "I have listed all the RIGHT sketches that Chaplin played – but *not necessarily* in the RIGHT order."

Hopefully, as my research continues, a more definite pattern of Chaplin's movements will emerge, which will then be revealed in the second edition of this book.

Karno Companies

The following is a list of sketches in which Chaplin is believed to have appeared, but the actual dates of his involvement are unknown – except where otherwise named. You need to select one from each date to plot his personal path.

1909

Date	Venue	Sketch	Notes
10 May	HOLBORN, Empire	*Skating*	Syd Chaplin
	GLASGOW, Empire	*The G.P.O.*	Fred Kitchen as 'Perkins'
	HALIFAX, Grand	*The Bailiff*	Albert Bruno, Gilbert Childs
	SOUTH SHIELDS, Empire Palace	*The Smoking Concert*	
17 May	EDINBURGH, Empire Palace	*The Smoking Concert*	(week 1)
	HAMMERSMITH, Palace	*The G.P.O.*	Fred Kitchen as 'Perkins'
	HOLBORN, Empire	*The G.P.O.*	Fred Kitchen as 'Perkins'
	WOOLWICH, Hippodrome	*Skating*	London DEBUT. Syd Chaplin
	SHEFFIELD, Empire	*The Bailiff*	Albert Bruno
24 May	EDINBURGH, Empire Palace	*Mumming Birds*	(week 2)
	EXETER, New Hippodrome	*Dandy Thieves*	George Hestor
	NOTTINGHAM, Empire	*The Bailiff*	Albert Bruno
31 May	BRIXTON, Empress	*Skating*	Sydney Chaplin
	CAMBERWELL, Palace	*The Bailiff*	Albert Bruno
	SHOREDITCH, Olympia	*The Bailiff*	Albert Bruno
	GLASGOW, Coliseum	*The Smoking Concert*	I(week 1)
7 June	SHOREDITCH, Olympia	*Skating*	Sydney Chaplin, Jimmy Russell
	BRISTOL, Palace	*The Bailiff*	Albert Bruno
	GLASGOW, Coliseum	*Mumming Birds*	(week 2)
	LIVERPOOL, New Olympia	*The G.P.O.*	Fred Kitchen as 'Perkins'
14 June	BERMONDSEY, Star Palace	*Mumming Birds*	[possibly Charles Chaplin]
	ARDWICK, Empire	*The AG.P.O.*	Fred Kitchen as 'Perkins'
	BELFAST, Empire	*The Smoking Concert*	(week 1)
	BURY, Royal and Palace	*Mumming Birds*, and *Skating*	Sydney Chaplin
	PLYMOUTH, Palace	*The Bailiff*	Albert Bruno, Gilbert Childs, John Basofti
21 June	BELFAST, Empire	*Mumming Birds*	(week 2)
	EXETER, New Hippodrome	*The Bailiff*	Albert Bruno, Gilbert Childs
	SWANSEA, Empire	*The G.P.O.*	Fred Kitchen as 'Perkins'
28 June	NEW CROSS, Empire	*The G.P.O.*	Fred Kitchen as 'Perkins'
	BRIGHTON, Alhambra	*The Bailiff*	Albert Bruno
	DUBLIN, Empire Palace	*The Smoking Concert*	(week 1)
	HALIFAX, Grand	*Mumming Birds*, and *Skating*	Sydney Chaplin
5 July	PUTNEY, Hippodrome	*Skating*	Sydney Chaplin
	WILLESDEN, Hippodrome	*Skating*	Sydney Chaplin, Jimmy Russell
	DUBLIN, Empire Palace	*Mumming Birds*	(week 2)
	PORTSMOUTH, Hippodrome	*The G.P.O.*	Fred Kitchen
	RAMSGATE, Royal Victoria	*The Bailiff*	Albert Bruno, Gilbert Childs
12 July	CAMBERWELL, Palace	*Skating*	Sydney Chaplin
	POPLAR, Hippodrome	*Skating*	Sydney Chaplin
	BRIGHTON, Alhambra	*Dandy Thieves*	
	LEICESTER, Palace	*Perkins MP*	DEBUT. Fred Kitchen
	LIVERPOOL, New Olympia	*The Smoking Concert*	(week 1)

(continued on next page)

Karno Companies

1909 (continued)

19 July	HOLBORN, Empire	*Mumming Birds*		
	LIVERPOOL, New Olympia	*Mumming Birds*		(week 2)
	NEWPORT, Empire	*Perkins MP*	Fred Kitchen	
26 July	SHOREDITCH, Olympia	*The Casuals*		
	ISLINGTON, Empire	*Skating*	Sydney Chaplin	
	BRADFORD, Empire	*Mumming Birds*		
	CARDIFF, Empire	*Perkins MP*	Fred Kitchen	
2 August	HOLBORN, Empire	*Perkins MP*	London DEBUT.	(week 1)
	BIRMINGHAM, Empire Palace	*The Bailiff*	Albert Bruno	
	CARDIFF, Empire	*Mumming Birds*		
	SOUTHSEA, King's	*Skating*	Copyright performance. Sydney Chaplin	
9 August	BALHAM, Hippodrome	*Skating*	Sydney Chaplin	
	BRIXTON, Empress	*The G.P.O.*	Fred Kitchen	
	HOLBORN, Empire	*Perkins MP*	Fred Kitchen	(week 2)
	BIRMINGHAM, Grand	*Mumming Birds*		
	The Bailiff	no trace		
16 August	HOLBORN, Empire	*Skating*	Sydney Chaplin.	(week 3)
	KILBURN, Empire	*Perkins MP*	Fred Kitchen	
	POPLAR, Hippodrome	*The Bailiff*	Albert Bruno, Gilbert Childs	
	NEWPORT, Empire	*Spring Cleaning*	DEBUT. Albert Darnley, Tom Nelson	
		Mumming Birds	no trace	
23 August	ISLINGTON, Empire	*Perkins MP*	Fred Kitchen	
	POPLAR, Hippodrome	*Perkins MP*	Fred Kitchen	
	PUTNEY, Hippodrome	*The Bailiff*	Albert Bruno, Gilbert Childs	
	RICHMOND, Hippodrome	*The Bailiff*	Albert Bruno, Gilbert Childs	
	ROTHERITHE, Hippodrome	*Mumming Birds*		
	WOOLWICH, Hippodrome	*Spring Cleaning*		
	OLDHAM, Empire	*Jail Birds*, and *Skating*	Syd Chaplin	
	BOLTON, Empire & Hippodrome	*Dandy Thieves*		
30 August	CAMBERWELL, Palace	*Mumming Birds*		
	BRISTOL, People's Palace	*Dandy Thieves*		
	BOSCOMBE, Hippodrome	*Fred Karno Company*	[sketch not named]	
	GLASGOW, Empire	*Perkins MP*	Fred Kitchen	
	NORWICH, Hippodrome	*The Bailiff*	Albert Bruno	
6 September	LONDON, Canterbury	*The Casuals*		
	SOUTHAMPTON, Hippodrome	*Mumming Birds*		
	DEVONPORT, Hippodrome	*Dandy Thieves*	George Hestor	
	BELFAST, Royal Hippodrome	*Perkins MP*	Fred Kitchen	
13 September	ISLINGTON, Empire	*Spring Cleaning*		
	EALING, Hippodrome	*Skating*		
	BALHAM, Hippodrome	*The Bailiff*	Albert Bruno, Gilbert Childs	
	BRISTOL, People's Palace	*London Suburbia*		
	BRIXTON, Empress	*Mumming Birds*		
	LIVERPOOL, New Pavilion	*The G.P.O.*	Harold Wellesley	
	PORTSMOUTH, Hippodrome	*Mumming Birds*		
		Perkins MP	no trace	
20 September	WILLESDEN, Hippodrome	*Spring Cleaning*		
	EALING, Hippodrome	*Mumming Birds*		
	OLDHAM, Empire	*The G.P.O.*	Fred Kitchen	
	OLDHAM, Empire	*Perkins MP*	Fred Kitchen	
	WIGAN, Grand Hippodrome	*Early Birds*		
	WIGAN, Grand Hippodrome	*Jail Birds*		

(continued on next page)

Karno Companies

1909 (continued)

Date	Venue	Sketch	Performer/Notes
27 September	BRIXTON, Empress	*The Football Match*	
	BALHAM, Hippodrome	*Mumming Birds*	
	ROCHDALE, Hippodrome	*Mumming Birds*	
	OLDHAM, Empire	*Perkins MP*	Fred Kitchen
4 October	BOLTON, Grand	*Skating* and *Mumming Birds*	Syd Chaplin
	CLAPHAM, Grand Palace	Fred Karno Company	[sketch not named]
	KILBURN, Empire	*Mumming Birds*	
11 October	BRISTOL, People's Palace	*London Suburbia*	
	EALING, Hippodrome	Fred Karno Company	[sketch not named]
	ISLINGTON, Empire	Fred Karno Company	[sketch not named]
	RICHMOND, Hippodrome	*Perkins MP*	Fred Kitchen
	SHOREDITCH, Olympia	Fred Karno Company	[sketch not named]
	COVENTRY, Hippodrome	*Dandy Thieves*	
18 October	LONDON, Oxford Music Hall	*The Bailiff*	Fred Kitchen
	CLAPHAM, Grand	*The Bailiff*	Albert Bruno
	POPLAR, Hippodrome	*Spring Cleaning*	
	ROTHERITHE, Hippodrome	Fred Karno Company	[sketch not named]
		Perkins MP	no trace
25 October	BIRMINGHAM, Grand	*Perkins MP*	Fred Kitchen
	BELFAST, Hippodrome	*Dandy Thieves*	George Hestor
	CHATHAM, Gaiety	*The Casuals* and *Mumming Birds*	
	HOLBORN, Empire	*Spring Cleaning*	
	MILE END, Paragon	*Skating*	Syd Chaplin
	PECKHAM, Hippodrome	*The Bailiff*	
1 November	EDINBURGH, Empire Palace	*Perkins MP*	Fred Kitchen
1 November	**PARIS, Folies Bergere**	***Mumming Birds***	**Charles Chaplin**
8 November	**PARIS, Folies Bergere**	***Mumming Birds***	**Charles Chaplin**
15 November	**PARIS, Folies Bergere**	***Mumming Birds***	**Charles Chaplin**
22 November	**PARIS, Folies Bergere**	***Mumming Birds***	**Charles Chaplin**
29 November	EALING, Hippodrome	*The Bailiff*	
	IPSWICH, Hippodrome	*Mumming Birds*	
	LEICESTER, Palace	*Perkins MP*	Fred Kitchen
	RICHMOND, Hippodrome	Fred Karno Company	[sketch not named]
	ROTHERITHE, Hippodrome	Fred Karno Company	[sketch not named]
6 December	BRADFORD, Empire	*Perkins MP*	Fred Kitchen
	HULME, Hippodrome	*Mumming Birds*	(1) Stan Jefferson's DEBUT
	MILE END, Paragon	*Spring Cleaning*	
		The Bailiff	no trace

13 December   **LONDON, Oxford Music Hall** *The Football Match*   Will Poluski, Gilbert Childs, Fred Newham,
CHARLES CHAPLIN (confirmed in theatre programme, but not playing 'Stiffy'.)
(doubling at)   **WILLESDEN, Hippodrome**   ***The Football Match***   **Charles Chaplin as 'Stiffy'**

> *The sketch is received with roars of laughter, much being due to the efforts of Charles Chaplin, Gilbert Childs, and Will Poluski Jun.*

> [Chaplin says he played the lead but, on the first night, flu complicated by laryngitis led to him having to pull out.]

*[20 December   MANCHESTER, Palace   *Skating*]   [Sydney & Minnie Chaplin, Jimmy Russell]

20 December	LONDON, Oxford Music Hall	*The Football Match*	[Chaplin OUT]	(week 2)
27 December	CHELSEA, Palace	FKC	[missing FOOTBALL??]	
*[27 December	MANCHESTER, Palace	*Skating*	Sydney & Minnie Chaplin, Jimmy Russell]	

1910

3 January	**EDGWARE, Metropolitan**	***The Football Match***	**Charles Chaplin as 'Stiffy'**

----

3 January   EDGWARE, Metropolitan

The Football Match Charles Chaplin

3 January   WAKEFIELD, Empire

Mumming Birds and *Skating* (1st company)

Sydney Chaplin, Stan Jefferson

10 January   LIVERPOOL, New Pavilion

Mumming Birds (2nd company) [1st company splits into two. Sydney leaves, Charlie joins Stan's company.]

10 January   SHOREDITCH, Olympia

Skating (1st company) Sydney Chaplin.

17 January   PUTNEY, Hippodrome

Skating (1st company) Sydney Chaplin

17 January   ROCHDALE, Hippodrome

Skating (2nd company – DEBUT) and *Early Birds* Charlie and Stan

24 January   BURY, Royal and Palace

Skating (2nd company) and *Early Birds*

Charles Chaplin, Ernie Stone, James Beresford Ted Banks. [They play their first hockey match.]

24 January   HAMMERSMITH, Palace

Skating (1st company) and *Mumming Birds*

Sydney Chaplin, Jimmy Russell, Geo. Craig, Jack Royal, Geo. Hoare, Frank Melroyd

31 January   HULME, Hippodrome and Floral Hall

Skating (2nd or 1st company?) and *The Casuals* [doubling with WIGAN?]

31 January   WIGAN, Grand Hippodrome

Skating (2nd company) [DOUBLING with Hulme?]

Charles Chaplin, Johnny Doyle

7 February   GLASGOW, Pavilion

Skating (2nd company) Charles Chaplin

7 February   ILFORD, Hippodrome

Skating (1st company) Sydney Chaplin

14 February   LEEDS, Hippodrome

Skating (2nd company) Charles Chaplin, Johnny Doyle

21 February   BIRMINGHAM, Hippodrome

Skating (2nd company) Charles Chaplin, Johnny Doyle [Saturday – Play hockey match at the City Rink.]

28 February   SHEFFIELD, Hippodrome

Skating (2nd company)

Charles Chaplin, and Johnny Doyle are in good form. The cast had great fun everyday at the American Rink.

7 March   LIVERPOOL, Royal Hippodrome

Skating (1st and 2nd company) Sydney joins Charlie's company. Johnny Doyle, Arthur Dando

14 March   NEWCASTLE, Pavilion Music Hall

Skating (1st and 2nd company)

Sydney Chaplin and Charles Chaplin, Stan Jefferson

21 March   ECCLES, Crown

Skating (1st and 2nd company)

Sydney Chaplin and Jimmy Russell

28 March   LONGSIGHT, King's

Skating (1st company) Charles Chaplin and Stan Jefferson. [Play Hockey match at Levenshulme.]

4 April   HACKNEY, Empire

Skating (1st company)

11 April   [Charlie switches to *Jimmy the Fearless*.]

"SKATING"
List of known Karno players:
1910

Charles Chaplin, Johnny Doyle, Stan Jefferson, Ernie Stone, Fred Gordon, James Barrasford, Miss M. Jackson, Ted Banks, Gertie Jackson; Arthur Dando, Charles Griffiths, George Farnley and, sometimes, Sydney Chaplin.

Manager: Frank O' Neil

WIGAN EXAMINER

25 JANUARY 1910

(w/c 24 January 1910)

THE HIPPODROME

KARNO'S COMEDIANS AT THE HIPPODROME

"*Roller Skating,*" which is Fred Karno's latest sketch is certainly one of the funniest he has yet presented to Wigan audiences. On Monday evening the efforts of his company in burlesquing this latest craze sent the house into screams of laughter, and especially humorous were **Charlie Chaplin** and Johnny Doyle. The merriment is present from start to finish, and some clever exhibitions of roller skating is also given when the scene is laid inside the rink.

The Casuals, another of Karno's absurdities is also very mirth provoking, the incidents taking place at the exterior and interior of the casual ward.

HIPPODROME

King Street, Wigan.

TO-NIGHT AT 7-30. TO-NIGHT

FRED KARNO'S LAUGHING COMEDIANS

in

"THE CASUALS"

and

"SKATING"

Two of the Funniest Sketches ever seen in Wigan

Two hours of continued Laughter.

Also a First-class Company of Vaudeville Artistes.

Popular Prices. Half-price at Nine to all parts.

Programme reversed after Wednesday.

"JIMMY the FEARLESS"
1910

11 April   LONDON
Jimmy the Fearless (rehearsals)
[Saturday 16th April – Charlie's 21st Birthday]
18 April   EALING, Hippodrome
Jimmy the Fearless ((production try-out)
Stan Jefferson as 'Jimmy'
(doubling at)   WILLESDEN, Hippodrome
Jimmy the Fearless (production try-out)
Stan Jefferson as 'Jimmy'.
25 April   STRATFORD, Empire (DEBUT)
Jimmy the Fearless – with Charles Chaplin as 'Jimmy'

2 May   HOLLOWAY, Empire
Jimmy the Fearless
[Alf Reeves offers to take Chaplin to the U.S.]
9 May   SHEFFIELD, Empire Palace
Jimmy the Fearless

16 May   SOUTH SHIELDS, Empire Palace
Jimmy the Fearless

23 May   NEWCASTLE, Empire Palace
Jimmy the Fearless

30 May   GLASGOW, Coliseum (week 1)
Mumming Birds

6 June   GLASGOW, Coliseum (week 2)
Jimmy the Fearless

13 June   WALSALL, Her Majesty's
Jimmy the Fearless

20 June   LEICESTER, Palace
Jimmy the Fearless

27 June   CARDIFF, Empire
"Jimmy the Fearless" is in the hands of a clever comedian
4 July   NEWPORT, Empire
Jimmy the Fearless

11 July SWANSEA, Empire
Jimmy the Fearless
Charles Chaplin enacts the title role.
18 July   LEEDS, Empire Palace
Jimmy the Fearless

25 July   BIRMINGHAM, Empire Palace
Jimmy the Fearless
[Reeves confirms Chaplin for the U.S. tour.]
1 August   HULL, Palace
Jimmy the Fearless

8 August LIVERPOOL, Empire
Jimmy the Fearless was billed to appear but Mike S.
Whallen is deputising. [The company were probably
summoned to London to rehearse *The Wow-Wows*.]

(continued in right-hand column on this page)

"JIMMY the FEARLESS"
and "THE WOW-WOWS"
1910

8 August   EAST HAM, Palace
The Wow-Wows (DEBUT) Entirely new production.
Sydney Chaplin
(doubling at)   TOTTENHAM, Palace
The Wow-Wows (DEBUT) Sydney Chaplin
15 August   ARDWICK GREEN, Empire
Jimmy the Fearless
22 August   NOTTINGHAM, Empire
Jimmy the Fearless

29 August   BRADFORD, Empire
Jimmy the Fearless
               [ENDS HERE]
5 September   WOOLWICH, Hippodrome
The Wow-Wows

12 September   ILFORD, Hippodrome
The Wow-Wows [Syd's company??]
SHOREDITCH, Olympia
The Wow-Wows [Charlie's company??]
               TOTTENHAM, Palace
Jimmy the Fearless Charlie Chaplin as 'Jimmy'. [There
could be 2 companies, or just one doing all 3 venues.]
Saturday 17 September
   Charles Chaplin and Stan Jefferson leave here. Sydney
Chaplin continues U.K. tour with *The Wow-Wows*
19 September   ISLINGTON, Empire
The Wow-Wows – Sydney Chaplin.
22 September. Charles Chaplin sails for the United States.

"JIMMY THE FEARLESS"
1910
List of known Karno Players

Charles. Chaplin, Stan Jefferson, Arthur
Dandoe, Bert Williams, Mrs. Bert Williams,
Mike Asher, Emily Seaman, Ernest Stone,
Harry Daniels, Albert Austin.

Manager: FRANK O'NEIL

NOTES

DATE-SHEETS

Chaplin's stage appearances in the

United States of America

On the following pages are "Date-Sheets" containing every known stage appearance which Chaplin made in the U.S.A. between October 1910 and November 1913.

Whereas, in the U.K., the usual "week" for theatre engagements is Monday to Saturday, in the U.S.A. there is no such standardisation. The length of stay at any one theatre depended upon the size of the theatre itself and the number of regular clientele it attracted. On which night they opened seemed to depend not only on how many nights the presentation was to play for, but when the company could actually get there. The availability of trains seemed to be the governing factor in all of this. Thus we find many instances of the Karno company's "week" beginning on a Saturday, or a Sunday, or a Monday, and even on a Wednesday; with the length of stay being anything from two days to five weeks. And not here was the Sabbath held sacred, which is probably why so many theatres were hit by a bolt of fire from heaven!

So, the date of the opening night has been given in all cases were known but, even then, it was not always possible to discern just when the week finished.

HOW TO READ THE TABLES.

The date on the left is what is termed as "Week Commencing" (often abbreviated to w/c) which, as has been explained, is not always a Monday.

The next entry is the "State;" then the "Town or City" where the theatre was located; followed by the name of the actual "Theatre." Where the same theatre was played two or more weeks by the same company, this has been highlighted in brackets, on the extreme right of the column.

On the second line of each entry: the text in *italics* is the name of the "Sketch" being played – that particular week at that venue. Text in [brackets] is the "Author's Comments."

It has taken the author, and a dedicated team of researchers, over two years to find and collate all these dates, so the publishers are keen to point out that, just because they are now in print, this does gives someone the right to take them and use them for their own publication. So, please note that:

THESE DATE-SHEETS ARE COPYRIGHTED

KARNO COMPANY – First U.S. Tour (1910-1911)

1910

3 October		NEW YORK, NEW YORK CITY, Colonial
	The Wow-Wows	
10 October		NEW YORK, NEW YORK CITY, Alhambra
	The Wow-Wows	
17 October		NEW YORK, BROOKLYN, Orpheum
	The Wow-Wows	[St George's Society and Usonas are in during the week]
24 October		NEW YORK, BRONX, Bronx
	The Wow-Wows	
31 October		NEW YORK, BROOKLYN, Greenpoint
	The Wow-Wows	
7 November		MASSACHUSETTS, FALL RIVER, Savoy
	A Night in a London Music Hall	
14 November		NEW YORK, BRONX, National
	A Night in a London Music Hall	
21 November		PENNSYLVANIA, PHILADELPHIA, Nixon
	A Night in a London Music Hall	
28 November		NEW YORK, NEW YORK CITY, American Music Hall
	A Night in a London Music Hall	
	[Sennett sees Chaplin sometime during the next five weeks.]	
5 December		NEW YORK, NEW YORK CITY, American Music Hall
	The Wow-Wows	
12 December		NEW YORK, NEW YORK CITY, American Music Hall
	A Night in a London Club	
19 December		NEW YORK, NEW YORK CITY, American Music Hall
	A Night in London Slums	
26 December		NEW YORK, NEW YORK CITY, American Music Hall
	A Night in an English Music Hall, and A Harlequinade in Black & White	

1911

2 January		NEW YORK, NEW YORK CITY, Plaza
	The Wow-Wows, and A Harlequinade in Black & White	
9 January		PENNSYLVANIA, PHILADELPHIA, Nixon
	A Night in a London Club	
12 January	(Thursday only)	PENNSYLVANIA, PHILADELPHIA, Academy of Music
	A Night in a London Club	(one-off Benefit performance)
16 January		PENNSYLVANIA, PHILADELPHIA, Park (Nixon house)
	A Night in an English Music Hall	
23 January		PENNSYLVANIA, PHILADELPHIA, Nixon
	The Wow-Wows	

[First Sullivan & Considine tour begins here, in Chicago]

30 January		ILLINOIS, CHICAGO, American Music Hall
	A Night in a London Club	
6 February		ILLINOIS, CHICAGO, American Music Hall
	The Wow-Wows	
13 February		ILLINOIS, CHICAGO, American Music Hall
	A Night in an English Music Hall	
20 February	- no trace.	(possibly) OHIO, CLEVELAND; or ST. LOUIS, MISSOURI; or DETROIT, MICHIGAN
26 February – 03 March		OHIO, CINCINNATI, Empress
	A Night in an English Music Hall	

(continued on next page)

KARNO COMPANY – First U.S. Tour (continued)

1911

4 March-11 March   ILLINOIS, CHICAGO, Empress
A Night in an English Music Hall

12 March   WISCONSIN, MILWAUKEE, Empress
A Night in an English Music Hall

20 March   MINNESOTA, MINNEAPOLIS, Unique
A Night in an English Music Hall

26 March – 02 April   MINNESOTA, DULUTH, Empress
A Night in an English Music Hall

3 April – 8 April   MANITOBA, WINNIPEG, Empress
A Night in an English Music Hall

10 April-11 April   (probably) MONTANA, MILES CITY [2 nights only?]

12 April-13 April   (probably) MONTANA, BILLINGS, Majestic [2 nights only?]

15 April – 21 April   MONTANA, BUTTE, Majestic (opens Saturday)
A Night in an English Music Hall

23 April – 29 April   WASHINGTON, SPOKANE, Washington
A Night in an English Music Hall

1 May – 6 May   WASHINGTON, SEATTLE, Majestic
A Night in an English Music Hall

8 May – 13 May   BRITISH COLUMBIA, VANCOUVER, Orpheum
A Night in an English Music Hall

15 May   WASHINGTON, TACOMA, Majestic
A Night in an English Music Hall

22 May   OREGON, PORTLAND, Grand
A Night in an English Music Hall

29 May   no trace

4 June   CALIFORNIA, SAN FRANCISCO, Empress
A Night in an English Music Hall

11 June – 17 June   CALIFORNIA, SACRAMENTO, Grand
A Night in an English Music Hall

18 June   CALIFORNIA, OAKLAND, Bell
A Night in an English Music Hall

25 June – 2 July   CALIFORNIA, LOS ANGELES, Empress
A Night in an English Music Hall

3 July   CALIFORNIA, SAN DIEGO, Empress
A Night in an English Music Hall

10 July   (possibly) SALT LAKE CITY

17 July – 22 July   COLORADO, DENVER, Empress

24 July   COLORADO SPRINGS
A Night in an English Music Hall

30 July – 5 August   MISSOURI, KANSAS CITY, Empress
A Night in an English Music Hall
[Stan Jefferson and Arthur Dando leave at the end of the week in Kansas City]

[FIRST SULLIVAN & CONSIDINE TOUR ENDS HERE, IN KANSAS.]

KARNO COMPANY – Second and Third U.S. Tours

1911

7 August – 13 August Week out between tours.

14 August – 19 August	MINNESOTA, MINNEAPOLIS, Unique
A Night in a London Club	
20 August – 26 August	MINNESOTA, ST. PAUL, Empress
A Night in a London Club	
27 August – 2 September	MINNESOTA, DULUTH, Empress
A Night in a London Club	
4 September – 9 September	MANITOBA, WINNIPEG, Empress
A Night in a London Club	
11 September	(probably) MILES CITY, or BILLINGS, or both [split week]
16 September – 22 September	MONTANA, BUTTE, Empress
A Night in a London Club	
24 September – 30 September	WASHINGTON, SPOKANE, Washington
A Night in a London Club	
2 October	WASHINGTON, SEATTLE, Majestic
A Night in a London Club	
9 October – 14 October	BRITISH COLUMBIA, VANCOUVER, Orpheum
A Night in a London Club	
16 October – 21 October	WASHINGTON, TACOMA, Empress
A Night in a London Club	
23 October – 28 October	OREGON, PORTLAND, Empress
A Night in a London Club	
30 October – no trace	
6 November	CALIFORNIA, SAN FRANCISCO, Empress
A Night in a London Club	
12 November – 18 November	CALIFORNIA, SACRAMENTO, Grand
A Night in a London Club	
20 November – no trace.	(possibly) CALIFORNIA, SAN DIEGO, Garrick
27 November	CALIFORNIA, LOS ANGELES, Empress
A Night in a London Club	
4 December	UTAH, SALT LAKE CITY, Empress [unconfirmed]
11 December	COLORADO, DENVER, Empress [unconfirmed]
18 December	COLORADO, COLORADO SPRINGS, Majestic
A Night in a London Club	
25 December – 30 December	MISSOURI, KANSAS CITY, Empress
A Night in a London Club	

[SECOND SULLIVAN & CONSIDINE TOUR ENDS HERE, IN KANSAS.]

1912

1 January 1912	ILLINOIS, CHICAGO, Hamlin
A Night in an English Music Hall	
8 January – 14 January	ILLINOIS, CHICAGO, Hamlin (Mon-Sun)
A Night in a London Club	
15 January	no trace

KARNO COMPANY – Third U.S. Tour (continued)

1912

21 January – 27 January	OHIO, CINCINNATI, Empress
A Night in an English Music Hall	
29 January - no trace.	(probably) ILLINOIS, CHICAGO, ?? (Mon-Wed?)
1 February – 3 February	ILLINOIS, CHICAGO, Empress (Thu-Sat)
A Night in the Slums	
4 February – 10 February	WISCONSIN, MILWAUKEE, Empress
A Night in an English Music Hall	
11 February – 17 February	MINNESOTA, MINNEAPOLIS, Unique (opens Sunday)
A Night in an English Music Hall	
19 February – 24 February	MINNESOTA, ST. PAUL, Empress [unconfirmed]
26 February	IOWA, WATERLOO, Majestic [unconfirmed]
4 March – 9 March	MANITOBA, WINNIPEG, Empress
A Night in an English Music Hall	
11 March	MONTANA, MILES CITY (Mon-Tue) [unconfirmed]
13 March – 14 March	MONTANA, BILLINGS, Acme (Wed-Thu)
16 March – 22 March	MONTANA, BUTTE, Empress (Sat-Fri)
A Night in an English Music Hall	
24 March – 30 March	WASHINGTON, SPOKANE, Empress (opens Sunday)
A Night in an English Music Hall	
1 April – 6 April	WASHINGTON, SEATTLE, Empress
A Night in an English Music Hall	
8 April – 13 April	BRITISH COLUMBIA, VANCOUVER, Orpheum
A Night in an English Music Hall	
15 April	WASHINGTON, TACOMA, Empress
A Night in an English Music Hall	
22 April	SOREGON, PORTLAND, Empress
A Night in an English Music Hall	
29 April	(possibly) CALIFORNIA, OAKLAND,
5 May – 11 May	CALIFORNIA, SAN FRANCISCO, Empress
A Night in an English Music Hall	
12 May	CALIFORNIA, SACRAMENTO, Empress
A Night in an English Music Hall	
20 May – 25 May	CALIFORNIA, LOS ANGELES, Empress
A Night in an English Music Hall	
27 May – 01 June	UTAH, SALT LAKE CITY, Empress [unconfirmed]
A Night in an English Music Hall	
3 June	no trace
10 June	COLORADO, DENVER, Empress [unconfirmed]
17 June	MISSOURI, KANSAS CITY, Empress
A Night in an English Music Hall	

[THIRD SULLIVAN & CONSIDINE TOUR ENDS HERE, IN KANSAS]
Company sail back to England, from New York, 6 July 1912

KARNO COMPANY

Summer in England

July 1912 – October 1912

1912

6 July Karno company set sail from New York, bound for England

15 July – 20 July   ENGLAND LONDON, Euston
 The Hydro (Sydney Chaplin)
 [The former U.S. company possibly went to watch, as this is the sketch they were scheduled
 to take with them on the next U.S. tour.]

22 July – 27 July   ENGLAND LONDON, Hackney Empire
 The Hydro (Sydney Chaplin)
 [The former U.S. company possibly went to watch.]

29 July – 3 August   ENGLAND SURREY, Kingston Empire
 The Hydro (Sydney Chaplin)
 [The former U.S. company possibly went to watch. In fact, they might well have appeared in it.]

5 August – 10 August   ENGLAND LONDON, Metropolitan
 Mumming Birds   [Charles Chaplin named as lead character.]

5 August – 10 August   ENGLAND LONDON, Tivoli
 Mumming Birds   Charles Chaplin

12 August – 15 August   CHANNEL ISLANDS, JERSEY, Opera House
 Mumming Birds, and *The Wow-Wows* Charles Chaplin

16 August – 16 August   CHANNEL ISLANDS, GUERNSEY, St. Julian's (Friday only)

19 August – 24 August   ENGLAND LONDON, Shepherds Bush Empire
 Mumming Birds

26 August – 31 August   ENGLAND LONDON, Middlesex
 Mumming Birds   [doubling with the Hackney Empire]

26 August – 31 August   ENGLAND LONDON, Hackney Empire
 Mumming Birds   [doubling with the Middlesex]

2 September – 7 September   ENGLAND ESSEX, Colchester Hippodrome
 The Village Sports, and *Mumming Birds* with Charles Chaplin as the lead character in both.

9 September – 14 September   ENGLAND BIRMINGHAM, Empire
 The Village Sports

16 September – 21 September   ENGLAND WARRINGTON, Hippodrome
 The Village Sports   [doubling with Liverpool]

16 September – 21 September   ENGLAND LIVERPOOL, Olympia
 The Village Sports   [doubling with Warrington]

23 September – 28 September   ENGLAND
 [no trace. Company probably returns to London to prepare for next U.S. tour.]

2 October   ENGLAND SOUTHAMPTON, En route

[Karno company set sail from Southampton, on board the SS Oceanic.]

KARNO COMPANY – Fourth and Fifth U.S. Tours
October 1912 – November 1913

1912

late 9 – early 10 October	*SS OCEANIC* arrives at NEW YORK
10, 11 or 12 October	NEW YORK, NEW YORK CITY, Proctor's, 5th Avenue
	A Lesson in Temperance – Billie Reeves. [Chaplin and Alf Reeves go to watch.]
14 October	[Karno Company hire a room, and spend time rehearsing.]
20 October – 26 October	OHIO, CINCINNATI, Empress (Tour starts here, Sunday)
The Wow-Wows	
28 October – 1 November	ILLINOIS, CHICAGO, Empress
The Wow-Wows	
3 November – 8 November	WISCONSIN, MILWAUKEE, Empress
The Wow-Wows	
10 November – 16 November	MINNESOTA, MINNEAPOLIS, Unique
The Wow-Wows	
18 November – 23 November	MINNESOTA, ST. PAUL, Empress
The Wow-Wows	
25 November – 31 November	MANITOBA, WINNIPEG, Empress
The Wow-Wows	
2 December – 3 December	(probably) MONTANA, MILES CITY, (2 nights only)
4 December – 5 December	(probably) MONTANA, BILLINGS, Babcock (2 nights only)
7 December – 13 Decemberq	MONTANA, BUTTE, Empress (opens Saturday)
The Wow-Wows	
15 December – 21 December	WASHINGTON, SPOKANE, Empress
The Wow-Wows	
23 December – 28 December	WASHINGTON, SEATTLE, Empress
The Wow-Wows	
30 December – 4 January	BRITISH COLUMBIA, VANCOUVER, Orpheum
The Wow-Wows	

1913

6 January – 11 January	WASHINGTON, TACOMA, Empress
The Wow-Wows	
13 January – 19 January	OREGON, PORTLAND, Empress
The Wow-Wows	
20 January	(possibly) CALIFORNIA, OAKLAND, Empress
26 January – 1 February	CALIFORNIA, SAN FRANCISCO, Empress
The Wow-Wows	
2 February – 8 February	CALIFORNIA, SACRAMENTO, Empress
The Wow-Wows	
10 February – 15 February	CALIFORNIA, LOS ANGELES, Empress
The Wow-Wows	
17 February – 22 February	CALIFORNIA, SAN DIEGO, Empress
The Wow-Wows	
24 February – 1 March	UTAH, SALT LAKE CITY, Empress (probably opens Wed 26 March)
The Wow-Wows	
3 March	(possibly) week 2 in SALT LAKE CITY or week 1 in DENVER

KARNO COMPANY – Fourth U.S. Tour (continued)

1913

10 March – 15 March	COLORADO, DENVER, Empress	
17 March – 19 March	COLORADO, PUEBLO, Empress (Mon-Wed)) [unconfirmed]	
20 March – 22 March	COLORADO, COLORADO SPRINGS, Empress (Thu-Sat)	
The Wow-Wows		
23 March – 29 March	MISSOURI, KANSAS CITY, Empress	
The Wow-Wows		

[FOURTH SULLIVAN & CONSIDINE TOUR ENDS HERE, IN KANSAS.]

----

31 March	PENNSYLVANIA, PHILADELPHIA	
[The Karno company have a week out, in Philadelphia.]		
3 April	NEW YORK, NEW YORK CITY, Metropolitan Opera House (Thursday only)	
Tannhäuser. [Chaplin travels to New York. In the evening he goes to the opera.]		
4 April	Chaplin returns to Philadelphia where telegram is awaiting him.	
5 April	Chaplin returns to New York, for meeting with Kessell and Bauman.	
6 April	Chaplin returns to Philadelphia.	

[Start of 11 week run of Nixon-Nirdlinger houses]

7 April – 12 April	PENNSYLVANIA, PHILADELPHIA, People's	(week 1)
14 April – 19 April	PENNSYLVANIA, PHILADELPHIA, People's	(week 2)
21 April – 26 April	PENNSYLVANIA, PHILADELPHIA, Nixon	(week 1)
A Night in an English Music Hall		
28 April – 3 May	PENNSYLVANIA, PHILADELPHIA, Nixon	(week 2)
A Night in a London Club		
5 May – 10 May	PENNSYLVANIA, PHILADELPHIA, Nixon	(week 3)
The Wow-Wows		
12 May – 17 May	PENNSYLVANIA, PHILADELPHIA, People's	(week 2)
19 May – 24 May	PENNSYLVANIA, PHILADELPHIA, Metropolitan	
A Night in an English Music Hall (Mon-Wed) then *A Night in a London Club* (Thu-Sat)		
26 May – 31 May	MARYLAND, BALTIMORE, Victoria	(week 1)
A Night in an English Music Hall		
2 June – 7 June	MARYLAND, BALTIMORE, Victoria	(week 2)
A Night in a London Club		
09 June – 14 June	District of Columbia, WASHINGTON DC, Cosmos	(week 1)
A Night in an English Music Hall		
16 June – 21 June	District of Columbia, WASHINGTON DC, Cosmos	(week 2)
A Night in a London Club		
[11 week run of Nixon-Nirdlinger houses end here, in Washington DC.]		
23 June – no trace	[probably a week out, between tours.]	

[Start of Fifth tour on Sullivan & Considine circuit]

29 June	MICHIGAN, DETROIT, Broadway [unconfirmed]	
07 July – 12 July	ILLINOIS, CHICAGO, Empress [unconfirmed]	
A Night in a London Club		
14 July	no trace	

KARNO COMPANY – Fifth U.S. Tour (continued)

1913

21 July   MINNESOTA, MINNEAPOLIS, Unique [unconfirmed]

27 July – 2 August   MINNESOTA, ST. PAUL, Empress
    A Night in a London Club

4 August – 9 August   MANITOBA, WINNIPEG, Empress
    A Night in a London Club
    [Groucho Marx sees Chaplin performing.]

11 August – 13 August   MONTANA, MILES CITY, Liberty [unconfirmed]

14 August – 16 August   MONTANA, BILLINGS, Babcock [unconfirmed]

16 August – 22 August   MONTANA, BUTTE, Empress
    A Night in a London Club

24 August – 30 August   WASHINGTON, SPOKANE, Orpheum

1 September – 6 September   WASHINGTON, SEATTLE, Empress
    A Night in a London Club
    [Chaplin had told Sennett his contract ended here. It didn't]

8 September – 14 September   BRITISH COLUMBIA, VANCOUVER, Orpheum
    A Night in a London Club

15 September – 20 September   WASHINGTON, TACOMA, Empress
    A Night in a London Club
    [Kessell and Bauman issue revised contract.]

22 September – 27 September   OREGON, PORTLAND, Empress
    A Night in a London Club
    [25 September: Chaplin signs revised contract from Kessell and Bauman.]

29 September – 4 October   no trace

05 October – 11 October   CALIFORNIA, SAN FRANCISCO, Empress
    A Night in a London Club

12 October – 18 October   CALIFORNIA, SACRAMENTO, Empress
    A Night in a London Club

20 October – 25 October   CALIFORNIA, LOS ANGELES, Empress
    A Night in a London Club

26 October – 1 November   CALIFORNIA, SAN DIEGO, Empress
    A Night in a London Club

2 November – 4 November   no trace (Sun-Tue)

05 November – 08 November   UTAH, SALT LAKE CITY, Empress (opens Wed)
    A Night in a London Club

10 November   (possibly) SALT LAKE CITY, or COLORADO SPRINGS, or PUEBLO

17 November – 22 November   COLORADO, DENVER, Empress

23 November – 29 November   MISSOURI, KANSAS CITY, Empress
    A Night in a London Club

[FIFTH SULLIVAN & CONSIDINE TOUR ENDS HERE, IN KANSAS.]
[Chaplin leaves here at the end of the week in Kansas. The rest of the
company tread water for three weeks while awaiting a replacement.]

LAUREL & HARDY – The British Tours

Part 1 – Screen to Stage [1926 to 1951]

Second Edition – Extensively revised, reformatted. and expanded

The story starts where our comedy heros meet up at the Hal Roach Studios, and become an inseparable partnership. We then fast forward to the promotional tour of major cities in England and Scotland, which they undertook in the summer of 1932.

Fast forward again to their 1947 British stage tour, for which readers are given a full account of every theatre engagement and every act they worked with; their travel arrangements; the hotels they stayed in; the people they met; previously undocumented public appearances. and descriptions of the crowds of thousands who mobbed them and left them reeling from the onslaught.

Second Edition. 210 pages. Lavishly illustrated — Softback — A4 [297mm x 210mm]
(ISBN 978-0-9521308-8-8) — Available via lulu.com

-----0-----

LAUREL & HARDY – The British Tours

Part 2 – 'The Last Stage.' [The 1952 and 1953-4 Tours]

Second Edition – Extensively revised, reformatted. and expanded

This engaging book is the story of the love which the British and Irish retained for these two comedy legends after the USA had turned its back on them, and how they adapted from film- to stage-work, and survived through the changing *modes* of comedy, and the changing *moods* of theatre audiences. Readers are given a full account of the theatres they played, the acts they worked with, their travel arrangements; the hotels at which they stayed; the people they met; and their many public appearances – all complemented by scores of rare photographs from these tours.

Second Edition. 208 pages. Lavishly illustrated — Softback — A4 [297mm x 210mm]
(ISBN 978-0-9521308-8-8) — Available via lulu.com

-----0-----

LAUREL and HARDY – The European Tours

"The European Tours" details not only the 1947-48 stage tours Laurel and Hardy played around Denmark, Sweden, France, and Belgium, but the year the two Hollywood comedians spent in France, during the making of their 1950-51 film *Atoll K*. Included in this is a promotional visit to Italy; plus details of two earlier visits to France — one by Laurel in 1927, and one by both comedians in 1932.

Readers will get to see the real men behind the screen characters of "Stan and Ollie" — how they coped with being mobbed everywhere they went; the exhaustion of a life of touring; and how they both worked on through serious illness to complete their last film.

From it all, Stan Laurel and Oliver Hardy emerge as lovable, but vulnerable, men – and readers will experience their every emotion throughout these previously undocumented tours.

Second Print. 128 pages – 200 illustrations. Softback – A4 [297mm x 210mm]
(ISBN 978-0-9521308-4-0) — Available via lulu.com

LAUREL and HARDY – The U.S. Tours

Second Edition – Extensively revised, reformatted. and expanded

After the two comedians meet at the Hal Roach Studios, the story takes an unexpected route. Instead of following them through the making of their films, we are led into a parallel world of public appearances, show business events, theatre tours, wartime fund raising tours, and troop shows. Revealed for the first time ever are details of three major U.S. city-to-city stage tours; numerous trips from the West to the East coast; three junkets to Mexico; and even a tour of Caribbean islands. On their travels, Laurel and Hardy meet a whole constellation of Hollywood stars; befriend a future President; and are invited to the White House. Stan and Babe emerge as warm and lovable, but vulnerable, men – and the reader will experience their every highlight and emotion throughout their long partnership.

Second Edition. 334 pages. Lavishly illustrated. Softback – A4 [297mm x 210mm]

(ISBN 978-0-9521308-6-4) — Available via lulu.com

-----0-----

LAUREL – Stage by Stage

"LAUREL - Stage by Stage" is the prequel to Marriots previous Laurel and Hardy's "Tours" books; and is a companion to "CHAPLIN – Stage by Stage."

It narrates for the first-time-ever all of Stan Laurel's stage shows, from his earliest appearances in British pantomime (as the teenage Stanley Jefferson), right up to his last-ever stage show before entering films.

Along the way he spends over three years touring with Charlie Chaplin, in the most-famous of all comedy troupes – the Fred Karno Company.

The next eight years are spent touring in U.S. vaudeville, playing in song-dance-and-comedy sketch acts with various partners.

Readers will experience every low and high as this comic genius tries to unshackle himself from the hardship and tedium of vaudeville, during a number of attempts to get into the world of film comedy. The amount of detail revealed about these "lost" tours is astounding.

272 pages – 200 illustrations. Softback – A4 [297mm x 210mm]

Second print (ISBN 978-1-78972-555-1) — Available via lulu.com

-----0-----

The many celebrities who have bought previous books written by "A.J" Marriot range from among Britain's best-loved British comedians; TV, film, and stage actors; and rock and pop stars, to some of Hollywood's most famous film directors and actors. Have you bought your copies yet?

A sincere "Thank You" to those who have.

"A.J" Marriot

o-o-o-0-o-o-o

For information on the First Editions, and how to purchase, go to the author's website:

www.laurelandhardybooks.com

OR e-mail: ajmarriot@aol.com for any enquiries.

LAUREL & HARDY – The British Tours
(First Edition)
What they said:

I am delighted to have a copy of your wonderful book. It is an absolute joy to read. (KEN DODD)

A.J. Marriot has given the fans of Stan Laurel and Oliver Hardy an exceptionally skilful, accomplished and memorable book, and I applaud him. (ERIC NICHOLSON – Comedy Lecturer)

The book is superb - a veritable treasure-trove of fascinating insights and anecdotes.
(PETER GOODWRIGHT – TV, Radio, and Theatre comedy star)

To say that I am delighted with this book is an understatement. It is a pleasure to read and Mr Marriot has captured the charm of Laurel and Hardy throughout.
(ROY WALTON – Comedy and Magic Shop owner)

You have done what I did not think possible, you have enhanced and increased my love for Laurel and Hardy - and for that you have my thanks. (JOHN ROCHE – Pembroke)

This book is a must for theatregoers weaned on the music halls, as they will revel in the wealth of theatrical detail recorded. (WORDS & MUSIC)

.. it certainly is required reading, not only by Laurel and Hardy fans, but anyone interested in the British Variety theatre. (BIRMINGHAM POST)

..... a fascinating read ... (SUNDERLAND ECHO)

The author's research is staggering, but from it Laurel and Hardy emerge as kind, sensitive men, always ready to spend time with their fans. (GRANTHAM JOURNAL)

All fans of Laurel and Hardy will relish this meticulous, wonderfully researched book... and learn in the process about the vanished variety stage and the pleasure it brought to us all in the days before television. (GRIMSBY EVENING TELEGRAPH)

Mr Marriot has produced an awesomely researched book which is absolutely unmissable for any Laurel and Hardy devotee. (MOVIE COLLECTOR)

The book manages to paint portraits of the two men that showed they could be human, upset or occasionally cranky, yet their basic kind humanity showing through. I think you get more of a sense of them as people than from any other of the Laurel and Hardy books. (PEPPER BOOKS – Ca.)

It made me laugh and made me cry. How strange to have such strong feelings about two people I never met, but then your book brought them alive. What more could one wish for?
(TANIA M. EDWARDS – London W14)

Unlike most recent books, your book documents much that was not known by Sons. It's truly outstanding. (GINO DERCOLA – Columbia, USA)

Words fail me in adequately expressing my heartfelt appreciation to you for writing this important history in the lives of Laurel and Hardy. (MARK A. MILLER – Columbus, Ohio)

I read your book in one go, and felt I was actually there. Every Son should have a copy.
(ARTHUR WESTWOOD – Atherton)

I don't think I have ever enjoyed a book so much as Laurel and Hardy - The British Tours.
(DAVID KING – New Milton)

o-o-o-0-o-o-o

Printed in Great Britain
by Amazon

31211947R00143